# Final Causality in Nature and Human Affairs

**STUDIES IN PHILOSOPHY
AND THE HISTORY OF PHILOSOPHY**

General Editor: Jude P. Dougherty

Studies in Philosophy
and the History of Philosophy      Volume 30

# Final Causality in Nature and Human Affairs

edited by Richard F. Hassing

THE CATHOLIC UNIVERSITY OF AMERICA PRESS
Washington, D.C.

The paper used in this publication meets the minimum requirements of American
National Standards for Information Science—Permanence of Paper for Printed
Library materials, ANSI Z39.48–1984.
∞

LIBRARY OF CONGRESS CATALOGING-IN-PUBLICATION DATA
Final causality in nature and human affairs / edited by Richard F. Hassing.
     p. cm.—(Studies in philosophy and the history of philosophy ; v. 30)
    Includes bibliographical references and index.
   1. Teleology.  I. Hassing, Richard F., 1944– .  II. Series.
B21.S78 vol.30
[BD541]
124—dc21
96-30050
ISBN 0-8132-0891-2 (alk. paper)

# Contents

# 1

# Introduction

## RICHARD F. HASSING

We first know a final cause from within our own daily experience. We intend to meet a friend, or we intend to build some bookshelves. We know that, as soon as we have the time and means to do or make what we intend, our purpose will determine a sequence of mental processes and physical motions, culminating in an action or product that fulfills or fails our intention. The goal, purpose, or end at which we aim is that for the sake of which plans are made and materials moved.

Staying within our own daily experience, we next discover our knowledge of luck. When something good but unintended happens to someone, we call it a lucky event. Luck means a peculiar kind of causality leading to effects that appear as intended and normally are so, but in lucky instances really are not intended. We know lucky effects as such because of our knowledge of intended effects; we cannot say, "that was unintended," unless we know what it means to do something on purpose.

Thus we know by our common, ordinary experience what human purposes and chance events are. Ignoring for the moment the paradoxical turn of thought at the origins of modernity,[1] our common knowledge of the difference between purpose and chance is neither problematic nor surprising—with one deep and perennial exception that arises spontaneously and never gets a complete answer from science or philosophy. This is the question whether chance events of great significance, rare events not humanly intended but with crucial outcomes and implications for human life, are really just a matter of chance, or whether they express some sort of purpose, one not seated in, and which transcends, human individuals and groups.

1. The paradoxical turn is necessitarianism, the doctrine that, against the appearances, all is necessitated, so that there is no privileged moment in any physical process, everything happens as it must. Therefore, the distinctions between voluntary human action, forced behavior, and chance events have no ground in the nature of things. Necessitarianism in early modern philosophy is discussed in section 5 of this introduction.

If we shift the field of inquiry from the mundane to the transcendent, asking questions about purpose and chance in the whole universe, or in the whole of human history, then the solidity and mundanity of our knowledge give way to philosophic wonder and practical concern.

Are there purposes or ends in nonhuman nature, in beings without foresight and choice? Indeed, somatic health, and organic structure and function in general, exemplify natural ends. What then about nonliving nature: the chemicals, and the weather and, above all, the sun, on which all living things depend? Is the emergence of the biosphere—an event of great significance—a matter of chance? Do the principles of *origin* of living species display a purposiveness commensurate with that of their *present natures* (for example, of organic structure and function)? Within the present Darwinian understanding, it seems not. Yet what are we to make of the spectacular picture of the evolution of the universe emerging from modern science? This is a picture whose dominant characteristic (despite catastrophist ups and downs) is an overall increase in the complexity and performance of natural structures.[2]

Is there a purpose to a whole human life, to the whole of human history, or is life "a tale told by an idiot,"[3] as the current spectacles of violent crime and factional conflict seem to suggest? Can political right be derived from a rationally discernable human end; do we desire the good, or just call "good" whatever we desire? Does an account of what is humanly right entail purposive notions of general nature or universal history?

## 1. Platonic Background

The idea of the good and the image of the sun in Plato's *Republic* constitute an emblematic introduction to the teleological problem. In *Republic* VI, Socrates tells Adeimantus and Glaucon that "the idea of the good is the greatest study" (505a2), and that it is "what every soul pursues and for the sake of which it does everything" (505d11–e1).[4] Here, the account is teleological: the good is the highest object of de-

2. The literature is large. For especially useful examples, see Bruce H. Weber, David J. Depew, and James D. Smith, eds., *Entropy, Information, and Evolution* (Cambridge: The MIT Press, 1990), 3 and 11–39, and David J. Depew and Bruce H. Weber, *Darwinism Evolving* (Cambridge: The MIT Press, 1995), chap. 15, especially 421–27. Depew and Weber proceed to argue for a thermodynamic perspective that would exclude both design teleology and Aristotelian natural form in favor of energy flows in informational systems; see *Darwinism*, chap. 17.

3. Shakespeare, *Macbeth*, 5.5.

4. Plato, *The Republic of Plato*, trans. Allan Bloom (New York: Basic Books, 1968). All quotations are from this edition.

sire, the supreme goal of human life.[5] But, unfortunately, Socrates' grasp of the idea of the good is uncertain; it seems he can only "divine" (505e1) that it is something, and so he must speak of it imperfectly, by means of analogy and supposition. The good is like the sun. The idea of the good does, in the realm of the intelligible, what the sun does in the realm of the visible. The sun yokes together sight and visible things (508a1), it "provides what is seen with the power of being seen" (509b2). But this is not all, for it provides them "also with generation, growth, and nourishment although it itself isn't generation" (509b3–4). By analogy, the idea of the good is "the cause of knowledge and truth" (508e3); that is, in virtue of the good, "being known is present in the things known" (509b6). But this is not all, because finally "existence and being are in them [the things known] besides as a result of it, although the good isn't being but is still beyond being, exceeding it in dignity and power" (509b7–10). Here, the account seems not to be teleological. We need the sun for visual perception, but we do not look at things and see them for the sake of the sun but rather for the pleasure of seeing itself. Furthermore, the operation of the biosphere, and thus the conservation of the living species, depend crucially on the sun but do not occur for the sake of the sun. If the good is the principle of the intelligibility of the world, do we then know for the sake of the good? According to the analogy, it would seem not; rather, we would seek knowledge for the pleasure of knowing as an end in itself.

In the Platonic account, knowing must be good (we do it instinctively), and, obviously, as animals we must be alive and healthy in order to know. Thus, the sun as cause of the generation and conservation of living things is a necessary condition of our enjoyment of knowing. What, therefore, is the relation between the sun and the good; are they simply unrelated? Socrates' remarkable answer, and he says it three times, is that the sun is an offspring, a child of the good (506e3, 508b13, 517c3). This must mean that the good is *somehow* a cause of the sun and its motion; the good somehow generates and is responsible for the sun, like a parent in relation to the child; there is some sort of causal relation between the good and the cosmic physical processes on which terrestrial life depends. Thus, the four great characteristics of the good are: principle of knowledge, cause of motion, ultimate *telos*, and ground of being. In the *Republic*, these four are, however, not unified in one account. Their meanings and the relations among them are

---

5. It is fairly clear from the context that "every soul" (*hapasa psychê*, 505d11) means every *human* soul. The absence of a Platonic biology will be important for the following analysis.

problematic. What, for example, is the relation between the intelligible forms and the sensible things that we see and point at? Plato's forms are notoriously separate from the sensible changeable things that participate in them. In the subsequent account of the divided line (509d–511e), sensible things are knowable (through *dianoia*) only insofar as they supply the figures and numbers of geometry and arithmetic; hence, *as changeable,* sensible things are excluded from the domain of *epistêmê* (both *noêsis* and *dianoia*). Accordingly, with respect to their knowability or opinability, Socrates makes no distinction among the sensibles between natural things and artifacts (510a5–6); both are relegated to the realm of opinion. Hence, there is no Socratic-Platonic biology. In the *Republic,* therefore, Socrates seems to deny the possibility of a science of nature, *epistêmê physikê.* Is this not the well-known characteristic of Socrates' "second sailing" (*Phaedo* 99d1)?

In the *Phaedo,* 95–99, Socrates recounts his disappointment with his own early studies in physics and his hope that Anaxagoras could save the endeavor by showing that "it is mind that arranges and causes all things."[6] This means something very specific: it means an explanation "of each thing and of all things in common" in terms of "what is best for each and what is good for all in common."[7] Indeed, "to find the cause of the generation or destruction or existence of each thing, [one] must find what sort of existence, or being acted upon, or activity is best for it."[8] This specific prescription for a detailed physical cosmology—absent from the account of the good and the sun in *Republic* VI—sounds like what will become most basic in the Aristotelian tradition of natural philosophy: proper operation according to the nature of each substance (for example, somatic health), the different natures being composed in a harmonious hierarchy ultimately grounded in a metaphysical principle (for example, first unmoved mover). Here, however, in the *Phaedo,* the desired account of mind, good, part and whole is not forthcoming. For Anaxagoras fails to deliver (98b8), and, rather than attempting his own comprehensive natural teleology, Socrates-Plato turns away from physics toward political philosophy, toward the analysis of opinion and the study of things as reflected in speech, not as they present themselves directly to us. The reasons for the Socratic abandonment of natural science are unclear: is it because of the reductionism of pre-Socratic physics which makes the human compound unintelligible (98c3–99b8), or is it, more fundamentally, because Socrates-

6. Plato, *Phaedo,* 97c1–2, trans. H. N. Fowler, Loeb Classical Library (1982).
7. *Phaedo,* 98b2–3.
8. *Phaedo,* 97c7–10. Translation slightly modified for greater literalness.

Plato thinks that a comprehensive teleology is not accessible to natural human reason?[9] What is clear, against this Platonic background, is the daring character of Aristotle's founding of final causality. Aristotle's comprehensive teleology—the union of his science of nature and theory of knowledge by means of natural form culminating in the pure actuality of the first unmoved mover—is his grand attempt to solve Plato's problem. For Aristotle's natural forms are both causes of motion in natural substances (*Phys.* 193b7) and sources of knowledge in the human soul (*De An.* 429a16), and each substance lovingly imitates, according to its form, the perfect actuality of the first unmoved mover (*De An.* 415b1–2, *Meta.* 1050b29). In this way, the cosmos of Aristotle not only *incorporates* the Socratic-Platonic idea of the good, it also *exemplifies* the type of natural teleology that Anaxagoras failed to provide and Socrates chose not to attempt. Apparently against Socrates-Plato's better judgment, Aristotle persisted in Socrates' first sailing.[10]

## 2. Regional Teleologies

We know that Aristotle's daring physics involves theories of local motion (*Phys.* 255b15) and astronomical phenomena (198a32) that, as discussed in the following, cannot be sustained today. This does not prevent us from seeking, in the spirit of the founder, partial or "regional" teleologies in the other classes of phenomena—the chemical, the biological, the human, and, although always speculative, even in cosmogony. The ten essays in this volume address issues attendant to the abiding questions of final causality. They are arranged in historical order, from Aristotle through Hegel, to the contemporary issue of anthropic-principle cosmology.

A glance at the table of contents, however, reveals a large gap. There is only one paper (Ernest Fortin's on political theory) on the roughly 2,000-year period from Aristotle to Kant. The purpose of the present introduction is accordingly twofold: to present the essays, but also to comment on certain of the most salient features of the period from Aristotle up to Kant. Specifically, the following issues are discussed: the problem of chance and providence (mentioned above) in Thomas

9. It may be unavailable to natural human reason because of the abiding problem of reconciling the good (and bad) of the part with the good of the whole, for example, the lion and the zebra, and the related difficulty of knowing why it is good that just these kinds of things exist and not other kinds.

10. Aristotle thus employs both dialectic and induction; see *Parts of Animals*, 642a25–30. See also Jacob Klein, "Aristotle, an Introduction," in *Jacob Klein Lectures and Essays*, ed. Robert B. Williamson and Elliott Zuckerman (Annapolis, Md.: St. John's College Press, 1985), 187.

Aquinas and its implications for Aristotelian teleology; the essential connection between the rise of laws of nature and the attack on formal and final causality that is the hallmark of the seventeenth-century origin of modern science and philosophy. These issues clearly presuppose familiarity with Aristotle's teleology. This is the subject of the papers by William A. Wallace and Allan Gotthelf.

*William A. Wallace* presents an overview and problematic of nature and causality. He proceeds within the Aristotelian tradition but with a special concern for comprehension of modern science as well. His guiding question is this: how are agent and end as *extrinsic* causes related to the concept of nature as *intrinsic* principle of change and stability? This question arises as soon as we appreciate the highly coordinated interactions between living species in an ecosystem. But it arises perhaps even more pointedly on grounds of two impressive products of modern natural science: technology and physical cosmology. Technology always involves transformative operations on natural materials by human agents yielding new effects and products for a vast range of human purposes. For example, is there a way to integrate within a single conception of nature the properties of uranium, silicon, nucleic acids—the material bases of nuclear, information, and genetic technologies—and the desires and actions of the human beings who work on these materials? And the massively evolutionary cosmology of the twentieth century provokes questions of ultimate agency and purpose that could not arise on grounds of the Aristotelian cosmos of fixed and eternal species. Wallace raises these questions and, in the context of his careful review of material, formal, efficient, and final causality, offers provocative answers both positive and negative. He argues that notions of agency and finality (operative through external relations between natural substances) are indeed implicit in Aristotle's definition of nature in a way that facilitates extension of the Aristotelian account to particular results of present science. But for Aristotle, as Wallace interprets him, the being-at-work of the forms aims finally at the conservation and perfection of the natures we now see and not at reaching beyond to the future production of new natures after the destruction of antecedent ones. Indeed, as Maimonides reports Aristotle's teaching, "it is impossible that a thing from among the existents should change as far as its nature is concerned."[11] For this reason, evolution cannot be brought within a purely Aristotelian understanding of nature.

---

11. Maimonides, *The Guide of the Perplexed* II.19, 39b; trans. Shlomo Pines (Chicago: University of Chicago Press, 1963), 303.

In *Allan Gotthelf*'s view, we must begin with living things, including ourselves, in order to understand adequately the meaning of teleology in Aristotle. Indeed, Aristotle says that "things which have a nature . . . are all substances" (*Phys.* 192b34), that "a man or a plant" exemplifies substance "in the highest degree" (*Meta.* 1032a19), that "the form [of a natural substance] . . . is the end or final cause" in generation (198b3, 199a33, 1015a12). And Aristotle's argument for formal cause depends crucially on the paradigmatic biological phenomenon: reproduction (193b8–12). This affirmation of the primacy of the biological, however, implies the rejection of a competing view, namely, that to understand Aristotle's teleology we must look first, not at living things, but at the natural local motion of the nonliving elements.[12]

Now Aristotle's account of the natural locomotion of the elements is part and parcel of his cosmology of essential distinctions—distinctions between up and down in place and between celestial and terrestrial motion and matter. These distinctions cannot survive the developments in physics culminating in Newton's gravitational theory. This is discussed in the concluding essay of this book in the context of the crucial question whether other distinctions essential within the Aristotelian understanding—above all the distinction between the human and the nonhuman—can survive in the face of modern natural science. My present point is that to base a defense of Aristotelian teleology on elemental local motion will lead to disappointment (and loss of credibility). For I believe that what we today call gravitational systems exhibit a type of intelligibility that cannot be accommodated to Aristotle's universal natural principles of form and matter. The reasons for this are not historical but essential to Aristotle's understanding of the completeness and goodness of the natural whole. That understanding—Aristotle's general or *comprehensive* teleology expressed through his detailed cosmology—is, therefore, untenable. This issue is introduced by way of my comments on Leo Strauss, Thomas Aquinas, and the seventeenth century, in sections 3–5 of this introduction. In the concluding essay of this book, I explain in detail the non-Aristotelian type of intelligibility exhibited by Newton's law of gravitation, a type of intelligibility on which Bacon and Descartes pinned all their hopes—to enjoy, however, only partial success: for it is precisely organisms that prove most resistant to explanation by Baconian-Cartesian-Newtonian laws of nature.[13] It is no accident that the scientific revolution was fought, not on the terrain of biology, but of physics.

12. Avicenna seems to be an important source; see *Sufficientia* I.5, in *Opera omnia* (Venice, 1508), 16v1B.

13. Atoms and molecules, of course, demand a radical departure from classical phys-

Proceeding within the biological view then, Gotthelf 's first objective is "to identify, and group . . . the range of issues on which one has to have a position if one can claim an understanding of Aristotle's theory." Most fundamental among these issues is the question, "What fact or facts ground or license Aristotle's use of teleological explanation?" Gotthelf 's second objective is to categorize and comment on recent answers to this question. His resulting typology of interpretations is structured in terms of two distinctions crucial for the philosophy of nature: the distinction between holism and reductionism and the distinction between *per se* and *per accidens* causality in the production of organic beings. Specifically, in certain lines of interpretation, teleological explanation is warranted by the (ontological, not just explanatory) *irreducibility* of organic wholes to their parts. In other lines of interpretation, teleological explanation is warranted by the existence of an intrinsic mechanism guaranteeing the regular production from seed of each species of organism; the essential point here is that, *regardless of the question of reducibility,* that is, regardless of whether they are ultimately amenable or not to explanation by material and efficient causes, organisms and their parts do not come to be *by accident,* as Empedocles had claimed (198b26–33). In these interpretations, Aristotle can thus be accommodated to contemporary accounts of genetic programming in molecular biology without resolving the holism-reductionism problem. Gotthelf 's third and final objective is to criticize certain of these interpretations in a way that elucidates relations between the notions of whole-part irreducibility and non-accidental production. He concludes with a defense of his own strong irreducibility thesis, and he places Aristotle's natural teleology in a distinctive position that cannot be assimilated either to mechanism or to design.

*Francis Slade,* in a brief but incisive comment, insists on a distinction between the terms 'end' *(telos)* and 'purpose'. Ends "are characteristic of all kinds of things . . . [and] exist independently of our willing them," whereas "purposes take their origin from our willing them." In our use of things, our purposes must be congruent with the ends intrinsic to the things—otherwise the things will be destroyed. Slade elaborates on the art of medicine, its intrinsic end, and certain incongruent purposes by which doctors are presently tempted. But his sharpest point follows (implicitly) from his assertion of what is perhaps the most

---

ics. Quantum physics exhibits certain Aristotelian features, namely, holism and in a sense potentiality but also certain Baconian features, namely, the primacy of the subsensible and the malleability of matter to experimental penetration beyond the common order of nature. And in its idealistic aspect, quantum physics would probably pose difficulties for both Aristotle and Bacon.

important and, unfortunately, most controversial claim in the history of philosophy: man has an end *(telos)*. Therefore, mankind can be destroyed through deficiencies, not of external conditions, but of human will and purpose. Slade's comment thus prepares the vexed question of the origins of our tradition of political right: does the basic concept of individual liberty derive from an account of human ends, or, on the contrary, from a denial that human beings have an end beyond self-preservation and its instrumental conditions?

*Ernest Fortin* takes us into the problem of natural right in the political theory of liberal democracy. The issue is timely. Both the post-communist transition in the former Soviet Bloc and the social pathologies of the United States pose with renewed urgency the historic question of the relation between politics and ethics. For according to Aristotle, "Virtue must be a care for every city" *(Pol.* 1280b7).[14] But according to Kant, "The problem of organizing a state . . . can be solved even for a race of devils, if only they have sense" *(wenn sie nur Verstand haben).*[15] These two quotations are radically opposed. They bound the problem of the relation between politics and ethics from opposite sides of the divide between ancients and moderns. We shall discuss this divide, and the emergence of German philosophy therefrom, in sections 4–6 of this introduction.

For Aristotle and Aquinas, politics and ethics are intimately connected; for the moderns they are quite separate.[16] The separation of politics and ethics makes politics seem easy.[17] Hence, Kant's formulation reflects the audacious optimism of Machiavelli (about whom, see more below): by the right method, a good form of government can be imposed on (to put it crassly) any human material.[18] But if Aristotle and Aquinas are, in some fundamental way, right, then a politics of liberty such as American constitutionalism that is, or becomes, ethically

14. Aquinas repeats this sixteen centuries later, under conditions very different from those of the small Greek city-states: "the proper effect of law is to lead its subjects to their proper virtue" *(Summa Theologiae,* Q. 92, A. 1, reply). The reasoning is thus not historical but essential to the Aristotelian-Thomistic understanding of human nature in relation to political order.

15. Kant, "Zum ewigen Frieden," in vol. 8 of *Kants gesammelte Schriften,* Prussian Academy (Berlin: Walter de Gruyter and Predecessors, 1902– ), 366, hereafter *Kants gesammelte Schriften;* trans. Lewis White Beck, "Perpetual Peace," in *Kant on History,* ed. Lewis White Beck (Indianapolis: Bobbs-Merrill, 1963).

16. To illustrate this point, it is often noted that neither Locke, the major philosophical founder of liberal democracy *(The Second Treatise on Government),* nor Marx, the philosophical founder of Communism, has a doctrine of moderation.

17. "Democracy—just do it!" was the logo on buttons worn by a group of young Americans heading to Eastern Europe to observe elections in 1990.

18. Machiavelli, *The Prince,* trans. Harvey C. Mansfield, Jr. (Chicago: University of Chicago Press, 1985), chap. 6, 23.

neutral can undermine its own conditions. It can with the best of intentions—for the noble cause of freedom from oppression—nevertheless facilitate the development of people unable to govern themselves. We are then forced back to the sobering question, "What is [political] freedom without [ethically] free people?"[19] Much is at stake in the issue Fortin addresses. His intention in this paper is to contribute to a knowledgeable understanding of our own victorious tradition of rights. This entails seeing clearly the theoretical break between medieval natural law and natural rights, on the one hand, and modern natural right, on the other. It is well worth noting that, in Fortin's judgment (although he does not elaborate here), the theoretical break does not necessarily rule out possibilities for rapprochement.

Fortin's detailed analysis of major recent debates and primary sources centers on the concept of right in relation to duty. The medieval accounts of law and right are based on a conception of human nature as essentially political, wherein authority is natural, and law mandates duties for the sake of the common good. A subject's rights—the things I can claim for myself—are conditioned on the prior performance of duties. In contrast, the modern accounts, for example, Hobbes and Locke, posit a state of nature in which human beings are free to conduct themselves as they will; they are by nature subject to no authority. All authority thus originates in the convention whereby I consent to be ruled by others *if and only if* they protect my natural right to life and liberty. For better or for worse—as is clear today for better *and* for worse—my rights are prior to my duties. The difference ultimately consists, Fortin concludes, in "the implications of a teleological versus a nonteleological understanding of human life." And so we must confront, in however brief and inadequate a manner, the enormously rich and complex period from medieval to modern, from Aquinas through the seventeenth century.

## 3. Science in Strauss's *Natural Right and History*

Let us begin with the basic premise of the Aristotelian parts of this anthology: the disruption of Aristotle's general teleology by modern gravitational theory does not prevent us from seeking partial or regional teleologies in the other classes of phenomena. It is precisely this premise that Leo Strauss seems to deny in the introduction to *Natural*

<hr />

19. The quotation, "What is freedom without free people?" is from Francesco de Sanctis, *Saggi critici* (Milan, 1933), Vol.3, 269. James Madison's remark in *Federalist* 63 is apt: "[L]iberty may be endangered by the abuses of liberty as well as by the abuses of power" (*The Federalist Papers* [New York: Mentor New American Library], 1961, 87).

*Right and History,* the writing to which readers of Strauss often recur for his view of natural science.[20] There Strauss says:

> The teleological view of the universe, of which the teleological view of man forms a part, would seem to have been destroyed by modern natural science. From the point of view of Aristotle—and who could dare to claim to be a better judge in this matter than Aristotle?—the issue between the mechanical and the teleological conception of the universe is decided by the manner in which the problem of the heavens, the heavenly bodies, and their motion is solved [*Phys.* 196a25 ff., 199a3–5]. . . . The fundamental dilemma, in whose grip we are, is caused by the victory of modern natural science.[21]

Let us call this Strauss's opening argument on natural science in *Natural Right and History,* a book in which the meaning of teleology is a fundamental theme.[22] The opening argument is indeed that the refutation of Aristotle's teleology of the heavens infects his teleology of the other parts of the cosmos. Since the human species is a part of the universe, a teleological understanding of man in the spirit of Aristotle is impossible.

Aside from the tentative sense of the words "would seem," this passage prompts questions, the first of which is explicit: who might be a better judge in this matter than Aristotle? The background to Aristotle's teleology in *Republic* and *Phaedo* makes clear that the answer to this question is, Plato. Strauss himself goes on in *Natural Right and History* to give an account of natural right that is both premodern (there are human excellences by nature) and—in the spirit of Plato—independent of general physics.[23] The crucial requirement on physical nature (examined in the concluding essay of this volume) is that it not be universally reductionist; that there can be natural compounds nonreducible to their parts and conditions, thus "that there are phenomena that form a class by themselves."[24] For Strauss, as well as Socrates-Plato, the class of first importance is, of course, that of the human phenom-

20. Leo Strauss, *Natural Right and History* (Chicago: University of Chicago Press, 1953), 7–8. Roger D. Masters, "Evolutionary Biology and Natural Right," in *The Crisis of Liberal Democracy: A Straussian Perspective,* ed. Kenneth L. Deutsche and Walter Soffer (Albany: SUNY Press, 1987), 48–66, offers a vertiginous analysis of this text in terms of Nietzsche, Boscovich, and quantum physics. My interpretation is quite different.

21. Strauss, *Natural Right,* 7–8.

22. This point is forcefully made and carefully explained by Richard Kennington, "Strauss's *Natural Right and History,*" in *Leo Strauss's Thought,* ed. Alan Udoff (Boulder: Lynne Rienner Publishers, 1991), 227–52.

23. Strauss, *Natural Right,* chap. 4. Note also Strauss's reference to "the difficulty with which every teleological physics is beset," 172; see note 9 above. John Finnis, *Natural Law and Natural Rights* (Oxford: Clarendon Press, 1980), 52, notes the disjunction between the introduction and the later account of natural right in chapter 4.

24. Natural Right, 129.

ena. This requirement on physical nature is less stringent than the demand for an Aristotelian theory of celestial body and motion. It seems
"the fundamental dilemma" of the opening argument has changed (by
Chapter 4 of *Natural Right and History*) into something that, in terms of
natural science, may be easier to handle. But there is a further, crucially
important specification of the irreducibility requirement: wholes, or at
least the human wholes, must be irreducible to their parts and conditions *in such a way* that, "the completed thing cannot be [adequately]
understood as a product of the process leading up to it, but, on the
contrary, the process cannot be understood except in the light of the
completed thing or of the end of the process."[25] On this point, Aristotle,
too, is unambiguous: "what each thing is—for example, a human
being, a horse, or a household—when its coming into being is complete
is, we assert, the nature of that thing" (*Pol.* 1252b32–33). Not the process but the product defines the primary intelligible. Fulfilling this prescription is clearly problematic in view of prevailing evolutionary theories, but, again, it does not require Aristotle's celestial physics. Thus
it is another valuable question, prompted by Strauss's opening argument, whether Aristotle himself ties his ethics and politics so tightly to
his distinctive physical cosmology. It is more likely that the decisive requirement for ethics and politics in Aristotle is that (consistent with the
primacy of product over process) the human specific difference be de-
fensible. By this I mean the following. We experience ourselves as
moved by desire for knowledge and, at least in certain crucial instances,
for excellent performance through freedom of the will. Are these two
uniquely human things—reason and virtue—genuine causes of our actions, or are they merely apparent and thus deceptive and false causes?
Is our belief that we can act *voluntarily*, in ways thus worthy of praise
and blame (*Nic. Eth.* 1109b30–35), really just a peculiar effect of causes
aimed at something quite different, something that in no way merits
praise or blame? To take an example from popularizations of the prevailing evolutionary theory, is our experience of free choice just an illusion, being in reality an accidental effect of random genetic variation
and environmental selection,[26] principles which aim *per se* simply at the
biological survival that is common to all living things, and is in no way
specific to the human? If the answer to the latter question is yes, then
what *seems* to differentiate the human kind from other living species—
reason, opinion, virtue and vice—is in fact illusory and gives no access

25. Ibid., 123.
26. Examples appear frequently in science journalism. See, for example, Natalie Angier, "Matter over Mind: the Curse of Living Within One's Genes," *The New York Times*,
18 December 1994, sect. 4.

to the true principles of human action. If the answer is yes, then there is no human specific difference, and so the *scientific* account of the human can only be in terms of the nonhuman. This is the point repeatedly made by Strauss in other published writings and in unpublished discussions, namely, that modern natural science undermines the idea of specific difference.[27] And here the Darwinian tradition in biology would be at least as relevant as classical physics.

Two large items remain in our examination of Strauss's opening argument: first, we must look at the cited passages in Aristotle's *Physics;* second, we must address the obvious question of Strauss's intention in the introduction to *Natural Right and History.* The first leads to essential material in Aristotle and Maimonides, the second to Thomas Aquinas and the problem of chance and providence.

In *Physics* II.4–6, Aristotle presents his account of chance: what it is, and in what way chance and its subspecies, luck, are causes of physical effects. We know that chance refers to a type of accidental causality. Chance effects proceed *per accidens* from causes, not *per se* aimed at those effects. The distinction between *per se* and *per accidens* causality is conveyed by means of a typical Aristotelian example: "in the case of a house . . . a cause which is *per se* is the art of building, but one that is

27. Leo Strauss, "An Epilogue," in *Essays on the Scientific Study of Politics*, ed. Herbert J. Storing (New York: Holt, Rinehart and Winston, 1962), 309, reprinted in Strauss, *Liberalism Ancient and Modern* (New York: Basic Books, 1968), 207; Strauss, *The City and Man* (Chicago: University of Chicago Press, 1964), 19 and 21. In chapter 4 of *Natural Right and History*, we find a complex account of several forms of premodern natural right, among which a Socratic-Platonic and an Aristotelian form, about which Kennington comments that, "[t]he common premise of both is the Socratic discovery of kinds, and the specific heterogeneity of the human kind" ("Strauss's *Natural Right*," 244). Accordingly, see Strauss, "Political Philosophy and the Crisis of Our Time," in *The Post-Behavioral Era*, ed. George J. Graham and George W. Carey (New York: David McKay Company, Inc., 1972), 230. In "The Three Waves of Modernity," in *Political Philosophy: Six Essays by Leo Strauss*, ed. Hilail Gildin (Indianapolis: Bobbs-Merrill, 1975), 87, Strauss says something akin to his opening argument in *Natural Right and History:* "The rejection of final causes [in modern natural science] . . . destroyed the theoretical basis of classical political philosophy. The new natural science differs from . . . the older one not only because of its new understanding of nature but also and especially because of its new understanding of science: knowledge is no longer understood as fundamentally receptive; [rather] . . . knowing is a kind of making." I believe that this is a statement about the self-understanding of modern science, not a statement about its (always partial) established results, for example, the refutation of Aristotle's celestial physics cited in *Natural Right and History*. Strauss is not saying here that modern science has proven that there are no final causes in nature. Although it is rarely conducted in canonical Aristotelian terms, the debate remains open in chemistry, biology, and ecology. Strauss's point, rather, is that, to the extent that a science of human things tries to imitate physics (or the positivist interpretations of its methodology), there will be no place for anything like classical political philosophy in that science. This is quite true, but it is a different issue from the question of the real implications (regardless of methodological fashion) of established results in science for the study of ethics and politics.

*per accidens* is the white or the musical" (196b26–27). The builder just happens to be white and a musician, attributes concomitant in the builder along with the builder's art. To understand chance, we must now see that effects as well as causes can be *per accidens*.[28] A squirrel's nest in the chimney of the house is a *per accidens* effect of the builder's art. Or consider a man who goes to the market for the sake of buying food but meets someone who owes him money and pays up (196b34–197a5). The effect is getting money—something for the sake of which human beings strive. It was here unintended, by both debtor and creditor, each of whom went to the market for other, unrelated purposes. We recognize that the creditor got the money by luck (a type of chance specific to human affairs). Here we recognize that the effect came about by chance because we know the distinct causes of the event were directed at other things. In general, as Aristotle makes clear, we can know that a cause-effect connection is accidental only against a background of cause-effect connections that are regular or stable, that is, non-accidental or essential (198a8). Aristotle's great and daunting task in *Physics* II.4–8 is to extend the notions of chance and purpose from the domain of human action, where we know our own intentions, to biological and astronomical phenomena, and finally to the cosmological processes on which all life depends (194b14, 200b3). The task is great because here we confront the question whether the ultimate principles of the universe stand in any meaningful relation to the human good. For this reason, the importance of the distinction between *per se* and *per accidens* effects cannot be overstated. As Aquinas says, concerning the momentous dispute between Plato and Aristotle over the sensible and the intelligible, "He [Plato] made [a] mistake because he failed to distinguish what is essential from what is accidental. Thus it happens that by accident even the wise fall into error. . . ."[29] Although he is speaking of Plato, Thomas's lapidary remark could apply to others in the history of philosophy, as we shall see. And Aristotle's task in *Physics* II.4–8 is daunting because we, the human species, are only a part of a much larger whole that we did not make, and so our access to the remote past and the distant parts of the universe is ineluctably conjec-

28. Thomas Aquinas, *In octo libros physicorum Aristotelis expositio* (Turin and Rome: Marietti, 1965), n. 214, 114–15; trans. Richard J. Blackwell, Richard J. Spath and Edmund Thirlkel, *Commentary on Aristotle's Physics* (New Haven: Yale University Press, 1963), 101.

29. Thomas Aquinas, The Division and Methods of the Sciences, Questions V and VI of the Commentary on the De Trinitate of Boethius, Q. 5, A. 2, reply; trans. Armand Maurer, The Division and Methods of the Sciences (Toronto: The Pontifical Institute of Mediaeval Studies, 1963), 20. The mistake is Plato's apparent rejection of a science of natural (sensible, changeable) beings.

tural. And here we find the first passage to which Strauss refers, 196a25 ff:

> There are some who say that chance is a cause both of this heaven (*t'ouranou*) and of all things in the cosmos (*tôn cosmôn pantôn*); for they say that the vortex came to be by chance, and so did the motion that separated the parts and caused the [present] order of the all (*tên taxin to pan*). And this is really worth wondering at; for they say, on the one hand, that animals and plants neither exist nor are generated by chance (*apo tyches*) but that the cause is nature or intellect or some other such thing (for it is not any chance thing that is generated from a given seed, but an olive tree from this [kind] and a man from that [kind]), and, on the other, that the heavens and the most divine of the visible things were generated by chance, which cause is not such as any of those in the case of animals or plants. Yet if such is the case, it deserves attention, and it is right that something should be said about it. For besides the fact that the statement is strange in other ways, it is stranger still to speak thus when they observe nothing generated by chance in the heavens but many things happening by chance among things which [according to them] neither exist nor are generated by chance. . . .
> There are also others who seem to think that chance is a cause but is not revealed to human thought, that it is something divine and rather godlike. (196a25–b7)[30]

I do not know whether Strauss intended to include or exclude the last sentence. It points to the problem of chance and providence on which Thomas Aquinas comments in a way that is relevant for the study of final causality in nature and human affairs, as discussed in section 4 of this introduction.

What is Aristotle's most basic point? Is it that, without a teleological science of the heavens (certification of a humanly meaningful good at which cosmological processes are aimed), there can be no teleological account of any other part of the universe, neither of the biological nor of the human? It seems not. I believe Maimonides states Aristotle's most basic point succinctly; it is the posing of the question, "if the particular things of the world are not due to chance how can the whole of it be due to chance?"[31] The particular things that are clearly not by chance (but by nature or intellect) are living things. Aristotle speaks of reproduction, Maimonides mentions organic structure:

> You know that the veins and nerves of any individual dog or ass have not happened fortuitously, nor are their measures fortuitous. Neither is it by chance that one vein is thick and another thin. . . . How then can one who uses his intellect imagine that the positions, measures, and numbers of the

30. Aristotle, *Aristotle's Physics,* trans. H. G. Apostle (Grinnell, Iowa: The Peripatetic Press, 1980), 30–31. The translation is slightly modified for greater literalness.
31. Maimonides, *Guide* II.20, 45b.

stars and the motions of their various spheres are without an object or fortuitous?[32]

Living things conspicuously exemplify purposiveness in nature. They do so through their structures, as well as their embryological development through a craft-like succession of stages completed in a well functioning whole of a determinate kind. The regular local motions of celestial bodies do not display purposiveness in this manner; in astronomical phenomena, final causality is obscure. But, obviously, astronomical processes are vitally necessary conditions of the biosphere (for example, if the sun operates out of typical parameters, we all perish; 194b14). Aristotle, Maimonides, and many others, including anthropic-principle cosmologists today, endeavor to answer the question, if the part is not by chance, how can the whole be by chance? In other words, do not manifestly purposive operations in one part of the universe entail purposiveness in their (not manifestly purposive) necessary conditions? The analysis and evaluation of Aristotle's answer in *Physics* II.4–8 forms the subject of a large literature.[33] The problem is complicated by the question whether Aristotle's main conclusions (at 198a6– 13 and 199a3–5) presuppose, or are independent of, his *detailed* and *refuted* cosmology of eternal species in their natural places within perfectly encased and indestructible Eudoxian concentric spheres moved by separate intelligences.[34] That cosmology encountered a major difficulty well before the rise of modern science, namely, in Ptolemaic mathematical astronomy. The difficulty—"the true perplexity"[35]—is

32. Ibid., II.19, 43b.

33. See *Aristotle on Nature and Living Things*, ed. Allan Gotthelf (Pittsburgh, Pa.: Mathesis Publications, 1985), and *Philosophical Issues in Aristotle's Biology*, ed. Allan Gotthelf and James G. Lennox (Cambridge: Cambridge University Press, 1987), with extensive bibliographies. See also the articles by Lindsay Judson and David Charles in Lindsay Judson, ed., *Aristotle's Physics: A Collection of Essays* (Oxford: Clarendon Press, 1991). In *Guide* II.19–24, Maimonides disagrees with the necessitarianism of Aristotle's cosmo-theology: Aristotle's God does not knowingly and freely will the sequential creation of this particular universe; the biblical God does.

34. For example, the importance of the eternity of the species is discussed by John Cooper, "Hypothetical Necessity and Natural Teleology," in *Philosophical Issues in Aristotle's Biology*, 243–74. A less stringent question is that of the relation between *Physics* II.4– 8 and the argument from motion with which the *Physics* concludes. This excellent question would require a much longer study, for it strikes deeply into the question of the unity of Aristotle's *Physics*. In any case, Strauss does not refer to the argument from motion in his report on Aristotle's view of teleology. For the importance of material causality in the argument from motion, see William A. Wallace, "Cosmological Arguments and Scientific Concepts," in *From a Realist Point of View* (Washington, D.C.: The Catholic University of America Press, 1983), 309–23.

35. Maimonides, *Guide* II.24, Pines, 326. See also Averroes's criticism of the contemporary astronomy, *In meta.* XII, C. 45, 1664; trans. Charles Genequand, *Ibn Rushd's Metaphysics*, (Leiden: E. J. Brill, 1984), 179.

clearly presented by Maimonides in *The Guide of the Perplexed,* II.24. Since Strauss wrote the introduction to the common (1963) edition of this work, he was undoubtedly aware of the serious premodern problems attendant to Aristotle's physics of the heavens.[36] Let us then make the questionable assumption (in order to reach a decision on Strauss's opening argument) that Aristotle's basic conclusions are independent of his detailed Eudoxian cosmological model. The two most important of these conclusions are:

Now chance and luck are causes of effects caused for the most part by intellect or nature, when some cause of these is accidental; but further, nothing that is accidental is prior to what is essential, thus it is clear that no accidental cause is prior to an essential cause. Thus chance and luck are posterior to intellect and nature. Hence, however it may be that chance is the cause of the heavens, even to the greatest extent, intellect and nature are of necessity a prior cause of many other things and of this all. (*Physics* II.6, 198a6–13)

So if these [rainfall, growth of grain, parts of animals] be thought to occur either by coincidence or for the sake of something and if they cannot occur by coincidence or by chance [because of their frequency, 198b35], then they occur for the sake of something. (*Physics* II.8, 199a3–5)

The second quotation is also the second of the two passages cited by Strauss in his opening argument.

The first of these excerpts expresses the persuasive conclusion that it makes no sense to speak of *per accidens* causes and effects in nature without acknowledging the prior or antecedent reality of *per se* causes and their effects, without which the accidental could not exist. This rule is then applied to two things: the whole universe, "this all," and to the spatial or temporal parts of which it is composed, one such part being "the heavens."[37] Today, in place of "the heavens" in Aristotle's argument, we have the solar system and the earth's biosphere. Aristotle shows that there must be *per se* principles of the universe, that is, stable,

36. Leo Strauss, introduction to Maimonides' *Guide,* xi-lvi. On xi, Strauss writes that he has been thinking about the *Guide* for twenty-five years, thus for twelve years prior to writing *Natural Right and History* in 1950. If we take Strauss's opening argument at face value (problems with Aristotle's celestial physics imply problems in the teleological understanding of the other parts of the cosmos), then, since the subhuman animals are also parts of the cosmos and since the teleological view of them (our grasp of the intrinsic tendencies toward somatic health specific to each kind) grounds veterinary medicine, would we not be forced to conclude that Ptolemaic astronomy caused veterinary science to be riddled with doubt?

37. The distinction between the all *(to pan)* and the heavens *(t'ouranou)* is important. It seems fairly clear at 196a27–28, that Aristotle knew of (and was addressing) opinions according to which this presently visible order of "the heavens" is but one in a long temporal sequence of worlds. Aquinas, *In phys.,* n. 202, attributes a many-worlds hypothesis of this type to Empedocles, based presumably on *Physics* VIII.1, 250b19 ff.

intelligible entities and processes that make knowledge of nature possible, even if certain parts of the universe proceed *per accidens* from those principles, even if "chance is the cause of the heavens, even to the greatest extent." This is an exceedingly delicate point. For here we find the problem of the relation between intelligibility and goodness.

Let us grant that Aristotle demonstrates the reality of *per se* cause-effect links in the universe, which are thus objects of human knowledge (197a20). There is, in other words, intelligible pattern rather than the unintelligible chaos of the absolutely accidental. But it is consistent with Aristotle's argument that the principles of the universe may be *per se* directed to intelligible but very general effects. An ancient example of this would seem to be the Empedoclean account of the natural tendencies of elements. Here, a great variety of compounds and worlds emerge through the general principles of "friendship and strife" (for example, attraction and repulsion) particularized according to the manner in which elements happen to fall together.[38] (Note the great importance of *particularization* throughout Maimonides' account in *Guide*, II.19–24.) We could say, following Aquinas, that, in this type of theory, there would be material and efficient causes that produce general effects, but particular effects (for example, "the heavens," or the biosphere) would be unexplained since they would not proceed *per se* from their causes.[39] For a significant example of a general cause that grounds the production of particular effects *per accidens*, listen to Descartes on the relation between God (as conceived by Descartes) and nature: "with God always acting in the same way and consequently always producing the same effect in substance [conservation of total quantity of motion], there occur, *as by accident (comme par accident)* many diversities in that effect."[40] In Descartes, of course, the particular effects that "occur as by accident" are not only explainable, they are controllable—through experiment under the aegis of laws of nature.[41] This surprising possibility is the subject of section 5 in this introduction. My point for now is to highlight by means of examples what Aristotle indicates: the possibility of intelligible general causes that are

38. *Physics* II.8, 198b12–17 and Aquinas's report on Empedocles, *In phys.*, n. 202.
39. Ibid., n. 250.
40. Rene Descartes, *Le Monde*, chap. 7; in vol. 11 of *Oeuvres de Descartes*, ed. Charles Adam and Paul Tannery (Paris: Vrin, 1964–76), 435, hereafter Descartes, *Oeuvres*, Adam and Tannery, eds.; *Le Monde*, trans. Michael S. Mahoney (New York: Abaris, 1979), 61, hereafter Descartes, *Le Monde*, Mahoney, trans.; emphasis mine.
41. Rene Descartes, *Discourse on Method*, part 6, in *Oeuvres*, Adam and Tannery, eds., vol. 6, 64 and 75; *The Philosophical Writings of Descartes*, trans. John Cottingham, Robert Stoothoff, Dugald Murdoch, vol. 1 (Cambridge: Cambridge University Press, 1985), 144 and 149; hereafter Descartes, *Philosophical Writings*, Cottingham, et al., trans.

related to particular sensible effects in a manner that, at some point in the linkage, involves chance.

Today, gravitational and nuclear physics yield a good theory of the formation of stars. But the problems of the subsequent formation of the solar system and the emergence of the biosphere (including biogenesis) remain open. More generally, in contemporary physics we find global principles like conservation of total mass-energy and angular momentum, or maximum energy flow and entropy production in open systems. We might say that the fulfilment of these principles by physical processes exemplifies a kind of teleology. But the "ends" in question are so broad that they are compatible with a large variety of distinct, *particular* cosmic arrangements, or variously ordered subparts of the universe, "many other things" (198a12). Examples might include Big Bang universes that recollapse too quickly for stars to form, or universes in which carbon, an essential element of organic material, is too scarce for life to emerge, or a universe in which a biosphere emerges but is subject to an erratic solar energy flux that causes all living things to die in protracted agony.[42] The poignant feature of Empedocles' account of the chance generation of the parts of animals (198b28–33), aside from its grotesqueness, is the great physical suffering to which malformed organisms would be subject. Such universes or parts of the universe—each a possible product of the same general principles— would not be *good* in a humanly meaningful sense. Aristotle's demonstration does not permit us to conclude, therefore, that the net *good* arrangement of "the heavens," that is, the solar system and our particular biosphere, is an effect proceeding *per se* and not *per accidens* from its causes. Aristotle's demonstration does not go far enough to connect the intelligible pattern of general *per se* principles to humanly meaningful good, unless the only humanly meaningful good is knowing, a possibility that might be sufficient for us as philosophers but not for nonphilosophical life. To clinch the full argument for cosmic teleology, we must show that this determinate visible order of ours proceeds *per se* from the principles; we must link intelligibility and goodness essentially and not accidentally. It will not do to stand neutral before this fundamental alternative and say that the universe is good simply because it is intelligibly determinate in any manner whatsoever; killer asteroids and unstable solar systems exhibit beautifully intelligible physics but their possibility puts big question marks over the goodness of nature.[43] I believe that Aristotle, Maimonides, Aquinas, and, therefore,

42. John Leslie, a contributor to this volume, presents detailed examples of alternative universes in *Universes* (London: Routledge, 1989).

43. In addition to the mortality of all living things, natural disasters and diseases call

Strauss, know this, and know that Aristotle's conclusion at 198a6–13 does not clinch the argument. Aquinas's comment is, again, exemplary:

If [after Aristotle's proof of the priority of intellect and nature] it should be held [consistent with Aristotle's proof] that chance is the cause of the heavens, . . . it would follow that intellect and nature are first of all causes of some other things and afterwards causes of the whole universe.

Moreover, the cause of the whole universe seems to be prior to the cause of some part of the universe, since any part of the universe is ordered to the perfection of the universe. But it seems to be unfitting (*hoc autem videtur inconveniens*) that some other cause is prior to that which is the cause of the heavens. Hence it is unfitting that chance is the cause of the heavens.[44]

St. Thomas judges it to be more *fitting* that this determinate order is a *per se* rather than *per accidens* effect of the principle. For Aquinas, it is not by demonstration that one links pattern and good *per se* but by an act of *phronesis*, the highest moral virtue in the premodern understanding, and finally, for Aquinas, not Aristotle, by faith. In spite of their difference, Aristotle and Aquinas have this in common: for both, the whole is beneficent. The disposition of Descartes, the founder of modern philosophy, will be very different.

The second of the two quotations above (199a3–5) is the culmination of Aristotle's famous reply to the materialists' claim that living things come about by chance and necessity (198b18–33) and not for the sake of an end and a good. The argument consists in the conjunction of a proposition and a hypothesis: what happens always or for the most part cannot happen by chance (198b35); *if* things happen either by chance or for the sake of something, *then*, we necessarily conclude, what happens always or for the most part happens for the sake of something. The account is provocative in its logically formal and hypothetical character. At least two difficulties would need to be resolved before an adequate assessment could be given. First, Aristotle seems to omit the possibility of purposeless regularities (necessary regularities, which, we could say, might be for the sake of ends too general to qualify as good, like conservation of energy, as discussed above). Second, in *Physics* II.2, Aristotle criticizes a poet who said that one has an end for the sake of which one is born, namely, death. The poet, says Aristotle, should

---

into question the goodness of nature, but always at a local level, thus against a continuing background of life that is, on balance, worth living. Global extinction is another, more radical matter.

44. Aquinas, *In phys.*, n. 237; *Commentary on Aristotle's Physics*, 109. The assertion that "any part of the universe is ordered to the perfection of the universe" is not in the Aristotelian text and may be an analogy based on the organization of animals. If so, we must note that the organized unity of an animal is evident to sense, whereas the parts of the universe are not nearly so tightly composed.

understand that "not every last thing tends to be an end, but only the best" (194a33). But death happens *always* to living things. Therefore, by the formal demonstration of *Physics* II.8, 198a3–5, death must be for the sake of something; isn't the poet right?[45] This is hardly to say that Aristotle's famous conclusion that nature acts for the sake of an end is wrong. My point is simply that, like any argument concerning the most fundamental issues, it is, in its full generality, problematic. Perhaps most interesting, finally, is the fact that all of Aristotle's many examples in the ensuing argument (199a8–14) are taken from human *technê* and from biology; there are no examples of astronomical phenomena. Therefore, even if we grant Aristotle a demonstration that, *within the biosphere,* nature acts for the sake of ends, it would still be the case that the proof of a *final* causal connection between the prior cosmological principles of the universe and the particular order of the biosphere remains elusive.[46] This elusiveness, to repeat, and in view of Aquinas's judgment of the fitting, above, (and his teaching on providence, below) is something of which I believe Aristotle, Maimonides, Aquinas, and Strauss are all aware. It clearly does not stop Aristotle from proceeding to argue, by means of many persuasive examples, for final causality in human and biological phenomena. It is, however, a sign that there has been (in fact there still is) a problem at the boundary or "joint" between the astronomical and the biological parts of the universe.[47]

This completes my comment on the two passages cited by Strauss. Unlike the issues encountered in these texts, my basic conclusion is simple: Strauss is not to be taken at face value in his opening argument on science in *Natural Right and History*. I base this conclusion on (1) Strauss's deep knowledge of Plato, (2) his subsequent account in *Natural Right and History*,[48] (3) the problems of *Physics* II.4–8 and of Aristotle's detailed cosmology, of which Strauss was aware through Maimonides. Strauss's true position, as indicated, is that modern natural science undermines the idea of specific difference and thus distorts our self-understanding. How this happens is described in the concluding essay of this volume.

45. I am indebted to Adam Shulman for pointing this out to me.
46. To get a proof, it is *sufficient* to plug in Aristotle's detailed Eudoxian cosmological model. Is it also necessary?
47. The problem of biogenesis is situated at this boundary today. Anthropic-principle debates examine the sequence of cosmic events leading from the origin of the universe (estimated at very approximately 15 billion years ago) up to, but not including, the origin of life (currently dated at around 3.8 billion years ago), focusing on evidence that the universe is "fine tuned" for the production of the materials necessary for the eventual emergence of life.
48. See especially Kennington's assessment, "Strauss's *Natural Right*," 231.

Therefore, having removed Strauss's apparent objection, we can affirm that the refutation of Aristotle's detailed cosmology by the physics culminating in Newton does not prevent us from seeking final causality—partial or regional teleologies—in other classes of phenomena: the chemical, the biological, the human, and even, as we shall see in the essays by John Leslie and George Gale, in contemporary physical cosmology. But the comprehensive teleology, the complete science of the essential connection between intelligible pattern and human good, remains a desideratum. It is an object of reason's natural eros never fully possessed by reason.[49] I suggest below that alternative positions on the relation between ultimate principles and human good define certain of the great traditions in the history of philosophy: Platonic, Aristotelian, medieval, early modern, and German philosophy. Let us turn to the obvious question of Strauss's intention in the introduction to *Natural Right and History* and to the problem of chance and providence. This will prepare the discussion of laws of nature and the attack on formal and final causality in early modern philosophy.

## 4. The Problem of Chance and Providence

What is Strauss's intention in his opening argument on science in *Natural Right and History?* I conjecture that it is to persuade two groups with different opinions about ultimate things to make much-needed (and still needed) common cause, and then, perhaps, quietly to indicate the philosophical source of the difference of opinion, namely, the problem of chance and providence. The two groups are the religious believers with a serious interest in Thomas Aquinas and nonbelievers or agnostics who would come to have a serious interest in Strauss's understanding of the history of philosophy. For both groups, premodern philosophy and the guiding question—What is nature?—are of principal concern. Both disagree with "the liberals of various descriptions."[50] In forty-five years, the situation has not changed.

At *Physics* II.4, 196b5–7, Aristotle says, "There are [those] who seem to think that chance is a cause but is not revealed to human thought, that it is something divine and rather godlike." Aquinas comments that, "this opinion has a radical truth," for "we [believers in the biblical God] hold that all things are ordered by divine providence."[51] Aquinas notes

49. Kant, *Critique of Pure Reason*, trans. Norman K. Smith (New York: St. Martin's Press, 1965), 7.
50. Strauss, *Natural Right and History*, 7.
51. Aquinas, *In phys.*, n. 206; *Commentary on Aristotle's Physics*, 98. Other important references to providence are in nn. 238, 250, and 268.

that Aristotle does not inquire into this opinion in the *Physics*, "because it exceeds the bounds of natural science."[52] Now in *Metaphysics* IX.8, Aristotle discusses the ways act and potency are mutually determined in motions and mobiles. He concludes concerning astronomical motions that "the sun and the stars and the whole heaven are always active, and there is no fear that any of them will ever stop (although natural philosophers do fear this)" (1050b23–25).[53] The naturalists presumably fear that the most powerful parts of the cosmos might bring about the total destruction of mankind. Would this event be providential, or mere chance, in the sense of a particular effect to which the general cause is not *per se* determined? This is the cosmological problem of chance and providence. We must compare what Aristotle has just said in *Meta.* IX.8 with Aquinas's view in *De potentia Dei:*

> We assign as the end of the heavenly movement something outside heaven that is obtained by that movement, and which can remain when that movement ceases. . . . We hold then that . . . it is a definite number of souls that is the end of the heavenly movement: and when this is reached the movement will cease.[54]

Presumably, and as Thomas could know by natural reason, the cessation of earth-sun relative motion would cause the death of all living things on earth, thus the extinction of the human species, due to the extreme temperatures that would result on opposite sides of the planet.[55] Now Aristotle's detailed cosmology makes such an event impossible, and thus it secures the overall goodness of the natural whole wherein, for Aristotle, the human *telos* takes place. The impossibility follows from the very specific nature of celestial substance within Aristotle's detailed (Eudoxian) model of the cosmos. Celestial substance has potency only to angular position, that is, Aristotelian celestial bodies are concentric spheres that can be other than they are only through continuous rotation about the earth's center. As a result of this specific structure, the visible celestial bodies can neither stop nor collide with the earth (since they move always at constant radius). In particular, the sun cannot stop, go out, or blow up, nor can comets or asteroids hit the earth. Accordingly, within the Aristotelian universe—an eternal, self-

---

52. Aquinas, In phys., n. 206; Commentary on Aristotle's Physics, 98.

53. Aristotle, *Aristotle's Metaphysics*, trans. H. G. Apostle (Grinnell, IA: The Peripatetic Press, 1979), 156.

54. Aquinas, *De potentia Dei*, Q. 5, A. 5, response; trans. The Dominican Fathers, *On the Power of God*, (Westminster, Md.: The Newman Press, 1952), bk. II, 113.

55. In *De potentia Dei*, Q. 5, A. 5, ad 17; *On the Power of God*, bk. II, 118, Thomas cites Apoc. 21:23, in support of the hope that the consummation of the world may not be so terrible. But, in view of the central symbol of Christianity, it is clear that suffering unto death is part of the imitation of Christ.

contained, very genteel life-support system—the cosmological problem of chance and providence does not arise.[56] As explained in the concluding essay of this volume, the physics culminating in Newton reveals that the most powerful parts of the universe—astronomical systems—are governed in part by a gravitational law (Newton's or, later on, Einstein's) that is *per se* structure-neutral. This means that, in their motions under gravitation, astronomical systems are intrinsically indifferent to the good operation of the terrestrial order. Therefore, the fear of the naturalists cannot be removed, because, for example, in the cometary collision of July 1994, the target could have been Earth instead of Jupiter. And so the cosmological problem of chance and providence cannot be avoided. It is not possible, as it was in Aristotle's specifically structured cosmos, to maintain by reason that the natural whole is simply beneficent. This is the main implication of the refutation by classical physics of Aristotle's theory of the heavens.

What can be said about the relation between ultimate principles and human good in the wake of the above result? We can identify at least two surviving alternatives: First, the natural whole is not good, but indifferent or hostile, due to the range and power of chance in the production of particular, and humanly crucial, physical effects. Accordingly, there is no *telos* of mankind *by nature*. This is the view most directly opposed to Aristotle. Second, the whole *is* beneficent but transcends the natural; accordingly, the *telos* of mankind is destined to take place not wholly in the natural order but only partially. The second alternative is obviously a biblical, theological view long antedating the scientific revolution, which revolution strongly modifies our physics, but in a way that leaves intact—and in fact, sharpens—the biblical theology of the ultimate destiny of the physical universe. The theological position is represented, as we have just seen, by Thomas Aquinas and, more generally, by medieval philosophy. Accordingly, for Aquinas and in contrast to Aristotle, the natural whole is itself only a part and an instrument in the service of a larger plan not fully disclosed to human reason.[57] For both Aristotle and Aquinas, the whole is beneficent; but the whole is understood by each in a fundamentally different way. For

---

56. The adjective "genteel" is John Dewey's, who aptly remarks in *Experience and Nature* (La Salle, Ill.: Open Court, 1929), that "[t]he empirical impact and sting of the mixture of universality and singularity and chance is evaded by parceling out the regions of space so that they have their natural abode in different portions of nature" (43–44). As a result, the man hit by a stone at 197b31–32 is a victim of chance, but the whole earth cannot be hit by a very big stone. The fact is that, in Aristotle, the natural whole is so good, it is almost comical.

57. Aquinas, *De potentia Dei,* Q. 5, A. 5, response, ad 7, A. 6, response; *On the Power of God,* bk. II, 114, 116, 122.

Aristotle, it is natural; for Aquinas, both natural and supernatural.[58] Of these two, only the theological position can survive, since Aristotle's detailed cosmology of natural goodness is refuted. We should not forget, however, that Plato did not attempt a comprehensive teleology[59] and thus in some way stands outside of the present analysis. Perhaps this is why Strauss, in view of his own decision regarding reason and revelation, turned in his later years to the study of Socrates.[60] It remains to discuss the first alternative, above, the position most directly opposed to Aristotle's cosmology of natural goodness. Let us call it the cosmology of indifference.

The cosmology of indifference underlies the attitude of modern philosophy: the natural whole is at best indifferent, and man has no *telos* by nature. Within this attitude, we could further distinguish early modern philosophy from German idealism. In the early moderns, nature is "material to work on,"[61] and reason is an instrument in the service of self-centered passions. How then should we live? We ought to get busy and try to gain control over all that affects us; that is, the wonder and reverence of the Greeks and medievals are inappropriate to our situation. There is no ground for non-self-interested virtue and reason has no eros of its own. Bleak realism combined with great optimism for the aggressive and progressive mastery of nature are the marks of early modern philosophy. This provokes a pressing question: how do we get from the power of chance in nature—the waterloo of Aristotle's physics of the heavens—to the mastery of nature? Aren't chance events unpredictable and thus uncontrollable? The relevant feature of early modern philosophy is a new and liberating conception of chance and necessity. This is the subject of section 5 of this introduction.

The transition, finally, to German idealism begins in reaction to the deficiencies of the early moderns. For the instrumentalization of both reason and virtue is not adequate to human life as we experience it. Despite impressive successes in technology and economics, the achievements of early modern philosophy are partial. In a larger perspective, its enlightened ideas of science and self-interest are one-sided; they are impoverishing doctrines. German idealism thus restores reason and

58. Aristotle's first and separate unmoved mover is, as such, metaphysical, but it has no plan or design and no will concerning the cosmos whose eternal motion it produces through final causation. See *Meta.* XII.9, and Thomas Prufer, *Recapitulations* (Washington, D.C.: The Catholic University of America Press, 1993), 35–42.

59. The *Timaeus* account seems to be a serious or plausible and important myth, but a myth nevertheless, and not science.

60. Strauss, *Natural Right and History*, vii.

61. John Locke, *The Second Treatise of Government*, ed. Thomas Peardon (Indianapolis: Bobbs-Merrill, 1952), sec. 35, 21.

morality, and, therewith, teleology, to privileged status. But the restoration of reason and morality in German idealism takes place on
grounds of history, not nature, for the latter is now merely phenomenal
and subordinate to the successive self-development of mind or spirit.
Not the natural whole, but the whole of human History becomes the
vehicle for the attainment of the human end.

Let us turn to the final sections of this account of the enormously
rich and complex period from medieval to modern, from Aquinas up
to Kant. The fundamental issue that orients these reflections is that of
the relation between the two questions that define philosophy: What is
the human good? What are the ultimate principles of the universe?

## 5. Laws of Nature versus Natural Forms and Ends

### Cosmology of Indifference

We begin from the cosmology of indifference arising in response to
the problem of chance and providence: the natural whole, the universe
in its particular determinacy, including the human part, is at best indifferent to what we call "good" and "bad." Accordingly, the human
species has no end or *telos* by nature. The cosmology of indifference in
early modern philosophy is illustrated by Descartes.

In *Le Monde,* Descartes constructs a model of the universe. It is
based, as indicated above, on "the very firmness and immutability that
is in God."[62] Grounded thereon are three laws of nature, one of which
is that each individual part of matter "tends always to continue its motion along a straight line."[63] Descartes says that "[t]his rule rests on the
same foundation as the two others and depends only on God's conserving everything by a continuous action . . . not as it may have been
some time earlier but precisely as it is at the same instant that He conserves it."[64] How is God related to the particular effects that we sense
and experience in nature? Consider any animal: it is bounded in space
by a physical surface within which fluids circulate. In fact, Descartes
says explicitly that "all the motions which take place in the world are
in some way circular."[65] Therefore, none of the motions we observe

---

62. Descartes, *Le Monde,* in *Oeuvres,* Adam and Tannery, eds., vol. 11, 439; in *Le Monde,* Mahoney, trans. 69.

63. *Le Monde,* in *Oeuvres,* Adam and Tannery, eds., vol. 11, 440; in *Le Monde,* Mahoney, trans., 71. For the other two laws, see *Le Monde,* Mahoney, trans., 61 and 65.

64. *Le Monde,* in *Oeuvres,* Adam and Tannery, eds., vol. 11, 440; in *Le Monde,* Mahoney, trans., 71.

65. *Le Monde,* in *Oeuvres,* Adam and Tannery, eds., vol. 11, 419; in *Le Monde,* Mahoney, trans., 29.

proceeds *per se* from God's conserving action. And what God conserves is not the well-functioning of living things in the biosphere. On the contrary, if the fluid particles in any organism actually moved according to God's conserving action, the organism would explode, which would not be good for it. Since this does not happen due to the circulatory flow of matter in the Cartesian plenum, God is not evil. But is He good? Could we perhaps say that God intends *indirectly* a beneficent fluid dynamics that holds all of us living things together? Descartes indeed says that

> even if we suppose that He creates nothing more than [matter and motion], and even if He does not impose any order or proportion on it but makes of it the most confused and most disordered chaos that the poets could describe, they [the laws] are sufficient to make the parts of that chaos untangle themselves and arrange themselves in such good order that they will have the form of a most perfect world, in which one will be able to see not only light, but also all the other things, both general and particular, that appear in this true world.[66]

How does this work? In Descartes's cosmology, the determinacy of the universe comes about from Cartesian matter, God's initial impulse, the three laws of nature, chance and necessity. God's initial impulse consists in imparting to matter a total quantity of motion randomized over the colliding corpuscles of matter.[67] The roles of necessity and chance are subtly allocated by Descartes, as follows: First, the laws of nature themselves are necessary; God has no choice in creating them.[68] Next, all the effects we observe are divided into two classes: the phenomena of elements and the phenomena of compounds. There are three corpuscular elements, called "fire," "air," "earth," which compose the stars, the heavens, and the planets; in other words, the elements are the emitters, transmitters, and reflectors of light that constitute the large structures of the universe. Under the aegis of the laws of nature, the sun and stars, the heavens, comets and planets—each of which consists of a single element—come to be from the initial chaos *always*, thus, necessarily in any imaginable universe.[69] The compounds, or mixed

66. *Le Monde,* in *Oeuvres,* Adam and Tannery, eds., vol. 11, 432; in *Le Monde,* Mahoney, trans., 55.

67. *Le Monde* in *Oeuvres,* Adam and Tannery, eds., vol. 11, 432, 434, 439; in *Le Monde,* Mahoney, trans., 55, 59, 69; *Discourse on Method,* part 5, in *Oeuvres,* Adam and Tannery, eds., vol. 6, 44; *Discourse on Method,*in *Philosophical Writings,* Cottingham, et al., trans., vol. 1, 132. Descartes's God grounds an early version of the postulate of equal apriori probabilities in equilibrium statistical mechanics.

68. *Le Monde,* in *Oeuvres,* Adam and Tannery, eds., vol. 11, 443; in *Le Monde,* Mahoney, trans., 77.

69. *Le Monde,* chap. 8–15. Note that at *Le Monde,* in *Oeuvres,* Adam and Tannery,

bodies, are another story. "We do not perceive mixed bodies in any place other than on the surface of the earth."[70] Four pages before his reference to the "good order . . . of a most perfect world," Descartes gives a striking characterization of compounds: "these mixed bodies taken all together are but as a crust *(écorce)* engendered on top of the earth by the agitation and mixing of the matter of the heavens surrounding it."[71] This sounds—provocatively—as if the order of the biosphere would indeed come about *per accidens,* from initial conditions and particle dynamics in no way aimed at this particular arrangement of species and ecosystems. That this is in fact Descartes's teaching can be discerned from a careful look at the summary of his cosmology in the *Discourse on Method,* parts V and VI.

In *Discourse* V, Descartes recapitulates results of his unpublished *Le Monde.* He says that in speaking "of the earth in particular," he showed "generally how all the bodies we call 'mixed' or 'composite' could come into being there."[72] Unfortunately, the extant editions of *Le Monde* do not contain this material.[73] But the *Discourse*—the first work Descartes chose to publish—explains that the class of compound bodies contains an important problem. Descartes says, concerning animals, that he "did not yet have sufficient knowledge to speak of them in the same manner as [he] did of the other things, that is, [logico-deductively] by demonstrating effects from causes. . . ."[74] The difficulty is made clear in *Discourse* VI. Here we finally see the basic distinction between the phenomena of elements and the phenomena of compounds in terms of chance and necessity. Descartes recapitulates his derivation of "the heavens, the stars, and an earth; and, on the earth, water, air, fire, minerals, and other such things which being the most common of all and the simplest are easiest to know."[75] These are the phenomena of elements, and, as noted, their generation follows with necessity from the

eds., vol. 11, 433–34, *Le Monde,* Mahoney, trans., 57–59, the humanly imaginable is identified with whatever is free of logical contradiction, which is in turn identified with the divinely possible. The crucial turn will be from the divinely possible to the humanly possible.

70. *Le Monde,* chap. 5, in *Oeuvres,* Adam and Tannery, eds., vol. 11, 428; *Le Monde,* Mahoney, trans., 47.

71. Ibid.

72. Descartes, *Discourse on Method,* part 5, in *Oeuvres,* Adam and Tannery, eds., vol. 6, 44; *Philosophical Writings,* Cottingham, et al., trans., vol. 1, 133.

73. See *Le Monde,* Mahoney, trans., xx, and *Philosophical Writings,* Cottingham, et al., trans., vol. 1, 99. Chapters 16 and 17 of *Le Monde* are apparently lost.

74. *Discourse on Method,* part 5, in *Oeuvres,* Adam and Tannery, eds., vol. 6, 45; in *Philosophical Writings,* Cottingham, et al., trans., vol. 1, 134.

75. *Discourse on Method,* part 6, in *Oeuvres,* Adam and Tannery, eds., vol. 6, 64; *Philosophical Writings,* Cottingham, et al., trans., vol. 1, 144.

laws of nature, and the initial chaos of matter and motion. Now come the more particular effects, including the phenomena of living compounds that, ever since book II of Aristotle's *Physics,* fueled the argument for natural teleology. Descartes says:

> When I sought to descend to more particular things, I encountered such a variety that I did not think the human mind could possibly distinguish the forms or species of bodies that are on earth from an infinity of others that might be there if it had been God's will to put them there.[76]

Now the role of God's will in Descartes's cosmology is restricted to the creation of Cartesian chaos: a necessarily conserved total quantity of motion is *randomly* imparted to the particles of matter.[77] Accordingly, two sentences later, the will of God becomes the power of nature:

> I must . . . admit that the power of nature is so ample and so vast, and these principles [the laws of nature] so simple and so general, that I notice hardly any particular effect of which I do not know at once that it can be deduced from the principles in many different ways. . . .[78]

Taken together, these two assertions imply that what determines or specifies the principles to a particular effect is not itself entailed by the principles, but rather is logically external to them. The principles are *per se* neutral to the vast range of their effects. Therefore, God or nature is not essentially determined to this particular order of compounds on "the crust" of the earth. There might be an infinity of other forms or species. Particular effects—such as the good order of the biosphere—follow "as by accident" *(comme par accident)* from God, not in the sense that God *intends* effects but, on rare occasions, misses them, like the natural and human agents of *Physics* II.4–6. Rather, particular effects are unintended by God or nature *because God or nature has no humanly meaningful intention.* This is why Descartes says, concerning material things, that "their nature is much easier to conceive if we see them develop gradually in this way than if we consider them only as entirely completed *(toutes faites).*"[79] Recall what Aristotle said about the primacy of product over process: "what each thing is . . . when its coming into being is complete *(telestheisês)* is, we assert, the nature of that thing"

76. Ibid.

77. See note 67, above.

78. *Discourse on Method,* part 6, in *Oeuvres,* Adam and Tannery, eds., vol. 6, 64–65; *Philosophical Writings,* Cottingham, et al., trans., vol. 1, 144. Of course, one sentence later, Descartes states the new conception of chance and necessity as experimentally controllable. This will be discussed momentarily.

79. *Discourse on Method,* part 5, in *Oeuvres,* Adam and Tannery, eds., vol. 6, 45; *Philosophical Writings,* Cottingham, et al., trans., vol. 1, 134.

(1252b32–33). If we look at natural things in their completed forms, we will be deceived into believing that they embody a divine design (*Genesis* I) or a natural intention; we will believe that "nature does nothing in vain" (1253a9). The truth is that nature does nothing for a purpose. Thus, Descartes's God is neither good nor evil; He is simply indifferent. Descartes's cosmology of indifference is subtly but precisely targeted against both Aristotle and the Bible.[80]

Let us pause and survey the terrain we have crossed. In doing so, we should not take for granted the successes of modern science, because it will obscure our view of the surprising position at which we have now arrived. For as it stands, this position—the cosmology of indifference—should lead us either to gloom and depression or to a life of self-forgetting abandon, because powerful forces over which we have no control are simply blind to our happiness or misery. It is remarkable that early modern philosophy leads to neither of these, neither to passive resignation nor to apolitical hedonism but rather to a vast reorientation of knowledge: the transition from the premodern understanding, in which nature and God are most fundamental, to the exaltation of human creativity that is the mark of modernity. We need to see how this could happen. The key idea must be that the blind forces of nature over which we have *heretofore* had no control are of such a type that, unlike the chance and necessity of ancient materialism, they will be *henceforth* subject to our control. This, in fact, is precisely what Descartes says in *Discourse* VI immediately after his statement on God's will or the power of nature in relation to particular effects. To discover in which of various ways a desired effect follows from natural forces, we do experiments "whose outcomes vary according to which of these ways provides the correct explanation."[81] The crucial premise is that under the same conditions, the laws of nature guarantee that the same things happen. Thus, by varying the initial or boundary conditions on natural processes, we can repeatedly sample, predict, and control outcomes. "God's will" can henceforth be subsumed within human will through controlled experiments on "the forms or species of bodies." In general, the historical turning point consists in the removal of our ignorance concerning the true causes and principles of things, or Enlightenment.[82]

80. For a fuller discussion, see Richard Kennington's excellent and very accessible article, "Rene Descartes," in *History of Political Philosophy*, ed. Leo Strauss and Joseph Cropsey, 3rd ed. (Chicago: University of Chicago Press, 1987).

81. Descartes, *Discourse on Method*, part 6, in *Oeuvres*, Adam and Tannery, eds., vol. 6, 65; *Philosophical Writings*, Cottingham, et al., trans., vol. 1, 144.

82. For the central importance of the Cartesian *cogito* in conjunction with the mastery of nature, see Kennington, "Rene Descartes," 431, 437–38.

*Transformism*

The productions of modernity are so striking in their good and bad qualities, especially in the twentieth century, that they have been the subject of intense and incessant critical reflection for at least fifty years. Against this towering background, I focus on a single point, but it is essential for the study of final causality in nature and human affairs. It is a new conception of necessity and chance that facilitates human control of natural processes. This new conception explains the paradoxical development and Promethean claims of early modern philosophy. On the side of nonhuman natural phenomena, it is crystallized in the experimental and mathematical *law of nature,* central to Bacon and Descartes, which finds its strongest confirmation in classical physics, in mechanics, electromagnetism, and thermodynamics. Essential here is the connection between the argument *for* laws of nature and the argument *against* formal and final causality in nature; they go hand in hand. On the side of human nature itself, the new conception is found in Machiavelli's transformation of virtue. Without a view of this broad development, it is difficult to see the rationale for the greatly reduced status of nature in German idealism.

First and foremost, it must be made clear that the idea of laws of nature is not coeval with human thought but rather began to emerge historically between the thirteenth and sixteenth centuries.[83] This means that laws of nature as we understand them—as principles of natural phenomena rather than human moral prescriptions—are not to be found in Greek antiquity. For example, in Plato there are only two instances of the term 'law of nature' *(nomos tês phuseôs),* at *Timaeus,* 83e and *Gorgias,* 483e. The latter—on the rule of the strong over the weak—is deliberately paradoxical. In Aristotle, there is only one usage, namely, at *De Caelo,* 268a14, concerning three-dimensionality; it has nothing to do with physical process or *kinêsis.* In keeping with the Aristotelian understanding, Aquinas excludes nonhuman natural beings from the domain of law.[84] This should be no surprise: for Aristotle, *form* is the fundamental intelligible in nature. We shall need to be clear about the meaning of natural form in the Aristotelian teaching and why it cannot be assimilated to law of nature. In Stoic

---

83. Recent scholarship has made this clear. See especially John R. Milton, "The origin and development of the concept of the 'laws of nature'," *Archives Européennes de Sociologie* 22 (1981): 173–95, and Jane E. Ruby, "The Origins of Scientific 'Law'," *Journal of the History of Ideas* 57 (July–Sept. 1986), 341–59.

84. Thomas Aquinas, *Summa Theologiae,* Iᵃ IIᵃᵉ, Q. 91, A. 2, ad 3; *Treatise on Law* (Chicago: Henry Regnery, 1965), 16.

writings, there is natural law but, again, it governs human beings, not natural processes. In contrast, the period from the thirteenth to the sixteenth centuries provides three clear, and apparently independent, precursors to the concept of physical law; specifically, the ideas of divine legislation in late (non-Thomistic) scholasticism, especially Ockham; the laws of optics in Roger Bacon; and laws of planetary motion, primarily in Copernicus.[85] At the risk of seeming dismissive, I maintain that, despite their intrinsic fascination and genuine value, none of the studies of the late medieval theological and Renaissance scientific origins of the concept of physical law really get at what is most essential (and disquieting). This is *transformism,* or the proclaimed *malleability* of nature and human nature to human, not divine, power.[86] It is the heart of the opposition between laws of nature and natural forms and ends. To see it, we must look again at Descartes, but also at Francis Bacon, and first of all at Machiavelli. It is Machiavelli who provides an original and nontechnical account of the issue; we do not have to be physicists to understand what he is saying. Whether we will be persuaded by Machiavelli concerning human things as much as we are persuaded by subsequent physics concerning natural phenomena is another matter.

For our purposes, the most important philosophical point in Machiavelli resides in the connection between the following two statements in *The Prince:*

85. Milton brings out nicely the importance of voluntarist theology for the "rejection of the Aristotelian physics of substantial forms and real qualities" (183) in favor of a created world radically contingent on "the absolute freedom and omnipotence of God" (184), Who thus decrees the properties and operations of matter according to laws divinely chosen from a great number of alternative possibilities. Accordingly, there is no necessity in nature other than the will of God (188). Ruby looks at the history of optics and astronomy and finds texts in Roger Bacon, Copernicus, and others wherein the terms "laws of refraction," "laws of nature," "laws of motion" are used in a manner completely compatible with our present scientific discourse. According to Ruby, these cases do not derive from or depend on the theological conception of divine legislation.

86. Milton, "The Origin and Development," 193–94, attributes the abandonment of the "idea that there exists a fundamental difference between natural and artificial bodies," to fourteenth-century voluntarist theology, since all natural things are artifacts, namely, products of God's art. But any biblical theologian must hold this. See, for example, Thomas Aquinas, *In phys.*, n. 268. Yet, for Aquinas, it does not follow (from nature as divine artifact) that we humans have the power to override the distinction between natural and artificial and, thus, for example, transform nonliving material into living material (Bacon, *New Organon* II.4). It is a long way from the radical contingency of the world in the face of God's power to the radical malleability of nature in the face of human power. I take the term "transformism" from one of its most extreme practitioners, Joseph Stalin. See Robert C. Tucker, *The Soviet Political Mind: Studies in Stalinism and Post-Stalin Change* (New York: Praeger, 1963), 92.

Men can be seen in the end that each has before him, namely, glories and riches. . . .[87]

one does not see that [the most excellent founders] had anything else from fortune than the opportunity, which gave them the matter enabling them to introduce any form they pleased.[88]

The connection, hardly obvious at first glance, consists in Machiavelli's notion of *necessity* as the fundamental cause of human action, as opposed to the traditional understanding of virtue based on free choice of the will. We shall see, in a moment, how this works by means of a simple example, using Strauss's *Thoughts on Machiavelli*. First, however, we must begin to see the parallel between what Machiavelli has said, above, and what Bacon says concerning the causes of natural phenomena.

It is widely acknowledged that the origins of modern science and philosophy are characterized by (1) an attack on formal and final causality, (2) an exclusive emphasis on efficient and material causality, and (3) a proclamation of the future enhancement of human power. Bacon's *New Organon* provides classic text on this tripartite scheme:

It is a correct position that 'true knowledge is knowledge by causes.' And causes again are not improperly distributed into four kinds: the material, the formal, the efficient, and the final. But of these the final cause rather corrupts than advances the sciences, except such as have to do with human action. The discovery of the formal is despaired of. The efficient and the material (as they are investigated and received, that is, as remote causes, without reference to the latent process leading to the form) are but slight and superficial, and contribute little, if anything, to true and active science.[89]

We get a taste of what Bacon means by the final cause of human action in *New Organon* I.129: "to establish and extend the power and dominion of the human race itself over the universe."[90] Now two crucial points emerge from the comparison of Machiavelli on politics with Bacon on natural phenomena. First, Machiavelli's two statements—on the ends and on the founders, the matter, and the form—express precisely the tripartite scheme, above, at the level, not of natural phenomena gen-

87. *The Prince*, chap. 25; Mansfield, 99.
88. *The Prince*, chap. 6; Mansfield, 23.
89. Francis Bacon, *The New Organon*, ed. Fulton H. Anderson (Indianapolis: Bobbs-Merrill, 1960), book 2, aph. 2, 121; hereafter Bacon, *New Organon*. See also *New Organon* 1.48 and 1.51., pp. 52–53.
90. *New Organon* 1.129, pp. 118–19. It is well known that, in the same aphorism (1.129), Bacon seems to proclaim theoretical contemplation as the highest end of life. For a discussion of this point, see Richard Kennington, "Bacon's Critique of Ancient Philosophy in *New Organon* I," in *Nature and Scientific Method*, ed. Daniel O. Dahlstrom (Washington, D.C.: The Catholic University of America Press, 1991), 235–51.

erally but of human nature and political life (the founders being the efficient cause). Second, the key term in these quotations is *form*. By considering what Machiavelli and Bacon imply about form, we can begin to see the idea of transformism.

Bacon says that it is pointless to seek formal causes. He then indicates the general reason why: natural forms—the visible species of things, like gold, or rose, or dog—are not causes at all, as Aristotle had mistakenly taught, but effects of something prior to form, namely, "the latent [thus heretofore hidden] process leading to the form." For Machiavelli, the regime or form of government is produced out of human material in a way that is fully determined by the agent cause, that is, the founder. Therefore, despite their differing focus, in both Machiavelli and Bacon, the term 'form' refers to a product and effect of prior causes. As such, form cannot be a principle and cause. Although clearly anti-Aristotelian, this is hardly a new idea. Anyone sensitive to the biblical revelation knows that, one way or another, God's creative activity is the process of which all form is the product. But in all philosophical reflection that respects the Bible, form is an effect that proceeds *per se* from its divine cause, for God knows and wills this particular order of creation.[91] What is new and radical in Machiavelli, Bacon, and Descartes is the further teaching that form has heretofore been an effect not *per se* but *per accidens* (meaning unintended) of forces henceforth subject to human control. We, or some of us, will control the previously unrecognized necessities at work in nature and human nature, and thereby control the future production of natural form and human performance. This means we can bring about new natures and new performances. In short, by removing our ignorance and false opinion concerning the causes of things, we can *transform* both natural and human material. In natural phenomena, the previously unrecognized sources of motion are the particles of bodies and their laws of interaction. To get at them, we must do violence to Aristotle's natural forms or species wherein the laws and particles have lain (and would otherwise continue to lie) hidden: "the nature of things betrays itself more readily under the vexations of art than in its natural freedom."[92] In human phenomena, the previously unrecognized principles are the powerful and self-centered passions for self-preservation, material acquisition, and, in a special few, glory. In both cases, false opinion has been the cause of our failure to see, false beliefs about forms and ends, virtue and vice, and the nature of God. Bacon sets out his audacious

91. *Genesis* I.
92. Bacon, *New Organon*, "The Great Instauration," 25.

project in the opening axioms of *New Organon* II. At first glance, however, Bacon's formulations seem almost bizarre. Let us, therefore, prepare for Bacon by way of Machiavelli, who speaks not in the arcane language of natural philosophy but of political phenomena familiar to all.

According to the first statement of Machiavelli, above, the human species has an end: glories and riches. This assertion rejects the traditional Greek and medieval ethical teaching according to which the natural ends of man are not merely bodily self-preservation (health and comfort), but also and most importantly, the activity of reason and the practice of moral virtue. "[T]he supreme good is happiness . . . the human good is the activity *(energeia)* of soul according to virtue . . . and this in a complete lifetime" (*Nic. Eth.* 1097b22, 1098a16–18). Hence, "virtue must be a care for every city" (*Pol.* 1280b7).

Machiavelli shrinks or contracts, and transforms, the traditional teleology. Glory in the traditional account accrues to a person as a side effect of our spontaneous admiration of his or her excellence; glory is not in itself an activity or actuality *(energeia)*, not an end in itself. In Machiavelli, it becomes an end in itself, the desire for glory necessitating the actions of great founders. The second of Machiavelli's "ends," riches, corresponds to the lowest of the traditional human ends, self-preservation, but, again, in a transformed way. In the traditional account, the desire to acquire would have to be ordered and limited in relation to our higher ends, for example, using reason and judging well in action (1280a33, 1295b6); in Machiavelli, there is no human-natural limitation to acquisitiveness, for we are told simply that "truly it is a very natural and ordinary thing to desire to acquire."[93] Machiavelli's "ends" are posited by self-centered desires having no intrinsic limitation; with respect to the individual, they are open-ended. Our principal conclusion: philosophy and moral virtue have been removed by Machiavelli from the list of human perfections; this constitutes an attack on final causality in ethics and politics.

The puzzling character of Machiavelli's two emblematic claims about the ends, the founders, the matter and the form, is this: the ability to impose any desired form on the human material represents a vast enhancement of human power to establish stable, effective government. In contrast, recall Aristotle's account of the middle class in *Politics* IV.11: "those cities are capable of being well governed in which the middling element is numerous. . . . It alone is without factional conflict."[94] But, for Aristotle, it is not within our power to produce a middle

---

93. Machiavelli, *The Prince*, chap. 3, p. 14.
94. Aristotle, *Politics*, 1295b36–37, 1296a7; *The Politics*, trans. Carnes Lord, (Chicago: University of Chicago Press, 1984), 134–35.

class by design, since "it is the greatest good fortune *(eutychia megistê)* for those engaged in politics to have a middling and sufficient property."[95] Chance limits virtue; this is the reason for the cautious reserve of ancient political thought. Against this background Machiavelli's audacious optimism stands out in sharp relief. But how exactly does his transformation of the causes work; that is, how exactly does contracting the ends bring about the expansion of our power? Here Strauss's comments from *Thoughts on Machiavelli* are indispensable:

> The common understanding of goodness had found its classic expression in Aristotle's assertion that virtue is the habit of choosing well and that choosing well or ill as well as the habits of choosing well or ill (the virtues or vices) are voluntary: man is responsible for having become and for becoming virts or vicious. Man can choose the good or the bad; he possesses a free will. . . . But freedom of the will is incompatible with the necessity of compulsion through which a man is literally compelled by other agents to act against his natural inclination. . . . acts of virtue consist in freely choosing the right means for the right end. . . . *Actions prompted by virtue are fundamentally different from actions prompted by necessity; only the former deserve praise.* . . . To act virtuously means to follow reason and in so doing not to be subject to necessity.[96]

Necessity is a fundamental theme in Machiavelli because of his revised understanding of virtue, one that runs counter to "the common understanding of goodness." In the *Discourses,* he says:

> We have already pointed out the advantage of necessity in human actions, and to what glorious achievements it has given rise. . . . The ancient commanders of armies, who well knew the powerful influence of necessity, and how it inspired the soldiers with the most desperate courage, neglected nothing to subject their men to such a pressure, whilst, on the other hand, they employed every device that ingenuity could suggest to relieve the enemy's troops from the necessity of fighting.[97]

Strauss comments:

> Man's doing his work in the best manner—the fullest exercise of his virtue—is due to necessity and not to choice. . . . [S]oldiers fighting against a superior enemy operate perfectly if they have no choice except to die or to fight; they cease to operate perfectly if they can achieve safety by flight or surrender, . . . since men are compelled by nature to try to avoid death; fighting is chosen because it is the only way in which in the circumstances certain and imminent

---

95. Aristotle, *Politics,* 1295b39; *The Politics* (Lord), 135. Note the other references to chance at *Politics* 1295b4 and 1295b14, *The Politics* (Lord), 134.

96. Leo Strauss, *Thoughts on Machiavelli* (Seattle: University of Washington Press, 1969), 244–45; emphasis mine.

97. Niccolo Machiavelli, *The Discourses,* book 3, chap. 12; in *The Prince and the Discourses,* trans. Christian Detmold, ed. Max Lerner (New York: Random House, 1950); 450–51.

death could possibly be avoided: the choice of fighting is imposed by necessity. If the soldiers can save their lives by flight or surrender, they choose flight or surrender. . . . *Fighting as well as flight or surrender aim at the same end, namely, the preservation of one's life;* this end is imposed, as we may tentatively say, by an absolute and natural necessity.[98]

The truly natural end of the majority of men is self-preservation. This general principle of human action is determined to particular effects by constraints imposed from without. Thus one and the same "end" manifests itself in vividly distinct empirical patterns of behavior —as what we praise as courage or as what we condemn as cowardice— according to the external conditions imposed on men by commanders and founders who know "the effectual truth [rather] than . . . the [traditional and erroneous] imagination of it."[99] The source of the crucial difference between courageous and cowardly performance is not internal to the soldiers themselves. Human beings have no intrinsic or *per se* directedness to goodness, where "goodness" means behavior or activity which is perfective of our specifically human nature, like the virtues of courage, justice, wisdom, and moderation. Rather, human nature is "virtue-neutral." In Machiavelli's new doctrine, to be virtuous means to be effective in dominating necessity by imposing constraints on others: "men will always turn out bad for you unless they have been made good [for you] by a necessity [that you impose on them]."[100] Those who are best at this are the founders; they act freely because they are necessitated *from within* (not, like the material on which they work, from without) by their compulsory desire for glory.[101] They are able "to introduce any form they pleased."

Let us look at the example of the soldiers, as understood by Aristotle and as understood by Machiavelli, in terms of the four causes:

ARISTOTLE

| | |
|---|---|
| *The End:* | The noble (*to kalon,* 1115b12–13) |
| *The Agent:* | The soldiers, voluntarily choosing, willing to fight for what is right. |
| *The "Form":* | Courageous combat performance. |
| *The "Matter":* | Honorable men |

Agent and subject of motion (the soldier) are the same; the agent acts for the end it itself intends. The subject is responsible for its own cour-

98. Strauss, *Thoughts on Machiavelli,* 247–48; emphasis mine.
99. Machiavelli, *The Prince,* chap. 15, p. 61.
100. Ibid., chap. 23, p. 95.
101. Strauss, *Thoughts on Machiavelli,* 249–50.

ageous performance. But the matter limits the form; without the right matter, the form cannot be attained.

MACHIAVELLI

*The End:*
*Of the soldiers:* Self-preservation, indifferent to "courage" or "cowardice."
*Commander's:* Glory
*The Agent:* The commander, imposing external constraints (fight or die).
*The "Form":* "Courageous" combat performance.
*The "Matter":* Whatever!

The agent (commander) is external to the subject of motion (soldier); the agent acts for the end it intends, and to which the nature of the moved subject is neutral. Because it is "homogeneous," the matter does not limit the imposition of form. Therefore, the external agent, not the subject of motion, is responsible for the essential difference between courageous and cowardly performance.

Machiavelli's radical message is that the traditional judgment of the essential distinction between courageous and cowardly performance is erroneous because both are caused by the "boundary conditions" imposed from without on one and the same matter. The traditional judgment, deceived by false beliefs, mistook what is accidental to the material (distinct performances) for what is essential and thus failed to recognize what is truly essential (the effects of necessity). Failing to link cause and effect accurately, mankind has heretofore been hostage to fortune or chance. Correction of our judgment by the methods of enlightenment will henceforth facilitate mastery of chance by the recognition and control of the determining conditions on natural forces. As Strauss puts it:

Contrary to Aristotle's view according to which multitudes have a natural fitness either for being subject to a despot or a life of political freedom, fitness for either form of life can be artificially produced if a man of a rare 'brain' applies the required degree of force to the multitude in question; compulsion can bring about a 'change of nature.'[102]

This is the kernel of transformism. Implicit therein is a new conception of chance as lack of complete knowledge in a necessitarian universe. Whereas in Aristotle a chance effect is both unforeseen and unfore-

102. Ibid., 252–53.

seeable (197a20, 198a5), in the new understanding, it is unforeseen but in principle foreseeable.[103]

It would not be difficult to trace this line of thought into political economy: from chapters 15–17 and 25 of Machiavelli's *Prince* to Locke's "wise and godlike" prince, who, by the liberation and canalization of acquisitiveness, creates (or seems to create) a whole new virtue, industriousness, and therewith (perhaps) the middle class that Aristotle thought was dependent on fortune.[104] Our purpose here, however, lies in another direction. It is to make clear the connection between the rise of laws of nature and the attack on formal and final causality in the seventeenth century. I maintain that the decisive component of the idea of laws of nature is transformism, of which Machiavelli's nonteleological, necessitarian account of human nature is a major source. Whether Machiavelli is the only source, is a large question.[105] Similarly, it is a large question whether we find his account of human things persuasive, especially in view of our continuing, spontaneous, and genuine admiration for that most basic of virtues, the courage of soldiers in combat. It is beyond question, however, that the necessitarian understanding of nature fits certain classes of nonhuman physical phenomena. Before turning to the arcane language of Bacon's philosophy, wherein law of nature is central, let us look at an example familiar to all students of contemporary physics: the Newtonian account of gravitational local motion.

Consider the local motion of a falling stone, a projectile, a satellite orbiting the earth. Each of these three exemplifies a two-body gravitational system (the earth plus the stone, projectile, or satellite) whose total mechanical energy is conserved. We could say that the "end" of the two-body system is conservation of mechanical energy. But this "end" is equally fulfilled by all three motions. Thus, one and the same end manifests itself in sharply distinct visible patterns of motion. The differences between the trajectories arise from the conditions (relative

103. Pierre Simon Laplace, *A Philosophical Essay on Probabilities*, trans. F. W. Truscott and F. L. Emory (New York: Dover, 1951), 4 and 6.

104. Locke, *Second Treatise of Government*, sec. 42, p. 26. For Machiavelli's account of liberality, see Clifford Orwin, "Machiavelli's Unchristian Charity," *American Political Science Review* 72 (1978): 1217–28. It is a large question whether the middle class apparently artificed through liberal capitalism does not in reality *presuppose* the middle class of moral character described by Aristotle in *Politics* IV.11.

105. Roger D. Masters, *Beyond Relativism* (Hanover, N.H.: University Press of New England, 1993) notes the likely significance of the relationship between Machiavelli and Leonardo da Vinci. For brief but suggestive examples, see *The Notebooks of Leonardo da Vinci*, ed. Jean Paul Richter (New York: Dover, 1970), vol. 2, nn. 1134, 1135, 1139.

position and velocity) imposed on the moved bodies by experimenters at the initiation of motion. Quite generally, the source of the differences between terrestrial and celestial local motion is not internal to the mobile subjects. It is not—as the Aristotelians mistakenly believed—the different natures of terrestrial and celestial bodies. Rather, a rock and the moon are made of the same stuff; their matter is homogeneous and not specified according to distinct forms (194b9). In their local motions, inanimate bodies have no intrinsic or *per se* directedness to one trajectory or another as perfective of their natures. Given the right initial conditions, what falls down today could be in orbit tomorrow or vice versa; that is, one trajectory can be transformed into another according to the will of human agents. This is the sense of transformism in Newton's gravitational theory.

We parenthetically insert the good question whether there is any evidence that Newton understood his physics as transformist. The answer is, yes. The generalization and extension of the basic principles of the gravitational theory to all phenomena is proposed by Newton in his preface to the first edition of the *Principia*.[106] As discussed in the concluding essay of this volume, the radical malleability of nature is implicit in the resulting reductionist research program. That Newton was aware of this is clear from Hypothesis III of the first Latin edition of the *Principia*: "Every body can be transformed into another, of whatever kind, and all the intermediary degrees of qualities can be successively induced in it."[107] Let us return to the main argument.

The premodern science of motion and matter mistook what is accidental to the mobile—distinct trajectories—for an essential effect of what it thus falsely judged to be different natural species. It thereby failed to recognize what is truly essential: the necessity of gravitational force and contingent (often controllable) initial conditions. On this point, both Aristotle and Aquinas commit the error into which fall "even the wise."[108] Correction of this error by classical mechanics has made possible modern astrophysics and the exploration of space.

106. Newton, *Principia*, trans. Motte and Cajori (New York: Greenwood Press, 1962), vol. 1, xviii.

107. Isaac Newton, *Philosophiae Naturalis Principia Mathematica*, ed. Alexandre Koyre and I. Bernard Cohen (Cambridge: Harvard University Press, 1972), 550. See also *Opticks*, 4th ed, Query 30 (New York: Dover, 1979), 374–75. Why did Newton delete this assertion from subsequent editions of the *Principia*? A sufficient reason would be that, regardless of Newton's awareness of the radical Baconian possibility expressed by hypothesis III, the hypothesis plays no role in the strict argument of the *Principia*. For the Baconian character of this hypothesis, see the following discussion, also *Wisdom of the Ancients* XIII, on Proteus.

108. Aquinas, *In de trinitate*, Q. 5, A. 2, reply; *De Trinitate*, Maurer, trans., 20. For

The point of this brief review of Newton's physics is to make clear against the premodern background the similar senses of 'nonteleological' in these two accounts of very different classes of phenomena: Machiavelli's nonteleological account of human nature, and the later nonteleological physics of universal gravitation. It must be emphasized, against a common tendency to argue by superficial analogy, that Newton's physics does not prove Machiavelli's politics and that no claim is being made for the reduction of human action to the terms of Newton's physics. Indeed, the similarities between Machiavelli and Newton can be correctly understood only against the premodern background of nature as internal principle of specific visible patterns of behavior, a concept of nature common to both Aristotle's ethics and his physics. Now the root of classical mechanics (from which is derived the conservation of mechanical energy) consists in Newton's *laws* of motion and gravitational force. Newton's gravitational theory thus affords a familiar example of a law of nature, as well as a sense of transformism (in gravitational locomotion) similar to that in Machiavelli (on human behavior). Let us turn then to a less familiar but more radical source, to laws of nature and transformism in Francis Bacon. Our goal is to see how the argument for Baconian laws of nature is essentially related to the argument against Aristotelian formal and final causality in nature. The crux of the matter is simply that, for Bacon, a law of nature is mainly about changing one kind, form, species, or quality of thing into another. This directly contradicts the Aristotelian understanding of natural form as *per se* unchangeable and normative.[109] As Aquinas succinctly puts it, "the soul and other natural forms are not *per se* subject to motion . . . they are, moreover, the perfections of mutable things."[110] This is why natural form in the Aristotelian teaching cannot be assimilated to law of nature in early modern philosophy and classical physics.

Bacon begins *New Organon* II in a way that seems at first glance both outlandish and obscure:

On a given body, to generate and superinduce a new nature or new natures is the work and aim of human power. Of a given nature to discover the form, or true difference, or nature-engendering nature, or source of emanation (for these are the terms which come nearest to a description of the thing), is the work and aim of human knowledge. Subordinate to these primary works are two others that are secondary and of inferior mark: to the former, the trans-

Thomas's acceptance of the heterogeneity of terrestrial and celestial matter, see Q. 5, A. 2, ad 6, and Q. 5, A. 3, ad 8; *De Trinitate*, Maurer, trans., 24 and 38–39.

109. Aristotle, *Metaphysics*, 1043b17, *Physics*, 193b8, 194a33, 198b3.
110. Aquinas, *In de trinitate*, Q. 5, A. 2, ad 6; *De Trinitate*, Maurer, trans., 24.

formation of concrete bodies, so far as this is possible; to the latter, the discovery, in every case of generation and motion, of the latent process carried on from the manifest efficient and the manifest material to the form which is engendered. . . . [111]

Bacon clearly wants knowledge in the service of human transformative power, the power to "superinduce a new nature" on a body, for example, "vegetation on some body that is not vegetable[!]"[112] The word 'form' appears twice, above, and means something different in each case. Form$_1$, "or true difference . . . ," means a Baconian law of nature: "in nature nothing really exists besides individual bodies, performing pure individual acts according to law. . . . And it is this law with its clauses that I mean when I speak of *forms*."[113] Form$_2$, "which is engendered," means Aristotelian form, now taken not as cause and principle but as effect and product of laws and law-governed process latent in bodies. Bacon's extraordinary idea is that discovery of laws will enable the transform$_2$ation of what we erroneously thought were Aristotelian natures normatively or ethically limiting human action. This is possible because Baconian laws underlie, conjoin, and unify what appear to our senses to be distinct and unrelated natures: "whosoever is acquainted with forms [i.e., Baconian laws] embraces the unity of nature in materials the most unlike, and is able therefore to detect and bring to light things never yet done. . . ."[114] Consider, for example, two things that appear to be quite different: the sun and terrestrial fire. Bacon says that "the doctrine that the heat of the sun and of fire differ in kind . . . tend[s] wholly to the unfair circumscription of human power."[115] For Bacon, heat is not *specific* to the hot subject, but *species-neutral* (a major theme of the concluding essay of this volume). In general, "it is most unskillful to investigate the nature of anything in the thing itself, seeing that the same nature which appears in some things to be latent and hidden is in others manifest and palpable."[116] What does Bacon mean? He means this: The same gravitational force hidden in celestial matter and motion is manifest in falling stones. Similarly, a lodestone manifests magnetism, while lightning appears to be completely different. But both present aspects of an underlying, "latent and hidden" Baconian nature, the electromagnetic field, the knowledge of which is accessible only to human practice and which accordingly "bring[s] to light things never yet done," like electric power, radio and television, lasers, the immense

---

111. Bacon, *New Organon* II.1, p. 121.    112. Ibid., II.4, p. 123.
113. Ibid., II.2, p. 122.    114. Ibid., II.3, p. 122.
115. Ibid., I.88, p. 86.    116. Ibid.

world of electromagnetic technology. In general, gravitation, electromagnetism, and thermodynamics—the principal theories of classical physics—exhibit laws of nature facilitating the transformation of phenomena and the production of new effects. (The quantum physics of atomic structure has Baconian features but is, overall, another story.) Here, Bacon seems prescient, and we wonder how far he himself intended to go.

## 6. Reason Transcending Nature

Is human nature included in Bacon's transformist project? His answer, as given in *New Organon* I.127, seems to be, yes:

> It may also be asked . . . whether I speak of natural philosophy only, or whether I mean that the other sciences, logic, *ethics and politics*, should be carried out by this method. Now I certainly mean what I have said to be understood of them all. . . . For I form a history and table of discovery for *anger, fear, shame,* and the like; for matters political; and again for the mental operations of memory, composition and division, judgment, and the rest; not less than for heat and cold, or light, or vegetation, or the like.[117]

There is a provocative echo of this disquieting proposal in Descartes's posthumously published *Treatise on Man*. In this work, Descartes constructs a human-like machine whose functions follow "from the mere arrangement of the machine's organs every bit as naturally as the movements of a clock or other automaton follow from the arrangement of its counter-weights and wheels."[118] The cause of motion in this machine is not soul but heat, which is explicitly described as being universal in the Baconian or species-neutral sense:

> In order to explain these functions, then, it is not necessary to conceive of the machine as having any vegetative or sensitive soul or other principle of movement and life, apart from the blood and its spirits, which are agitated by the heat of the fire burning continuously in its heart—a fire which has the same nature as all the fires that occur in inanimate bodies.[119]

Among the functions of this machine are the passions of anger, fear, and shame, and they are subject to a new and remarkable type of control by Cartesian reason. In preparation for a look at this, let us note

117. Ibid., I.127, pp. 115–116; emphasis mine.
118. Descartes, *L'Homme*, in *Oeuvres*, Adam and Tannery, eds., vol. 11, 202; *Philosophical Writings*, Cottingham, et al., trans., vol. 1, 108. *Discourse* V and VI repeat the account but with modifications that, I believe, make it less striking.
119. *L'Homme*, in *Oeuvres*, Adam and Tannery, eds., vol. 11, 202; *Philosophical Writings*, Cottingham, et al., trans., vol. 1, 108. See also *Discourse* V, in *Oeuvres*, Adam and Tannery, eds., vol. 6, 46; *Philosophical Writings*, Cottingham, et al., trans., vol. 1, 134.

that the role of fire in Descartes's cosmology of indifference is very special. In *Discourse* V, it becomes clear that fire is in fact Descartes's first transformist principle:

I took pains to make everything belonging to the nature of fire very clearly understandable, because I know nothing else in the world, apart from the heavenly bodies, that produces light. Thus I made clear . . . how it can produce different colors and various other qualities in different bodies; how it melts some bodies and hardens others; how it can consume almost all bodies, or turn them into ashes and smoke; and finally how it can, by the mere violence of its action, form glass from these ashes—something I took particular pleasure in describing *since it seems to me as wonderful a transmutation as any that takes place in nature.*[120]

Let us conclude with a remarkable example of the new conception of chance and necessity as humanly controllable: the analogy of the fountain in Descartes's *Treatise on Man*. Here we find an account of reason and passion quite unlike the human-natural teleology of Aristotle's *Ethics*.

In explaining how the human-machine responds to external stimuli, Descartes introduces the example of large, intricately designed "grottos and fountains in the royal gardens."[121] Just as animal spirits move the parts of the human-machine, the elaborate piping and water flows in the gardens can produce all sorts of effects according to the corresponding trigger mechanisms:

External objects, which by their mere presence stimulate [the human-machine's] sense organs and thereby cause them to move in many different ways . . . are like visitors *(estrangers)* who enter the grottos of these fountains and unthinkingly cause the movements which take place before their eyes. For they cannot enter without stepping on certain tiles which are so arranged that if, for example, they approach a Diana who is bathing they will cause her to hide in the reeds, and if they move forward to pursue her they will cause a Neptune to advance and threaten them with his trident; or if they go in another direction they will cause a sea-monster to emerge and spew water onto their faces; or other such things according to the whim *(caprice)* of the engineers who made the fountain. And finally, when a *rational soul* is present in this machine it will have its principal seat in the brain, and reside there like the fountain-keeper *(fontenier)* who must be stationed at the tanks to which the fountain's pipes return if he wants to produce, or prevent, or change their movements in some way.[122]

120. Descartes, *Discourse in Method*, part 5, in *Oeuvres*, Adam and Tannery, eds., vol. 6, 44–45; *Philosophical Writings*, Cottingham, et al., trans., vol. 1, 133; emphasis mine.
121. Descartes, *L'Homme*, in *Oeuvres*, Adam and Tannery, eds., vol. 11, 130; *Philosophical Writings*, Cottingham, et al., trans., vol. 1, 100.
122. *L'Homme*, in *Oeuvres*, Adam and Tannery, eds., vol. 11, 131; *Philosophical Writings*, Cottingham, et al., trans., vol. 1, 101.

Do not the movements of the Diana, the Neptune, the sea-monster represent Descartes's understanding of the causal processes underlying our experience of shame, fear, anger? (Note that being spit upon is traditionally regarded as an outrageous insult demanding immediate response in defense of one's honor. But if we saw it in Descartes's terms, what would become of our anger?) Needless to say, the passions play a decisive role in our own happiness or misery. It is thus remarkable that Descartes characterizes the physical basis of our emotions as existing "according to the whim of the engineers who made" our body-machines. "[T]he engineers" means God or nature. This is the most directly and immediately personal example of the cosmology of indifference. The passions, which dominate our lives, are essentially physical, and the designer of our emotional mechanism didn't much care about how the system happens to affect us. By nature, therefore, the human kind has no good or normative mode of operation, no *telos*. We have heretofore failed to appreciate this, believing instead in the traditional accounts of virtue based on the soul's ability to order itself through moral preachments and heroic but painful self-restraint. These are like "proud and magnificent palaces built only on sand and mud."[123] Descartes's enlightening claim is rather that, correctly understood, our psycho-physical system is such that the "I" can stand over its material like the fountain-keeper. The fountain-keeper enjoys liberating detachment from the physical processes over which he presides. Is this not the seed of reason's transcendence of nature, the growing self-awareness of reason's supremacy, culminating in the concepts of self, spirit and freedom in German idealism? Here in Descartes, not the arduous rule of right opinion over the passions—attainable only by the few—but a new fluid-dynamical medicine open to all will be the ground of ethics. As in Machiavelli, virtue becomes the control of previously unrecognized natural forces. But in Descartes, mastery of indifferent but malleable nature consists in the technology of the human passions based on a mathematical physics employed by a transnatural mind.[124] That minds have special, transnatural status is demanded by the astounding fact that human (or at least Cartesian) reason was able to figure all of this out, over against a powerful aggregate of natural forces indifferent to human success. In its recognition of necessity and chance, reason thus begins to recognize its own transcendence of na-

123. Descartes, *Discourse on Method*, part 1, in *Oeuvres*, Adam and Tannery, eds., vol. 6, 8; *Philosophical Writings*, Cottingham, et al., trans., vol. 1, 114. Thus the approach of the dialectician at *De Anima*, 403a31, is misconceived.
124. *Discourse on Methods*, part 6; in *Oeuvres*, Adam and Tannery, eds., vol. 6, 62; *Philosophical Writings*, Cottingham, et al., trans., vol. 1, 143.

ture and human nature. Let us draw our major conclusions concerning early modern philosophy.

The philosophies of Bacon and Descartes find validation in the theories of classical physics (optics, not mechanics, being Descartes's forte). Against Aristotle's thoroughgoing natural teleology, Bacon and Descartes's nonteleological accounts of nature are thus partially true. But, at least in the case of Descartes, the highest intention is a transformation of human nature itself through a liberating physics of the human passions. This intention is unfulfilled. Against Bacon and Descartes, Aristotelian ethics is far more reasonable.[125] And not only in the domain of human phenomena but more generally in the domain of biology, Bacon and Descartes are disappointing. They have no theory of organism, to which, as noted earlier, Baconian-Cartesian-Newtonian laws of nature are not adequate. For the unity, characteristic activity, and self-replication of an organism demand an account wherein general causes (for example, the species) are tightly linked to their particular effects (for example, the individual). Aristotelian notions of form and matter, as well as Kantian notions of natural purpose (see below), thus remain serious contenders in philosophical discussions of modern biology. Hence we return to the possibility of regional teleologies today.

Unfortunately, however, the mastery of a partially malleable nature presents us with a problem Aristotle and his students did not have. Modern natural science provides powerful means of control and transformation unguided by a commensurately authoritative understanding of ends. The decision at the inception of German idealism seems indeed to have been that no scientific understanding of physical nature could yield humanly meaningful goods, purposes, or ends by which to guide our choices. Nature is merely the spatio-temporal arena of material transformations under physical laws. Not nature, but the progressive self-awareness and self-determination of reason must provide the ground of ultimate intelligibility and human morality. This completes my account of the period from Aristotle through medieval and

125. This is my own opinion. It is not shared by contemporary proponents of the Baconian-Cartesian project, who are pressing with vigor the claim for scientific control of human nature. Paul Churchland, *Engine of Reason, Seat of the Soul* (Cambridge: MIT Press, 1995), 277–78, provides a striking example: "If we—all of us—were systematically to replace our humble common sense concepts with their more powerful scientific counterparts . . . then each of us would gain a cognitive grip on the world, and a continuing control over it, that far exceeds one's current feeble grasp. . . . We might as well know [these scientific counterparts] for what they are. And make practical use of them with what that knowledge brings . . . today's common sense can become tomorrow's forgotten mythology. The scientific enterprise, accordingly, is . . . the leading rung of a ladder the entire human race is climbing."

early modern philosophy. Let me resume the presentation of the essays in this volume.

*Richard L. Velkley* addresses the fundamental problem of intelligibility and goodness on the plane of Kant. In Kant, of course, the intelligibility of the natural, phenomenal world arises not from things as they are but from the a priori structure of theoretical reason. Morality, on the radically other hand, "must not be sought in the nature of man [nor be based] in the least on empirical grounds."[126] In the *Critique of Judgment*, Kant seeks indications of the unity of the realms of nature and morality he so sharply divided in the earlier *Critiques*, those of *Pure Reason* and of *Practical Reason*. What, for example, is the relation between the fact that we possess just these particular categories of understanding and forms of intuition, and the fact of the moral law, which governs human practice and defines the goal of human history? Are these two ultimate contingencies themselves related in some essential way or merely contingently? These questions arise necessarily in Kant because the emotional and physical performance of human beings (for example, exploitation of some by others) must alter (for example, cessation of exploitation) consequent to the progressive realization of the moral *telos*. The possibility of reason's transformation of nature must be, in some way, intelligible, for the human being is a compound of self-determining reason and deterministic nature. Yet the comprehension of this unity falls neither within the theoretical reason of the first *Critique* nor within the practical reason of the second *Critique*. Velkley examines how the unity of the human species—a particular empirical determination within the natural whole—is understood in terms of necessity and contingency in Kant's third *Critique*. Velkley concludes that, in Kant, "it is necessarily true that human beings are the unity of reason and desire only if they are contingently so." Rather than giving an ultimate account of the necessary grounding of human rationality in the whole, like Aristotle's detailed cosmology, Kant gives an ultimate account *"in terms* of fundamental contingencies."

*David A. White* focuses on Kant's understanding of organism, or natural purpose, in the *Critique of Judgment*. The type of causality exhibited by a living thing is quite unlike the causality accessible to scientific understanding in classical physics. In the case of an organism, Kant describes the cause-effect relation as being "such that we can see it as law-governed only if we regard the cause's action as based on the idea

126. Kant, *Grundlegung zur Metaphysik der Sitten*, in *Kants gesammelte Schriften*, vol. 4, 389; *Foundations of the Metaphysics of Morals*, trans. Lewis White Beck (Indianapolis: Bobbs-Merrill, 1959), 5.

of the effect, with this idea as the underlying condition under which the cause itself can produce that effect."[127] This elusive Kantian formulation means at least this: the relation between cause and effect in the unity and specificity of an organism is more intimate or essential than the external and contingent relation between, say, Newton's universal law of gravitation and the particular orbital structure of the solar system. The law of gravitation is not *in* the solar system the way the form or species is *in* the living individual. Now for Kant, "a natural purpose is not a constitutive concept either of understanding or of reason. But it can still be a regulative concept for reflective judgment. . . ."[128] White's concern is to examine precisely how the concept of natural purpose regulates judgment. To this end, he explicates the terms 'form' and 'unity' by means of a close textual analysis of sections 64, 65, and 77 of Kant's third *Critique*.

*John W. Burbidge* discusses Hegel's concept of final causality, first its logical structure, then its function in human history, the domain most important for the understanding of Hegel. Nature and spirit, the two sides of the essentially temporal whole, must interact in the realization of some type of final stage. "On the one side are mechanical movements and chemical combinations, instinctive desires and blind passion. . . ." Here, the Machiavellian, Baconian, and Cartesian teachings on nature and human nature are taken up within the Hegelian synthesis. "[O]n the other [side] is some kind of direction that has a sense of a unified whole." The cunning of transnatural reason consists in the achievement of harmony by natural means having no intrinsic directedness to harmony. Burbidge helps us understand how this works in Hegel. Most interesting, in view of recent debates on the end of history, is his account of the endless recurrence of divisions within unification, of natural passions and new conflicting interests within reason's conventions of freedom. According to Burbidge, "[t]here is no end to history."

Anthropic-principle cosmology addresses the problem of intelligibility and goodness in the terms of contemporary physics. Within the evolution of the universe, is the present order of astronomical systems, chemical elements and compounds, and living things an effect of the principles *per se* or *per accidens*? In anthropic-principle cosmology, the principles are the laws and initial conditions (previously mentioned), and the fundamental constants (not previously mentioned). These gov-

127. Kant, *Kritik der Urteilskraft*, sec. 63, in *Kants gesammelte Schriften*, vol. 5, 366–67; *Immanuel Kant Critique of Judgment*, trans. Werner S. Pluhar (Indianapolis: Hackett Publishing Co., 1987), 244.
128. *Kritik der Urteilskraft*, sec. 65, in *Kants gesammelte Schriften*, vol. 5, 375; Pluhar, trans., 255.

ern the cosmological and stellar processes that gave rise to at least one biosphere in which emerged intelligent living observers. To appreciate anthropic-principle cosmology, it is necessary to understand what is meant by the term "fundamental constants." In the basic equations of physics, there appear quantities whose numerical values are (unlike those of variable quantities) fixed and unchanging in time and space. For example, the well-known equations, $F = -GMm/R^2$, $E = mc^2$, $E = h\nu$, contain the quantities G, c, h, representing the universal gravitational constant, the speed of light in a vacuum, and Planck's constant. Similar examples of fundamental constants are the electron charge, e, and the electron and proton masses, $m_e$, $m_p$. Why do these constants have the particular numerical values that they do? For example, why is the speed of light 186,000 miles per second instead of 185,000 miles per second? This question was long considered unanswerable because the numerical values of the fundamental constants were taken as irreducibly contingent facts not subject to further explanation. Thus, mainstream physics took little interest in the question, "what difference would it make if the values of the fundamental constants were different?" Over the last fifty years, calculations done primarily by physicists in their spare time have made clear that, in fact, the universe in its particular detail is extremely sensitive to the values of the fundamental constants. Specifically, minute changes in their values derail the processes whereby stars and galaxies are formed and whereby the higher chemical elements, especially carbon, are then produced through nuclear fusion in stars and distributed in space (amazingly) through supernova explosions. In other words, it is now an established fact that the universe is "fine-tuned" for the production of the materials—the chemical elements beyond hydrogen and helium—necessary for life. The debates and discussions of anthropic-principle cosmology concern especially the scientific and philosophical interpretation of the fine-tuned universe. There are two broad alternative interpretations: (1) The fine-tuning is best explained as the *per se* effect of a designing mind. This interpretation is thus the most scientifically up-to-date version of the design-teleological argument for the existence of God. (2) The fine-tuning is best explained as a *per accidens* effect as follows. Within a huge number of alternate universes—separate and distinct either in space or time—all conceivable values of the fundamental constants will occur. It just happens that life-permitting values occur in our universe, which we intelligent organisms accordingly observe. In the myriad other universes, different values of the fundamental constants preclude the production and distribution of the chemical elements and/or the stable operation of stars needed for life, and so in those universes, nothing able to observe them evolves. This interpretation is thus the most scientifically up-to-date version of the Empedoclean many-worlds cosmology of chance and necessity.

*John Leslie* clarifies and addresses the many questions that arise in response to the discoveries and theories of the fine-tuned universe. He reviews the empirical evidence for fine tuning and describes different types of many-worlds theories. He takes up the important question of what the anthropic principle itself is, distinguishing weak and strong forms thereof, and the very important question of how it can contribute to explanation and even to testable predictions. He concludes with a discussion of the teleological interpretation "and the predictions it might encourage."

*George Gale* reviews the history of twentieth-century physical cosmology from its origins in Einstein's general theory of relativity and Hubble's observational discovery of galactic recession. The conception of the universe as expanding from a singular initial state, now called the Big Bang, was in place by 1931. This is the essential background for the development of anthropic-principle cosmology. Gale's concern is then to address the question whether anthropic-principle arguments are physics or metaphysics. To this end, he distinguishes types of anthropic-principle arguments, including but going beyond weak and strong anthropic principles to consider the more speculative quantum theories of multiple universes. Gale concludes that imputation of final causality to physical processes relegates the respective theory to metaphysics, rather than to physics. Different anthropic principles are thus physics or metaphysics according to their teleological content.

*Richard F. Hassing,* in the concluding essay, addresses the problem of natural science and human self-knowledge: How does our belief in science affect the way we understand ourselves? Here the promissory notes of this introduction must be paid off. Accordingly, the non-Aristotelian type of intelligibility—called species-neutral or structure-neutral—featured by early modern philosophy and characteristic of classical physics is explicated in terms of its first scientifically successful example, Newton's gravitational theory. The step from Newton to universal reductionism is described and, therewith, the traditional idea of the unity of science that has predominated from the seventeenth century up until the recent decline of logical positivism. Hassing maintains that there has never been a sound, science-based argument for universal reductionism. The new, nonreductionist (and as yet inchoate) unity-of-science conception is then described and evaluated. This conception is based on evolutionary emergence and, in its details, derives from recent developments in self-organizing systems, nonlinear science (chaos theory), and molecular biology. Hassing's fundamental point is that both unity-of-science models—the old reductionist and the new evolutionist—are species-neutral and, therefore, lead to the same basic difficulty: our ordinary, prescientific experience of specific difference loses its scientific ground. Therefore, no account of the human on its own terms can count as science. The solution defended (although not elaborated) is a problematic, but non-contradictory dualism of natural science and human experience.

# 2          Is Finality Included in Aristotle's Definition of Nature?

## WILLIAM A. WALLACE

The question I propose in the title of this paper may seem simplistic. Everyone knows that Aristotle's cosmology is teleological and that final causes are pervasive in his system of explanation. "Nature acts for an end" is so axiomatic in Aristotelian natural philosophy that one might well ask what can be problematic about finality in nature. So, to be clear from the outset, my problem is not with finality in nature but rather with the way or ways in which finality is or is not included in the definition of nature that Aristotle proposes at the beginning of the second book of the *Physics*. After the briefest of prologues in that book, Aristotle offers a classical definition of nature that is known to most philosophers. In literal translation the definition reads, "Nature is a principle and a cause of motion and of rest in the thing to which it belongs primarily and essentially, and not merely accidentally" (192b21–23).

Now the problem with this definition can be seen by focusing on the way the word "cause" occurs in it and then on the way Aristotle subsequently goes about explaining his concept of causality and how it relates to his concept of nature. Briefly put, for Aristotle "nature is a cause of motion and of rest," and it is a cause that is "in the thing" whose nature it is. Being in the thing, it is an internal cause, and so nature is an internal cause of motion and of rest. But, as we read along in Book II of the *Physics*, we find that, of the four types of cause Aristotle enumerates there, only two are internal causes, namely, matter and form. The remaining types, agent and end, are external causes; they are not "in the thing" but rather are external to it. So we are not surprised to find that Aristotle identifies a thing's nature with its matter and with its form, and thus sees nature functioning both as a material cause and as a formal cause. But, if "nature is an internal cause of motion and of rest," is it not also an *efficient* cause of motion, for that is what we normally mean when we say that something is a cause. And, in view of our pervasive notion of teleology, is nature not also a *final* cause of motion, as Aristotle explicitly states later in Book II (199a33). If we give affirmative answers to these questions, then two *external* causes will have become *internal* causes also, and the problem I propose is, how can this be? How can external causes become internalized, as it were, to function also as internal causes?

The problem, so stated, seems to be little more than a textual exercise for Aristotelian scholars, but I wonder if it is not more far-ranging than that. It continues to offer difficulty for natural scientists, especially those dealing with evolution, and with their concerns in mind as well as those of the exegetes I propose to look more deeply into the problem.

## The Causal Model

Let me start with Aristotle's causal model, a simple explanatory scheme that takes its origin from the world of artifacts and which he applies to the world of nature.[1] The four factors involved in that scheme are usually identified as matter, form, agent, and end. Analyzing an artifact such as a chair on this basis, it is easy to identify the first two factors, matter and form. The matter is the stuff or material out of which the chair is made and which remains in it—for example, wood, or, to be more precise, cherry or oak. The form is the shape or design imposed on the wood during the chair's making. Both of these factors are internal to the chair, that is, they are within it and serve to explain its composition in the order of being, and so we call them internal causes. The remaining two factors are external to it and are mainly of help in explaining how and why the chair came to be. The agent is the carpenter or craftsman who fashioned it from raw materials, and the end is the goal or objective he had in mind when so doing, say, to construct a piece of furniture on which one can sit comfortably. They are principles more in the order of becoming than in the order of being, though once made, the chair retains a relationship to its maker and also embodies the goal he had in mind when making it.

Applying this causal model to a clarification of Aristotle's definition of nature—to understand, for example, what is meant by the nature of sulphur—it would appear that only the first two factors, matter and form, are immediately relevant. If nature is the source of distinctive

1. Much of what follows in this essay is excerpted from my recent book, *The Modeling of Nature: Philosophy of Science and Philosophy of Nature in Synthesis* (Washington, D.C.: The Catholic University of America Press, 1996), which should be consulted for the further development of my thesis. The basic idea behind this work is outlined in my "The Intelligibility of Nature: A Neo-Aristotelian View," *Review of Metaphysics* 38 (1984): 33–56.

activities that originate within a thing and are not imposed on it from without, only internal factors here seem relevant. These are sulphur's matter, or the stuff out of which it is made, and its form, the structure or design assumed by that matter when sulphur comes into being. This is not to say that no agents or efficient causes are operative in the order of nature or that no goals or ends are intended or achieved through nature's operations. But with regard to sulphur, it is difficult to identify the agent that produced it or the end for which it was produced, and thus these external causes would seem not to be part of its nature.

Perhaps one gets the impression that we have moved too fast here, that I have been superficial in applying Aristotle's treatment of the four causes to his definition of nature. Possibly true, so let us probe more deeply into his teaching on causality, which is also found in the second book of the *Physics,* to see how agency and finality might be included in the classical definition. I shall start by reviewing quickly Aristotle's teaching on nature as matter and nature as form, and then proceed from that to his teaching on nature as agent and nature as end, the source of the present difficulty.

## Nature as Matter

According to Aristotle, the matter or material cause of a natural entity is the stuff from which it is made and which remains in it. The Greek term for stuff is *hulē.* Precisely how to identify *hulē* is the puzzle involved in considering nature as matter, as we can see by considering the artificial analogue. If asked to identify the material out of which the chair was made, we would reply "wood," or perhaps "cherry" or "oak." That is open to inspection and often can be identified as having a nature in its own right, say, oak. Not so simple is the identification of the matter out of which sulphur, or an oak tree, or a horse is made. If it is to satisfy the requirements of a material cause as seen in the artifact, it must be some underlying stuff out of which the natural entity is made and that continues to remain in it. That there *is* such a stuff seems obvious on the face of it, but precisely *what* it is poses the problem.

For those who have some knowledge of modern science, it might appear that Aristotle's stuff is nothing more than the naturally occurring elements listed in the Periodic Table. That is a good answer, but it breaks down as soon as we consider one of the examples I have just given, namely, sulphur. That substance is itself one of the elements, and so the question recurs: what is the stuff of which elements are made? So we can think of the atom of sulphur and its components: its nucleus and orbital electrons, and then the parts of the nucleus, say, neutrons and protons, and regard these as the basic stuff of which natural things are made. But again, electrons and protons and neutrons come to be and pass away, they themselves are natural entities, and so we are back to our question, what is the stuff of which subatomic particles are made? Aristotle's answer to this type of question would be that, to understand nature, we have to go all the way back to some primordial stuff, a *hulē prōtē*, a *materia prima* or protomatter, that underlies all the changes going on in the world of nature. To use the language of modern science, protomatter is a kind of conservation principle that regulates all natural transformations. The closest scientists in the present day come to such a conservation principle is mass-energy. Whatever quarks may be, or leptons and hadrons in their various forms, it seems generally agreed that all are manifestations of mass-energy. This is the ultimate matrix to which science has come in identifying the material cause of the universe. To say this is not to identify protomatter with mass-energy as though that were all it is, but no doubt there are similarities between the two concepts, despite the fact that they are arrived at by very different modes of reasoning.

A surprising implication of such lines of reasoning is that matter, seen as nature and as a basic constituent of all natural entities, is not the passive and inert principle it has long been pictured to be. It is a powerful and potential principle that lies at the base of the most cataclysmic upheavals taking place on our planet and in the remote depths of space. And not only does nature explore its potentialities, but man, through his ingenuity, has succeeded in triggering some of them himself. The most breath-taking achievement of the twentieth century, the unleashing of nuclear energy, focuses our attention anew on how potent matter can be when it is unveiled in its primordial state.

## Nature as Form

Returning to the causal model based on our artifact, the chair, we note that its form is intimately related to its matter, in the sense that the form is the shape or figure the matter assumes during the chair's manufacture and becomes, as it were, part of its being. Moreover, although the wood, say, oak, was not always formed as a chair, as long as it was identifiable as oak, it was always seen under one form or another, and from this point of view the two, matter and form, seem quite inseparable. We might think from this correlative status that both are equally intelligible, that just as there is something mysterious about the basic matter of the universe, so the forms it assumes or to which it is united are difficult to grasp as well. This is not exactly the case, for though matter is to a large degree refractory to our understanding, form is surprisingly intelligible. It provides a window through which the world of nature is seen and through which many of the natures that inhabit it can be readily understood.

That this is true may be seen from the ways we speak about the natural objects, and not merely the artifacts, that fall under common observation. We are able to identify most of the animals, plants, and minerals with which we come in contact, and we are also able to classify them in ways that show our awareness of the differences among them. Moreover, though many of these objects have a multiplicity of parts and are far from homogeneous in structure, we grasp them in a unitary way and ascribe one nature to them. It is this formality, or form, that we name and define as we become acquainted with natural kinds, with substances of different types found in our environment.

How to describe or characterize this natural form in a way that differentiates it from the shape or configuration of an artifact presents more of a problem. Obviously the outline or silhouette of a cow or a giraffe is a help in identifying it and is closely associated with its nature. In this respect, it resembles the form of an artifact. But the shapes of organisms vary over a wide range, in one individual throughout time and indeed from one individual to another, even though the natures underlying the shapes may be the same. Similar statements could be made about most of the quantitative and qualitative attributes with which natural substances are endowed. All of these can be understood as so many forms that make the particular substance intelligible and enable us to distinguish it from others in number and kind. So as to differentiate these sensible forms from the form that gives unity to a nature, what we here refer to as "nature as form," we call this natural form a substantial form, that is, a form that underlies its attributes and makes it a substance in its own right. Incidental attributes or properties we then speak of as accidental forms, intending by this forms that are adventitious to the nature and can vary in degree or in presence and absence without affecting its basic character.

It is this natural or substantial form that is apprehended when we grasp the nature of an entity and attempt to define it. Like nature itself, this formal component is not an empirical concept: it is not given immediately in sense experience, though it is derivable from such experience. It has more the features of a universal than of a particular representation. That is why the defining notes or attributes of sulphur and lead, of rose bushes and oak trees, of mosquitoes and kangaroos apply not only to this or that sulphur, copper, rose bush, etc., but to each and every instance of them. Were this not so, it would be impossible to have universal knowledge of the world of nature, and, *a fortiori,* any science of nature. We would be limited to cataloging individual after individual, without ever being able to discern natural kinds, that is, the substantial features they have in common, notwithstanding the many ways they differ numerically within a species or class.

The simplicity and unity of the natural form should not obscure the many attributes and activities that derive from it and of which it is the inner source. To speak of a horse as a mammal, for instance, signifies that it belongs among higher vertebrates that nourish their young with milk secreted from glands of a special type. This entails a complex organism with structures and organs that function in interrelated ways to assure the well-being of the whole. More will be said later about the ways in which activities originate within such natural agents, but for now it need only be mentioned that the unifying form, no less than the underlying matter, is the internal source from which all such activities ultimately spring. Behaviors, actions, and reactions are natural for a substance precisely to the extent that they proceed from within it and thus from its matter and form as its basic intrinsic constituents.

Much the same point can be made by contrasting the natural or unifying form with the artificial form of chair in our causal analogue. The shape or design of a chair is basically a matter of geometry and is no more the source of activity than is the shape of triangle when this is abstractly conceived and not embodied in wood or plastic. A wooden triangle can fall and be broken, whereas an abstract triangle cannot. Similarly, a chair can undergo change: it can be scratched or gouged, thrown down stairs, burned in a fire. But it cannot be so changed *precisely* as chair, but rather as something made of oak or other material. Indeed, it is the nature of the substance out of which it is made that determines what can be done with it, how it reacts to forces impressed upon it. It is in this sense that the natural form is the inner source of activities and reactivities, whereas the artificial form, or any other accidental form, for that matter, is not.

## Nature as Agent

Here we have obviously made the opening to agency and finality as these are included in Aristotle's definition of nature, so we move now to the third explanatory factor in our causal model, the agent or efficient cause. Now, what is there in nature that corresponds to the maker of the chair in the case of the artifact? To answer this, note that the making of the chair is an activity of the maker and as such can be correlated with a capability that preexists in the maker and is the proximate cause of his activity. A general principle is latent in the example: operations and activities, and reactivities as well, proceed from abilities and potentials that are lodged in the natures of agents and so can serve to explain the ways in which they act and react with neighboring objects. Natural forms are the inner source of these activities, but such forms are endowed with powers that can be activated and so enable substances to act on, and interact with, things external to them in distinctive ways. It is the ability of one substance to act on another that explains why we are able to identify agents and reagents in the order of nature.

Now man is a natural organism endowed with many powers and capabilities, and, on this account, he can serve as a paradigm for the investigation of agencies in nature. The carpenter's making of a chair is an instance of a natural agent at work on other bodies, pieces of wood, forming their material into a useful artifact. The example can be extended indefinitely as we range through all of the constructive, mechanical, and industrial arts, the feats of engineering, the products of modern technology. Man is a powerful agent who acts, directly or indirectly, on the substances around him, appropriating them and transforming them in countless ways to suit his needs and desires.

Similar instances can be adduced in the animal and plant kingdoms. Beavers build dams, birds their nests, and spiders their webs, and in all these natural activities they use or affect objects with other natures to the benefit of themselves and their species. Animals give birth to young and plants bear seeds, thus serving as agents for bringing new organisms into the world. And through the balance of nature, fauna and flora convert chemical substances and direct solar energies to provide food and nutriment for a wide range of species. All living organisms, in their life processes, are so many agents that interact with their environment and produce changes in other things in the course of their development.

At the level of the non-living, on the other hand, agencies are not so easy to identify and, on this account, have been poorly understood for centuries. But the Chemical Revolution of the eighteenth century led to remarkable insights into the ways elements interact with each other to form compounds, how minerals are formed in the bowels of the earth. Chemicals have affinities, and, given the proper circumstances, these manifest themselves as abilities to enter into combination with other substances, thus affecting them and, in many instances, giving rise to new natures. Although such reactions can be studied and realized in the laboratory, they are natural processes that are initiated by the agents and reagents that enter into them. Strictly speaking, there are no chemical artifacts: all new substances are the work and product of nature, bringing to actualization the potentials latent in the materials from which they are formed, under the influence of the initiating conditions and catalysts that bring them about.

Physical agents are frequently seen as exerting forces on surrounding objects and thus causing motions and changes of state in them. In this view, a force is itself an instance of an efficient or agent cause. Physicists link forces with energies and fields, and these provide an even deeper source of information about natural agents. Four major forces or potentials are now believed to underlie all of nature's transformations: the electromagnetic force, the gravitational force, the strong nuclear force, and the weak nuclear force. (The latter nuclear force has recently been shown to be related to the electromagnetic force such that one can now speak of the "electroweak" force.) Through their use, we are now able to explain how all objects, animate as well as inanimate, act on each other and produce the phenomena observable throughout the entire universe.

Obviously, there are difficulties in understanding nature as agent in terms of these basic forces and the subatomic entities with which they are associated. One instance is the way in which external agents function within evolutionary theory. Chemists feel reasonably sure that they know how elements evolve into compounds of more and more complex structures, all the way to DNA with its replicating potentials. Physicists are confident of their ability to explain how chemical elements have originated and have come to be spread through the universe in their present abundances. Biologists understand genetic and reproductive mechanisms and know how one pair of mice produce other mice, the same in species and similar in family characteristics. Yet when we consider the entire chain of being, from the simplest particles to the most developed organisms now living or preserved in the fossil record, we find it difficult to identify the cosmic agents that cause one species to come from another or to evolve into a higher species that possesses capabilities not found in its antecedent. How to get more from less, or something from nothing, is a real puzzle. And nothing seems more puzzling than uncovering the agent causes that permit its occurring on a grand scale throughout our universe.

## Nature as End

This brings us to the fourth and final factor in our causal analogue, the end or final cause. The Greek word for end is *telos*, source of our "teleology," so with this type of cause we come to the disputed question of teleology in nature. For Aristotle, as we have said, nature acts for an end. If evolution is viewed as a natural process, does this also entail that it is a teleological process, one that is goal-directed in the sense that higher and more developed species are not merely the result of chance but are somehow determined in advance? There is no easy answer to this question, but I promise to return to it later.

It can be helpful first to distinguish three different meanings of the word "end," not all of which are equally identifiable in natural processes. The first and simplest meaning is that of end in the sense of terminus, the point at which a process stops. In a journey from New York to Washington, the nation's capital is the end of the trip, the place where the traveler comes to rest. Similarly, the natural fall of an object terminates when the heavy body reaches the center of gravity to which it is tending or encounters some obstacle that impedes its motion and brings it to rest. A plant grows from a seedling to full maturity, at which point it stops growing; the same could be said of the developmental process of a flea or an elephant. Natures are stable kinds, that is, within a certain range, they represent regions of stability in a world of flux. In our experience, fleas do not grow and grow indefinitely, say, until they reach the size of elephants, nor are elephants found as small as fleas. Growth processes terminate, and to the extent that they are natural processes, the states at which they terminate are ends reached by nature and so satisfy the first meaning of final cause.

This same meaning applies also to the more fundamental processes that bring natural substances into being and are readily seen in the realm of the inorganic. Hydrogen and oxygen combine to form water, sodium and chlorine to form salt. In such reactions, each of the reagents loses its own being and properties; new substances or natures emerge, and these have different, in many cases radically different, sets of properties. Chemists are interested in what makes such reactions go, but no less interesting is the question what makes them stop. Elements or isotopes with high atomic number break down radioactively, but again they do not do so in an unending and completely indeterminate way. At some stage, the radioactive breakdown ceases, and this, as in the case of chemical combination, occurs when a stable nature has been reached. In the plant and animal world, similar examples abound. Sperm and ovum unite to form a zygote, which divides and subdivides repeatedly, eventually to form a stable organism of a given kind. Monsters occasionally occur, but with astounding regularity mosquitoes generate other mosquitoes, squirrels other squirrels, and so on. In this way, nature is more than an inner source of change and activity; it is also a source of permanence and stability. When such stability terminates a natural process, whether inorganic or organic, it is the end of the process and, as such, its final cause.

A second meaning of end or goal adds to the idea of terminus the notion that it is somehow a perfection or good attained through the process. In some instances of natural change this meaning is easily verified, in others it is not. Clearly in cases of organic growth the end product represents a superior grade of being over the stage at which it began. It is also more perfect, in the etymological sense of *per-factum*, as that which is thoroughly made and possesses no *de-factum*, that is, is lacking in nothing it should possess as a member of its species. In inorganic changes, it is difficult to see in what sense a compound is better than an element, or an element of higher atomic number better than an element of a lower. Perhaps one should differentiate here between processes that are good for a particular nature, say, to conserve it in being, the way in which salt crystallizes and so preserves its identity, and those that are good for nature as a whole, the universe made up of many different kinds. Elements are good in themselves, but compounds may more readily serve the needs of the organic world; plants and vegetables represent a higher stage of being than complex molecules but less than that attained by the animals that eat them and incorporate them into their substance. If this seems true in the observable order of nature, it would be even more so in the evolutionary order, if such is indeed the work of nature. The successive production of higher and higher types undoubtedly represents some type of progress, some greater good or perfection that is attained over time, presuming that the later types are not mere freaks or the result of chance occurrences.

The third meaning of end is more specialized still, for it adds to the notion of termination and perfection that of intention or aim. This serves to identify the type of final causality found in cognitive agents. Animals and humans are natural agents of this type: many of their activities are planned or intended in advance and so can be seen as end-directed from their beginning. A person building a house or a bird a nest must have in advance some notion of what is intended, for otherwise neither builder would know what materials to gather. There seems to be a difference in the two cases, however, for the bird does its work by instinct and tends to make the nest in a form predetermined by its species, whereas man is not so limited and can generate the multiplicity of dwellings recorded throughout human history.

Much of the difficulty with teleology in nature arises from conceiving all final causality as intentional or cognitive and not sufficiently distinguishing the cognitive from the terminative and the perfective. St. Albert the Great gave expression to this mentality with the aphorism:

*opus naturae est opus intelligentiae,* the work of nature is the work of intelligence.[2] If by saying this, one means that every natural agent consciously is aware of the goal at which it is aiming, there is little evidence that such could be the case throughout the entire order of nature. The word "intelligence," however, can take on a variety of meanings, as is clear from the way people talk of artificial intelligence in the present day. Perhaps in this way of speaking one could say that the double helix is programmed to replicate in a certain way and so "knows" how to do it, or that an asteroid "knows" how to find its path through the solar system without performing the calculations we make to predict its path. In this sense, natural agents seem to foreknow what they aim to achieve and so implicitly substantiate the claim that nature acts for an end.

Such considerations open up the complexity and mystery of final causality in nature, analogous to those already seen when posing questions along the lines of the other three causes. Matter and form are easy enough to grasp in a general way, and yet understanding ultimate matter and unifying form presents difficulties of considerable magnitude. Natural agents are pervasive in the universe and are readily identifiable, but cosmic agents are largely hidden and so have managed to escape detection for centuries. Final causes exert their influence in terminative and perfective ways, yet they, too, give rise to serious problems. Is there an ultimate goal to which nature tends? Is there an intelligence behind its operations that organizes its matter and its agents so as to achieve that goal? Again I'll take out a promissory note, but you will have to admit that these are interesting questions, as much for the scientist as for the natural philosopher.

## Aristotle's Definition of Nature

Let us return at this point to Aristotle's definition of nature and inquire whether nature as agent and nature as end are included in any way in that definition. After our foregoing survey, we would have to admit that they are. To say that nature is a principle and cause of motion and of rest is implicitly to recognize, apart from material and formal causality, these two additional types of cause, efficient and final causality. If nature is the cause of motion, it is in some way an efficient cause, for the very definition of an efficient cause is that it is causative of motion. And if nature is the cause of rest, it is equivalently a final

---

2. A study of this interesting expression is made by J. A. Weisheipl in his "The Axiom 'Opus naturae est opus intelligentiae' and its Origins," in *Albertus Magnus—Doctor Universalis 1280–1980,* ed. G. Meyer and A. Zimmerman (Mainz, Germany: Matthias-Grünewald-Verlag, 1980), 441–63.

cause, for rest is the terminus, the end, that brings a motion to its nat-ural completion.

But that still leaves us with the problem of how to reconcile the two opposites we have been analyzing in this essay, the internal and the external, to provide an integrated view of nature as the "inner dimension" of material substance. How is it possible to internalize agency and finality within a natural body, and to do so in a general way so as to be applicable to the living and the non-living as well?

Aristotle himself suggests, later on in Book II of the *Physics*, that sometimes there is a simple answer to this question, namely, that the formal cause, the efficient cause, and the final cause "often amount to one." He explains this by saying that "both the whatness [the formal cause] and the final cause are one, and the first cause of motion [that is, the efficient cause] is the same in kind as these, for man begets man . . ." (198a24–27). But this is a special case, and Aristotle signals this by saying that the three causes (form, agent, and end) *often* amount to one. Are all natural or substantial forms efficient causes, or is this true only in the realm of the living, where the natural form is a soul that animates the plant or animal body? Are all natural or substantial forms final causes, and if so, how can this be true in the realm of the inorganic? What is the final cause of sulphur, for example, assuming that sulphur is a natural substance and has a nature much as do an oak or a squirrel? Questions such as these could bother a scientist in the present day, for whom the answer that "man begets man" might not prove altogether satisfactory.

## Models of Nature

With the scientist's interests in mind, as well as those of the Aristotelian scholar, I propose to use two schematic models to probe more deeply into Aristotle's teaching on nature in search of an answer. These are shown on Figures 1 and 2. Fig. 1 shows the generic factors that enter into the composition of what I call "A Natural Body," that is, a body or substance that comes to be and passes away in the order of nature, without regard to the particular kind of body it may happen to be. Fig. 2, entitled "Models of Various Natures," is borrowed from an essay of mine that has recently appeared in print.[3] Actually, it is a further expansion of the first diagram showing how various kinds of

3. "Aquinas's Legacy on Individuation, Cogitation, and Hominization," in *Thomas Aquinas and His Legacy*, ed. David Gallagher, Studies in Philosophy and the History of Philosophy, vol. 28 (Washington, D.C.: The Catholic University of America Press, 1994), 173–93.

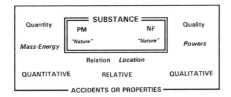

*Figure 1. The Individual Natural Body*

bodies, that is, those with inorganic natures, plant natures, animal natures, and human nature variously flesh out the generic factors identified in the first. Through an examination of these figures, perhaps we can determine where and how agency and finality are lodged within natural bodies of different kinds and serve, along with matter and form, to make up their "inner dimension."

As diagrammed in Fig. 1, a natural body is composed of substance and accidents: the first, substance, is shown enclosed in double outline, and the second, entitled "accidents or properties," in single outline. The substance of a natural body, its inner core, is itself composed, the two essential components being matter and form. These are now identified, on the basis of the foregoing exposition, with the letters PM and NF. PM stands for protomatter, Aristotle's *hulē prōtē* or the *materia prima* of the Latins, and NF for natural form, Aristotle's *morphē* or *natura* of the Latins. Alternate ways of designating this form are substantial form, the *forma substantialis* of the Latins, or again, specifying form, or yet again, stabilizing form—expressions that in some circumstances provide a better indicator of its functions.

Aristotle's explicit statements in Book II of the *Physics* leave little doubt that both protomatter and natural form are to be identified with the body's nature: for him, natural form is nature in the primary sense as determining and actual, whereas protomatter is nature in a secondary sense as generic and potential.[4] The actual nature of a thing or its natural form is what specifies it as a natural kind and further stabilizes

4. Aristotle lays the groundwork for this identification in chapters 7–9 of the first book of the *Physics*, where he refers to matter as the "underlying nature" (191a8) and form as the "natural form" (192b1). He elaborates further on this in chapters 1 and 2 of the second book, where, having given his definition of nature, he goes on to state: "One way, then, of regarding nature is as the first underlying matter . . . ; from another point of view we may think of the nature of a thing as residing rather in its form, that is to say, in the 'kind' of thing it is by definition" (192a28–31). Later he explicitly affirms that "the form is nature to a higher degree than the matter," and gives as his reason that "each thing receives a name when it exists in actuality rather than when it exists potentially" (193b7–9).

it in being. Thus the NF not only informs PM and makes of it a composite substance, but it also makes the substance be what it is, that is, it organizes and specifies it. Again, the form confers on the protomatter a stable mode of being, so that the composite it forms, the natural substance, underlies its accidents in more than transitory fashion.

The accidents of a natural body are also shown on Fig. 1, arranged somewhat arbitrarily around the inner core. They are grouped into three categories: quantitative, qualitative, and relative. The most important of the first group is quantity itself, shown next to PM or protomatter, and the most important of the second is quality, shown next to NF or the natural form. The relative accidents then include relation and the last six species of accident listed in Aristotle's *Categories*, of which only one, location, is shown at the lower center of the diagram.

With regard to quantity, we may note that its basic function as an accident is to ground bodily extension by putting part outside of part and so enabling matter or substance to be divisible into parts. Such parts can then be conceptualized as discrete and so become the basis for numbering in the order of nature. On this ground, there are two kinds of quantity: continuous, associated with magnitude or extension, as in the length of a line; and discrete, associated with multitude or number, as in a positive whole integer. Medieval commentators on Aristotle, such as St. Thomas Aquinas, also saw extensive quantity, when taken together with protomatter (*materia signata quantitate*, matter signed with quantity), as the individuating principle in a natural substance.[5] In the late seventeenth century, Sir Isaac Newton focused on the related concept of "quantity of matter" (*quantitas materiae*) and thought of it as mass.[6] More recent science has furnished the related concept of mass-energy—which I have already associated with protomatter, its quantitative measure, as it were—shown beneath quantity on the left of the diagram.

As a proper accident, quality stands for the distinctive attributes of an object through which we come to know its nature. There are various ways of classifying qualities: the most obvious kinds are sensible qualities, those that fall directly under the senses such as a particular color, temperature, odor, and taste, and the particular shape or figure a body assumes, such as the outline of a cat. These collectively make up the accidental features through which we differentiate one individual from

5. In his *Summa theologiae*, Part 1, quest. 75, art. 4, and parallel places.
6. His first definition in the famous *Principia* reads: "The quantity of matter is the measure of the same, arising from its density and bulk conjointly." Then, explaining the definition, he states, "It is this quantity that I mean hereafter everywhere under the name of body or mass."

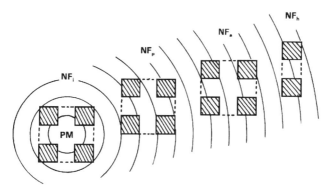

*Figure 2. A Powers Model of Various Natures*

another—individuating characteristics—while being aware that they are not essential to the nature itself. Less obvious are the various powers or dispositions with which substances are endowed and which are more directly linked to their natures; it is from the exercise of such powers that their natures can be ascertained. On this account, since a thing's actions and reactions enable us to determine its powers and from these we judge its nature or say what it is, we here regard its powers as proper accidents or properties. We thus indicate only powers as representative of the distinctive attributes in which we shall now be interested, and show it below quality on the right of the diagram.

This last consideration, which assumes importance for understanding Fig. 2, enables us to rejoin the problem of extrinsic causality and show how this is related to the concept of nature. The various models shown in Fig. 2 schematize the relationships between characteristic activities, natural powers, and the stable natures that are their underlying source.[7] Stable natures we consider as pertaining to three broad genera: inorganic natures, plant natures, and animal natures; in addition, we treat human nature as adding a further specification to animal nature. All are stable in the sense that substances with these natures have a fairly permanent mode of being and acting. The key differences among them lie in the characteristic activities and reactivities that are proper to the various genera. These proceed from agencies

---

7. Actually Fig. 2 is a generic model, a composite of several specific models I have sketched in fuller detail in two previous publications: "Nature as Animating: The Soul in the Human Sciences," *The Thomist* 49 (1985): 612–48, and "Nature, Human Nature, and Norms for Medical Ethics," in *Catholic Perspectives on Medical Morals: Foundational Issues*, ed. E. D. Pellegrino, J. P. Langan, and J. C. Harvey, Philosophy and Medicine, vol. 34 (Boston: Kluwer Academic Publishers, 1989), 23–53.

or powers located within species that are subsumable under each genus and on this account are intrinsic to both genera and species. At the same time, such powers are what enable the individual bodies that instantiate the species to act on other things and so incorporate within themselves the notion of agency or efficient cause. In thus acting, they achieve ends consonant with their natures and so give indication of how nature is teleological or acts for an end. Through them, therefore, we can go beyond seeing nature as restricted only to matter and form, as though nature were to function as an intrinsic cause alone. They enable us to see nature as both agent and end along the lines sketched earlier in this essay, and thus as involving elements of extrinsic causality as well. Some idea of how this can be done may now be gained from a brief discussion of Fig. 2.

You will note that the basic polarity of PM and NF, that is, of protomatter and natural form, structures Fig. 2 as well as Fig. 1. The primary difference is that Fig. 2 separates the two vertically rather than horizontally and then shows four kinds of substantial form, designated by the different subscripts attached to the letters NF across the top. The first or lowest order, indicated by $NF_i$, with the subscript "i" standing for inorganic, determines the protomatter to be a substance with an inorganic nature; that next to the right, indicated by $NF_p$, with the subscript "p" standing for plant, determines the protomatter to be a substance with a plant nature; that to the right of it, indicated by $NF_a$, with the subscript "a" standing for animal, determines the protomatter to be a substance with an animal nature; and the last to the right, indicated by $NF_h$, with the subscript "h" standing for human, determines the protomatter to be a substance with a human nature. Within each of these types, with the exception of the last, there is the possibility of many different species. Thus, among inorganic substances we might have copper or sulphur; among plants, geraniums or oaks; among animals, squirrels or cows, and so on. The natural form is said to be a specifying form because it determines the substance to have a particular nature, that of copper or sulphur, geranium or oak, squirrel or cow. In fact, the natural form itself may be referred to as the nature of the substance it determines. And we recognize this when we observe a particular substance and note its nature, saying this is copper, and that is an oak, and the animal running there is a squirrel. A nature, moreover, is a durable thing, and that is why we can speak of a natural form as a stabilizing form. If a substance is copper, or oak, or a squirrel, it is not a transient entity but tends to stay that way—copper perhaps for years or centuries, the oak and the squirrel over their life spans.

Apart from surface appearance, we should add that natures are categorized on the basis of the powers from which the activities or reactivities of various substances originate. These are indicated in Fig. 2 by the little boxes grouped under the four NF's. For the inorganic, note that we have updated Aquinas's four elements and their qualities by the four forces of modern physics: gravitational force, electromagnetic force, the weak force, and the strong force. Plant powers include those of nutrition, growth, and reproduction, all noted by Aquinas, to which we have added homeostasis as a basic power of life control. Animal powers are those of sensation, both external and internal, those that originate movement, and those that activate the sense appetites or the emotions, all of which were likewise known to St. Thomas. And finally, there are the two distinctively human powers about which St. Thomas knew the most, those of thought and personal decision, known as the intellect and the will respectively.[8]

It is important to note that all these powers, except the last two, require bodily parts or organs for their operation. That is why plants and animals are called organisms, for their bodies are differentiated into organs with which they perform various life functions. The organs are parts of their bodies; the powers that activate or energize them may be thought of as parts of their souls or substantial forms, so let us call them "power parts" to distinguish them from bodily parts. Inorganic substances, of course, do not have organs in a proper sense, and so we do not refer to their forms as souls, though we speak of plant souls, and animal souls, and human souls. Yet we now know something that St. Thomas did not, namely, that inorganic substances likewise have bodily parts: molecules, atoms, nuclei, electrons, all controlled by the four basic forces that we might say "energize" the world of the non-living.

Notice now a curious feature of the model in Fig. 2. It may be viewed as picturing four different kinds of natural substance, or it may be seen as picturing only one particular kind of substance, depending on how much of the figure is taken into account. But, when considering any one kind of natural substance, note this further fact: one can disregard the powers that are found on its right, but one is forced to take into account the powers that are found on its left. A plant, for example, shown as $NF_p$, does not have the powers of sensation, movement, and reasoning that are found in animals and humans, and so these are not required for its understanding. Yet, as biochemistry has taught us, it cannot exercise its own powers of nutrition and growth if it is not a physico-chemical composite endowed with the basic forces of the in-

8. These powers are sketched in a general way in his *Summa theologiae*, Part 1, quest. 77, and in more detail in questions 78 to 80.

organic. Similarly, a brute animal, shown as $NF_a$, does not have the powers of intellect and will, and so these are not necessary to understand it; but it cannot be an animal if it does not have the vegetative powers of nutrition, growth, and reproduction, as well as the physicochemical components on which these in turn are based. And finally, the human being, shown as $NF_h$ farthest on the right, requires everything on the left to carry out its life functions. The human soul, as Aquinas explains it, includes virtually within itself an animal soul, a plant soul, and the form of an inorganic substance—and so it contains all their powers as power parts.[9] Through them, it is able to energize its many bodily parts, the organs and components of which the human body is composed.

## Aristotle's Definition Again

With this we return to Aristotle's definition of nature from a new vantage point and ask, once again, where are agency and finality, two extrinsic causes, contained within nature as part of its inner dimension? Note now that, apart from the letters and boxes on Fig. 2, we have also included there circular lines to create the impression of a field radiating out from protomatter (PM). That field should be thought of as an energizing or enlivening field, and indeed as a model of the natural form (NF) or the soul itself, for the soul is what energizes or enlivens the body. Not only does the form energize protomatter to form the body, as it were, but it also energizes the various activities in which the body comes to be engaged. But the form or soul is strictly speaking a formal cause, and so we have to be careful in labeling it an efficient cause. The reason for this is that the natural form does not produce any activity *directly;* rather it does so through the powers that, ontologically speaking, are its proper accidents. The form acts, but only *through* the natural powers with which it is endowed, and it is in this way that agency can be attributed to it. And when it acts in this way, it acts for ends that are consonant with its nature, and so can also be seen as a final cause. So finality comes to be included in the definition of nature, and in a surprising way, under the concept of form. Not that the formal cause is strictly speaking a final cause, but rather that natures as forms are possessed of powers that are end-directed and so actually incorporate agency and finality in their very understanding.

We have been examining Aristotle's definition of nature given at the beginning of the second book of the *Physics*, where it is characterized

9. *Summa theologiae*, Part 1, quest. 76, arts. 3 and 4.

as an internal principle of motion and of rest. In conclusion, let me return to my promissory note and ask how far the notions of agency and finality that are implicit in this definition can be pushed, particularly whether they can be extended to include the process we now refer to as evolution. My answer to the latter question is that they cannot. Nature as there defined by Aristotle, to adopt Richard Dawkins' expression, is a selfish principle.[10] It applies to natures as they are intrinsic principles within bodies, whose natures they are intent on conserving and perfecting, not reaching beyond themselves to give rise to new natures or species. On this view, there is no finality within a nature that leads it to self-destruct and give rise to a nature different from its own.

If we wish to account for evolution, therefore, it seems that we have to look outside the natures we know and study in the sciences of our day to some kind of external principle that can account for an overall evolutionary process. In effect that means that we have to leave nature with a small "n," the natures we experience, to speak of Nature with a capital "N," the universe or cosmos made up of *all* the natures we presently know. And when we wonder how this Nature with a capital "N" has come to exist in its present form, invariably we are led to think of "Mother Nature" or the "Author of Nature" or some transcendent being as its proportionate cause. I leave you at this point, for as a philosopher of nature I sense that to go further I would be moving into metaphysics and so might find myself on unfamiliar ground. But I suspect that many scientists in our day agree with such reasoning and feel the urge to become metaphysicians—an outcome quite unexpected in an age dominated by positivist thought.

10. As in the title of his book, *The Selfish Gene* (Oxford: Oxford University Press, 1976).

# 3   Understanding Aristotle's Teleology
## ALLAN GOTTHELF

Final Causality is the mode of causation that characterizes human action, and it extends throughout the living world. I believe, too, that it is the goal-directed character of life—and the biological basis of that goal-directed character—which provides the foundation for the very concept of value.[1] Understanding final causality is thus essential to understanding man's nature as the distinctive biological entity he is, and to understanding a great part of the natural world of which he is a part, and how his good is to be found in that world.

Aristotle shared this view of teleology's importance. His teleology—his thesis that final causality is operative both in human action and in the development, structure, and functioning of living organisms generally—is central to his philosophical thought, and an understanding of Aristotle's teleology has been a central concern of my own research over the years. In several previous papers, I have offered an interpretation of Aristotle's teleology: its logical structure, its ontological basis, its empirical character, its relation to his theory of the good, its consequences for the axiomatic structure of biological science, and its implications for his metaphysical theory of substance and essence.[2] There

1. Harry Binswanger, "Life-Based Teleology and the Foundation of Ethics," *The Monist* 75 (1992): 84–103; Ayn Rand, *The Virtue of Selfishness: A New Concept of Egoism* (New American Library, 1964), ch. 1.
2. Allan Gotthelf, *Aristotle's Conception of Final Causality.* (Ann Arbor, Mich.: University Microfilms, 1975). "Aristotle's Conception of Final Causality," *Review of Metaphysics* 30 (1977): 226–54; reprinted with additional notes and "Postscript 1986" in Allan Gotthelf and James G. Lennox, eds., *Philosophical Issues in Aristotle's Biology* (Cambridge: Cambridge University Press, 1987), 204–42; hereafter Gotthelf and Lennox, *Aristotle's Biology*. "First Principles in Aristotle's *Parts of Animals*," in Gotthelf and Lennox, *Aristotle's Biology*, 167–98. "The Place of the Good in Aristotle's Natural Teleology," in J. J. Cleary and D. C. Shartin, eds. *Proceedings of the Boston Colloquium in Ancient Philosophy*, vol. 4 (1988) (Lanham, Md.: University Press of America, 1989), 113–39; hereafter Gotthelf, "The Place of the Good." "Teleology and Spontaneous Generation: A Discussion," in R. Kraut and T. Penner, eds., *Nature, Knowledge and Virtue: Essays in Memory of Joan Kung. Apeiron* Special Issue 22.4 (1989), 181–93; hereafter Kraut and Penner, *Nature, Knowledge and Virtue.*

has been, in addition, an enormous literature on these topics since 1976.[3] In this paper, although I will have occasion to summarize my own line of interpretation and to comment briefly on other lines, I want rather to focus on three other matters. First, I would like to step back from the various controversies regarding Aristotle's teleology to identify, and group, the range of issues involved—the range of issues on which one has to have a position if one can claim an understanding of Aristotle's theory, quite apart from what interpretation one ends up with. I find three such groups of questions, which I call "Analysis," "Basis," and "Extent." Second, focusing on the questions I group under "Basis," which I consider to be the most fundamental set of questions, I will provide a typology of interpretations I have found in the literature from 1976 through 1992. Third, I would like to comment on one particular line of interpretation other than my own which raises in a very interesting way the question of the relevance of Aristotle's natural teleology today: Is Aristotle's conception of final causality, as I interpret it—a conception developed in the context of a very different physics, chemistry, and biology—still applicable in today's scientific context?[4]

## Three Groups of Questions

First, then, the range of issues on which any full interpretation must decide. I divide them into three, which, as mentioned, I call: Analysis, Basis, Extent. According to my own interpretation, these three sets of issues are logically connected, even interwoven, so the division is not a radical one; nevertheless, I think the issues still need distinguishing, since whatever their connections they must each be worked through separately, and in the recent literature they are occasionally discussed in isolation from each other.

Under "Analysis," I include questions about the basic categories of teleological causation Aristotle appears to find, and how they relate to each other. For instance, Aristotle finds teleological causation at work both in human action and in nature, in living organisms. Is the pattern of causation the same in both cases? Teleological causation in human action involves desires and beliefs. In the famous example in *Physics* II.3 with which Aristotle introduces the fourth way of being a cause,

3. Allan Gotthelf, "Report on Recent Work," in David M. Balme, trans., *Aristotle's De Partibus Animalium I and De Generatione Animalium I (with passages from II.3)* (Oxford: Clarendon Press, 1992).
4. For the main theses and supporting arguments of my own line of interpretation, see "Aristotle's Conception of Final Causality," rev., in Gotthelf and Lennox, *Aristotle's Biology*, 204–42, and Gotthelf, "The Place of the Good," 113–39.

viz., as being an *end* or *aim*, a health-sustaining digestion is the aim that causes the walk after dinner (194b33–35). The aim, as discussions in various other treatises make clear, is embodied in a desire (and the conception of the good it represents), and gets translated into a walk only through the belief (craft-knowledge in the case of the doctor) that walks after dinner facilitate a health-sustaining digestion. But the development of a living organism also occurs for the sake of some end or aim the living organism has. How is that aim embodied? Surely not in any desire or conception of the good, or any belief about means, since the embryo has no desires or beliefs, and Aristotle does not recognize any sort of cosmic *design*.[5] So how are these two cases of teleological causation to be analyzed, and how are they related?

And in the case of natural organisms, Aristotle not only speaks of processes of formation as being for the sake of the whole organism that results, but also of parts of developed organisms (or of features of these parts) as being for the sake of the whole organism. These are not obviously the same patterns. Let's call the former mode of teleological causation "coming to be for the sake of " and the latter "being for the sake of." How are they each to be analyzed and what is their relationship? In my own work, for example, I have argued that for Aristotle, paradoxical as it might sound, "being for the sake of " is defined in terms of "coming to be for the sake of ": A part is for the sake of its contribution to the whole only if it has come to be for the sake of that whole.[6] Others have suggested that it is the other way round.[7] Whatever the answer, the question of how these different ascriptions of teleological are to be analyzed and of what their relationship is, both fall under my heading, "Analysis."

Some scholars have suggested that what helps unite the various patterns is the fact that in each case the end is something *good*. While accepting of course that all ends are indeed good (or apparently good), I have argued in a recent paper against the view that a proper analysis of what it is to be an end must or, indeed, should refer to that fact.[8] In any case, I locate the question of the place of the good in Aristotle's analysis of teleological causation under the heading, "Analysis."

David Charles in a recent paper has argued that *Physics* II.8 provides no basis for precise answers to any of these questions (except possibly

5. In the sense in which design implies a designer: see n. 13 below.

6. See "Postscript 1986" in Gotthelf and Lennox, *Aristotle's Biology*, 237–42.

7. See, for example, Richard Sorabji, *Necessity, Cause, and Blame: Perspectives on Aristotle's Theory* (Ithaca: Cornell University Press, 1980), 173.

8. Gotthelf, "The Place of the Good."

the last), and I agree.[9] I said as much in my dissertation and in my 1976 essay. I suggested that the route to answering the questions that fall under my heading, "Analysis," is to turn first to the questions that fall under the heading "Basis." For only after we understand the overall ontological basis of Aristotle's ascriptions of teleological causation to nature, would we be in a position to provide a proper analysis and comparison of each of the categories.

Under the heading "Basis," I group all questions that have directly to do with the question: What fact or facts ground or license Aristotle's use of teleological explanation? On my own view, as I have already intimated, there is an *ontological* basis for that use—something different *in the world* in those cases to which teleological explanation is applicable and those cases where it is not, and something different about the causation of the phenomena in question. But since some people deny this, at least for the natural teleology, and insist that the difference is only epistemological, or pragmatic, depending somehow on our own mode of understanding, the question needs to be put more generally. I will review a variety of answers that have been put forward to this question shortly, but let me first indicate what I have in mind for the third category of issue, which I call "Extent."

It is uncontroversial that Aristotle applies final causality to human action, and to the development, structure, and functioning of living organisms generally, and it is uncontroversial that in most cases the end in question is the good (however ultimately analyzed) of the agent or organism whose development, structure, or functioning is being explained. But in recent papers, some scholars have argued that Aristotelian teleology extends beyond those cases, downwards to the inanimate, and upwards to the Prime Mover. Thus, Charles Kahn has revived the older view that the Prime Mover is a *direct* teleological cause not just of the motion of the outermost sphere but of all natural motion in the cosmos, both living and inanimate.[10] And David Furley has argued that in *Physics* II.8, Aristotle supports the view that rainfall is for the sake of something.[11] David Sedley has endorsed Furley's analysis but has gone beyond it in claiming that the rainfall is for the sake of man. Joining this passage (198b16–199a8) with the notorious one in

9. David Charles, "Teleological Causation in the *Physics*," in Lindsay Judson, ed., *Aristotle's Physics: A Collection of Essays* (Oxford: Clarendon Press, 1991), 101–28.
10. Charles H. Kahn, "The Place of the Prime Mover in Aristotle's Teleology," in Allan Gotthelf, ed., *Aristotle on Nature and Living Things* (Pittsburgh, Pa.: Mathesis Publications, 1985), 183–205.
11. David Furley, "The Rainfall Example in *Physics* II.8," in Gotthelf, *Living Things*, 177–82.

*Politics* I in which Aristotle states that plants are for the sake of animals and animals for the sake of man (1256b15–22), as well as with other passages, Sedley has argued that Aristotelian teleology is *anthropocentric*, with man the ultimate beneficiary of all sublunar teleological action. God, or the Prime Mover, is the ultimate aim or aspiration of teleological action, but man is its ultimate beneficiary.[12] These are, needless to say, deeply important questions for our overall interpretation of Aristotle.

As with the issues under "Analysis," I do not myself think in the end one can decide how to read the key texts that bear on questions of "Extent" without appeal to one's view on the questions under "Basis." So I will focus in this paper on that issue. I have found it helpful in considering the recent literature on this issue to group the various positions that have been defended according to the typology which follows.[13]

## Five Lines of Interpretation

1. *Strong Irreducibility.* Living organisms and their parts do not come to be by material necessity alone. The use of teleological explanation is sanctioned by the absence of such a material level account, since that absence alone entails that the form of the living organism has a real causal role (as aim) in the organism's generation.

This view, which is mine, is also defended by Charlton, Waterlow [Broadie], Cohen, and several others, and as one of Aristotle's two lines of argument for natural teleology, by Cooper.[14] In my view, the absence

12. David Sedley, "Is Aristotle's Teleology Anthropocentric?" *Phronesis* 36 (1991): 179–96.

13. In this typology, I of course omit the view that Aristotle's teleology rests on design (in the sense in which that requires a designer). Although this view was held by several scholars in nineteenth-century Germany, it has no basis in the text and contradicts Aristotle's conception of the Prime Mover. (See Kahn, "The Place of the Prime Mover," 185). At the beginning of his commentary on Aristotle's *Physics* II.8, Thomas Aquinas seems at first glance to be attributing such a view to Aristotle, but arguably he is simply asserting his own view, without distinguishing it, as he more typically does, from Aristotle's. See Thomas Aquinas, *Commentary on Aristotle's Physics*, trans. R. J. Blackwell, R. J. Spath, and E. Thirlkel (New Haven: Yale University Press, 1963), lec. 12, §250, 115–116.

14. William Charlton, *Aristotle's Physics, Book I and II, with a report on recent work* (Oxford: Clarendon Press, 1992). Sarah Waterlow [Broadie], *Nature, Change and Agency in Aristotle's Physics* (Oxford: Clarendon Press, 1982). Sheldon Cohen, "Aristotle on Hot, Cold, and Teleological Explanation," *Ancient Philosophy* 9 (1989): 255–70. John M. Cooper, "Aristotle on Natural Teleology," in M. Schofield and M. C. Nussbaum, eds. *Language and Logos* (Cambridge: Cambridge University Press, 1982), 197–222, and "Hypothetical Necessity and Natural Teleology," in Gotthelf and Lennox, *Aristotle's Biology*, 243–74. A summary statement of my own view may be found in Gotthelf and Lennox, *Aristotle's Biology*, 230–34.

of a full material-level account requires the presence of an irreducible potential for form, and this irreducible potential provides a *primitive directiveness upon* an end which is the ontological basis of Aristotle's natural teleology. Some others (for example, Charlton, Cooper) treat something other than a potential for form as ontologically basic for natural teleology.

2. *The Pragmatic View.* Living organisms and their parts *do* come to be by simple material necessity alone; material-efficient causes are the only actual *causes* involved. Teleological explanation is sanctioned rather by the fact that material level accounts fail to satisfy some pragmatic or subjective need we (sometimes) have for a certain type of explanation, a need which teleological explanation *does* satisfy.

Wieland defends a Kantian version of this theme.[15] Nussbaum speaks of the superior simplicity and generality of teleological explanation over material-level explanation.[16] There is an ontological element to Nussbaum's line, although it is not developed (it gets more developed in her later papers[17]), and her interpretation there remains significantly pragmatic or epistemological. Sorabji speaks of "the relativity of explanation to the questions asked."[18]

3. *Limited Irreducibility.* Living organisms and their parts do indeed come to be of material necessity, at least if they (and their actions and processes) are described materially (including geometrical properties). But certain feature(s) of these organisms and parts are not explained by that fact, namely their *goodness* (or: the organism's status as an *organism*). The irreducibility of the outcome's goodness (or organismic status) is what sanctions the use of teleological explanations, which do explain those features of organisms and their parts. That material/efficient causes necessitate but do not explain teleological outcomes is a consequence of the fact that explanation proceeds from essence, and essence is given by the organism's goal and thus good, and not by its material constitution.

15. W. Wieland, *Die aristotelische Physik* (Göttingen: Vandenhoeck Ruprecht, 1970), chap. 16.
16. Martha C. Nussbaum, *Aristotle's* De Motu Animalium: *Text with Translation, Commentary and Interpretive Essays* (Princeton: Princeton University Press, 1978), 70.
17. Martha C. Nussbaum, "Review of *Substance, Body, and Soul: Aristotelian Investigations,* by E. Hartman," *Journal of Philosophy* 77 (1980): 355–65. "Aristotle," in T. J. Luce, ed., *Ancient Writers* (New York, 1982). "The 'Common Explanation' of Animal Motion," in P. Moraux and J. Wiesner, eds., *Zweifelhaftes in Corpus Aristotelicum: Studien zu Einigen Dubia: Akten des 9. Symposium Aristotelicum* (Berlin, 1983). "Aristotelian Dualism: Reply to Howard Robinson," *Oxford Studies in Ancient Philosophy* 2 (1984): 197–207.
18. Sorabji, *Necessity, Cause, and Blame,* 29–31 and 158.

This view is defended by Charles.[19] Cooper finds a *per impossibile* version of this argument in the first argument in *Phys.* II.8, supplementing the basic line of argument found in II.9 (see 1 above): even if, *per impossibile,* organisms and their parts came to be of material necessity, that would still not explain the fact of the good arrangement of the parts in these organisms.

4. *Weak Irreducibility.* While Aristotle did in fact believe that living organisms and their parts do not come to be by material necessity alone, and while he did believe that the presence of an irreducible potential for form is what sanctions the use of teleological explanation, his defense of the existence of such an irreducible potential does not depend on the unavailability of a full account in terms of material necessity. On this view, there will be an irreducible potential for form so long as there is a "program" in the seed which controls and regulates organic development ensuring that it results in an organism of that form, a "program" which is defined in terms of that form. Whether the operation of such a "program" is reducible to current physico-chemical laws is irrelevant to the question of its irreducibility in the weaker sense which is relevant here. That weaker sense is roughly that biological explanation must make reference to such a "program."

This is the view presented by Bradie and Miller[20] and (to some extent) in Balme.[21] Bradie and Miller compare it to the contemporary analysis of teleological explanation offered by Ernest Mayr.[22] I discuss their interpretation in the next section below.

5. *Intrinsic Causes/Anti-Eliminativism.* Whether or not Aristotle thought living organisms and their parts come to be by material necessity (in any of the ways advocated or denied in lines of interpretation 1–3) is *irrelevant* to his endorsement of teleological explanation. This endorsement depends rather on a denial that the coming to be of living organisms and their parts is *accidental.* (One could deny accidentalness either because one thought there was a primitive directiveness upon the relevant forms, *or* because one thought there was a material mechanism which guaranteed that such forms would be a regular outcome.) That denial derives from Aristotle's insistence, against his accidentalist

19. David Charles, "Aristotle on Hypothetical Necessity and Irreducibility," *Pacific Philosophical Quarterly* 69 (1988): 1–53.
20. Michael Bradie and Fred D. Miller, Jr., "Teleology and Natural Necessity in Aristotle," *History of Philosophy Quarterly* 1 (1984): 133–45.
21. David Balme, "Teleology and Necessity," in Gotthelf and Lennox, *Aristotle's Biology,* 275–86.
22. See Ernst Mayr, *Towards a New Philosophy of Biology* (Cambridge: Harvard University Press, 1988), chap. 1, and the references to Mayr in Bradie and Miller, "Teleology and Natural Necessity."

rivals, that the coming to be of an organism and its parts has an *intrinsic (efficient) cause* of the appropriate sort. Aristotle was thus an *anti-eliminativist*, not an *anti-reductionist*, as interpretations 1, 2, and 4 hold. There are two versions of this view:

5a. The appropriate sort of intrinsic efficient cause is something "program"-like which insures a regular outcome, much as in the contemporary view defended by Mayr (see 4 above). There is a material structure of some sort within the material supplied by the female which responds to the material supplied by the male in much the way that the system of "marvelous automatic puppets" Aristotle speaks of several times responds to the release of the tension holding it fixed: a simple initial motion produces a "pre-programmed" sequence of motions generating a very complex, structured result (in the automatic puppets perhaps a dance, in biological generation an organism).[23] The formal character of the outcome, the regularity of its production, and the need to define the initial material structure in terms of its ability to produce such a result, allow us to speak of that result as a final cause. This view is defended by Matthen[24] (and is probably what the Bradie-Miller view turns into when one asks for a definition of "program," and an explanation of the sort of "irreducibility" involved).

5b. The appropriate sort of intrinsic efficient cause is one which not only guarantees that a living organism of a certain form regularly results, but one in which that intrinsic efficient cause is present *because the result it produces is good.* This view is defended by Irwin and Meyer.[25] Irwin claims that Aristotle's critique of the Empedoclean "selectionist" position shows that he, Aristotle, held that the intrinsic efficient cause present in the seed is present *because* its presence in the parent contributed to the good result which is the parent's survival and reproduction; Meyer claims that it at least shows one possible way in which Aristotle could have supported this position (5b). The appeal to selective success in past generations as the basis of teleological explanation in present generations is a central part of the contemporary "aeteolog-

23. I actually believe that the standard reading of the relevant passages, which takes the initial motion to act only once at the beginning of the development, causing some motion which then causes another motion, etc., like falling dominoes, is not correct. The text suggests rather that the initial source of motion, the active potentiality that resides first in the father's seminal material and then primarily in the fetus' heart, is continually active, all the way through the development, as I will discuss in detail elsewhere.

24. Mohan Matthen, "The Four Causes in Aristotle's Embryology," in Kraut and Penner, *Nature, Knowledge and Virtue*, 159–80.

25. Terence H. Irwin, *Aristotle's First Principles* (Oxford: Clarendon Press, 1988), chap. 5. Susan Suavé Meyer, "Aristotle, Teleology, and Reduction," *Philosophical Review* 101 (1992): 791–825.

ical" analysis of teleological explanation by Harry Binswanger and Larry Wright.[26]

## Aristotle and Contemporary Thought

I have commented on versions of line 1 other than my own, and on versions of line 2 elsewhere, and will comment on lines 3 and 5 in a subsequent paper.[27] I would like here to discuss the version of line 4 developed in the 1984 paper by Michael Bradie and Fred D. Miller, Jr. referred to above (n. 20), since it raises important questions regarding the relationship of Aristotle's natural teleology to contemporary biological teleology.

In a review of the literature to 1983, Bradie and Miller conclude (i) that advocates of line 1 are right to claim that for Aristotle material-efficient causality could not by itself produce living outcomes, and (ii) that I was right to stress the role of a potential for form in grounding teleological explanation. They agree with me too that Aristotle thought the potential for form was not reducible to potentials of the material elements. But they distinguish two irreducibility theses:

26. Harry Binswanger, *The Biological Basis of Teleological Concepts* (Los Angeles: Ayn Rand Institute Press, 1990), and Binswanger, "Life-Based Teleology." Larry Wright, *Teleological Explanations* (Berkeley and Los Angeles: University of California Press, 1976). It is interesting, in view of Meyer's explicit claim that Aristotle was an anti-eliminativist rather than an anti-reductionist, that one section of "Life-Based Teleology" is titled "Reduction vs. Elimination."

27. I mention here one difficulty for each. With respect to line 3, there is a *prima facie* problem for the view that Aristotle holds that there is a full material and efficient causal account but gives primacy to the teleological over the material-efficient account on grounds that teleological factors go into the essence of animals and their parts, since according to a common reading of the *Analytics* and *De Anima* I.1, we determine what goes into the essence by *first* seeing what is explanatorily primary. (David Charles's forthcoming book will attempt to address this issue.) With respect to line 5, it must be said that, while one can agree that *for us* (with contemporary biochemistry), the non-accidentalness and consequential teleological character of the production of animals and their parts is compatible with their having come to be by material necessity (witness, for example, the Binswanger-Wright analysis), it does not follow from this that *Aristotle himself* thought it was compatible: that is, it is precisely the claim of line 1 that, *for Aristotle,* given the limitations of the only sort of matter theory in principle plausible to him, and the consequent unavailability of any "reliable mechanism" (Meyer, "Teleology and Reduction," 812, n. 21) that could serve as a material-level-based intrinsic efficient cause, if an outcome were to be of material necessity (as, for example, spontaneous outcomes are), it would *not* be in any way due to form or final cause. (In speaking of "spontaneous" outcomes, I have in mind the sort discussed in *Physics* II.6, and exclude spontaneous generation, which as explained in *Gen. Animalium* III.11, I believe is not captured by the *Physics* II.6 account. See Gotthelf, "Teleology and Spontaneous Generation.") But all these matters require further discussion.

i. The potential for form is irreducible to the potentials of earth, air, fire, and water.

ii. The potential for form is irreducible to any potential on any level of explanation.[28]

They say that I have argued successfully that Aristotle held (i) but that my claim that (i) was the core of Aristotle's teleology requires Aristotle to also hold (ii). However, they claim, there is no evidence that Aristotle ever held (ii), and in fact it would be anachronistic to attribute (ii) to Aristotle, since that would require him to rule out in advance theories he could not have imagined, such as contemporary DNA theory. That leads them to distinguish two claims about movement involved in Aristotle's teleology:

T1. In a life process, the goal is produced by means of a potential existing from the outset, through movement conforming to a formal principle ("containing a certain *logos*").

T2. The source of the movement through which life processes occur is vital heat, which cannot be identified with the potentials of the simple sublunar elements.

About these claims they write:

Claim T2 has been thoroughly discredited by modern biology, but T1, which is the core of Aristotle's teleology, has been vindicated by modern biology. For the point of T1 is that life processes are self-regulating in virtue of inherent forms or structures. The type of movement required on Aristotle's account for a potential for form is the type of movement exemplified by the DNA molecule. The genetic "program" contained in the molecule's structure directs and limits the organism's growth in the manner set forth in Aristotle's biological writings.[29]

In outline, my response encompasses four points.

1. I find their claim that it is anachronistic to attribute (ii) to Aristotle puzzling, for there is a single, simple premise, available to Aristotle, that gets one from (i) to (ii). It is that the level of earth, air, fire, and water is the *basic* level. To deny Aristotle that premise and attribute to him the view that there might be a more basic level from which development could be accounted for wholly by material-efficient causes, is what strikes me as anachronistic, on two counts: First, there is no tentativeness whatsoever in Aristotle's theory of the elements (nor is the sort of general denial of certainty that is common today any part of Aristotelian epistemology). Second, as Waterlow [Broadie] and Cohen

28. Bradie and Miller, "Teleology and Natural Necessity," 147.
29. Ibid., 148.

point out, all of Aristotle's instincts regarding matter theory are in the direction of the view that the lower you go the less structure you get, and the less possibility of explaining complex, highly structured, highly functional outcomes.

2. Bradie and Miller do indeed make clear, with their T1, that there is a nontrivial generic similarity between Aristotle's account of the basis of teleological explanation and the contemporary genetic program account. But Aristotle could not have projected such an account and thus did not himself countenance such a generic version, much less endorse it. But *we* can see it, and we can call any view that endorses T1 *Aristotelian* (but not "Aristotle's").

3. Actually, point 2 requires qualification: As suggested in the parenthesis attached to the description of line of interpretation 5 in the previous section, the Bradie and Miller view would seem, if pressed in the ways indicated, to turn into a version of line 5, and in particular into a version of 5a. But for reasons both Irwin and Meyer on the one hand, and Binswanger on the other, have suggested, 5b is to be preferred over 5a, both in the contemporary context and as the generic "Aristotelian" view. The point may be put simply. If there is a regular direction upon an end, guaranteed by an intrinsic efficient cause of a material sort, this seems only to *mimic* teleological causation; what we need is that the intrinsic cause's activity that leads to the end occurs *because* it leads to that end. In my interpretation, as I elaborate it in my "Postscript 1986," sec. I, the addition to Aristotle's ontology of potentials for form entails that when some potential for form is being realized, everything needed for that form is also being realized. These latter needs, then, occur *because* the form is coming to be. But if an actualization of such a potential is only a redescription of some set of actualizations of material level potentials, I don't see that anything happens or comes to be *because* it is needed for the end. Under these circumstances, teleological explanation would seem to be applicable only if the "program" itself is present solely because of the success of its outcome in previous generations, and this is interpretation 5*b*.

4. Taking the previous three points into account, then, the best we can say on behalf of the Bradie and Miller thesis is that, in the face of contemporary physics and biochemistry, Aristotle would very likely *retreat* to a version of 5b. But it remains the case (given Bradie-Miller's declared agreements with me together with point 1 just above) that on Aristotle's view a "potential for form" involves a *primitive* directiveness upon an end, not a directiveness that is in any way derivative from any material level "mechanism" or "structure" or "intrinsic efficient cause." The existence of such a *primitive directiveness,* made possible by a

strongly irreducible potential for form, is the core of Aristotle's teleology, and what differentiates that teleology from the various modern theories to which some interpreters have tried to assimilate it, and with which it indeed has important generic similarities.[30]

From a contemporary standpoint, these generic similarities are not to be dismissed, and the contemporary physicist and biological theorist Max Delbrück was perhaps only slightly exaggerating in insisting that Aristotle ought to be awarded a posthumous Nobel Prize "for the discovery of the principle implied in DNA."[31] And comparing contemporary biological teleology with Aristotle's own may help illuminate for us the generic features of our favored theory. But if we are to be historically accurate, and to understand what it was that was missed by the early modern critics of Aristotelian teleology, for whom the only alternatives were mechanism or design, we need to understand what it is that is *distinctive* about Aristotle's natural teleology. And if I am right in thinking that much else in Aristotle's thought, from his ethical theory to the theory of substance in the central books of the *Metaphysics*, depends centrally on his natural teleology, understanding the teleology aright will be crucial for understanding much else in his philosophy, and thus for learning the great amount there still is for us to learn from Aristotle today.

30. For Miller's current view, see *Nature, Justice and Rights in Aristotle* (Oxford: Clarendon Press, 1995).

31. Max Delbrück, "Aristotle-totle-totle," in Jacque Monod and E. Borek, eds., *Of Microbes and Life* (New York: Columbia University Press, 1971), 50–55.

# 4                                                    Ends and Purposes
## FRANCIS SLADE

"End" as a translation of *telos* means what a thing will be that has
become fully determined in its being; the defined; the complete; a condition of perfection, completion, fulfillment. "End" as a translation of
*telos* does not mean "termination," as when a road ends in a "dead end";
it does not signify that something no longer exists, as when we say that
"death is the end of life." End, as *telos*, signifies a continuing state of
perfectedness; it is akin to the meaning of "finish," where we are speaking about what the cabinet maker does last in making a piece of furniture: he puts the finish on it, that is, brings it to perfection in
completion.

End, as *telos*, is not synonymous with "purpose," although the words
are commonly understood to be, and are used as, synonyms. But *telos*
does not mean purpose. Agents and actors have "purposes" by which
they determine themselves to certain actions. Purposes are motives,
"motors" propelling us toward destinations. Ends, on the other hand,
are characteristic of all kinds of things; the end of the axe is "cutting,"
but the axe executes no purpose in its cutting. Those who use axes, the
agents, have many purposes: to clear land, to obtain firewood, to blaze
trails, to attack someone, etc. Ends are not executed by agents. Purposes require agents. Purposes belong to agents as they determine
themselves to actions.

The end of the art of medicine, a body of knowledge and skills, is
the restoration and maintenance of the condition called health. A
man's purpose in practicing medicine can be various, from the making
of money to the relief of suffering humanity out of a love of mankind,
just as long as the purpose is congruent with the end for which medicine
exists. The art of medicine does not exist in order to provide the people
who practice it with money; nor does it exist in order to allow those who
practice it to demonstrate their sympathy with, and benevolence towards, their fellow human beings. One may, of course, execute such
purposes in the practice of the art of medicine. But suppose that the

money-making physician finds that he can make enormously more money using his medical skills to kill people rather than to cure them; or, suppose again, that the philanthropic physician's sympathy for the suffering leads him to kill his patients "mercifully." These purposes, that is, making money and demonstrating one's love for fellow men, are no longer congruent with the end of the art of medicine. For if such purposes were systematically executed by most physicians, they would lead to the destruction of the art itself, since, if physicians acquired a reputation for killing rather than for curing, no one would wish to consult them. Since everyone would do everything possible to avoid them, there would soon be no physicians, for without patients, the art cannot be practiced, and so could not be learned.

> *Ends exist independently of our willing them;*
> ends do not originate in our willing them to be.
> *Purposes take their origin from our willing them;*
> purposes would not be if agents did not give them being.

The Hippocratic Oath taken by physicians forbids the use of the art of medicine to kill people. This prohibition is for the sake of the art rather than for what are known as "moral reasons." Killing those upon whom they attend is forbidden to physicians by the Hippocratic Oath, not because it is morally wrong to murder people—the wrongness of murder is something that applies to all men, and it is forbidden by whatever laws they acknowledge themselves to be subject to—but because to use the art of medicine to kill people destroys the art. The Oath, then, is for the sake of the art. The Hippocratic Oath does not forbid murder by medicine to physicians on account of the patients, but on account of the art of medicine. Nor would a physician violate the Oath by murdering someone in a manner that did not depend upon the art of medicine. Should a physician shoot someone with a shotgun and kill him, he does not thereby violate his Hippocratic Oath. The physician who murders someone with a shotgun may be indicted and tried for murder, convicted, and incur the legal punishment for the act, but he is not for that reason excluded from the practice of medicine.

Purpose is synonymous with "intention." I define it, following Oakeshott, as "an imagined and wished-for satisfaction."[1] Aristotle's term *proairesis* is "purpose" in this sense. Man has an end *(telos);* individual human beings have "intentions" or "purposes" in executing their acts. Purpose *(proairesis),* the efficient cause of action, is what we *propose* to ourselves to do.

---

1. Michael Oakeshott, *On Human Conduct* (Oxford: Clarendon Press, 1990), 39.

"The idea is that you start out with certain ends—things that you favor or want."[2] This is precisely *what ends are not,* but certainly what they are frequently, and mistakenly, taken to be. What we "favor," or what we "want," describe purposes, not ends. "Favoring" and "wanting" are words indicating what can be loosely described as some kind of "mental activity." While purposes presuppose such activity, ends do not. They do not originate out of "mental activity"; their reality does not derive from being constituted by such activities, activities which have their being in "consciousness." An end is "out there" beyond favoring and wanting. Ends do not come to be out of what I favor, or what I want.

2. Gilbert Harmon, *The Nature of Morality* (New York: Oxford University Press, 1977), 31.

# 5     On the Presumed Medieval Origin of Individual Rights

## ERNEST L. FORTIN

Few issues pertaining to the history of ethical and political thought have proved more intractable over the years than that of the relationship of individual or subjective rights to the more traditional natural law approach to the study of moral phenomena. Some prominent theorists, such as C. B. Macpherson and Leo Strauss, have long argued that the two doctrines are irreducibly different and incompatible with each other,[1] whereas other scholars—Jacques Maritain, John Finnis, and James Tully, to name only three[2]—see the rights doctrine, not as a substitute for its predecessor, but either as a more polished version of it or a useful complement to it. The matter is of no small consequence for decent citizens who worry about a possible tension between the biblical component of the American founding and the framers' apparent commitment to an Enlightenment concept of rights that, to paraphrase Tocqueville, promotes egoism to the level of a philosophic principle. It is also a source of concern for Catholic ethicists who are uneasy with the gradual erosion of the once ubiquitous natural law and its supersession by a focus on rights in recent Church documents and Catholic theology generally. If the rights doctrine is not only compatible but essentially continuous with the natural law doctrine, any qualms that one may have about acquiescing in it may be safely laid to rest. If, alter-

1. C. B. Macpherson, *The Political Theory of Possessive Individualism* (Oxford: Oxford University Press, 1962). Leo Strauss, *Natural Right and History* (Chicago: University of Chicago Press, 1953), esp. 181–83. This is not to suggest that Strauss and Macpherson are in complete agreement with each other. See in this connection Strauss's review of Macpherson's book, reprinted in Leo Strauss, *Studies in Platonic Political Philosophy*, ed. Thomas L. Pangle (Chicago: University of Chicago Press, 1983), 229–31.

2. Jacques Maritain, *Les Droits de l'homme et la loi naturelle* (New York: Éditions de la Maison Francaise, 1943); *The Person and the Common Good*, trans. John J. Fitzgerald (Notre Dame, Ind.: University of Notre Dame, 1966). John Finnis, *Natural Law and Natural Rights*, (Oxford: Clarendon Press, 1980). James Tully, *A Discourse on Property: John Locke and His Adversaries* (Cambridge: Cambridge University Press, 1980).

natively, the two doctrines are demonstrably at odds with each other, the qualms may not be wholly unwarranted. One way to tackle the problem is to inquire into the intellectual pedigree of the rights theory. Unfortunately, scholarly opinion is sharply divided on this issue as well, as can be seen from a brief survey of the recent literature on the subject. Three names stand out among others in this connection.

The first is that of Michel Villey, the distinguished French legal historian and philosopher, who in his book on the formation of modern juridical thought[3] and numerous other publications stretched out over a fifty-year period has sought to prove that the father of the rights theory as we know it is William of Ockham. For Villey, everything hinges on the distinction between objective right—"the right thing" *(ipsa res iusta)*, "one's due" or one's proper share, Ulpian's *suum ius cuique tribuere*—and subjective right, by which is meant a moral power *(potestas)* or faculty *(facultas)* inhering in individual human beings. How and to what extent the two notions differ from each other becomes plain when we recall that "right" in the first sense does not necessarily work to the advantage of the individual whose right it is. In Rome, the right of a parricide was to be stuffed in a bag filled with vipers and thrown into the Tiber. Ockham, the villain of Villey's story, is the man who would have consummated the break with the premodern tradition by accrediting that monstrosity known as subjective rights, or rights that individuals possess, as opposed to rights by which so to speak they are possessed. His would be the work that marks the "Copernican moment" in the history of legal science.[4] In Villey's view, a straight path leads from Ockham's nominalism, according to which only individuals exist, to the rights with which these individuals are invested; for not until the rise of philosophic nominalism in the late Middle Ages could such a novel conception of rights have seen the light of day.

The second author to be reckoned with is Richard Tuck, whose book on the origin of natural rights theories,[5] acclaimed by many as a breakthrough when it came out in 1979, is a history of the notion of subjective rights from its supposed twelfth-century origins to its full expression in the works of Locke and, before Locke, Grotius, who finally

3. Michael Villey, *La formation de la pensée juridique moderne* (Paris: Dalloz, 1975). This paragraph and a few others that follow incorporate materials previously used in my "Sacred and Inviolable: *Rerum Novarum* and Natural Rights," *Theological Studies* 53 (1992): 203–33.
4. Michel Villey, "La Genèse du droit subjectif chez Guillaume d'Occam," *Archives de philosophie du droit* 9 (1964): 97–127, quotation on p. 127.
5. Richard Tuck, *Natural Rights Theories: Their Origin and Development*, (Cambridge: Cambridge University Press, 1979).

"broke the ice"[6] by casting off the shackles of Aristotelian philosophy. Tuck distinguishes between *passive* rights, by which he means rights reducible to duties incumbent on other people, and the more pertinent *active* rights or rights understood as the absolute liberty to do or to forbear.[7] Two great periods mark this history: 1350–1450, which witnessed the flowering of Nominalism, and 1590–1670, the period in which the rights doctrine finally came into its own with the publication of the great works not only of Grotius and Locke but of such other eminent theorists as Suarez, Selden, Hobbes, Cumberland, and Pufendorf. I note in passing that, with admirable intellectual integrity, Tuck has since repudiated in private conversation part of the argument of his book. I do not know whether he has yet done so in writing.

The third protagonist in this unfolding saga is Brian Tierney, who in the last ten years or so has inundated us with a spate of articles purporting to demonstrate that the now triumphant rights doctrine is indeed an early- rather than a late-medieval or a specifically modern contribution to the development of political and legal theory.[8] Against Villey, Leo Strauss, and a number of Strauss's followers, among them Walter Berns (Tierney's one-time colleague at Cornell) and Arlene Saxonhouse,[9] Tierney argues that there is no significant hiatus or breach

6. Tuck, *Natural Rights Theories,* 175. The expression is a quote from Barbeyrac, *An Historical and Critical Account of the Science of Morality,* preface to Samuel Pufendorf, *The Law of Nature and Nations,* trans. B. Kennet (London, 1749), 55, 63, 98.
7. Tuck, *Natural Rights Theories,* 5–6.
8. These articles include Brian Tierney, "Tuck on Rights, Some Medieval Problems," *History of Political Thought* 4 (1983): 429–40; "Villey, Ockham and the Origin of Individual Rights," in *The Weightier Matters of the Law: A Tribute to Harold J. Berman,* ed. John Witte, Jr. and Frank Alexander (Atlanta: Scholars Press, 1988), 1–31; "Conciliarism, Corporatism, and Individualism: the Doctrine of Individual Rights in Gerson," *Cristianesimo nella storia* 9 (1988): 81–111; "Marsilius on Rights," *Journal of the History of Ideas* 52 (1991): 5–17. "Origins of Natural Rights Language: Texts and Contexts, 1150–1250," *History of Political Thought* 10 (1989): 615–46; "Aristotle and the American Indians—Again," *Cristianesimo nella storia* 12 (1991): 295–322; "Natural Rights in the Thirteenth Century: A *Quaestio* of Henry of Ghent," *Speculum* 67 (1992): 58–68, and "1492: Medieval Natural Rights Theories and the Discovery of America," in *Moral and Political Philosophies in the Middle Ages,* ed. J. Carlos Bazan, Eduardo Andujar, and Leonardo Sprocchi (Ottawa: Legas, 1995), 167–76, which summarizes in readily assimilable form the results arrived at in the previous articles.
9. Tierney, "Conciliarism, Corporatism," 88: "One school of thought holds that all modern rights theories are rooted in the 'atheistic' philosophy of Hobbes and hence regards them as incompatible with the whole preceding Christian tradition." The reference is to an article by Walter Berns, "Comment on 'Christians, Politics, and the Modern State,' by E. R. Norman," *This World* 6 (1983): 96–101. See Tierney, "Villey, Ockham," 20, n. 74, where Berns is taken to task for having written that "natural rights and traditional natural law are, to put it simply yet altogether accurately, incompatible." In Tierney's opinion, "[s]uch views seem based on a mistaken idea that modern rights theories are derived entirely from Hobbes and on simple ignorance of the history of the concept of

of continuity between the medieval and modern understandings of right. His thesis in a nutshell is that the subjective rights to which Villey points as the hallmark of modernity are in fact an invention of the brilliant canonists and civil lawyers of twelfth- and thirteenth-century Europe, whose writings he subjects to a far more painstaking scrutiny than either Villey or Tuck had done. In Tierney's own words,

The doctrine of individual rights was not a late medieval aberration from an earlier tradition of objective right or of natural moral law. Still less was it a seventeenth-century invention of Suarez or Hobbes or Locke. Rather, it was a characteristic product of the great age of creative jurisprudence that, in the twelfth and thirteenth centuries, established the foundations of the Western legal tradition.[10]

Tierney's point against Villey is both well taken and ably documented. His articles have shown, convincingly in my opinion, that the definition of rights as "powers" antedates the Nominalist movement by some two centuries and that in this matter Ockham and his followers were not the radical innovators Villey makes them out to be. Further support for this conclusion is to be found in the fact that Ockham's treatment of the natural law, long a bone of contention among scholars, is anything but revolutionary,[11] as we know now that the egregious mistake contained in the printed editions of his classic statement on the subject has been corrected on the basis of a fresh reading of the manuscripts.[12] Ockham's threefold division of the natural law into principles that apply (a) to both the prelapsarian and postlapsarian stages of humanity and are therefore unchangeable (for example, the prohibition against lies and adultery), or (b) only to the prelapsarian stage (for example, the community of goods and the equality of all human beings), or (c) only to the postlapsarian stage (for example, private property,

---

*ius naturale* before the seventeenth century." In "Natural Rights in the Thirteenth Century," 58, Tierney takes issue with Saxonhouse's contention that prior to the seventeenth century, people did not think of individuals "as possessing inalienable rights to anything—much less life, liberty, property, or even the pursuit of happiness." See Arlene Saxonhouse, *Women in the History of Political Thought* (New York: Praeger, 1985), 7.

10. Tierney, "Villey, Ockham," 31.

11. On Ockham's conservatism, see Tierney's remarks in "Villey, Ockham," 19, citing John Morrall, who describes Ockham as "an interpreter and defender of the achievements of the past."

12. William of Ockham, *Dialogus*, Part III, Tr. ii, Book III, 6. The most recent edition is that of M. Goldast, ed. (Frankfurt, 1614), which merely reproduces the Lyons edition of 1494, along with its mistakes. The corrected text is to be found in H. S. Offler, "Three Modes of Natural Law in Ockham: A Revision of the Text," *Franciscan Studies* 15 (1977): 207–18. The mistake in the Goldast edition concerns the second level of natural law and consists in reading the unintelligible *quod ideo est naturale quia est contra statum naturae institutae* for the *quod ideo dicitur naturale quia contrarium est contra statum naturae institutae* of the manuscripts.

slavery, and warfare) does little more than systematize what the canonical tradition routinely taught. If Ockham can be said to have innovated, it is not in regard to this issue; it is rather in regard to the theoretical foundation of the natural law, whose principles are said by him to owe their truth, not to God's intellect, but to His will alone, to such an extent that God could command us to hate him if he so desired.[13] Simply put, no human act is intrinsically good or bad; it becomes such solely by reason of its being enjoined or forbidden by God.

For all its outstanding merits, however, Tierney's demonstration is not without problems of its own, one of them being, not that it uncovers traces of subjective rights in the Middle Ages, but that it constantly refers to these rights as "natural," something that few medieval authors, and none of those cited by Tierney himself, ever do, with the one exception of Nicholas of Cusa, to whom I shall return. In the vast majority of cases, the rights in question are called "rights" without qualification and appear to have been understood as civil or canonical rights. This is typically the case with Gerson, who discusses at great length the rights of popes, bishops, and local prelates, or the rights of mendicant friars to preach, hear confessions, and receive tithes, all of which manifestly belong to the realm of positive and specifically ecclesiastical rather than natural right.[14]

One does encounter the expression *iura naturalia* on a few scattered occasions not mentioned by Tierney, but its meaning bears little resemblance to the one that attaches to it from the seventeenth century onward. Augustine used it in the midst of the Pelagian controversy in an effort to explain how original sin, the sin committed by Adam and Eve, could have been transmitted to their descendants. The rights of which he speaks are the "natural rights of propagation"—*iura naturalia propaginis*—whereby the offspring, who are somehow precontained in the ancestor, are thought to inherit through birth the characteristic features of his fallen nature.[15] In a similar manner, St. Jerome speaks of incest as a violation of the natural rights—*iura naturae*—of a mother or a sister.[16] In other instances, the link with our modern rights theory

13. See William of Ockham, *Quaestiones in librum secundum Sententiarum*, II, qu. 15, ad 3 and 4, in *Opera Theologica*, vol. 5, ed. G. Gal and R. Wood (New York: St. Bonaventure, 1981), 347–48.

14. See, for example, Tierney, "Conciliarism, Corporatism," 94, who notes that *Consideratio* 12 of Gerson's *De potestate ecclesiastica*, which immediately precedes the formal definition of *ius* in *Consideratio* 13, "is devoted entirely to a discussion of *iura*—the rights of popes, kings, bishops, and lesser prelates in the conduct of church affairs."

15. Augustine, Contra Iul., *Opus Imperfectum*, 6, 22, in *Patrologia Latina*, ed. J. P. Migne, vol. 45, col. 1551.

16. Jerome, *In Amos*, in *Commentarii in prophetas minores*. Part I.6 of *S. Hieronymi Presbyteri Opera*. Corpus Christianorum (Turnhout: Brepols, 1969) i, 1.

is even more tenuous. Primasius of Hadrumetum describes the antlers that burst forth from the heads of certain animals and keep growing and growing as violating the "natural rights of places"—*naturalia locorum iura.*[17] None of this, needless to say, adds up to a *bona fide* natural rights theory imbedded in a coherent and properly articulated framework.

Nor, as I have intimated, can the concept of natural rights be said to play a significant role in medieval thought. Tierney himself acknowledges that Thomas Aquinas did not have a theory of natural rights,[18] but, to the best of my knowledge, no medieval writer either before or after him ever tried to elaborate such a theory. If the information at our disposal suggests anything, it is that rights as the medievals understood them were subservient to an antecedent law that circumscribes and relativizes them. For Ockham, a "right" was a "lawful power," *licita potestas.*[19] For his contemporary, Johannes Monachus, it was a "virtuous power," *virtuosa potestas,* or a power "introduced by law," *a iure introducta.*[20] As the adjectives used to qualify them imply, these rights were by no means unconditional. They were contingent on the performance of prior duties and hence forfeitable. Anyone who failed to abide by the law that guarantees them could be deprived of everything to which he was previously entitled: his freedom, his property, and in extreme cases his life. Not so with the natural rights on which the modern theorists would later base their speculations and which have been variously described as absolute, inviolable, imprescriptible, unconditional, inalienable, or sacred.

In support of his thesis that rights are an invention of the Middle Ages, Tierney notes that the precept "Honor thy father and thy mother" is not only a commandment; it also means that parents have a subjective right to the respect of their children.[21] Fair enough, although these are not the terms in which the medievals were wont to

17. Primasius of Hadrumetum, *Commentarius in Apocalypsin,* ed. A. W. Adams (Turnhout, Belgium: Brepols, 1985), 2, 5.
18. Tierney, "Natural Rights in the Thirteenth Century," 67. According to Busa's exhaustive *Index Thomisticus,* the word *iura* occurs a total of fifty-four times in Thomas's voluminous corpus but never in the sense of natural rights. In all cases, the reference is to canonical or civil rights, or to the ancient as distinguished from the new codes of law, or to the laws governing warfare and the like.
19. See Villey, "La Genèse du droit subjectif chez Guillaume d'Occam," 117. Even without the addition of *licita, potestas* often means a "legal" power, as distinguished from *potentia,* which can designate a premoral power. It is true that the distinction between the two is not always strictly observed.
20. Johannes Monachus, *Glossa Aurea* (Paris, 1535), fol. xciv, Glossa ad Sect. 1.6.16. Tierney, "Villey, Ockham," 30.
21. Ibid., 20.

92 ERNEST L. FORTIN

pose the problem. Their question was not whether parents have a right
to be respected by their children but whether it is objectively right that
they be respected by them. Even if one grants the legitimacy of Tierney's inference, however, one is still left with the problem of determining which of the two, the right or the duty, comes first and of deciding
what is to be done in the event of a conflict between them. Is this subjective right, assuming that it exists, inamissible, or could it sometimes
be overridden by more compelling interests?

Granted, one cannot conclude from the absence of any explicit distinction between objective and subjective right in their works that the
classical philosophers and their medieval disciples would have objected
to the notion of subjective rights or rights as moral faculties or powers,
for such they must somehow be if by reason of them human beings are
authorized to do or refrain from doing certain things. Since rights are
already implied in the notion of duty—anyone who has a duty to do
something must have the right to do it—there appears to be no reason
to dichotomize them. What they represent would be nothing more than
the two sides of a single coin. If, as was generally assumed in the Middle
Ages, there is such a thing as the natural law, one has every reason to
speak of the rights to which it gives rise as being themselves natural.

This is in fact what appears to have been done explicitly by a small
number of late-medieval writers such as Marsilius of Padua, Ockham,
and Nicholas of Cusa, in whose works the expression *iura naturalia*
makes an occasional appearance. Marsilius refers to certain rights
*(iura)* as "natural" because in all regions "they are in some way believed
to be lawful and their opposites unlawful."[22] Nothing suggests he had
any intention of breaking with his predecessors, at least as regards the
subordination of these rights to the natural law, about which, para-
doxically, he himself seems to have had serious doubts.[23] Ockham uses
the same expression at least once, but again within the context of a
discussion of the natural law.[24] Nicholas of Cusa, to whom I have already alluded, does something similar when he writes:

There is in the people a divine seed by virtue of their common equal birth and
the equal *natural rights* of all human beings *(communem omnium hominum aequa-
lem nativitatem et aequalia naturalia iura)* so that all authority, which comes from

22. Marsilius of Padua, *Defensor Pacis*, trans. Alan Gewirth (Toronto: University of
Toronto Press, 1990), II.12, 7.
23. The gist of Marsilius's argument is that universally admitted moral principles are
not fully rational and, conversely, that fully rational principles are not universally admitted. See Leo Strauss, "Marsilius of Padua," in *History of Political Philosophy*, ed. Leo
Strauss and Joseph Cropsey (Chicago: University of Chicago Press, 1987), 292–93.
24. Ockham, *Dialogus*, Part III, Tr. ii, Book III, 6.

God as do all human beings . . . is recognized as divine when it arises from the common consent of the subjects.[25]

Unfortunately, Nicholas does not volunteer any further information on what he means by a "natural right" or call special attention to the expression, as well he might have if he had wanted to give it a new and more pregnant meaning. He too merely echoes the traditional medieval view according to which the early humans were free and equal insofar as they knew nothing of political authority, slavery, or private property.[26] To repeat, nowhere in the Middle Ages does one come across a natural rights teaching comparable to the one set forth in the works of a host of early modern political writers, beginning with Hobbes. The most that can be said is that, on the basis of their own principles, the medievals could conceivably have put forward a doctrine of natural rights rooted in natural law. They never did. Why? The simplest answer is that in matters of this sort they tended to take their cue from the Bible, the Church Fathers, Roman law, the canon law tradition, and Aristotle's *Ethics and Politics* once they became available in Latin translation during the course of the thirteenth century. In none of these texts is there any thematic treatment of or stress on natural rights.[27] For better or for worse, natural rights in our sense of the term were largely alien not only to the medieval mind but to the literature of the entire premodern period.

One can certainly agree with Tierney that the surge of interest in

25. *The Catholic Concordance*, trans. P. Sigmund (Cambridge: Cambridge University Press, 1991), 230, translation slightly modified. The original text is to be found in Nicholas of Cusa, *Opera Omnia*, III.iv, 331, ed. G. Kallen, vol. 14 (Hamburg: Felix Meiner, 1963), 348. The text is cited by Tierney, who does not call attention to the rarity of the expression. See "Conciliarism, Corporatism," 109.

26. Nicholas's treatise was presented to the Council of Basel in early 1434. It clearly reflects Nicholas's conciliarist leanings and was calculated to support his views on this subject. See also G. de Lagarde, "Individualisme et corporatisme au moyen âge," in *L'organisation corporative du moyen âge à la fin de l'Ancien Régime* (Louvain: Bibliothèque de l'Université, 1937), 52.

27. The Bible certainly knows nothing of natural rights. If it is famous for anything, it is for promulgating a set of commandments or, as one might say, a Bill of Duties rather than a Bill of Rights. The term "rights" in the plural, *iura*, does not appear even once in the Vulgate, for centuries the standard version of the Bible in the West. *Ius* in the singular occurs approximately thirty times but always to designate some legally sanctioned arrangement. Gen. 23:4 speaks in this sense of a *ius sepulchri* or right of burial apropos of Abraham, who discusses with the Hittites the possibility of acquiring a tomb for Sarah. As is clear from the context, Abraham is not claiming any kind of right and has no need to do so, for the Hittites were offering him free of charge their "choicest sepulchres" to bury his dead. The Hebrew Bible itself makes no attempt to define this or any other right. Since it has no word for "nature" and, in any event, does not engage in philosophical speculation, it can hardly be expected to describe such rights as "natural."

94 ERNEST L. FORTIN

legal theory from the twelfth century onward is a remarkable phenomenon, but it does not of itself signal the emergence of a new concept of
right. The occasion was the recent adoption of Roman Law in the West,
necessitated by the pressing need to find solutions to such typical problems as the relation between the pope and the emperor, between the
emperor and the lesser rulers of Christendom, between rulers and subjects, between mendicants and seculars, and so on, or else to determine
such issues as the rights of property (particularly as these affected religious orders) or the rights of infidels—all of which called for an approach to moral matters that focused to an unprecedented degree on
rights and duties. Ockham himself, whose supreme ambition in later
life, as Tierney notes, was to have Pope John XXII declared a heretic,[28]
was motivated by a similar set of concerns. In all such cases, the rights
under consideration were legal rights, sanctioned either by the civil law,
the divine law, or, if one wants to go beyond what the medievals explicitly taught, the natural law. Tierney himself puts the matter in
proper medieval perspective when he writes:

In fact, one finds natural rights regarded as derivative from natural law at
every stage in the history of the doctrine—in the twelfth-century renaissance
of law, in the eighteenth-century Enlightenment and still in twentieth-century
discourse.[29]

Part of the confusion in this instance arises from the fact that what
Tierney has in mind when he refers to the eighteenth century is not
the characteristic Enlightenment view of rights but Christian Wolff's
assertion that "[t]he law of nature *(lex)* obliges man to perfect himself. . . . *ius* is called a faculty or moral power of acting. . . . *ius* provides
the means for what *lex* provides as an end."[30] Similarly, when he speaks
of "twentieth-century discourse," he is thinking not of Rawls and Dwor-
kin but of Maritain and Finnis, two authors who, like Wolff, are committed to a basically premodern understanding of justice and morality,
however much they may be influenced, as was Wolff, by modern modes
of thought. None of this meets the crucial question head-on, which has
to do, not with whether the premoderns had any notion of subjective
rights, but with the order of rank of rights and duties.

On this score, the likeliest supposition is the one according to which
there exists a specifically modern notion of rights that comes to the fore
with Hobbes in the seventeenth century and distinguishes itself from

28. Tierney, "Villey, Ockham," 19.
29. Ibid., 20–21.
30. Christian Wolff, *Institutiones Iuris Naturae et Gentium*, in *Gesammelte Werke*, vol. 26
(Halle, 1750), 23–24; quoted by Tierney, "Conciliarism, Corporatism," 102.

all previous notions not so much by its definition of right as a power as by its proclamation of rights rather than duties as the primary moral counter. Nowhere is the new position formulated more clearly than in chapter 14 of *Leviathan*, which begins with a forceful assertion of the primacy of the natural right of self-preservation, that is, of the right that each individual possesses to resist anyone who poses, or is thought to pose, or could conceivably pose a threat to his existence or well-being. From this primordial *right* of nature Hobbes goes on to deduce the whole of his simplified morality and, in particular, the various *laws* of nature—nineteen of them in all—that reason devises and to which human beings bind themselves when, for the sake of their own protection, they "enter" into civil society. In Hobbes's own words,

The RIGHT OF NATURE, which writers commonly call *ius naturale*, is the liberty each man has to use his own power, as he will himself, for the preservtion of his own nature—that is to say, of his own life—and consequently of doing anything which, in his own judgment and reason, he shall conceive to be the aptest means thereunto.[31]

This is precisely the teaching that was taken over by subsequent theorists, including Locke, who points out that "in the state of nature everyone has the executive power of the law of nature,"[32] a teaching that he himself tells us is not only strange but "very strange."[33] This teaching is clearly of a piece with the Hobbesian notion of the "state of nature," that prepolitical state in which one is not bound by any law whatsoever and is free to deal with others as one's sees fit.[34] Nothing could be further from the traditional view, which knows of no state in which human beings are not subject to some higher authority and views the meting out of punishments—Locke's "executive power of the law of nature"—as the prerogative of rulers and no one else. To refer to Thomas Aquinas once again, anyone is free to reward others for doing good but only the "minister of the law" has the authority to punish them for doing evil.[35] Gratian's Decree is even more explicit, calling any pri-



31. Thomas Hobbes, *Leviathan*, ed. C. B. Macpherson (New York: Penguin, 1985), chap. 14, first paragraph.
32. Locke, *Second Treatise of Civil Government*, nos. 6, 7, 8, and 13.
33. Ibid., no. 13. See also no. 9, where the same teaching is likewise described as "very strange."
34. See Thomas Hobbes, *De Cive*, ed. Howard Warrender (Oxford: Clarendon Press, 1983), I, 8–9. Benedict Spinoza, *A Theologico-Political Treatise and A Political Treatise*, Trans. R. H. M. Elwes (New York: Dover, 1951), II, 18: "In the state of nature, wrongdoing is impossible; or, if anyone does wrong, it is to himself, not to another."
35. Aquinas, *Summa Theologiae*, II–II, 64, 3. Also I–II, 92, 2, ad 3, and 90, 3, ad 2. Thomas's teaching follows roughly Aristotle, *Nichomachean Ethics*, Loeb Classical Library (1982), X, 15–24. Cf. Francisco Suarez, *De Legibus*, ed., Luciano Parena (Madrid: Consejo

vate individual who takes it upon himself to put a criminal to death a "murderer": *Qui sine aliqua publica administratione maleficum interfecerit velut homicida iudicabitur, et tanto amplius quanto sibi potestatem a Deo non concessam usurpare non timuit.*[36] The opposition between the old and the new views is equally striking when one turns to the question to which Tierney's article on Henry of Ghent is entirely devoted, namely, whether a criminal who has been justly sentenced to death is allowed to flee if the opportunity presents itself.[37] From Henry's text we learn that a convict does have that right, but only as long as he can exercise it without injuring anyone else—*sine iniuria alterius.*[38] This position is not essentially different from the one taken by Thomas Aquinas, who also argued that a prisoner is not morally obliged to stay in jail while awaiting his execution but is nevertheless strictly forbidden to use physical force to defend himself against the executioner.[39] The only point that distinguishes the two authors, and it is a minor one, is Henry's claim that under certain circumstances fleeing may be a "necessity" or a positive duty, the reason being that refusing to flee would be tantamount to committing suicide.[40] In this matter, Henry was followed by the well-known sixteenth-century canonist, Jacques Alamain, who agreed that a prisoner in this situation is

Superior de Investigaciones Científicas, Instituto de Francisco de Vitoria, 1971), III.3, 3; Hugo Grotius, *De Iure Belli et Pacis* (Lausanne, France: Bousquet, 1751–52), II.20, 3.

36. Gratian, *Decretum*, I, 23, qu. 8, can. 33, in *Decretum Magistri Gratiani*, ed. E. Friedberg, Corpus Juris Canonici, vol. I (Leibzig: Tauschnitz, 1879). The text follows Augustine, *City of God*, 1, 21.

37. The pertinent text by Henry of Ghent is *Quodlibet* 9, qu. 26, in *Opera Omnia*, ed. Raymond Macken (Leuven: University Press, 1983), vol. 13, 307–10.

38. Ibid., 308. See Tierney, "Natural Rights in the Thirteenth Century," 64.

39. *Summa Theologiae*, II-II, 69, 4, ad 2: ". . . *nullus ita condemnatur quod ipse sibi inferat mortem sed quod ipse mortem patiatur. Et ideo non tenetur facere id unde mors sequatur, quod est manere in loco unde ducatur ad mortem. Tenetur tamen non resistere agenti quin patiatur quod iustum est eum pati.*" The example in terms of which the problem was discussed in antiquity was that of Socrates, who could easily have fled with the help of powerful friends but chose instead to die, ostensibly in obedience to the laws of the city. As the *Crito* suggests, however, his real reasons for doing so were quite different. At the age of seventy, with at best only a few more years to live and faced with the unattractive prospect of having to spend them in some uncongenial place, Socrates had less to lose by accepting his sentence than would have been the case had he been younger.

40. See Tierney, "Natural Rights in the Thirteenth Century," 64–65. Pufendorf, who deals briefly with this issue, seems to be crossing a line of sorts when he says that the magistrate is the one who should be held responsible for the convict's escape and punished for neglecting his duty. See *De Iure Naturae et Gentium*, 8.3, 4: "The delinquent is not at fault if he be not put to death. The blame lies wholly upon the magistrate." Pufendorf's statement reflects the modern tendency to compensate for the greater freedom allowed to individuals by making greater demands on the government. Laws and institutions are now considered more reliable than moral character. On this general topic, see Harvey C. Mansfield, Jr., *Taming the Prince: The Ambivalence of Modern Executive Power* (New York: The Free Press, 1989).

not only permitted to flee but obliged to do so because he is required by natural law to preserve his life and body.[41] Tierney takes this as further evidence that the key concepts of the seventeenth-century rights theorists "often had medieval origins."[42]

But did they? To stick only to the issue at hand, Tierney overlooks the crucial fact that, by the time we come to the new seventeenth-century theorists, the ban against inflicting bodily harm on one's judge or executioner has been lifted. Hobbes is again the one who makes the case most pointedly when he says that

no man is supposed bound by covenant not to resist violence, and consequently it cannot be intended that he gave any right to another to lay violent hands upon his person. In the making of a commonwealth, every man gives away the right of defending another, but not of defending himself. . . . But I have also shown formerly that before the institution of commonwealth every man had a right to everything and to do whatever he thought necessary to his own preservation, *subduing, hurting, or killing* any man in order thereunto; and this is the foundation of that right of punishing which is exercised in every commonwealth. For the subjects did not give the sovereign that right, but only in laying down theirs strengthened him to use his own as he should think fit for the preservation of them all. (emphasis added)[43]

The same view is affirmed, albeit with greater caution, by Locke, whose political system issues, like Hobbes's, in perfect rights rather than perfect duties. For Locke, as for Hobbes, the right of self-preservation, from which all other rights flow, is inalienable, which means that it is not in the power of human beings to surrender it even if they should wish to do so.[44] Locke's most powerful statement to this effect

41. Tierney, "Natural Rights in the Thirteenth Century," 66.
42. Ibid., 67.
43. Hobbes, *Leviathan*, chap. 28. The earlier statement to which Hobbes alludes occurs in chap. 21, where it is stated that "if the sovereign command a man, though justly condemned, to kill, wound, or maim himself, or not to resist those that assault him . . . yet has that man the liberty to disobey." See, in the same vein, *De Cive*, 2, 18: "No man is obliged by any contracts whatsoever not to resist him who shall offer to kill, wound, or any other way hurt his body." See, on this topic, Thomas S. Schrock, "The Rights to Punish and Resist Punishment in Hobbes's *Leviathan*," *The Western Political Quarterly* 44 (1991): 853–90, who writes: "Thomas Hobbes was the first political thinker to declare a right in the guilty subject to resist the lawful and lawfully punishing sovereign." Schrock adds that this teaching precipitated a "crisis" in Hobbes's political theory, for "there are reasons to doubt that the would-be Hobbesian sovereign can acquire a right to punish if the would-be Hobbesian subject has a right to resist punishment. If these two rights cannot co-exist within the same conceptual and political system, and if Hobbes will not rescind his declaration of the right to resist, his punishment-dependent political theory is in trouble."
44. The term "inalienable," which the *Declaration of Independence* popularized, does not appear to have been used by Locke himself. It shows up in the *Virginia Declaration of Rights,* but only with reference to the right of revolution.

is the one that occurs in the *Second Treatise of Government*, where one reads:

[F]or no man or society of men having a power to deliver up their preservation, and consequently the means of it, to the absolute will and arbitrary dominion of another, whenever anyone shall go about to bring them into such a slavish condition, *they will always have a right to preserve what they have not a power to part with*, and to rid themselves of those who *invade this fundamental, sacred, and unalterable law of self-preservation for which they entered into society* (emphasis mine).[45]

To be sure, Locke is careful to add that, just as one is bound to preserve oneself, so one is bound, as much as one can, to preserve the rest of mankind, but—and this is the telltale qualification—only so long as one's own preservation does not "come into competition" with anyone else's.[46] I take this to be just another way of saying that in the final analysis, rights take precedence over duties. On this central point, both he and Hobbes stand together against all of their premodern predecessors.

Interestingly enough, it is often when they sound most alike that moderns and premoderns are furthest apart. The fact that in dealing with this matter both groups advert to the desire for self-preservation might lead us to think that they at least have this much in common; but closer examination reveals that this is not the case. For the medievals, self-preservation is first and foremost a duty: one is not allowed to commit suicide or do anything that is liable to impair one's health.[47] As Thomas Aquinas, good Aristotelian that he is, puts it, "anyone who takes his own life commits an injustice, not toward himself [by definition, justice and injustice are always *ad alios*, that is, directed toward others],[48] but toward God and toward his city, to whom he owes his

---

45. Locke, *Second Treatise of Government*, no. 149. On the derivation of all other rights from the basic right of self-preservation, see, for example, *First Treatise of Government*, nos. 86–88.

46. Locke, *Second Treatise of Government*, no. 6.

47. See Aristotle, *Nic. Ethics*, V, 1138a9–13. It is true that the laws do not expressly forbid suicide, but "what it does not expressly permit it forbids. . . . He who through anger voluntarily stabs himself does this contrary to the right rule of life, and this the law does not allow; therefore he is acting unjustly. But toward whom? Surely toward the city, not toward himself." A similar problem arises in connection with Socrates, who was accused of a crime for which, if found guilty, he could be sentenced to death. The question is whether he had a "duty" or a "right" to defend himself. In Plato, *Apology*, Loeb Classical Library (1982), Socrates' defense is presented as being first and foremost a duty: *philosophounta me dein Zēn* (*Apol.*, 28e). According to the modern view, it is without any doubt a "right." See Spinoza, *Theologico-Political Treatise*, chap. 20.

48. See Aristotle, *Nic. Ethics*, V, 1134b11: "No one chooses to hurt himself, for which reason there can be no injustice toward oneself." See Aquinas, *Summa Theologiae* II-II, 58, 2.

services."[49] The same view is reflected in a felicitous statement by Godfrey of Fontaines that brings together both the objective and subjective dimensions of the problem:

Because by the right of nature *(iure naturae)*, everyone is bound *(tenetur)* to sustain his life, which cannot be done without exterior goods, therefore also by the right of nature each has dominion and a certain right *(quoddam ius)* in the common exterior goods of this world, which right also cannot be renounced.[50]

A very different note is sounded by Hobbes, Locke, and their followers, for whom self-preservation is not in the first instance a duty but a right that justifies not only the use of physical force against one's lawful executioner but the taking of one's own life, an act that the religious tradition always regarded as more grievously sinful than homicide and to which it attached severe penalties.[51] If self-preservation is an unconditional right and if, as Hobbes and Locke contend, such rights are to be defined in terms of freedom, that is to say, if human beings are free to exercise or not exercise them, one fails to see why it would be forbidden to commit suicide or allow oneself to be enslaved by other human beings. Needless to say, most people will prefer life to death and freedom to slavery, but these have now acquired an altogether different status. They no longer appear as moral obligations laid upon us by a higher authority but as claims that one can assert against others. To quote Locke himself, the state that "all men are naturally in . . . is a state of perfect freedom to order their actions *and dispose of their possessions and persons as they think fit,* within the bounds of the law of nature, without asking leave or depending upon the will of any other man."[52] It is true that Locke limits the exercise of the rights that human beings enjoy in the state of nature to what is allowed by the "law of nature," but, as we saw earlier, in the state of nature, man and not God is the "executor of the law of nature." In that state, there are no restrictions other than the ones that an individual may decide to impose upon himself.

This observation is only apparently contradicted by Locke's state-

49. *Summa Theologiae* II-II, 59, 3, ad 2; cf. 64, 5, c. See also on the prohibition against suicide, Francisco Suarez, *De Triplici Virtute Theologica: De Caritate,* in vol. 13, *Opera Omnia,* ed. Charles Berton (Paris: Vives, 1859), 7, 18.

50. Godfrey of Fontaines, *Quodlibet* 8, qu. 11, *Philosophes Belges* 4 (1924), 105. See Tierney, "Villey, Ockham," 27.

51. If the suicide attempt was successful, the dead person's property could be confiscated by the state. If it failed, other grave penalties were imposed. Until very recently, Roman Catholic Canon Law stipulated that anyone who committed suicide was not to be given a Christian burial.

52. Locke, *Second Treatise of Government,* no. 4. See also, for a similar argument, no. 135.

ment that "everyone is bound to preserve himself and not to quit his station wilfully," inasmuch as all human beings are "the workmanship of an omnipotent and wise Maker . . . made to last during his, not one another's, pleasure."[53] Nowhere does Locke say that God has *commanded* human beings to maintain themselves in existence. What we learn instead is that human beings are directed by God to preserve themselves by means of their "senses and reason," just as the inferior animals are directed to preserve themselves by means of their "sense and instinct."[54] Both men and animals have, implanted in them by God, a desire for survival, but only in man does this desire give rise to a right, presumably because only men have reason and are thus able to figure out what is necessary for their self-preservation as well as their comfortable self-preservation.[55] The question then is what happens to the law prohibiting suicide once the desire for self-preservation in which it is rooted is lost because of intense pain or a hopelessly weakened physical condition. Clearly, the "law of nature" of which Locke speaks is his own natural law. It is strictly a matter of calculation and has nothing to do with the self-evident principles on which the moral life is said to rest by the medieval theorists. In short, it is not at all certain that in Locke's mind there were any compelling moral arguments against suicide.[56] On this score as on so many others, he and his medieval "predecessors," as Tierney would call them, could not be further apart.

Though unable on the basis of his own principles to deny the natural right of suicide, Locke may have been loath to defend it openly, not only because doing so would have been dangerous in the extreme—his teaching was already "strange" enough—but because the whole of his political theory stands or falls by the power that the fear of death and the desire for self-preservation are capable of exerting on people's minds. Absent this bulwark, any human being could, in the name of freedom, renounce the exercise of his most basic rights, whether they be the right to life, to limited government, or to freedom itself.[57] This could well be the point at which modern liberalism shows signs of re-

53. Ibid., no. 6.
54. *First Treatise of Government*, no. 86.
55. Ibid., no. 87.
56. For a valiant defense of the opposite view, see G. D. Glenn, "Inalienable Rights and Locke's Argument for Limited Government: Political Implications of a Right to Suicide," *The Journal of Politics* 46 (1984): 80–105. I am indebted to Professor Walter Berns for part of my interpretation of Locke's stance and posture in regard to suicide.
57. Such a concern would be analogous to that evinced by certain present-day antiabortionists who insist on calling all abortion murder lest, by excluding from that category abortions performed in the earliest stages of the pregnancy, they should weaken their case against it.

coiling upon itself. Is there or is there not at the heart of Locke's teaching a latent contradiction or, short of that, an irremediable tension?[58]
Whatever the answer to the question, the foregoing considerations
permit us to glimpse the reasons that motivated the sixteenth- and
seventeeth-century revolt against premodern thought and convinced
so many of its promoters of the need for a fresh start. The new rights
theory was perhaps not entirely consistent, and, by grounding all ethical principles in the desire for self-preservation, a self-regarding passion, it did not of itself conduce to a high level of morality. But it was
public-spirited. Its aim was to procure the good of society by putting
an end to the massacres and bloody wars that had hitherto marked its
life.[59] To paraphrase Mandeville, the trick consisted in turning private
vices to public advantage. A new kind of hedonism was born that sup-
posedly enables one to enjoy the rewards of moral virtue without acquiring virtue itself, that is, without having to undergo a painful and
chancy conversion from a concern for worldly goods to a concern for
the good of the soul. In the process, morality itself was drastically simplified. The only virtue needed for the success of the enterprise was
the one geared to the needs of society—"social virtue," as Locke called
it[60]—rather than to the proper order of the soul. Justice became not

58. The tension reminds us in some way of the one found in Hobbes's theory, according to which the state has the right to put a criminal to death and the criminal the
right to kill his executioner. Cf. above, p. 11, n. 1. Differently and more broadly stated,
Hobbes was of the opinion that a war could be just on both sides at the same time. Bec-
caria later tried to solve the dilemma by advocating the abolition of capital punishment.
In grappling with the same problem, some twentieth-century positivists have gone further and argued that survival or self-preservation is not an antecedently fixed goal or
end but a contingent fact. We are committed to it only because our concern happens to
be "with social arrangements for continued existence, not with those of a suicide club."
H. L. A. Hart, *The Concept of Law* (Oxford: Oxford University Press, 1961), 188. As far
as I know, the first modern philosopher to rule out suicide altogether is Kant, who argues
against it not on the ground of self-preservation but because it runs counter to the categorical imperative. See *Foundations of the Metaphysics of Morals*, trans. Lewis White Beck
(Indianapolis: Bobbs-Merrill, 1959), Sec. 2, and, for a fuller discussion, Immanuel Kant,
*Lectures on Ethics*, trans. Louis Infield (New York: Harper and Row, 1963), 148–54.
59. See Descartes, *Discourse on Method*, Part I: "I compared the ethical writings of the
ancient pagans to superb and magnificent palaces built only on mud and sand: they laud
the virtues and make them appear more desirable than anything else in the world, but
they give no adequate criterion of virtue; and often what they call by such a name is
nothing but cruelty and apathy, parricide, pride, or despair."
60. Locke, *An Essay Concerning Human Understanding*, ed. A. C. Fraser (New York:
Dover, 1959), vol. 1.2, 4. The essential difference between the old and the new morality
is well summed up by Locke, ibid., vol. 1.2, 5: "[I]f a Christian, who has the view of
happiness and misery in another life, be asked why a man must keep his word, he will
give this reason: Because God, who has the power of eternal life and death, requires it
of us. But if a Hobbist be asked why, he will answer: Because the public requires it and
the Leviathan will punish you if you do not. And if one of the old philosophers had been

only the highest virtue but the only virtue, now reduced to the requirements of peace.[61] Tocqueville knew whereof he spoke when he said that
America had managed to dignify selfishness by transforming it into a
passably decent if not particularly elevated philosophy.

In view of their revolutionary stand on a matter as grave as that of
the origin and goals of human existence, it is not surprising that the
leaders of the new movement should have been careful to express themselves in language that made them sound more conservative than they
actually were. One notion well suited to this purpose was that of the
"state of nature," which began to figure prominently in their works and
continued to do so for the next century and a half.

As used by Hobbes, Locke, and their many followers, the notion has
highly individualistic connotations, predicated as it is on a nonteleological understanding of human nature. It derives the moral "ought"
from the "is" or the "right" of self-preservation from the "desire" for
self-preservation and thus denies that to be and to be good are two
different things. One cannot portray human beings as atomic individuals who once existed in a so-called state of nature without implying
that they are not naturally political and social or without subscribing
to the view that their most basic impulse is not an attraction to the good,
including the good of society, but an aversion to physical evil, along
with an overpowering urge to overcome it.

By the middle of the seventeenth century, however, the "state of nature" had become a commonplace in political literature and was used
indiscriminately by authors on both sides of the divide. In his short but
illuminating essay *On the Natural State of Men*, Pufendorf distinguishes
at least four different meanings of the expression, which can designate
not only the prepolitical state postulated by the new theorists—the
Hobbesian war of every man against every man, a state only slightly
more politely described by Locke as "very unsafe, very unsecure . . .
full of fears and continual dangers"[62]—but the perfect state in which
Adam was created, the cultural state in which human beings are pre-
sumed to have existed prior to the emergence of civil society, or any
pagan or pre-Christian civil society, such as classical Greece.[63] This am-

---

asked, he would have answered: Because it was dishonest, below the dignity of man, and
opposite to virtue, the highest perfection of human nature, to do otherwise."

61. Cf. Hobbes, *Leviathan*, chap. 6, where all the other moral virtues—courage, liberality, magnanimity, and the like—are demoted to the rank of passions.

62. Locke, *Second Treatise of Government*, no. 123.

63. For a discussion of the different versions of the natural state available in the
seventeenth century and in Pufendorf, see M. Seidler's introduction to his edition and
translation of *Samuel Pufendorf's On the natural state of men* (Lewiston, N.Y.: Edwin Mellen
Press, 1990), 28–31.

biguity is precisely what made it possible for the new theorists to pass their "strange" doctrines off as more or less standard theological fare. Pufendorf 's essay is valuable in that it gives us a better idea of how much he and his contemporaries had learned from the opposition that the "justly decried Hobbes" had aroused and how circumspect they had become in dealing with issues as explosive as these.[64] Pufendorf himself leans heavily on Hobbes, for whom he evinces an obvious preference— he was known as the "German Hobbes"—but not without injecting into the discussion a series of disclaimers that give the impression of his wanting to dissociate himself from Hobbes's most extreme positions. It is almost as if he were using the state of nature as a shield with which to protect himself. After all, no less a figure than the eminently re- spectable Grotius, to say nothing of others, had made use of the ex- pression and thereby removed from it any taint of heterodoxy or impiety.

Virtually all the writers of Pufendorf 's and Locke's generation, it seems, had mastered the art of concealing their "novelties" by cloaking them in more or less traditional garb. The "state of nature," with its vague theological connotations, is only one example of this procedure. Francis Bacon had already admonished radical innovators to express themselves only in familiar terms, adding that one should always begin by telling people what they most want to hear, that is, what they are accustomed to hearing.[65] This appears to be exactly what most of our seventeeth-century writers did. As a result, it became customary to pass over the crucial differences that set Grotius apart from Locke and Pu- fendorf and lump the three of them together as fellow travelers or members of the same ideological camp. Grotius does mention the state of nature on two occasions, but to designate pre-Christian civil society and not Hobbes's or Locke's precivil state.[66] Unlike Hobbes, Locke, and Pufendorf, in whose works Aristotle's name hardly ever appears, he

64. See on this subject Locke's long discussion of caution and judicious concealment in *The Reasonableness of Christianity* (Washington, D.C.: Regnery Gateway, 1965), 39–123. See also, on the pains taken by Locke publicly to distance himself from Hobbes, Robert Horwitz's introduction to the translation of Locke's *Questions Concerning the Law of Nature* (Ithaca: Cornell University Press, 1990), 5–10.

65. Bacon, *The Plan of the Great Instauration, init.*, in *The New Organon*, ed. Fulton H. Anderson (Indianapolis, Ind.: Bobbs-Merrill, 1960), 17. On the use of esotericism in the premodern tradition, see Grotius, *De Iure Belli et Pacis*, III.1, 7–20. Also, for recent as- sessments of the problem as it posed itself in the early modern period, Paul Bagley, "On the Practice of Esotericism," *Journal of the History of Ideas* 53/2 (April-June 1992): 231– 47. D. Wootten, "Lucien Febvre and the Problem of Unbelief in the Early Modern Pe- riod," *Journal of Modern History* 60 (1988): 695–730.

66. Grotius, *De Iure Belli*, II.5, 15, 2. See also III.7, 1, where the expression *primaevus naturae status* is used in a similar sense.

holds Aristotle in highest esteem;[67] and he endorses wholeheartedly the patented Aristotelian teaching that human beings are political by nature.[68] His is still a basically classical and medieval outlook, now brought to bear on the problems of his time.

This brings us back to the question with which we started, namely, whether any ultimate reconciliation between modern and premodern ethical thought is possible. To restate that question in terms more germane to Tierney's argument: Is the seventeenth-century rights theory an offshoot of medieval theological and legal speculation or merely an accidental byproduct of its later development, if even that?

The early modern writers, with whom any discussion of the problem must begin, if not necessarily end, certainly understood themselves to be breaking entirely new ground and to be doing so on the basis of a radical critique of the premodern tradition. Many of them, from Machiavelli onward, thinking that they had discovered a new continent, likened themselves to Christopher Columbus and were ready to burn their ships behind them.[69] They, at least, were convinced of the fundamental irreconcilability of the two positions and hence of the necessity to choose between them. Accordingly, they saw the war in which they were engaged, not as a civil war pitting rival factions against each other within a divided city, but as a war between two continents neither one of which could survive unless the other was destroyed. Francis Bacon stated the problem as well as anyone else when he located the opposition between the two groups on the level of "first principles and very notions, and even upon forms of demonstrations," in which case "confutations [that is, rational arguments] cannot be employed." The

67. Grotius, *Prolegomena to the Law of War and Peace*, no 42: "Among the philosophers Aristotle deservedly holds the foremost place, whether you take into account his order of treatment, or the subtlety of his distinctions, or the weight of his reasons." Grotius nevertheless thought it possible to improve upon the teaching of his master by providing a more methodical treatment of the subject matter of his book and by illustrating his teaching by means of a larger number of historical examples. See ibid., nos. 1 and 38.

68. Ibid., 6: "Among the traits characteristic of human beings is an impelling desire for society, that is, for the social life, not of any and every sort, but peaceful and organized according to the measure of their intelligence, with those of their own kind. This social inclination the Stoics called 'sociableness.' Stated as a universal truth, therefore, the assertion that every animal is impelled by nature to seek only its own good cannot be conceded."

69. Machiavelli, *Discourses*, Book I, Introduction. Bacon, *New Organon*, I, 92: "And therefore it is fit that I publish and set forth those conjectures of mine which make hope in this matter reasonable, just as Columbus did, before that wonderful voyage across the Atlantic, when he gave the reasons for his conviction that new lands and continents might be discovered besides those which were known before; which reasons, though rejected at first, were afterwards made good by experience and were the causes and beginnings of great events."

only safe way to proceed, he concluded, was to insinuate one's new doctrines "quietly into the minds that are fit and capable of receiving it."[70]
Hobbes is no less explicit, particularly as regards the issue of rights and
duties. "Right," he says, "consists in liberty to do or to forbear, whereas
law determines and binds to one of them, so that law and right differ
as much as obligation and liberty, *which in one and the same matter are
inconsistent*."[71] If Hobbes is to be taken at his word, the modern rights
theory was no mere attempt to erect a new structure on the old foundation of classical and Christian ethics. Its ambition was to lay down an
entirely new foundation, to wit, a selfish passion—the desire for self-
preservation—and go on from there to devise a political scheme that
would be in accord with it from the start. As usual, Hobbes is the one
who stated the issue most forcefully when he wrote in the short Epistle
Dedicatory to his *De Hominis Natura:*

> To reduce this doctrine to the rules and infallibility of reason, there is no way
> but, first, to put such principles down for a foundation as passion, not mis-
> trusting, may not seek to displace, and afterwards to build thereon the truth
> of cases in the law of nature, which hitherto have been built in the air.[72]

Let us grant for the sake of argument that no ultimate synthesis between a consistent natural law theory and a consistent natural rights
theory is possible. Does this mean that any kind of rapprochement between them is out of the question? Not necessarily. One thing is nevertheless certain: no such rapprochement can be effected on the basis of
a principle that transcends the original positions, each one of which
claims supreme status for itself. This leaves only one possibility: a rapprochement effected on the basis of the highest principles of one or
the other of these two positions.

The need for some such mediation began to be felt in the Middle
Ages when important social and demographic changes gave rise to a
more complex juridical system. Tierney's studies may or may not have
shown that individual rights are a product of twelfth- and thirteenth-
century jurisprudence, but they do show with admirable lucidity how
far our medieval forebears managed to find a place for rights within a
human order that reflects the natural order of the universe. The modern world has been experimenting for close to four centuries with a
theory that subordinates law to rights. The results have been mixed at
best, and this is what lends a measure of credibility to the now fre-

70. Bacon, *New Organon*, I, 35.
71. Hobbes, *Leviathan*, chap. 14.
72. Hobbes, *De Hominis Natura*, part 1 of *Elements of Law*, ed. F. Tönnies (London: Cass, 1969), xv.

quently heard calls for a re-examination of the discarded alternative, which insisted on the subordination of rights to duties or the common good.

My immediate concern was not to argue for the superiority of either of these two distinct approaches to the study of ethics and politics but to clarify the difference between them and caution against any hasty identification of one with the other. A thorough grasp of the problem would involve us in a much more methodical investigation of the implications of an ethics of virtue or character versus an ethics of rights, as well of the implications of a teleological versus a nonteleological understanding of human life. Tierney, who is more interested in the historical and legal aspects of the question than in its philosophic or theological aspects, has not seen fit to undertake this kind of investigation and I shall not undertake it, either.[73] Still, one cannot help wondering whether the argument in favor of the medieval pedigree of the modern rights doctrine does not owe much of its appeal to the fact that it combines in neat if somewhat unexpected fashion a deep-seated longing for a glorious Christian past with a powerful attachment to the freedoms of the modern age.[74] It would not be the first time that scholarly judgment on matters as complex as this one is influenced to a greater or lesser degree by considerations of an extratheoretical nature.

73. A more adequate discussion would obviously have to take full account of the important modification that the modern rights doctrine underwent at the hands of Kant and his followers. For all its stress on duty, however, Kant's moral doctrine is still in the end a doctrine of rights rather than of virtues.

74. On the widespread trend to rehabilitate the once discredited Middle Ages and trace to them the major achievements of the modern age, see the provocative, if at times impressionistic, book by Norman F. Cantor, *Inventing the Middle Ages: The Lives, Works, and Ideas of the Great Medievalists of the Twentieth Century* (New York: W. Morrow, 1991).

# 6     Moral Finality and the Unity of *Homo sapiens:* On Teleology in Kant

## RICHARD L. VELKLEY

### I. The Problematic Unity of the Human

The German philosophic tradition since Kant has an underlying unity of theme and purpose distinguishing it from the philosophy of pre-Kantian epochs. Its central problem is the analysis of the theoretical deficiencies and practical dangers in the accounts of reason in earlier philosophy; its dominant purpose is the search for a new teleological principle to ground the unifying horizon for the understanding of human life and its relation to nature or being. The new principle would replace the scientific accounts of reason and nature of the seventeenth century, which proved inadequate to the task of supplying a coherent sense of the whole. Kant believed he found this new principle, with decisive inspiration from Rousseau, in self-legislative freedom. The later German systems or quasi-systems replacing Kant's have primary principles derived from his account of freedom. Here I have seven philosophers in mind—Fichte, Schelling, Hegel, Schopenhauer, Nietzsche, Husserl, and Heidegger—and their principles of the absolute ego, the creative unconscious, the historical dialectic, the will to life, the will to power, the prescientific lifeworld, and the primordial disclosure of Being. What these principles share is an attack on earlier modern accounts of scientific reason as abstract, mechanistic and narrow, as failing to do justice to the concrete wholeness or richness of nature and human experience, and thus impoverishing our conceptions of morality, political life, and human aspirations toward the noble, the sacred, and the beautiful.

The ultimate origin of this attack is the criticisms of early modernity in Rousseau and Kant. But in keeping with its origin, the attack undertakes to reform, not simply to reject, modernity. Most of the philosophers listed are seeking to ground the possibility of human unity or wholeness in a way consistent with modern ideas of freedom and au-

tonomy; or one could say that they are attempting to avoid the consequences of fragmentation and alienation by reason that seem inherent
in earlier modernity, while preserving the modern aim of progressive
emancipation of humanity. That aim is still evident, if distorted or dis-
guised, in the most recent Continental thinking derived from German
sources. The third of Kant's *Critiques,* the 1790 *Critique of Judgment,* can
provide essential insight into the character and motives of this later
tradition. With this work Kant provided his successors with much of
the ammunition they used to assault Kant's critical philosophy itself, as
presented in the two earlier *Critiques,* that of *Pure Reason* and that of
*Practical Reason.* In the *Critique of Judgment,* Kant is attempting to uncover possible indications of the unity of the realms of nature and freedom he so sharply divided in the earlier *Critiques.* In other terms, he is
seeking to understand the sources of human unity, specifically by investigating aesthetic experience and organic or teleological and non-
mechanistic aspects of nature. Several of the systematic programs of
German Idealism after Kant start from this work, as is evident in Schiller's *Letters on the Aesthetic Education of Man* of 1795, Schelling's *System
of Transcendental Idealism* of 1800, and Hegel's *Faith and Knowledge* of
1802. Indeed, after this *Critique,* a more insistent demand for a unification of all human experience, seeking closer identification of nature,
art, and history, is apparent in most of the major German philosophers.
    Yet there is something contradictory about this project, and the
problem is apparent already in Kant's third *Critique.* As I shall explain,
Kant in all three *Critiques* is seeking to provide a ground for the systematic unity of reason. And very centrally, this unity is meant to satisfy
the fundamental human metaphysical need or eros, for the unconditioned. But the last of the *Critiques* discloses how the goal of unity is
attainable only through certain contingencies that elude the systematic
legislation of reason. I would argue that those contingencies are inherent in metaphysical eros itself, and that it is eros which points to the
limitations of the goal of systematic unity.[1] The latter goal is a later
modern derivative of the project of universal self-emancipation by
means of the organon of unifying rationality, for whose sources one
must go back to Bacon's *New Organon* and Descartes's *Regulae ad direc-
tionem ingenii.* But the effort to incorporate the satisfaction of human
eros into this project is introduced by Rousseau and Kant. The subsequent development of German philosophy is a story of dramatic, al-

---

1. Some related issues in the *Critique of Judgment* have recently been discussed, but
with rather different aims and conclusions, by J. Lawrence, "Logos and Eros: The Underlying Tension in Kant's Third *Critique,*" in *Idealistic Studies* 12 (1992): 130–43.

most unbearable, tension, as one thinker after another strives to reconcile the moral aim of universal systematic unity with the satisfaction
of eros. Is such reconciliation possible? Is moral rationality ultimately
harmonious with the erotic striving of reason that is, perhaps, inherently unjust? Since investigating the origins of the later German tradition in Kant's reception of Rousseau, this is the question that has
occupied me in further reflection on this tradition. This reflection has
helped to make clearer to me that the frequent characterizations of
later modern philosophy in terms of radicalized autonomy, subjectivity
or mastery of nature are inadequate. In this paper I shall consider aspects of this question as it is posed by the central concerns and arguments of the *Critique of Judgment.*

## II. Eros and Contingency

But I shall approach this question in a rather oblique way by first
mentioning another. A question raised by any philosophy, including
surely that of Immanuel Kant, is the nature of the relation between
necessity and contingency. This question is whether human beings are
able to give ultimate accounts of their place in the whole of things that
satisfy a need for a necessary grounding of their own rationality; or
whether they are forced to acknowledge some fundamental inexplicable contingencies, and must forgo such ultimate accounts. There is
yet another possibility, one that is evident in a number of later modern
philosophers, and very notably in Kant. That is the possibility of giving
an ultimate account of the place of human reason in the whole of
things, *in terms* of fundamental contingencies. This approach, I shall
argue, is evident in Kant's treatment of the human being as the contingent unity of reason and desire in his third *Critique.*

Necessity and contingency are related to the question of eros. To
explore this connection as Kant understands it, one must reflect on the
first *Critique,* the critique of theoretical reason as undertaking to gain
metaphysical knowledge. In the prefaces to the two editions and the
introduction of that work, Kant presents his doctrine of "the natural
disposition to metaphysics," according to which human reason is characterized by a permanent and irresistible striving to uncover the ground
of the totality of things, including itself, in an unconditioned and hence
absolutely necessary ground. Kant uses the term "idea" for the various
conceptions of unconditioned totality that correspond to that ground,
as well as the language of impetuous need and desire to describe the
striving for it. Thereby he reveals his intention to explicate the meaning
and fate of Platonic philosophic eros. And one can say that the entire

critical philosophy, as elaborated chiefly in the three *Critiques*, is an effort to justify that erotic striving.

Kant proceeds from the fact that the metaphysical striving, being inherent in reason, has persisted into modern times and must persist in spite of the efforts of modern anti-metaphysical critics such as David Hume. But metaphysical reason also entangles itself in a seemingly insoluble dialectic (antinomies, paralogisms, etc.) that threatens all confidence in reason and thus exposes all higher culture of reason, including the scientific Enlightenment of modernity, to possible self-destruction. Kant then tries to justify the metaphysical eros in a fashion consistent with limitations of human reason exposed by modern philosophic and scientific principles (centrally those of Newton), and consistent with modern projects of furthering the progress of human self-determination and mastery of nature. Through the threefold reconciliation of metaphysical eros, modern mathematical science of nature and the moral dignity of enlightened self-determination, Kant believes he achieves a definitive and satisfactory completion of the requirements of human rationality. I must take time to describe in some detail how Kant claims to accomplish this goal, and underline the place of contingency in the project of critical philosophy as presented in the first two *Critiques*. Then it will be possible to turn to the consideration of fundamental contingency in the third *Critique*, the contingent unity of reason and desire or of justice and eros. Kant's last *Critique* can be considered his deepest reflection on the problems inherent in the effort to satisfy metaphysical eros through a modern form of unified system.

## III. The Forms of Contingency

I start on a very familiar note: Kant believes that his critique of reason's cognitive powers establishes the impossibility of attaining the goal of metaphysical eros by means of theoretical insight. According to this criticism, the phenomenal world that human reason can know only through the synthetic activity of the pure transcendental subject, cannot be intelligibly grounded in things in themselves, or in other words, in some ultimate condition lying outside the series of phenomenal conditions imposed by that subject. This means that the phenomenal world of our knowledge is in some sense an ultimate fact or contingency; while that world is governed by laws and rules that have an immanent universality and necessity, this order of laws defining intelligible experience for us issues from our own subjectivity only, which is not groundable in some deeper or higher cause. For Kant the peculiar discursive principles of our understanding (that is, the categories) and the peculiar forms of intuition we possess (that is, space and time) are capable of internal clarification and elaboration (for that is what transcendental analysis is), but they do not permit further explanation. Just why we have these principles and forms, rather than others, must remain forever mysterious to us; this is an ultimate contingency for our understanding, although perhaps not for some other possible understanding of which we can have no concept.

Kant also argues, however, that one form of unconditioned necessity is available to our reason. This is freedom as based on the recognition of the moral law. Such freedom is rational because it necessarily has the form of universal self-legislation, and it is unconditioned because that legislation cannot take its principle from some extraneous source, such as the inclinations and desires, or nature and God, regarded as authoritative grounds independent of reason. As self-legislative freedom, reason is thus the ground of a universal and necessary order of autonomous or self-determining agents, what Kant also calls the "kingdom of ends." Therefore in the sphere of the moral, but not of the theoretical, reason has access to absolute necessity. This access is only reason's recognition of its own inner nature as non-arbitrary or lawlike freedom. According to this recognition of the unconditioned within itself, moral reason gives itself primacy in the formulation of all doctrines, theological and metaphysical, concerning the ultimate ideas of God, the soul, and the world. All speculative metaphysics must ground its assertions on the premise of moral freedom, and on no other premise. That is to say that Kantian or critical theology and metaphysics take an immanent form as the elaboration by pure practical reason of the conditions that must be assumed or postulated if the same reason is to pursue without impediment and with confidence its own highest ends. Those conditions, as regulative ideas and postulates for the extension of reason, do not determine theoretically the nature of objects independent of reason. They only describe heuristically the characteristics of the totalities, or infinite incompletable projects, that our reason imposes on itself for its own purposes of inquiry or moral improvement.

But in this way the ideas of metaphysics receive, Kant claims, a satisfactory interpretation as the conditions for the practically unlimited, but theoretically limited, extension of human reason, which extension is governed by the unconditioned demands of the moral law. And hence the erotic striving for the unconditioned is satisfied in the realm of practical reason. This is the chief intent of the critical philosophy: to show that the metaphysical striving for absolute necessity is achieved only in the sphere of the practical. The displacement of metaphysical eros into the pursuit of ultimate practical goals gives new metaphysical

legitimacy to modern Enlightenment and its central concept of freedom. History takes on new metaphysical significance as the realm in
which humanity tries to realize the demands of the unconditioned inherent in its free rationality. The critical demonstration of the meaning
of metaphysical eros is a teleological one, displaying the true moral end
of the most essential need of our reason. Yet again one cannot forget
the background of irremovable contingency against which this demonstration is achieved. Not only are the basic elements of our theoretical understanding of nature ultimate contingencies, but the moral law
itself is an ultimate "fact of reason," not derivable from any higher
ground. Moral freedom has a rational form, but its possibility necessarily eludes our powers of insight.

There is yet another very central form of contingency in Kant's philosophy, and that is of the unity of the human being, as a compound
of reason having freedom as its essence, and of natural phenomena
determined by mechanical causation. From neither the standpoint of
moral reason, nor that of scientific inquiry into nature, is this compound of reason and nature intelligible as a unity. For our understanding, it is a merely contingent concurrence of utterly disparate types of
rational order. Yet of course the coexistence is actual in a particular
species (*homo sapiens* as it was beginning to be called in Kant's time),
and this coexistence has drastic implications for the exercise of both
moral rationality and theoretical inquiry. Most crucially for Kant, our
moral reason imposes on us the goal of achieving the maximum of
freedom in the sensible world, according to the ultimate end of the
highest good. That end means nothing if it does not mean the infinite
advance of the human species toward greater moral perfection and a
correspondingly appropriate satisfaction of natural inclination and desire. But this entails that humanity must advance toward a condition
of greater unity or harmony of reason and desire that seems utterly
unintelligible. How this greater unity or harmony might become more
intelligible to us is the theme of all the inquiries of the *Critique of Judgment*. And this *Critique* is also the work in which Kant most thoroughly
investigates the problem of contingency.

## IV. Reason's Autonomous Order

In order to gain a broader perspective for reflecting on Kant's treatment of this mysterious and contingent human unity, one must think
further on how Kant's entire critical project is concerned with unification. In the stages of Kant's philosophical development the first task
of unification, commenced already in the late 1740s, was the reconcil-

iation of metaphysical groundings of nature, for which the primary source was Leibniz, with the mathematical account of natural phenomena disclaiming insight into ultimate grounds, for which the paradigm was Newton. The implications of real influx or *influxus physicus* of Newtonian universal gravitational attraction decided the case, for Kant, against monadology, but they did not entirely sound the death-knell for metaphysics.[2] Kant later expanded the project of unification by taking a more epistemological turn in the early 1760s, so as to reconcile the characteristically modern starting point for theoretical knowledge in immediate certainties of consciousness, with metaphysical demands for necessity in the apprehension of an objective world. Thus the metaphysical need of reason for comprehension of unconditioned totality was not abandoned, yet its satisfaction remained elusive. The discovery in the middle 1760s that Rousseau could offer fundamental insight into the nature of human reason was the event that provided Kant with unexpected illumination in the metaphysical problem. For Rousseau offered the possibility of understanding all of human reason as a self-sufficient rational order of laws and principles or as a coherent and unconditioned totality that somehow satisfies its own demands for universality and necessity, while its grounding in some possible higher reality must remain unknown. It is not only the moral law that acquires this self-legislative form, but all of human reason, in the critical philosophy as it slowly matured over fifteen years after Kant received this decisive impulse from Rousseau.

This way of understanding reason as an autonomous self-legislative order has several advantages. Theoretically the necessary correspondence of our cognitions to their objects is intelligible if those objects themselves are merely the result of the syntheses of the same cognitive activities. If objects exist wholly independently of our cognitive legislations, our a priori grasp of them is a deep mystery. One could say this is the epistemological unification Kant was seeking. Metaphysically the free legislation of reason over itself suggests reason's unconditioned character as some sort of ultimate originative ground, the only one available to us, satisifying the erotic striving for the unconditioned, although not knowable through theoretical categories. The unconditioned as freedom lies beyond the empirical determination of phenomena, and thus it is a ground that in no way competes with the Newtonian legislation of nature (as long as natural phenomena are not regarded as things in themselves). So this is the metaphysical unification Kant was seeking.

2. See Michael Friedman, *Kant and the Exact Sciences* (Cambridge: Harvard University Press, 1992), 1–52.

Lastly, there is a teleological unification offered by the new account of reason. Kant had been disturbed in the early 1760s by the lack of satisfactory teleology in earlier modern accounts of human reason and action. The dominant teleologies of passion, sentiment, and inclination seemed to offer neither moral rigor nor intelligible rationality of principles. Reason as autonomous self-legislative order seemed to offer the needed kind of teleology. And perhaps most strikingly, it suggested an ultimate unification of theory and practice, for the metaphysical unconditioned could be seen as identical with the ground of moral self-determination. The Rousseauian insight proposed a way of ending the ancient and seemingly hopeless conflicts between metaphysical speculation and the moral needs of practical life. All theoretical and scientific inquiry could now be placed in clear subordination to a universal moral principle that would be satisfying to the metaphysicians because it is an ultimate ground, and to the common moral understanding because it possesses unquestionable moral integrity and rigor.

In summation: the principle of the self-unification of reason is the idea that only by conceiving reason as self-legislation can one make intelligible reason's ability to achieve universality and necessity in the various domains of metaphysics, knowledge of nature, morality, and teleology. At the same time, this conception renders thinkable the completion of metaphysics as a science solving all its essential problems definitively. In the Introduction to the *Critique of Pure Reason,* second edition of 1787, Kant writes: "It must be possible for reason to attain certainty whether we know or do not know the objects of metaphysics, that is, to come to a decision either in regard to the objects of its inquiries or in regard to the capacity or incapacity of reason to pass any judgment on them. . . . This science (the critique of reason) cannot be of any very formidable prolixity, since it has to deal not with the objects of reason . . . but only with itself and the problems which arise entirely from itself, and which are imposed on it by its own nature, not by the nature of things which are distinct from it."[3] This statement brings forth yet another crucial aspect of the conception inspired by Rousseau. Kant became fully convinced of the explanatory range of this conception, when in the late 1760s he proposed that the dialectical perplexities of metaphysics are the result of a self-inflicted misapplication of reason's own concepts and principles. That which reason inflicts on itself, it is able to correct. Again, viewing reason as self-legislation permits a hitherto unconsidered extension of reason's powers, and in this

---

3. *Critique of Pure Reason,* B 22–23. Norman Kemp Smith's translation, *Critique of Pure Reason* (New York: St. Martin's Press, 1965), is used throughout.

case, it enables one to regard reason as both the ground and the final dissolver of metaphysical illusion.

This is indeed a very Rousseauian idea, for Rousseau had proposed, as his novel contribution to the account of the origins of human society and its ills, the view that perfectible reason, not incorrigible nature, is the source of the perplexities whereby rational humanity comes into conflict with itself. If this is so, Rousseau argues, human beings can resolve many, if not all, of those conflicts through a self-imposed justice establishing an equality approaching that of the primordial natural state. In Kant's metaphysical version, only the spontaneous affirmations of an uncritical and dogmatic reason, not a determinate order independent of reason, is the source of reason's fundamental errors and illusions. Its errors are due to injustice, not merely to natural ignorance or weakness of human cognitive powers. Hence, the project of reason's self-criticism is characterized as the dispensation of justice by a "tribunal which will assure to reason its lawful claims, and dismiss all groundless pretensions."[4] While the problem of reason is then one of justice, it is a justice that is self-derived and self-imposed. This recalls the notion of horizontal justice, identical with the logic of the general will, that Rousseau offers in his *Social Contract,* and that replaces vertical derivations of justice from a higher principle of nature or God. Putting this all together, one can say the problem for Kant is the metaphysical eros of an unjust reason, with its very destructive internal dialectic, and the solution is reason's self-justification through discovering both the source of its errors and their resolution in its own activity. That both the problem and the solution must be seen in terms of justice is made perfectly evident by the terminology of the central "Transcendental Deduction of the Categories" in the first *Critique,* whose task Kant describes as answering the question of justice, the *quid juris,* which addresses the legitimate employment of the fundamental metaphysical concepts.

For Kant, the critical self-rectification of reason is the foundation for a more unified and coherent system of reason than any previously offered. Thus he speaks of attaining an account of a "systematic unity of ends," after completing the critical propaedeutic which first establishes basic justice by defining the boundaries of the different rational faculties, within which they can live in peaceful coexistence. Again, the basis of such systematic unity is the idea of reason as self-determining. But let us recall now, that self-determination implies fundamental contingency, for the ultimately free, spontaneous and unconditioned basis of the self-determination is inscrutable by our reason.

4. Ibid., A xi.

## V. The System of Particular Laws

We are nearly ready to turn to the third *Critique*, but first it is useful to consider briefly some of the concluding chapters of the *Critique of Pure Reason,* which already indicate certain features of the postpropaedeutical system. Thus the hopes grounded in moral teleology for unification of virtue and happiness in a moral world, a unification "grounded in freedom's own essential nature," give rise to "the investigation of nature . . . in the form of a system of ends."[5] Kant does not offer here a detailed account of this system, only rather cryptic suggestions. He seems to proceed on the assumption that if nature is to be understood as harmonizing with the ends of moral reason, then nature, already on an empirical level, must take the form of a systematic unity of particular natural laws. But the idea of such a system raises a special difficulty, which can be stated as follows. The transcendental foundation of possible experience in the first *Critique* has offered only the account of the conditions of objectivity in general, conditions that are identical with those of the general laws of Newtonian physics. These conditions, however, do not clarify the possibility of particular empirical laws and, therewith, the great diversity of empirical universals and species of the actual natural world. That diversity is utterly contingent with respect to the general transcendental laws of the pure understanding, which define "pure possible nature." The analytic part of the critique of theoretical reason is in fact concerned with the account of nature only to the extent that this account will validate the pure employment of the metaphysical concepts or categories as necessary conditions of experience. The central Transcendental Deduction of the Categories makes no attempt to characterize knowledge of the full object of ordinary experience, either as concrete individual or as member of an empirical species.

Yet the latter must be reflected upon, Kant says, because the human understanding would have no employment if nature did not exhibit differences as well as homogeneity.[6] More crucially, the philosophic interest of the understanding's empirical employment arises for Kant when he begins to make the transition from the critical propaedeutic to systematic unity. That transition is guided by reason's necessary interest in achieving the goal of the unity of nature and freedom in the moral world, for which the human species must try to understand its position in nature (since it must try to understand the prospects of

5. Ibid., A 816/B 844.
6. Ibid., A 657/B 685.

realizing freedom in nature), and thus it must try to grasp its situation in nature as a particular species. But how can human reason approach this problem? For the purpose of inquiry into the particular laws of nature, the understanding must prescribe to itself special regulative maxims, namely, the maxim of seeking higher species and genera for given individuals and species, and the maxim of seeking diversification of subspecies under given species.[7] Maximum unity, maximum diversity, and continuity between species are the regulative ideas governing the inquiry into nature as a system of empirical laws. Yet these heuristic maxims are not derived from nature, and they are not constitutive of nature a priori. All the same, the discovery of given empirical universals is what satisfies the understanding, not an arbitrary construction of universals. In other words, human reason cannot simply legislate the character of the system of nature as a totality of empirical laws. It only legislates to *itself* a certain goal—that of finding empirical generality—which it can only hope that nature will satisfy.

When this goal is satisfied, the occurrence is a contingency for our reason, and hence this search is a "problematic" one. In the discussion of the regulative ideas in the first *Critique*, Kant speaks of a search for "problematic universals," as he does in the third *Critique*. Indeed, the earlier passage describes the search in terms that are used later to describe reflective judgment: the "particular is certain, but the universality of the rule of which it (the particular) is a consequence, is still a problem."[8] That is to say, the universal, as a particular law or species, is not already determined by reason (unlike the transcendental principles of possible experience) but must be projected by reason and then confirmed by the empirical order. The first *Critique* here anticipates the distinction of the third *Critique* between determinative judgment, which employs the already determined universal to subsume particulars under it, and reflective judgment, which seeks the universal where only the particular is given. What then does the later *Critique* add to the discussion besides new terminology?

## VI. Lawful Contingency

The critical examination of reflective judgment in the third *Critique*, beginning with the very informative first introduction which Kant did not publish, treats judgment as a faculty possessing its own a priori principle, one independent of both practical or end-determining rea-

7. Ibid., A 651/B 679ff.
8. Ibid., A 646/B 674.

son and the theoretically legislative understanding. This is a status judgment did not enjoy in either previous *Critique*. Even the anticipation of judgment's reflective task in the account of the regulative maxims regards judging as carrying out the orders of reason in its search for systematic unity. Although the third *Critique* still places reflective judgment in the context of that search, such judgment is now given a rule that reason itself does not produce, that is, a "concept of things of nature insofar as nature conforms to our power of judgment," or of nature as purposive for our ability to gain knowledge of it.[9] This is a very peculiar a priori principle, for reason here neither legislates determinately what nature must be (as does the pure understanding employing the categories), nor does it merely prescribe a maxim to itself, without speaking about the character of nature. Instead, nature is ascribed a certain character, that of purposiveness, yet only for the aims of our inquiry into it, hence only subjectively. The rule anticipates an unenforceable fittingness of nature for our purposes, both moral and theoretical—a harmony that eludes our legislative activity, while it promotes our legislative aims.

That harmony is avowedly contingent with respect to what we can know a priori, yet it is orderly. The particular order of nature might be so infinitely diverse that it would confound all efforts to comprehend it. Instead, nature specifies itself as knowable universals, so that the particular order evinces lawfulness. Hence, Kant defines the purposiveness ascribed to nature as the "lawfulness of contingency."[10] A related joining of apparent opposites is found in another phrase Kant employs for the object of reflective judgment: the "technic of nature." With it, Kant describes the mode of production whereby nature specifies the general transcendental laws with the particular forms and universals of the empirical order. From a human standpoint, this mode of production must be understood by analogy with human art as an intentional production by design. The self-specification of nature wholly eludes the mechanistic terms of our theoretical understanding, and no other concepts are available to help us except those of artistic making, which are not theoretical. Thus the assumption that nature operates by design is subjectively necessary for us to render intelligible what is otherwise incomprehensible. But it is neither a theoretical description

9. Immanuel Kant, *Erste Einleitung in die Kritik der Urteilskraft*, in vol. 20, *Kants gesammelte Schriften*, Prussian Academy der Wissenschaften (Berlin: Walter de Gruyter and Predecessors, 1902–), 202–203.

10. *Erste Einleitung*, 20.217, 243, and Immanuel Kant, *Kritik der Urteilskraft*, in vol. 5, *Kants gesammelte Schriften*, Prussian Academy der Wissenschaften (Berlin: Walter de Gruyter and Predecessors, 1902-), 5.404.

of nature nor a metaphysical doctrine of supernatural or noumenal causation by design.

It is notable that Kant does not rest content with the postulation of a divine artificer on the grounds of moral theology, although that surely would be a possible move on the basis of the theoretical critique. Instead, he makes a special point of stressing that a possible nonhuman kind of understanding might have no need of the idea of technical intention or design to comprehend nature's nonmechanical mode of self-specification. Indeed, we are justified in ascribing to an unknown supersensible substrate a mode of production which is *neither* mechanical *nor* by intention or design to account for the mysterious particular order of nature. To regard nature as "technical" and to regard it as a realm of "lawful contingency" are merely necessities for our kind of understanding.

The lawful contingency of nature's self-specification for our faculties, that is, the a priori rule of reflective judgment, is the issue in both the aesthetic and the teleological discussions of the third *Critique*. For reasons of brevity, I cannot be too expansive about these discussions. On the aesthetic, it must suffice to say that Kant is interested there in how the apparent regard of nature for our faculties is the source of a peculiar disinterested pleasure, when nature produces mere forms that set into motion a harmonious play between the cognitive faculties of imagination and understanding, without offering a basis for a definite cognition by concepts. Here too, as in the self-specification through empirical laws, nature evinces a contingent lawfulness (in offering beautiful forms) that is the source of a delightful amazement, one not to be expected only on the foundation of transcendental legislation. In a similar fashion, the observation of organized living beings incites wonderment in us since their existence is wholly contingent with respect to our inevitably mechanistic manner of causal explanation.

But now one can ask: if the conception of nature as producing purposively for our faculties is admittedly only a subjective or regulative idea, wherein lies its advantage for us? Why not merely talk about various forms of regulative unity, as in the first *Critique,* and leave out the peculiar anthropomorphizing speech about nature's purposive regard for our faculties? Clarity about this can be acquired only from answering the question of why and how Kant moved beyond conceiving the satisfaction of the highest interest of reason, or its metaphysical eros, solely in terms of the unconditioned legislation of practical reason and its postulations, and moved toward greater acknowledgement of the conditioning of practical reason (and its highest end) by sensibility. This is the same as an inquiry into Kant's motives for taking up the problem of the unity of the human being as a contingent species.

## VII. The Sensible and the Intelligible

A full answer to this question would have to take into account nearly all of the critical writings of the 1780s, in particular those on politics, culture, and history that investigate the sensible conditions for the worldly realization of the highest good. But perhaps the metaphysical level of the answer is best indicated in a couple of remarkable sections (76 and 77) of the Dialectic of Teleological Judgment in the third *Critique*.[11] Here Kant reflects on the conditions of the intelligibility for us of some of the most fundamental concepts: possibility, actuality, necessity, contingency, freedom, and purpose. Going well beyond assertions of the previous two *Critiques*, Kant now proposes that these concepts (and as a consequence, as I will show, metaphysical eros) are for us meaningful only because we happen to be a compound of reason and sensibility. That is to say that our existence as a particular living species is crucial to the very possibility of metaphysical reason. Yet our sensible mode of existence is, from the standpoint of pure transcendental reflection, a mere contingency. Thus Kant has moved to a deeper level of fundamental contingency, from the fact of finite understanding and the fact of the moral law to the fact of the species. This contingency, unlike the other two, seems to involve a mysterious participation of nature as the source of the empirical differentiation of our being as species. Suggested here is the starting point of a new kind of natural philosophy. Just in passing, I remark that these two sections were highly regarded by Goethe, Schelling, and Heidegger. Schelling writes that "perhaps never have so many deep thoughts been pressed together into so few pages" as in these pages of the third *Critique*.[12]

I shall have to compress the argument and do great injustice to this rich passage. Kant seeks to demonstrate the following:

1. The distinction within our understanding between the two heterogeneous faculties of understanding to provide concepts and sensible intuition to provide immediate relation to objects, makes possible the distinction between possibility (dealt with by concepts) and actuality

11. *Kritik der Urteilskraft*, 5.401–10.
12. F. W. J. Schelling, *Vom Ich als Prinzip der Philosophie*, in vol. I/1, *Schellings Sämmtliche Werke*, ed. K. F. A. Schelling (Stuttgart: Cotta, 1856–61), 242; J. W. Goethe, "Anschauende Urteilskraft," in *Schriften zur Botanik und Wissenschaftslehre* (Munich: Deutscher Taschenbuch Verlag, 1963), 185–86; M. Heidegger, *Kants These über das Sein*, in *Wegmarken* (Frankfurt am Main: V. Klostermann, 1967), 297.

(given by intuitions). Thus the distinction between the possible and the actual holds, so far as we can tell, only for a finite understanding conditioned by sensible intuition, such as ours. Our reason, however, is also driven to think the problematic idea of an understanding that is intuitive, for which all thinkable possibility is actual. Since such a being would have no representation of the possibility that some objects might not exist, that is, of the contingency of existing objects, it would have no concept of necessity and contingency, as well as none of the distinction between actuality and possibility.

2. The distinction between necessity and contingency has, in turn, a crucial role in our conception of the distinction between the necessity of moral obligation, the *ought*, and the contingency of subjective actualization, the *is*. Moral freedom is not conceivable by us in any fashion except as an obligation under a law that declares what ought to be. But for another understanding, the moral law stating what is possible might coincide with the theoretical law stating what is actual, and for such an understanding, there would be no ought. Such an understanding would also not be free in any sense intelligible to us, for we can conceive freedom only in connection with consciousness of a command to realize the rationally possible in a distinct realm of sensible actuality. Thus we have the further implication that freedom is not thinkable for us apart from the conditions of a finite understanding conditioned by sensible intuition.

3. Lastly, the concept of purpose has the same limitation for us, of not being thinkable apart from our sensible mode of existence. Again, Kant starts from the distinction between actuality and possibility and now relates it to the heterogeneity of universal and particular. The universal, representing possibility, is unable to establish for us the actuality of the particular, which always has something contingent about it with respect to the universal. Thus we have no insight into the necessary wholeness of the concrete particular, which for our understanding must be grasped as a joining together of contingently-related universals. Our understanding must proceed from logical parts to wholes, that is, from universals toward the concretely determined particulars, in our theoretical knowledge of objects. Thus our aggregative way of understanding is mechanistic, and organisms, which appear to be causally produced through the prior unity of the whole, must remain incomprehensible to us. Yet another possible understanding might proceed from the whole to the part and have insight into organic production of individuals. But such an understanding would have no concept of purpose, at least, none that we can think. For the concept of purpose is inseparable from the lawfulness of the contingent, that is, the un-

expected harmonizing of particulars with our projected universals
(which are unable to produce the particulars). It also follows that the
purposive production of living beings by intention or design is also only
a humanly necessary way of thinking (so far as we can discern), and
one that cannot be meaningfully ascribed to a divine being.[13]
Kant cautions the reader about this entire passage that its propositions are set forth without proof, and that these propositions are "too
important and too difficult" to be accepted immediately.[14] Close reflection on them helps explain this caution, for this passage is perhaps
the most radical statement of immanent teleology and the immanent
satisfaction of metaphysical eros in all of Kant's writing. For in this
passage, Kant is trying to establish that unconditioned moral freedom,
with its function as ground of the highest purpose for rational beings,
becomes meaningless outside the context of finite sensible existence.
Therefore, the passage prepares the way for these extraordinary assertions just a few sections later: (1) that only a rational species capable
of giving itself purposes, such as the human species, can be the final
purpose of all of creation;[15] (2) that without the existence of the human
species, "all of creation would be a mere wasteland, gratuitous, and

13. The merely human need to conceive natural production in terms of design would
seem at first, following Kant's analysis, to be simply a consequence of the distinction of
faculties (understanding and sensibility) that as such defines any "finite understanding,"
human or otherwise. But the title and text of section 77 stress that the concept of design
in nature is a peculiarity of the specifically human understanding. One could say that
this further limitation of the genus "finite understanding" by humanness is brought
about by the sheer contingency of the embodiment of finite understanding in a species
of living being, one that as such finds itself interested in the organization and ends of a
living being. Without that interest, one does not see why the limitation of the finite understanding to an aggregative or mechanical mode of explanation would be experienced *as*
a limitation and an inadequacy in the effort to explain what can only be grasped, after
all, as phenomenal—namely the living organism. Yet this sheer contingency of the the
vital embodiment of understanding and sensibility in the human is of enormous consequence, for clearly it is an indispensable condition for the ideas of "contingent lawfulness" employed by the reflective judging of aesthetic and organic form, which ideas
are then in turn used regulatively by reason for conceiving the possible unity of freedom
and nature in humanity's approach to its final end. Thus in section 77, Kant reaches the
crucial structural element holding together the project of the third *Critique*. But that
project, one must note, is only a further stage in the critical effort to satisfy the highest
metaphysical and erotic interest of reason by non-theoretical means, the effort Kant announced and outlined in the first *Critique*. It can also be maintained that Kant's examination of the problem of embodiment is quite insufficient, and that this insufficency
discloses a fundamental weakness in the critical philosophy. For Goethe, Schelling and
Hegel, section 77 could serve as a central text for the "self-undermining" of Kantian
thinking, precisely through the dialectical penetration of its exploration of the presup-
positions of criticism.
14. *Kritik der Urteilskraft*, 5.401.
15. Ibid., sections 83 and 84.

without final purpose."[16] Since a divine understanding cannot be conceived as giving itself purposes, it also cannot be conceived as the final purpose of creation. Kant is certainly not proposing an anthropocentric atheism. Yet he is saying that, in our conceptions of our own final purpose and of that of creation itself, a certain anthropomorphism is inescapable. At the same time, he is saying that we lack all insight into how nature, or more accurately a supersensible substrate uniting nature and freedom, actually operates on our behalf through promoting the moral progress of the species. The very marvelous evidence of contingent harmony in aesthetic judging and in organic beings leads us to think that it is reasonable to make presumptions on behalf of a beneficent superhuman providence, although we cannot meaningfully ascribe to it our notions of causality, freedom, and purpose.

## VIII. Culture's Hidden Ground

I will have to rush quickly, unfortunately, through the very important account of cultural teleology that supports and gives more content to the idea of the human species as the final end of creation. Aesthetic judging has an obviously central role as refining the raw inclinations and making them more susceptible to moral legislation, through rendering them "communicable." Yet there are also the manifold ways in which the realm of culture promotes human advancement through more negative means, whereby the progress of the arts and sciences initially increases human misery—chiefly through luxury, inequality and war—only in order to force the human species to overcome its self-inflicted evils. Thus through the experience of evil, the human species becomes master of its passions and desires, achieves enlightened maturity, and earns its title as the final end of creation. It learns that nature has not constituted it for attaining happiness; rather, the destiny of our species as rational is to achieve autonomy, and, if possible, a corresponding sensible satisfaction. No doubt Kant regards the disinterested pleasures of the aesthetic as the indicator of a higher humanity that accomplishes the true harmonization of reason and desire. There is more than one element of Rousseau in this: in the account of culture as the realm of self-inflicted perplexities and in the suggested resolution through a concept of nature as embodying, not a teleology of utility, but a teleology of self-sufficient and unneedy freedom, such as Rousseau found in his solitary reveries. Culture can be interpreted as the human expression of a third—and to us necessarily unfathomable

16. Ibid., 5.442 (section 86).

—mode of natural causality, neither mechanical nor teleological by design. This *modus efficiendi* of nature or the supersensible substrate, as divested of all anthropomorphism of intention, can be humanly experienced (but not comprehended) in the beautiful art of genius, whose production unites the unconscious impulses of nature with the disciplined reflection of rational freedom. Genius is the primary human instance of purposive action without determinate purpose or of the contingent lawfulness of nature's "technic."

## IX. The Contradiction in Eros

I would like to close with a final remark on the apparent contradiction in this account of the final satisfaction of metaphysical eros. This is the contradiction between the unconditioned necessity of the moral system and the contingency of erotic fulfillment. The standpoint of the moral system is expressed in Kant's anthropocentrism, or his stark assertion that only the human species as freely self-legislating can be the final end of creation. The standpoint of the contingency that challenges this systematic standpoint is expressed in the profound arguments that the human sensible mode of existence is the locus of the mysterious apparent regard of nature, in its self-specification and empirical productivity, for forms of harmony that elude all free self-legislation. Yet these standpoints (of absolute necessity and of contingency) cannot be absolutely contradictory, for both are indispensable to Kant's account of the satisfaction of metaphysical eros. Their contradiction could be regarded as inherent in metaphysical eros itself. For if the striving for the unconditioned is that of a desire that seeks to ground itself in rational necessity, it is also the case that such desire can exist only if it relates to reason, and thus to its own goal, contingently. The desire for absolute justification has necessarily something unjust about it. Or put another way: it is necessarily true that human beings are the unity of reason and desire only if they are contingently so.

# 7 Unity and Form in Kant's Notion of Purpose

## DAVID A. WHITE

The *Republic* advises us that the study of unity is one of the principal avenues to "the contemplation of true being" (525a1). It may be noted here then that toward the end of the *Critique of Judgment*, Kant says that "the unity of a purpose is a very special kind of unity," since it always carries with it reference to "a *cause* that has understanding" (sec. 75, p. 275/ 5.393).[1] Now purpose and purposiveness are cognate notions that perform a variety of functions in the third *Critique,* and one of these functions is to help account for what Kant calls an "organized being." Only organized beings exemplify natural purposes, and Kant asserts that these beings "first give objective reality to the concept of a *purpose* that is a purpose *of nature* rather than a practical one, and which hence give natural science the basis for a teleology . . ." (sec. 65, p. 255/ 5.376).

The notion of a natural purpose is clearly crucial for Kant's philosophy of science, since only those beings that are organized—living beings—give rise to the notion of purpose in a way justifying the introduction of the teleological dimension in scientific inquiry. Thus in the final analysis, it is because some sciences concern living things that all sciences are capable of being structured according to a teleological framework. And it would follow, presumably, that the notion of unity will be no less special with respect to natural purpose—indeed, perhaps even more special—than unity is with respect to the notion of purpose itself.

In the same section (65), Kant asserts that the concept of a natural

1. All references to the *Critique of Judgment* are from Immanuel Kant, *Critique of Judgment,* trans. Werner S. Pluhar (Indianapolis: Hackett, 1987). Additional references to this *Critique* are cited in the body of the article and will include Kant's section number when relevant, page number from Pluhar's translation, as well as the citation (volume and page numbers) from *Kants gesammelte Schriften,* Prussian Academy (Berlin: Walter de Gruyter and Predecessors, 1902—). All italicized citations are Kant's emphases unless otherwise indicated. All bracketed passages in the translations are by Pluhar.

purpose is "not a constitutive concept either of understanding or of reason;" it can, however, "still be a regulative concept for reflective judgment, allowing us to use a remote analogy with our own causality in terms of purposes generally, to guide our investigation of organized objects and to meditate regarding their supreme basis" (p. 255/ 5.375). In short, the teleology of natural purposes is heuristic, not constitutive; it guides scientific inquiry through a "remote analogy" with our own use of causality. In the same vein, recall that, for Kant, the analysis of teleological judgment in the third *Critique* is "critique"—that is, it is not by itself metaphysics. As Körner puts the point:

While the first *Critique* justifies the mechanistic method on the basis of a mechanistic metaphysic, the third *Critique* justifies the teleological method in spite of the impossibility of a teleological metaphysic. This impossibility is insisted upon time and again. Kant admits only a metaphysic of nature and a metaphysic of morals. There is no metaphysic of purpose, but only a *Critique of Teleological Judgment.*[2]

Even if a teleological metaphysics is impossible, however, it does not follow that metaphysics is completely irrelevant to this aspect of Kant's program. We have seen Kant forthrightly assert that unity—a cardinal metaphysical notion—is "special" in the concept of purpose. Furthermore, the special character of unity includes the fact that the unity of a purpose refers to causality. Kant made this clear in section 53 (p. 244/ 5.366), when he asserted that the relation of cause to effect is essential in leading judgment to purposiveness that is "objective and material." And as we have seen, Kant maintained in section 65 that we use cause and effect (albeit in a way only analogous to more canonic senses) to comprehend how a natural purpose is related to scientific inquiry concerning organized beings.

It is true, as Körner maintains, that Kant often points out that the notion of a natural purpose applies only regulatively to the natural order. But even if this notion does function only regulatively, it still *regulates*, that is, it provides rules for interpreting experience in a certain way—and these rules *must* be followed. In this sense then, a regulative concept is no less constitutive—with respect to what is being regulated—than a constitutive concept is with respect to nature as such.[3] As a result, a regulative concept has a set structure developed by Kant in light of certain fundamental, and decidedly metaphysical,

2. S. Körner, *Kant* (Harmondsworth, England: Penguin, 1955), 209.
3. For a similar usage of the regulative understood in a constitutive sense, see p. 246 of Paul Guyer and Ralph Walker, "Kant's Conception of Empirical Law," *Proceedings of the Aristotelian Society*, Supplemental vol. 64 (1990): 221–58.

concepts. It is legitimate therefore to examine Kant's discussion of natural purpose from the standpoint of metaphysics—*as if* it were metaphysics, so to speak—since the explanation and justification of this concept borrows the discourse and argumentative procedures of metaphysics.[4]

The purpose of this paper is to show how the notion of form functions with respect to unity in Kant's description of a natural purpose. We shall see that unity in this context is complex in ways unremarked upon by Kant and that this complexity involves an important problematic with implications, not only for the regulative comprehension of living things, but also for the status of empirical concepts in general. Thus, a distinctively Kantian "contemplation of true being" will depend in no small measure on determining how unity functions in these contexts.

## I

Kant initiates a full-scale discussion of the concept of natural purpose in section 64 of the *Critique of Judgment* and continues the account in section 65.[5] In section 64, he says, "provisionally," that "a thing exists as a natural purpose if it is *both cause and effect of itself* (although in two different senses)" (p. 249/ 5.370). Kant warns us, however, that "though we can think this causality, we cannot grasp it" (p. 249/ 5.371), a point he repeats toward the end of section 65 when he affirms that, "strictly speaking," the "organization of nature has nothing analogous to any causality known to us" (p. 254/ 5.375). Kant makes explicit at the beginning of section 65 that the causality he has in mind is final rather than efficient. But it still must be shown why this sense of causality is so idiosyncratic when applied to the explanation of natural purpose.

Consider the application of causality Kant offers in section 64. The example is a tree. Kant asserts that within its species, a tree "is both cause and effect, both generating itself and being generated by itself

---

4. And, contra Körner, George Schrader claims that in the *Critique of Judgment,* "Metaphysical questions, among them the central issue of teleological organization in nature, occupy more attention than in the *Critique of Pure Reason.*" If so, there is all the more reason to focus attention on the strictly methodological phase of Kant's position. See George Schrader, "The Status of Teleological Judgment in the Critical Philosophy," *Kant-Studien* 45 (1953–54): 204–35, quotation on p. 206.

5. For sources offering systematic commentary on these two sections, see H. W. Cassirer, *A Commentary on Kant's Critique of Judgment* (New York: Barnes & Noble, 1938), 322–33, and John D. McFarland, *Kant's Concept of Teleology* (Edinburgh: Edinburgh University Press, 1970), 101–106. Neither Cassirer nor McFarland pursue the line of investigation advanced here.

ceaselessly, thus preserving itself as a species" (p. 249/ 5.371). However, the tree also "produces itself as an *individual*," that is, it grows,
but not in any mechanistic sense; rather, "the matter that the tree as-
similates is first processed by it until the matter has the quality peculiar
to the species, a quality that the natural mechanism outside the plant
cannot supply" (p. 250/ 5.371). Thus, the two senses in which causality
is operative in this analysis concern the tree as member of a species and
as individual material thing.

Kant is careful to emphasize in section 64 that the description of the
tree in terms of these senses of causality is "provisional," and in section
65, Kant clarifies this complex causality. Here Kant stipulates that "for
a thing to be a natural purpose, it must meet two requirements." First,
"the possibility of its parts (as concerns both their existence and their
form) must depend on their relation to the whole." Kant insists, however, that if we think of a thing just in this way, then "it is merely a work
of art," that is, "it is then the product of a rational cause distinct from
the matter of the thing (distinct from the thing's parts)" (p. 252/ 5.373).

It would appear that Kant raises this point against the first requirement because he wants to reduce, and if possible eliminate, the sense
in which we understand the existence and form of a natural thing to
depend on a cause existing *outside* that thing, in the way the artist exists
outside the artifact. What Kant wants is to conceive a natural thing as
somehow embodying, *within* its very nature as material, the rationality
of the cause accounting for the thing's existence and form. In fact, Kant
has introduced the function of causality *within* a natural purpose to
replicate the imputed causality *between* the supposed source of the
thing, its idea, and anything purposive thought as produced from that
source. To accomplish this shift in the context of causality, he asserts a
second requirement: "the parts of the thing combine into the unity of
a whole because they are reciprocally cause and effect of their form"
(p. 252/ 5.373). Presumably this requirement answers, or at least addresses, the problem raised against the first requirement.

It is well to note here that Kant's analysis of natural purpose in sections 64 and 65 includes, in addition to "cause and effect," the terms
"part," "whole," "form," "species," as well as "unity" (already mentioned above). Thus, although the analysis may have, in intent, no sub-
stantive metaphysical status, the description of how natural purpose is
purely regulative trades on the accrued metaphysical heritage these
terms unavoidably display. In other words, to follow Kant on this matter, we must come to grips with the metaphysical connotations of the
terms while viewing them in the light of their intended function as accounting for the regulative character of a natural purpose.

Let us consider more carefully the first way Kant describes the distinctive function of causality, this in section 64. Kant says that "within the species," the tree "is both cause and effect, both generating itself and being generated by itself ceaselessly, thus preserving itself as a species" (p. 249/ 5.371). Now when the tree causes as species, the tree does not cause another species; it causes a particular individual of that species. Thus, the tree is "generating itself " not only in the sense that tree A, having begun to exist, will grow and thereby continue to generate itself, but also in the sense that it is part of the generative nature of tree A to produce seeds capable, under appropriate conditions, of becoming tree B, another individual tree of the same species. As a result, "ceaselessly" refers to the species of the tree, not to the individual tree, that is, the species as such will maintain a "ceaseless" existence as long as trees A, B, C., et. al., continue to be produced.

Consider the causal relation between two trees, A (the older) and B (the younger, grown from A). Causality here, Kant says, preserves the species of the tree. But in order for such preservation to obtain, tree B, once caused, must continue to exist. If tree B grew from tree A but then tree B died as a sapling, then the species would not be preserved. Therefore, when Kant says of an individual tree that it is "being generated by itself ceaselessly," the meaning must be that tree A depends upon tree B *for the preservation of its species* just as much as tree B depended on tree A for its possibility as a tree of this species. For without the continued existence of tree B, the species of tree A would cease to exist when tree A ceased to exist.

But observe the consequences. Since *one and the same* species underlies this process, it cannot be said just that tree A causes tree B as an effect. For at the level of species, it must also be said that tree B causes tree A as an effect, since unless a second tree of the same species existed and continued to exist, it would not be possible to appeal to the species of the tree in the first place. In sum, at the level of species, tree A causes tree B *and* tree B causes tree A. But if A both causes B and is caused by B, then the directional factor of causality vanishes. And if causal direction cannot be preserved, then the notion of causality itself becomes suspect. If therefore the distinction between two trees in terms of causal direction cannot be drawn at the level of species, then it would appear otiose even to introduce the causal rubric, at least if causality is to function in preserving the species in the manner Kant intends.[6]

6. For different approaches to causality in this context, see Schrader, "Teleological Judgment," 223, who wants to broaden Kant's usage of causality with respect to teleology so that it becomes part of causality understood as a category. See also Alicia Juarrero

As already noted, Kant prefaces his discussion of causality in section 64 with the claim that it is "provisional," and also that "though we can think this causality, we cannot grasp it." This studied hesitation continues at the beginning of section 65, when Kant says that the description of a natural purpose as "both cause and effect of itself" is "not quite appropriate and determinate and still needs to be derived from a determinate concept." We have seen reason to suspect that Kant's introduction of causality in this context, if subjected to sustained scrutiny, does not succeed in the way he intends. Presumably then what Kant says in this section *will* be "appropriate and determinate" and will clarify, as much as possible, how to think the causality unique to a natural purpose.

Kant's procedure at this point in section 65 is subtle. He says that two requirements must be met to provide the requisite explanation. But after he states the first requirement, he immediately draws back from it and states the second requirement, almost as if the first requirement is merely a rough draft of the second, and, in this sense, not really a requirement at all. Consider again the first requirement: "the possibility of its parts (as concerns both their existence and their form) must depend on their relation to the whole" (p. 252/ 5.373).

Let us begin by considering, here in the first requirement, what Kant appears to mean by "form" *(Form)* and by "whole" *(Ganze.* Since Kant is discussing a particular instance of a natural purpose, "whole" would have to refer, minimally, to, for example, the whole tree. "Form" then would, apparently, have the sense of the physical shape of the constituent parts of the tree taken as a unity, as *one* tree. But notice that the second requirement (the one obviating the kind of objection Kant raises against the first requirement) stipulates that

the parts of the thing combine into the unity of a whole because they are reciprocally cause and effect of their form. For only in this way is it possible that the idea of the whole should conversely (reciprocally) determine the form and combination of all the parts, not as cause—for then the whole would be a product of art—but as the basis on which someone judging this whole cognizes the systematic unity in the form and combination of all the manifold contained in the given matter (p. 252/ 5.373).

---

Roque, "Self-Organization: Kant's Concept of Teleology and Modern Chemistry," *Review of Metaphysics* 39 (1985): 107–135, especially 119–20, for an application of "non-linear causality" to systems theory. But, on the other hand, consider this remark by R. Butts: ". . . I find his treatment of organisms as natural ends extremely difficult, resting upon important equivocations that cannot here be investigated in detail." Kant's use of causality might be considered one of the "equivocations" Butts has in mind. See Robert E. Butts, *Kant and the Double Government Methodology* (Dordrecht: D. Reidel, 1984), 269, fn 17.

According to this complex passage, the parts of the thing combine into the unity of a whole. Thus, here Kant must mean "whole" in the sense of the whole particular thing, since the parts of the thing could not refer to, say, the parts of the definition of that thing. But the interesting sense from this second passage concerns "form." When Kant says that the parts of the thing combine into the unity of a whole because they are "reciprocally cause and effect of their form," he cannot mean simply form in the sense of physical shape. For the determination that occurs here is not just of a spatio-temporal thing lacking any formal structure, an indeterminate mass of matter, but of a thing *of a certain type*. And it would follow that if "form" includes this sense of type, then "whole" would also include the same sense, since a "whole" tree is always and necessarily a whole tree *of a certain type*. It may be inferred then that Kant's terms "form" and "whole" presuppose the notion of species. And we have already seen Kant introduce this very term in section 64, when he says that within the tree's "species" *(Gattung)*, the tree is both cause and effect (p. 249/ 5.371).

To reinforce this conclusion, we recall that Kant explicitly says that the matter of a particular living thing has "the quality peculiar to the species." Therefore, even if form should be taken as referring initially to the tree's shape as a unified whole, this whole always possesses a formal dimension in exemplifying a given species. Thus, two maples may have different forms in terms of their respective shape, but they will share the same form as instances of one type of natural thing.[7]

It is vital to recognize the intimacy between the notion of form and that of species when examining the second requirement for a natural purpose. Recall that this requirement states that "the parts of the thing combine into the unity of the whole because they are reciprocally cause and effect of their form." Now if we can substitute species for form in this passage, then Kant posits a causal reciprocity between all parts of the thing taken as a unity and the form of that thing. Kant does not mean that the leaves of an maple tree, as one part of a whole, should be understood in causal reciprocity with that element of the species of the maple tree that includes the tree having this kind of leaf. The point is that the leaves, branches, trunk, bark, etc., as distinguishable parts

---

7. Occasionally Kant uses form as a synonym for physical shape, but these instances are infrequent and do not affect the primary sense of the term as developed above. See, for example, section V, p. 25/ 5.185; see also, in the so-called "First Introduction" to the third *Critique* (which is included in Pluhar's translation of the *Critique of Judgment*, 385–441), section II, p. 392/ 20.203 and section IV, p. 398/ 20.210. Kant replaced this introduction with the one now included in the *Critique* because the original was too long. For additional discussion concerning this alteration, see McFarland, *Teleology*, 69–70, fn 1.

of the maple, once combined into one whole maple, are understood as in causal reciprocity with the form (i.e., species) of the maple as a single form.

It should be noted, however, that Kant adds another, more complex dimension to this sense of causal reciprocity in the second requirement (a dimension already adumbrated toward the end of section 64). For on the next page of section 65, Kant says that "we must think of each part as an organ that *produces* the other parts (so that each reciprocally produces the other)" (p. 253/ 5.374). Unless thought in this way, the part could be construed as an "instrument of art," that is, the means whereby an external source could create a particular natural thing to assume the form that it possesses as a natural purpose. This sense is more complex because here each part of the thing should be thought as producing all other parts of the thing, rather than just as one element in a set of parts with only the unified set as such in causal interaction with the form of the whole thing.

It is generally clear what Kant wants to emphasize by characterizing the part/whole relationship in this way. For if each part of a whole thing (of a certain type) is considered as producing *every* other part, then there is a degree of intimacy, of vibrancy, of internal dynamism, that cuts across our experience of empirical facts such as that some parts (e.g., the roots of a tree) are at a distance from other parts (the leaves). But if we think of the roots as producing the leaves and of the leaves as producing the roots, then the relationship between these two parts of the whole tree becomes much "closer," that is, more dynamic. Furthermore, thinking of all the parts of this kind of whole in this way may lead to discovering hitherto unrecognized organic relationships between (and among) various parts and systems of parts within this whole, precisely because what binds all these parts and systems to one another is a kind of formal unity that is more fundamental than, say, the fact that the thing exists in a single spatial setting.

Strictly speaking, however, this heuristic characterization of the relation between and among the parts of a whole natural purpose is open to the same kind of objection as that raised against Kant's earlier account of the causal relation between the individual trees as preservers of the same species. For if we consider the leaves of the maple tree as producing (or causing) the roots of the tree, then, as noted, we must also think of the roots of the maple tree as producing the leaves of that tree. Multiply this single reciprocal relation by the number of distinct parts of a maple tree. If, therefore, *each* part must be thought of as causing *all other* parts, then the necessary result is loss of direction in terms of causal production and, I submit, consequent loss of any effective explanatory power in the appeal to production of parts "within" the tree, just as there was loss of explanatory power in the appeal to one tree causing another tree at the level of species.

It appears, furthermore, that one could also raise precisely the same kind of question in the context of the unified parts of a single tree in relation to the form of the tree as we did above in the contexts of (a) one tree producing another tree and (b) each part of that tree producing all other parts of the same tree. For if we are to think of one tree causing the form of that tree *and also* of the form of the tree causing the one tree, then there is no causal direction between the two, and the appeal to causality again ceases to be informative. The question still stands: How should we think a natural purpose in order to appreciate its uniqueness?

## II

Now it might be objected, particularly against this last line of criticism, that too much emphasis is being placed on the form of the thing existing in some sense "apart" from the thing as an embodied whole. But it is Kant who introduces this emphasis, and he does so in a variety of contexts. If, therefore, this emphasis is traced through a series of important passages in the third *Critique*, it is possible to determine, by setting in relief the relative status of causality and form with respect to a natural purpose, how unity becomes problematic.

1. Toward the conclusion of section 65, Kant calls our attention to the fact that his discussion of natural purpose is of an "inscrutable property of nature," a property that, as such, may be considered as an *"analogue of life"* (p. 254/ 5.374). If, in contrast to Kant's account, we were to attempt to explain a living thing by appealing to "organized matter," Kant contends that we do not make the notion of life "a whit more intelligible" (p. 254/ 5.375). Thus, to endow matter with the property of organization to explain why living things are alive is, for Kant, simply to hide behind an unanalyzed notion of organization, and nothing really has been explained. Thus, whatever makes a material thing a living material thing is other than its matter.

2. In section 64, Kant asserts (in a passage already cited above) that matter has the "quality peculiar to the species" (p. 250/ 5.371), which suggests that matter can at least be distinguished from the species that defines or characterizes it. Note also that this assertion means that the species is, again, in some sense "apart" from the matter that, as it were, receives it. Kant makes a similar point in section 78 (p. 296/ 5.411) when he contends that it is a property of matter to be receptive to other

forms *(Formen)* than it can get through mechanism. The implication is that matter is in principle indeterminate—perhaps akin to Aristotelian matter in this regard—but that it will remain the same regardless of variation in the species that informs it.[8] Furthermore, and relevant to our present inquiry, it may be inferred that whatever form does determine a given quantity of matter is in some essential sense distinguishable from the matter it so determines.

3. What then does organize matter into a living thing? Earlier in section 65, Kant asserts that "an organized being has within it *formative* force, and a formative force that this being imparts to the kinds of matter that lack it (thereby organizing them)" (p. 253/ 5.374). Kant is thus well aware of the explanatory power in the notion of form, and we may also recognize a distinction between the kinds of matter that belong to a living thing, and the "formative" *(bildende)* power present to the matter of that thing, thereby, presumably, accounting for the property of life displayed by that kind of thing.

4. Also in section 65, Kant equates "the matter *(Materie)* of the thing" with the thing's "parts *(Teilen)*" (p. 252/ 5.373). Thus, when Kant says that the formative force is imported to the kinds of matter that lack it, it would seem to follow that only this force can make the matter of the thing, that is, its parts, to be what they are and thereby to become capable of interacting causally in the way Kant has attempted to describe. Therefore, even if the respective parts of the natural purpose could be meaningfully preserved through the cause/effect interplay (which, I have argued, is not the case), what establishes them as parts *of a certain type of whole*, that is, a form or species, is precisely this "formative force."

There is then a concerted emphasis on form existing, at least logically, in some sense apart from matter but yet making a single material thing to be something of a certain sort. The importance of form in this regard thus sets in relief the critique offered above of Kant's use of causality. For if the parts of an organized whole cannot be effectively distinguished from one another by appealing to the cause/effect rubric in the way Kant has attempted (i.e., by mutual reciprocity), then the production and very existence of each part must be accounted for, not by interactive causality, but solely by this formative force.

---

8. Kant's position on the nature of matter is complex and variously interpreted. But for present purposes, the precise meaning of matter need not be determined, since the point here concerns the contrast between matter—however it may be defined—and form. For a brief but useful summary of Kant's approaches to matter, see Philip Kitcher, "Kant's Philosophy of Science," in *Self and Nature in Kant's Philosophy,* ed. Allen W. Wood (Ithaca: Cornell University Press, 1984), 204–206. See also the critical remarks in Kwang-Sae Lee, "Kant on Empirical Concepts, Empirical Laws and Scientific Theories," *Kant-Studien* 72 (1981): 398–414, especially 399ff.

In fact, the same conclusion concerning the priority of form may be established by another, more direct route. For, one might ask, what distinguishes parts A and B of a natural purpose in such a way that it is even possible to assert that A causes B (and vice versa)? Surely we can think of the roots of a tree producing the leaves of that tree only because the tree *has* leaves and roots. In other words, the parts of the tree exist only by virtue of the form that makes a tree what it is. In the end, therefore, the real work in the analysis of natural purpose is done not so much by our thinking the notion of causality, which Kant duly stresses, but by the notion of form underlying the process of causality, which Kant tends to leave without any particular emphasis. The fact that Kant says twice, in sections 64 and 65, that we cannot press the notion of causality too far suggests that he may have had some presentiment of its inadequacy. Indeed, Kant says that we bring teleological judgment into our investigation of nature "by *analogy* with the causality in terms of purposes, without presuming to *explain* it in terms of that causality" (section 61, p. 236/ 5.360); in other words, Kant effectively denies that the causal factor in the account of a natural purpose should be understood as explanatory—although sections 64 and 65 depend in large measure on the feasibility of causality in this regard.

If, therefore, the unity of a natural purpose becomes nugatory once the causality purported to be operative in that whole becomes "ungraspable" in the sense Kant intends, the question then becomes whether the unity of the species of that whole also becomes problematic. Will the notion of "form," once appropriately described and analyzed, suffer the same destiny of indeterminacy as that of reciprocal causality?

# III

There are various senses in which the form of a natural purpose exists, or at least can be thought of as existing, apart from a given individual thing. And this separation between form and particular—a separation of decided metaphysical cast—implies that the notion of unity will become especially crucial. For the formative force determining an individual instance of a natural purpose does not just produce *one* tree, but rather *one* tree of *one certain type*. Thus, two distinct senses of unity will emerge in Kant's account of natural purpose: (1) the unity of the individual living thing; (2) the unity of the species of which that individual thing is an instance.

That the two unities are distinct may be established as follows: in section 65, Kant says that "nature organizes itself, and it does so within each species of its organized products; for though the pattern that nature follows is the same overall, that pattern also includes deviations useful for self-preservation as required by circumstances" (p. 254/ 5.374). It has been argued that Kant's appeal to self-preservation here refers to species as such, and that he has thereby adumbrated an inchoate theory of evolution.[9] Thus, a given species will make adaptations in its structure in order to preserve itself as a species. But if so, then the adaptations are not made by the individual members of the species *as individuals,* but only as members of a given species. As a result, the adaptive direction "required by circumstances" will be identically exemplified by these members. But this identity is a function of the species, a function that will vary formally from species to species as each species strives to maintain its own existence. Therefore, the species has, so to speak, a life of its own and includes in that life the possibility of engendering "deviations" for purposes of preserving its own identity. In sum, the species, as a type, differs from the individuals whose form is determined, and is subject to gradual alteration, in accordance with the possibilities latent in that type.

The relevant point is that the species of a living thing is distinguishable from the individual members of that species. Thus, the relation between the parts of the definition of the species and the species as a whole is not the same as the parallel relation between the parts of the living tree and the tree as a whole. Otherwise put, the unity of the species maple has a structural latitude lacking in the unity of an individual maple tree. The unity of the species maple can admit differences (Kant's "deviations") that leave the existence of the species as such unaffected, differences that a single maple tree, lacking the introduction of an evolutionary alteration, cannot admit and continue to exist.

The difference between the unity of a species and the unity of an instance of that species also emerges from another discussion. In developing the second requirement (section 65), Kant contends that only if the parts of a natural purpose are reciprocally the cause and effect of its form, "is it possible that the idea of the whole should conversely (reciprocally) determine the form and combination of all the parts, not as cause—for then the whole would be a product of art—but as the basis on which someone judging this whole cognizes the systematic unity in the form and combination of all the manifold contained in the given matter" (p. 252/ 5.373). Note here Kant's continued insistence that "the idea of the whole" must not be separated from the thing itself

9. See Butts, "Teleology and Scientific Method," 1–16, esp. 7; and, for additional commentary on Kant and evolution, see Roque, "Self-Organization," 120–24.

by being construed as its cause, for then the idea is outside the thing, and the thing becomes "a product of art." Rather, the idea now becomes "the basis" for judging the thing as a natural purpose; thus, the idea of the thing has shifted from cause of that thing to the basis for our judgment of that thing.

But one may contend that if this shift is to preserve significance, then the way we must cognize the natural purpose is as a "systematic unity in the form and combination of all the manifold contained in the given matter." The key notion here is "systematic unity in the form." Presumably what we can cognize of the idea of the thing is precisely how the thing displays "systematic unity" in terms of the interaction between its various parts and the form, that is, the species, that determines those parts. In other words, the idea as basis, rather than as cause, becomes present to our cognition only as a certain kind of systematic unity. Therefore, without this notion of unity, it would not be possible for the idea underlying a natural purpose to become a relevant factor in determining the uniqueness of a natural purpose. For only if the form possesses unity can the parts of the whole vary among themselves, not to mention evolve over time, and yet remain parts of a determinate whole. It follows that what gives unity to the species maple tree, its form, is not the same as what gives unity to an individual maple tree as an instance of that species.

## IV

The form of a natural thing, it has been argued, is equivalent to the species of that thing. Therefore, given the importance of species and genera in the realization of empirical cognition, it becomes a vital concern to the teleological phase of the Kantian system to determine the status of form—what makes a natural purpose to be the kind of thing that it is. In Section IV of the introduction to the third *Critique* (p. 27/ 5.187), Kant speaks of "our being able to grasp nature and the unity in its division into genera and species that makes possible the empirical concepts by means of which we cognize nature in terms of its particular ideas." Relevant in this passage is not only the stated importance of species and genera, but the implied distinction between "genera and species" and "empirical concepts," as if a species, itself a concept, is, by virtue of priority in some sense, distinct from an empirical concept. We shall return to this point shortly.

How then are species and genera, as a type of concept, derived? It appears from Sections IV and V of the Introduction to the third *Critique* that they originate strictly in the understanding. Thus, in Section

V (p. 24/ 5.185), Kant says that the understanding, in laying "an a priori principle at the basis of all reflection on nature," includes in this principle "that there is in nature a subordination graspable by us of species under genera." Kant presupposes here that species are attainable; what the understanding must posit a priori is the subsumption of species under genera, not whether it is possible to grasp a species in the first place. But shortly thereafter in the same section, Kant speaks of the "conceivability" that empirical laws might be such that "it would be impossible for our understanding to discover in nature an order it could grasp—i.e., impossible for it to divide nature's products into genera and species. . . ." (p. 25/ 5.185). And here we observe that Kant is aware, at least as a theoretical possibility, that the things of nature could be so diversified that a species would not be available, that the character of unity requisite for a species remains hidden. Whereas the first a priori principle presupposed the unity of a species and posited only the unity of the genus under which species fell, the second point addresses the possibility that the understanding may have been structured so that it could not even grasp species, thus obviating any classificatory relation between species and genus, and also making it impossible to affirm an empirical law.

And yet, in the next paragraph, the accessibility of species seems to be beyond question. Kant says that:

if we say that nature makes its universal laws specific in accordance with the principle of purposiveness for our cognitive power—i.e., in a way commensurate with the human understanding with its necessary task of finding the universal for the particular offered by perception, and of finding interconnection, under the unity of this principle, with regard to what is different [across species] (though universal within any one species)—then we are neither prescribing a law to nature, nor learning one from it by observation (although observation can confirm the mentioned principle). (p. 25/ 5.186).

Here it seems that Kant finds the problem not with the species as such but with the universal insofar as it falls "within any one species." Thus, if the maple is a species, then it appears to be in some sense given (an implication discussed below). The difficulty Kant sees is determining whether some perceivable feature of the maple instances a universal that will also fall under some other species of tree (for example, whether the maple shedding its leaves is a property, a universal, shared by other species of tree). It appears that determining what is universal in the maple *as one species* is not problematic.

But, upon examination, such determination is indeed a problem for Kant. And in order to appreciate the complexity involved in determining a species, a concept delimiting a type of living thing, it is essential to recall some basic distinctions advanced in the third *Critique*. Judgment, generally described as the thinking of a particular under a universal (Section IV, p. 18/ 5.179), is distinguished by Kant into determinative (thinking the particular under the universal when the latter is "given") and reflective, when the particular is "given and judgment has to find the universal for it" (Section IV, pp. 18–9/ 5.179). Commentators differ on the import of this distinction.[10] For our purposes, the question is whether a species, if construed as a universal, also is a "given" of some sort. In other words, is the concept of a species derived in the same way as or differently from any other type of concept?[11]

Species, as concepts representing living things, embody a purpose in the Kantian sense. In section 63, Kant asserts that only in one case "does experience lead our power of judgment to the concept of a purposiveness that is both objective and material, that is, to the concept of a purpose of nature; namely, when we have to judge a relation of cause

10. Here are some of the stated positions. For McFarland, *Teleology*, 72, determinative judgment has both an "empirical and transcendental use," which implies that this type of judgment encroaches on the understanding. And the function of reflective judgment has inspired a wide diversity of opinion. Thus, for example, Butts claims that reflective judgments, "are neither true nor false, not even probable or improbable; they are rather rational *estimates* of the way nature operates, and express chosen normative research strategies thought to render nature intelligible." See Butts, "Teleology and Scientific Method," 4. However, Kant maintains that reflective judgments concerning natural purposes can provide empirical cognition (sec. 64, p. 248/ 5.370), a consequence that Butts's position would seem to preclude. Butts has overemphasized the process factor of reflective judgment and overlooked its essential product, and implications from this product. The most concentrated recent attempt to deal with the distinction is found in Paul Guyer's "Reason and Reflective Judgment: Kant on the Significance of Systematicity," *Nous* 24 (1990): 17–43. Guyer points to what he calls "intermediate concepts" (e.g., p. 18) as the special province of reflective judgment, and he envisions both determinate and reflective judgment working in tandem to supply the appropriate universals to particulars. Guyer also appeals to these intermediate notions in Guyer and Walker, "Kant's Conception of Empirical Law," 229, 232. As we shall see, the interpretation of the function of reflective judgment will have an important bearing on the type of concept this judgment produces, especially with respect to the possibility of determining species as a concept.
11. Schrader, "Teleological Judgment," 210, points out the almost complete lack of discussion of universals in the first *Critique*. However, this lack has not deterred one commentator from concluding that Kant is a "nominalist" in denying "the ontological reality of abstract entities." See Lee, "Kant on Empirical Concepts," 405, fn 39. The relevant question in the context of the third *Critique* concerns the object of reflective judgment's search for a universal. When such judgment discovers a universal, is it, *qua* universal, any different from a universal of determinant judgment? Thus, does the distinction between reflective and determinative judgment entail a difference between kinds of universal or does it pertain merely to the way these universals are approached and formulated? This question will be addressed below. It may be observed that Guyer's "intermediate notions" (mentioned in the previous note) represent one way of handling this issue.

to effect which is such that we can see it as law-governed only if we regard the cause's action as based on the idea of the effect, with this idea as the underlying condition under which the cause itself can produce that effect" (p. 244/ 5.366–67). The introduction of causality here, as based on an "idea" producing a certain "effect," requires that reflective judgment must be supplemented by reason. Thus, "seeing that a thing is possible only as a purpose requires that the thing's form could not have arisen according to mere natural laws, laws we can cognize by understanding alone as applied to objects of sense, but requires that even empirical cognition of this form in terms of its cause and effect presupposes concepts of reason" (p. 248/ 5.369–70). Noteworthy here is the fact that even though the form of a purpose of nature "could not have arisen according to mere natural laws," Kant posits that empirical cognition of this form is possible. However, this possibility rests on a cause-effect rubric that, as Kant adds, "presupposes concepts of reason." In other words, it now becomes clear that knowing the form of a purpose of nature, the species of a living thing, is not due simply to the activity of the understanding but is cognitively complex, since such cognition must also include reason.

The most direct explanation of reason's function in this regard appears in section 77, "[o]n the peculiarity of the human understanding that makes the concept of a natural purpose possible for us." Kant says that "the concept of a causality of nature which implies that nature is a being acting according to purpose seems to turn the idea of a natural purpose into a principle that is constitutive of the natural purpose." But, Kant insists,

the idea in question is a principle of reason for the power of judgment, not for the understanding. Hence it is a principle [that helps us] merely to apply understanding generally to possible objects of experience, namely, in those cases where we cannot judge determinatively but can judge merely reflectively. Therefore, even though in those cases the object can be given in experience, yet we cannot even *determinatively judge* it in conformity with the idea (let alone do so with complete adequacy) but can only reflect on it (p. 289/ 5.405).

Kant warns us here of the particular danger of thinking about natural purposes in ways that threaten to render such purposiveness constitutive of the thing, rather than merely registering how we must think about all living things, under the aegis of reason, in order to make them cognitively accessible. Furthermore, it is important to see that reason operates in this context as a *principle* underlying the "idea" of such purposiveness, that is, it guarantees only the possibility that we can conceive of natural things according to a species-genus format; it does not, by itself, specify the limits of the empirical unity found in each individual species.[12]

And the manner of such conception is intricate and difficult to determine. Kant says emphatically here that this principle is applied only to reflective judgment, *not* to the understanding. One might infer then that the understanding plays no part in the resulting conceptualization of a natural purpose. But the divorce is not so sharp. First, Kant does say that the object "can be given in experience;" in other words, the understanding must function just so that the categories can present the thing *as* an object of experience. And second, although the principle of reason is given to reflective judgment, Kant says that this is to help the understanding reflect on, but not determinatively judge, the natural purpose. In other words, the understanding works in league with reflective judgment,[13] although the result is that we cannot judge the natural purpose "in conformity with the idea," but can "only reflect on" the living thing. However constitutively understanding may grasp a natural purpose, our cognition of such objects never attains an "ideal" awareness of their complete nature, since such awareness is bestowed only as an approximation, that is, as a consequence of a principle of reason.

This consequence is crucial for determining the status of a species as a concept. For what effect does the fact that we can only reflect on living things and not judge them determinatively have on our cognition of the thing's form, that is, its species? Kant continues in section 77 by observing that there is "a certain contingency in the character of our understanding" (p. 290) and he explains as follows:

We find this contingency quite naturally in the *particular* that judgment has to bring under the *universal* supplied by the concepts of the understanding. For the universal supplied by *our* (human) understanding does not determine the particular; therefore even if different things agree in a common characteristic, the variety of ways in which they may come before our perception is contingent. For our understanding is a power of concepts, i.e., a discursive understanding, so that it must indeed be contingent for it as to what the character and all the

12. Cf. Butts's useful adaptation of A643/B671 of the first *Critique*: ". . . reason bears no relationship to objects, but only to attempts to understand. Only by ordering attempts to understand empirical objects does reason have any relationship at all to such empirical objects. Reason cannot create concepts of objects; it can only order these concepts and unify them [A643/B671]." As we shall see, however, the function of reason in the third *Critique* with respect to creating concepts, especially species, is more complex. See Robert E. Butts, *Kant and the Double Government Methodology* (Dordrecht: Reidel, 1984), 215.

13. The kinship between understanding and reflective judgment becomes so intimate that Schrader, "Teleological Judgment," 215, seems justified in describing them as "two species of the same genus." And this will not be the last time that Kant's main cognitive functions threaten to overlap one another in scope.

variety of the particular may be that can be given to it in nature and that can be brought under its concepts (p. 290/ 5.406).

Kant speaks of bringing a particular under the "universal" supplied by "the concepts of the understanding." It would seem then that a species must be a "universal," thus exhibiting the "discursive" character of our understanding—assuming that the "concepts of the understanding" are the categories. This implication can be fully justified, however, only when Kant's general position on empirical concepts has been detailed, a particularly troublesome area in Kantian exegesis.[14] Some comments on this matter are offered below; for now, let me sketch a preliminary investigation concerned with conditions for the possibility of securing a species as a type of universal.

Kant appears to have been aware of the difficulties deriving from the character of unity with respect to empirical concepts. For later in section 77, he introduces a distinction relevant to determining the unity of a species as one type of empirical concept. The discussion of this distinction, terse and dense, concerns the difference between what Kant calls an analytic and synthetic universal. And the development of this distinction, if applied to the problematic status of species, will indicate one way to understand Kant's position in this regard.

Our understanding is so ordered that when it deals with a natural object, it must "wait until the subsumption of the empirical intuition under the concept provides this determination for the power of judgment" (p. 291/ 5.407); in other words, our understanding

must start from the parts taken as bases—which are thought of as universal— for different possible forms that are to be subsumed under these bases as consequences. [We,] given the character of our understanding, can regard a real whole of nature only as the joint effect of the motive forces of the parts (pp. 291–2/ 5.407).

This, for Kant, is an analytic universal. It is analytic in the sense that the understanding must move from the parts to the whole, concluding about real wholes of nature that they are nothing more than the joint effects of the motive forces of their constituent parts.

But, Kant adds, "we can also conceive of an understanding that, unlike ours, is not discursive but intuitive, and hence proceeds from the *synthetically universal* (the intuition of the whole as a whole) to the particular, i.e., from the whole to the parts" (p. 291/ 5.407). This is a syn-

14. Thus, George Schrader says he is not sure "any of us know precisely what Kant's theory of empirical concepts actually is." See his useful study, "Kant's Theory of Concepts," in *Kant: A Collection of Critical Essays*, ed. Robert Paul Wolff (Garden City, N.J.: Anchor Books, 1967), 134.

thetic universal, and if it exists at all, it will be the product of an understanding constituted very differently from our own.

Relevant here is Kant's description of parts "taken as bases" and "thought of as universals." Consider maple leaves as part of a tree. If maple leaves fall from a tree in the autumn, then it might be thought that *all* trees will shed their leaves in autumn. The shedding of maple leaves might be taken as a base from which to form the universal that all trees shed their leaves. However, empirical observation informs us that this particular base cannot be thought of as universal for all trees (although, of course, it is universal for all maple trees), since some trees do not shed their leaves at all. The point is that the distinction between deciduous and non-deciduous trees takes its departure from the leaves themselves as a base and from attempting to take this base "as a universal."

Now our understanding produces analytic and not synthetic universals, and Kant provides an additional account concerning the way an analytic universal deals with the relation between part and whole, an account directly relevant to the question of unity in species representing a natural purpose. Thus, "the only way we can make the possibility of the parts dependent on the whole is by having the *presentation* of [the] whole contain the basis that makes possible the form of that whole as well as the connection of the parts required to [make] this [form possible]" (p. 292/ 5.407–408). The "make possible" here must mean relative to our experience of the whole, that is, it cannot mean that the existence of the form of an maple tree depends on our presentation of it, for this would make all such forms dependent solely on presentation—an outright idealism. Nonetheless, Kant insists that only if "the form of the whole" is so presented can the parts of the whole be dependent on the whole (rather than, as our understanding dictates, the other way around).

In this case, the "whole" is a natural purpose, that is, a living thing. But do we understand the whole tree just as an individual or as an individual necessarily belonging to a particular species?

In order to appreciate the complexity of this question, let us return briefly to Kant's implied distinction (cited above, the passage from Section IV of the introduction) between an empirical concept and a species. The question is whether a species is the same kind of concept as an empirical concept. There are, upon examination, significant differences between the two types of concept.[15] Distinguish, first of all,

---

15. Useful here is Philip Kitcher's observation concerning "two separate questions Kant would be prepared to ask about a given concept": whether "some experience of a

between the content of the species, that is, the reality of what it refers to and the structure of a species as a concept. The species of a maple tree will clearly differ, *qua* type of tree, from the species of a maple, but *qua* species, the two are identical. All species will include, as elements in their structure: (a) a set of characteristics delimiting the nature of the thing; (b) the fact of reproduction; (c) the spatio-temporal environment required for reproduction; (d) the things produced, living things, as unified wholes; (e) numerical differences between these wholes; (f) and variations in individual differences between (and among) these wholes. All these characteristics (and there may be more—this list is intended as representative rather than exhaustive) must be included under the notion of any species.

Consider now, by contrast, the structure of an empirical concept, for example, the deciduousness of certain trees. Whereas the species of a tree must include reference to the tree as a whole, an empirical concept can refer only to part of the tree, in this case the fact that the leaves of the tree will fall away and then regrow. And, in general, an empirical concept can refer to *any* part, or set of parts, of a natural thing. Now this difference between an empirical concept and a species is significant with respect to unity. For since an empirical concept can refer to only part of an organic whole, the principle of unity underlying this concept will be less complex than the principle of unity underlying the species of that organic whole. And this consequence implies that the principle of unity for a species will occupy a different level, whether ontological or methodological, than the principle of unity for an empirical concept.

Consider this approach to the structure of the concept of a species with respect to what Kant has said about presentation of wholes in section 77. Now if reproduction is essential to a natural purpose—a property Kant himself emphasizes in his treatment of reciprocal causality in the context of natural purposes—then the presentation of the whole would have to include not just that whole that is a single tree, but the generative relation between that tree and another tree, i.e., two distinct wholes, identical in form but materially distinct from one another. Thus, the requisite presentation could not be static, of just one maple, but must be temporally and spatially complex in having to encompass the process of one tree producing another tree of the same type.

---

particular kind is needed to *acquire* a particular concept" or whether "some experience of a particular kind is needed to *justify our use* of a particular concept," in "Kant's Philosophy of Science," 197–98, italics in text. The former question is relevant for determining the structure of species as a concept.

But even if we assume that such a complex presentation is at hand,[16] problems will remain, given that Kant concludes this phase of his analysis by asserting that the "real whole" is "only the joint effect of the motive forces of the parts." For one wants to ask what "moves" the parts to interact and cohere in the first place—indeed, to exist as parts of one form rather than another, not to mention existing merely as indeterminate quanta without form altogether—since the collocation of parts in a maple tree hardly results from nature's randomness (or even, as Kant himself often says, from nature's mechanisms). The form of the maple tree (i.e., its species) must, therefore, display a metaphysical priority over the parts of that tree.

It may be concluded then that the unity of the form remains problematic even if the form depends only, as Kant would have it in his discussion of universals in section 77, on the presentation of the whole rather than on an intuitive insight, *à la* classical realism, into the thing's nature. However, what has been gained from this discussion is a perspective on developing the presentation of the whole so that the unity requisite for its formal structure, as a species, can be determined.

## V

When Kant is describing reciprocal causality in a natural purpose, it is essential to recall that the causality he is considering pertains to the individual tree as a member of a certain species. Thus, the various causal interactions that can be specified will not vary from individual tree to individual tree (except, of course, for accidental reasons depending on the empirical conditions of a given tree). It is because the tree is an instance of a certain species that the causal interplay of that one tree will assume the course that it does. Now, as we have argued in Part I above, the discussions of causality and parts and whole in sections 64 and 65 depend on the notion of form, that is, species. But what provides the *unity* for establishing the concept of a species in the first place?

Consider a collection of unfamiliar trees, all similar in appearance. We might think that these trees could be grouped, thereby becoming

16. Kant's account of reflective judgment in the first introduction warrants the possibility of such a presentation. Thus, he defines reflection as "to hold given presentations up to, and compare them with, either other presentations or one's cognitive power, in reference to a concept that this [comparison] makes possible" (sec. V, p. 400/ 20.211). In this case, the relevant comparison would involve presenting both the tree engendering the seeds and the tree so engendered.

unified in some essential sense by that grouping. But such a unity would be based on the mere fact of similar appearance. If, therefore, we wanted this grouping to stand as one of specificity, the unity of the grouping would have to encompass processes of investigation involving more than merely noting the appearance of the trees. Now for Kant, the reflective judgment must "search" for the appropriate concept under which to subsume a particular. But if we must search for a concept to locate a particular empirical feature of an organic thing, then surely we must search just as much for the concept evoking the species appropriate to that thing. In other words, reflective judgment is no less essential for determining a species as it is for determining a particular empirical concept denoting a property belonging to members of that species.

I suggest, therefore, that the species as such, as a concept, can be determined only when the understanding, in company with reflective judgment, *is continuing to reflect on the conceptual structure of a species*, that is, to reflect on the set of characteristics given in part IV above as proper to the notion of a species. This reflection is directed at the complex presentation of the thing as an ensemble of parts and wholes, as developed in the discussion of section 73. One can infer then that all references to "form" in sections 64 and 65 are no less reflective and therefore, in their own way, heuristic, than the attempts to think reciprocal causality in the natural purpose grasped as an ensemble of whole and parts. As a result, the unity of a species is, so to speak, merely a *reflective unity*.[17] In this regard then, a species is never a fixed entity, but mirrors the fact that our cognition of living things, whether as single individuals or as types, can only approximate the full character of what it means to be alive, and to be alive according to formally determinate limits. In sum, the species of anything living is a delicately balanced product of (a) reflective judgment seeking a universal (and finding one), (b) understanding as the source of unity for particulars that fall under this universal, and (c) reason as the source for a formal unity that, insofar as it grounds the possibility of cognizing all particular living things of that species as well as the concept of the species, can never be fully cognized as such.[18]

17. Cf. Philip Kitcher, "Projecting the Order of Nature," in *Kant's Philosophy of Physical Science*, ed. R. E. Butts (Dordrecht: D. Reidel, 1986), 210, who correctly refers to the "mind-dependency" of "natural kinds," but without analyzing the complexity that goes into the constitution of species as a concept representing a natural kind. See also George Schrader's, "Teleological Judgment," 221, perceptive comment that "concept formation" in Kant is an "art," a particularly relevant rubric for those concepts that serve as species.
18. Cf. Schrader, "Teleological Judgment," 234–35, on teleology as a principle of judgment operative on all levels of cognitive experience.

The complex reflective unity of a species should be juxtaposed with the direct and unqualified appeals to species and genera in section IV of the introduction to the third *Critique* (cited in part IV above). There is no necessary inconsistency here; rather, we can take Kant to be just mentioning these two types of general concepts in a broad context circumscribed by the understanding, since the understanding is a principal—but not the only—architect of such concepts. At this early juncture in the work, Kant is merely introducing his subject matter, and, therefore, he need not detail the complexity involved in the full cognition of species, a matter taken up later in the *Critique*, although not perhaps in the systematic way that would have made his position more evident.

## VI

It is worth emphasizing how the relation between understanding and unity is crucial to Kant's overall position with respect to living things. There are two clear senses in which the understanding is related to unity in the *Critique of Judgment*. First, the natural object (e.g., a tree) appears as an object of experience. Kant explicitly says this in section 77. As noted earlier, such appearance presupposes the category of unity, as provided by understanding, in order to determine the tree as an object of experience. The second sense concerns the tree as the subject of scientific scrutiny, that is, something coverable by empirical laws. According to sections IV and V in the introduction, reflective judgment possesses a principle for insuring the necessity of particular empirical laws. This principle concerns "the form that things of nature have in terms of empirical laws in general," that is, with respect to "the purposiveness of nature in its diversity" (p. 20/ 5:180). These empirical laws must "be viewed in terms of such a unity as if they too had been given by an understanding (even though not ours) so as to assist our cognitive powers" (sec. 19, p. 19/ 5.180). As a result, the second sense of unity relates experience of individual trees to their inclusion under a given empirical law, with all such laws sanctioned in their systematic unity as elements of botany (and science in general)[19] by an understanding, even though this understanding is "not ours."

19. Butts, "Teleology and Scientific Method," 12, has maintained that "the maxim of teleology holds only for *some* products of nature, organisms," italics in text, and he cites as evidence Kant's claim, in section 73, that the possibility of a living matter (hylozoism) is not even coherently conceivable (15, fn 7). This claim is not incorrect as long as one keeps in mind that everything in nature, as treated in any science, will fall under teleology in the sense that all scientific laws, including the laws of physics, will be pur-

But now we see that a third sense of unity has emerged. For the empirical laws of botany do not concern this tree that I behold before me; they concern the *species* of this perceived tree. It has been argued that the unity of the species of a maple tree is not the same as the unity of the individual maple tree, but it is also not the same as the unity presupposed in the understanding "not ours" that allows empirical laws about such species to cohere into a systematic whole. In sum, just as reflective judgment must assume the "purposiveness of nature," that is, as if an understanding not our own contained the basis of the unity of what is diverse in nature's empirical laws, so also it must be assumed that reflective judgment, understanding, and reason, all working collaboratively, contain the basis of the unity of what is diverse in nature's concepts of species.[20]

Examining the concept of a species through the focal point of unity reveals the complexity of formulating such a concept for Kantian epistemology. An ancillary question is whether, and if so, to what extent, the unity requisite for a concept of species must be shared by other types of concepts. Consider, for example, empirical concepts such as deciduousness, brown, and mountain. If the species maple tree presupposes a reflective unity, does it follow that the concept of deciduousness also presupposes the same kind of unity? In short, does the conceptual structure of the whole dictate the conceptual structure of all organic parts of that whole? And what about a concept such as brown, which can pertain both to part of a tree and to mud—things both living and non-living? Finally, is the concept of mountain exempt from such unity because it represents something non-living?

This last type of empirical concept is of particular interest. Trees, as living things, reproduce instances of their species; mountains, as non-living, do not. But if masses of land exist in a variety of sizes, each of which falls under the concept "mountain," then the concept of mountain must be broad enough to cover these differences. It was asserted above that the unity of the concept maple tree must include (in part) a temporal and spatial factor in order to capture the fact of reproduction as an essential element of the species. In the case of mountains, the spatial factor would clearly be relevant, since the concept of

---

posive insofar as these laws are systematically deployed by Kant's hypothetical understanding.

20. And it will follow that empirical laws themselves, insofar as they depend on species for their subject matter, will also become no less regulative (a consequence noted by Guyer, "Kant's Conception of Empirical Law," 222, and McFarland, *Teleology*, 97, although not for the reasons argued above).

mountain does not depend solely on Mt. Everest, but also on Mt. Rainier—and the mountains in England's Lake District. In this respect then, parallel structure obtains between the concept of a species and this type of empirical concept.

Furthermore, the parts of a living maple tree are related to one another in a manner different from the way the parts of a mountain are related to one another. The question is whether the differences between (a) the parts of the mountain and the mountain as a whole and (b) the parts of a living thing and the living thing as a whole have any effect on the concept mountain versus the species maple tree. Otherwise put, does the differentiation between parts and whole in a non-living thing warrant the same demand for unity in the concept of a non-living thing that appears to be warranted for the unity in the concept of a species? If so, then the problems accruing to Kant's attempts to articulate the structure of empirical concepts pertaining to natural purposes will also apply to all empirical concepts that pertain to non-living things.

Kant realized that the order of science required an assumption about systematic unity, an assumption Kant gives to reflective judgment (rather than to reason, as he did in the first *Critique*).[21] It has been argued here, however, that according to Kant's approach to knowledge and natural purposes, the use of concepts to represent species (and genera) requires the same kind of assumption, produced, in part, by the same kind of faculty—although "not ours"—as that which secured unity for the systematicity of empirical laws as well as the categorical unity required for the very possibility of experiencing natural objects. Whether these concerns about unity also apply to other types of empirical concepts is, perhaps, a matter for future inquiry.[22] But it seems

21. Commentators differ on why Kant introduced this shift. McFarland, *Teleology*, 80, sees no special significance in the move. Schrader, "Teleological Judgment," 205, suggests that Kant gradually realized that reason should be reserved more for the moral sphere than for the strictly epistemological; therefore Kant had to introduce a new faculty to account for what reason had done. And Guyer, "Significance of Systematicity," 19, 34, contends that the shift reflects a fundamental rethinking of undeveloped areas in the epistemology of the first *Critique* (see the following note).

22. It may be observed that ramifications from inquiry concerning the effect of the teleological dimension on the critical philosophy as a system have already covered a wide gamut. Schrader, "Teleological Judgment," 215ff, argues that all empirical concepts (including, presumably, species) must be *a priori*, a conclusion forced on Kant's position, says Schrader, by the need for consistency. And, on the other end of the interpretive spectrum, Butts, *Double Government*, 260ff, 271–74, following a suggestion from Lewis White Beck, wonders whether the constitutive/regulative distinction, so fundamental to the epistemology and metaphysics of the first *Critique*, should be relaxed, if not eliminated, so that all cognitive claims become regulative. And, most recently, Guyer, "Significance of Systematicity," raises a similar problem with the constitutive/regulative

safe to conclude that the connection between true being and unity seen in the *Republic,* when appropriately applied, has significant repercussions on that aspect of Kant's thought marked by the intersection of science, nature, purpose, and knowledge.

---

distinction from the standpoint of internal consistency, a problem arising from Guyer's interest in the doctrine of systematicity in the third *Critique.* These fundamental revampings of the critical philosophy originate from tensions in Kant's theory of cognizing living beings, and from his desire to systematize the experience embodied in scientific laws. As we have seen, however, the roots of this tension go even deeper, that is, into the very formulation of concepts themselves, especially concepts concerned with specifying the structure of natural organisms.

# 8                      The Cunning of Reason
## JOHN W. BURBIDGE

There is no phrase more characteristic of Hegel's philosophy of history than 'the cunning of reason'. It suggests that there is some kind of purpose to history—a universal idea—that exploits the passions of finite humans to accomplish its ends, allowing them to grate against each other like stones on a wind-beaten shore until all awkward edges are rubbed away, and the smooth circles of eternity emerge. It expresses in a vivid image Hegel's concept of final causality.

In doing so, however, it is paradoxical. For reason, we tend to think, is the achievement of harmony, of perpetual peace, of the divine kingdom on earth. Everything is sublated into the absolute (to use the language of Hegelians). To achieve this by means of individual passions which wear each other down, however, is perverse. For the means contradicts the end. Wherever the means involves the conflict of passions, it is highly unlikely that the end can be perpetual peace. For each mediating moment communicates elements of its own character to the next. But in the continuing series that results there can be no leap into another genus: from conflict into harmony, from passion into reason, from the earthly Babylon into the heavenly Jerusalem. It is precisely this paradox that has led messianic thought of whatever sort to affirm, as at least part of the truth, that messiah will come only when men are so evil that there is no hope.

How can Hegel maintain this paradox? How can he combine cunning with reason? This question leads us to teleology, or the theory of final causes; for 'cunning' suggests using means to disguise the end being achieved. Indeed, as Hegel says in his chapter on Teleology in the larger *Logic*, reason is cunning when a subjective purpose sets up a mediated relation with the object it wants to accomplish by shoving another object in between. He captures the essence of this relationship in the final sentence of paragraph 209, the corresponding section of *Encylopaedia:* "As the power inherent in those processes by which the objective wears itself down by mutual friction and dissolves itself, the

152      JOHN W. BURBIDGE

subjective end nonetheless keeps itself *outside of them* and is that which *maintains itself* in them; this is what we mean by the *cunning* of reason."[1] We are, then, led directly into the logic of final causes. What does it really mean to talk of teleology, of means and ends? Hegel's analysis is very subtle and sophisticated. For our purposes we need only sketch that logical analysis very briefly.[2]

The first thing to notice is that the final cause, as cause, is other than what is caused. It is conceptual, an organized structure of reason— what we might call subjective—whereas its effect is to be objective, something that takes place in reality. This discrepancy means that final causes never are fully self-determining. They have to take account of that which is alien, even if their ultimate goal is to dissolve that barrier. Limited by their separation from the objective, they are inevitably finite.

The second thing to notice, however, is that the subjective final cause is necessarily directed toward that objective world; for it is not only something conceptual and general but also inherently dynamic, spelling out in some detail the way the objective world is to be determined. This process of determining its own content, its specific intention, has its own paradoxical consequence; for it presupposes that the objective world is not yet determined in that way. It distinguishes its own goal

1. In English, the 1830 *Encyclopaedia* has never been published as a unit. See, then, Wallace's translation of the first part, *Hegel's Logic*, trans. William Wallace (Oxford: Clarendon, 1975), or *The Encyclopaedia Logic*, ed. Geraets, et al. (Indianapolis: Hackett, 1991). Since references are to paragraph numbers, no page numbers are needed.

As far as I can determine, the phrase "cunning of reason" is peculiar to this section of the Logic, first appearing in the larger *Science of Logic* of 1816, and reappearing in all three editions of the *Encyclopaedia*. The only other appearance is in the lecture notes of students in the Philosophy of History. (As yet we cannot determine in which particular lecture series it was used.)

In 1831, however, Hegel introduced into his discussion of Measure an interesting comment: "To the extent that it is taken as an indifferent limit, quantum is the side with respect to which a being lies open to unsuspected attack and thoroughly condemned. It is the *cunning* of the concept to grasp onto this side, from which its quality does not seem to come into play—and indeed so much so that the aggrandizement of a state or of a fortune, etc., which leads finally to disaster for the state or for the owner, even appears at first to be their good fortune." G. W. F. Hegel, *Gesammelte Werke* (Hamburg: Meiner, 1968ff ) 21:332, 24–29. (This work is indicated hereafter by Hegel, *Gesammelte Werke;* in all references to this work, the first number indicates the volume, the number(s) after the colon the page(s), and the final set of numbers the lines.) *Hegel's Science of Logic*, trans. A. V. Miller (London: Allen and Unwin, 1969), 336. Cunning is involved when a simple adjustment of quantity produces a radical transformation of quality. This passage would appear to have benefited from Hegel's use of the phrase in the lectures on world history. In all places where Hegel used the term "cunning" for reason, he stressed it, using Sperrdruck.

2. The following *exposition de texte* is based on Hegel, *Gesammelte Werke*, 12:160–72; *Science of Logic*, 740–54.

from the reality in which that goal is to be realized. And so it defines its own status as something that exists outside of the objective world, while yet necessarily connected with it.

There is, then, an inherent tension between the content of any subjective goal and its form. Its content involves determining objectivity; formally, however, the goal as subjective lies outside that objectivity. This tension needs to be mediated, since it is a tension within the single meaning of purpose, or end as such. The logical structure of mediation is inference, or syllogism.

To resolve the tension between content and form, it must first be made explicit, and transformed from a simple tension into an exclusion of one from the other. The subjective goal relates directly with that which is radically other, and thereby discloses publicly its internal conflict. At the same time, the goal determines itself by abandoning itself to pure objectivity, its alien other.

That last paragraph hides a whole network of puns in Hegel's text. A syllogism, or mediated inference, is a *Schluss;* the process of mediating involves resolution, or *Entschluss,* exclusion, or *Ausschluss* and disclosure or *Aufschluss.* As is his wont, Hegel is delighting in making philosophy speak German.

The subjective intention is only the first moment in any complete analysis of final cause. For the resolve both to exclude oneself from, and to disclose oneself in, objectivity initiates a move towards the fully realized goal. Were that resolve not finite, not limited by an external world, the move would be sufficient of itself to accomplish its purposes. Since, however, its subjectivity must come to terms with an alien objectivity that is excluded from it, it uses what lies immediately at hand as an instrument, as *means* towards the end.

There is nothing special about the means it chooses to use. Any number of instruments could do the task. A particular object becomes the means because it is useful and available.

What we have is a syllogism in which the means used serves as the mediating or middle term. The subjective intention appropriates or subsumes the instrument: that is the minor premise. In its turn, the instrument is to lead to, and overreach, the objective world, incorporating it into the overall goal: that is the major premise. The means, however, lies outside of both the subjective intention and the realized goal. It is something purely mechanical. So the connection that links the terms of this syllogism is not provided by the means but stems from the goal intended.

While on the one hand, the means is thus incorporated into the reflective perspective of the end as proposed subjectively, it also, on the

other, gives to that end an immediate objectivity, and starts its transformation into achieved reality. So the means of accomplishing an end
is not simply an objective entity, an instrument; it is just as much activity—a dynamic that changes things.

Nonetheless the means is unstable. Implicitly it unites subjective intention and its realization, but the goal has not yet been fully achieved.
As an instrument, the means initiates natural processes, mechanical
and chemical, that will lead on to the fully achieved end. These processes are blind and simply follow their own necessity. It is the cunning
of reason that uses them for its ends and, through them, accomplishes
its purposes.

We have, then, subjective aim, instrument, and the realized goal.
They can be united in a single perspective because the content remains
the same throughout. Whether pure intention, utilized means, or final
achievement, it is a single conceptual organization of parts into a whole
that determines what each one will be. To be sure, there are significant
differences. The content starts as simply a concept; it becomes the governing principle that uses instruments; and in the end, it is objectively
realized. But the whole thing can be called a final *cause* only because
the conceptual content remains the same throughout.

In Hegel's analysis, however, this has a further paradoxical implication. For it means that in our objective world, we never do come to
an end. Each stage reached is itself transient and leads over to something else. Each end becomes in turn a means to another end . . . and
the process continues to infinity.

It is the external connection between the subjective end and its realization that has produced this infinite progress; this is the central core
of what is meant by final cause. Once we acknowledge that fact, however, the whole perspective shifts. For the concept that is the original
intention requires an objectivity that starts out as alien so that it can
then reincorporate that otherness back into its own integrated framework. In other words, its goal is to maintain itself by using the objective
world; and to transform the objective world in such a way that its own
internal processes will maintain a conceptually coherent dynamic. That
is to say, the whole causes its determinate division into parts, while the
parts constitute and create the whole. It is what Aristotle and Kant take
to be the ultimate truth of teleology.

But, says Hegel, it is misleading here to talk of final causes. For a
cause is always distinct from its effect. By contrast, in this interrelation
of whole and parts, the subjective concept is one with its objective realization; cause is the same as effect. The appropriate term to characterize this logical structure is not final cause or teleology, but life. And

instead of calling this a concept, with its overtones of subjectivity, we call it an Idea, a term used to capture the fully adequate concept—what is objectively true.[3]

I have spent some time sketching the logic of the term 'final cause', or teleology, to set the stage for my main task, which is to show how final causality functions in history. Hegel's logical analysis is much more intricate and detailed than I have suggested; however, it would take more than a single lecture to do justice to every nuance. In any event, I am not sure I as yet understand every nuance. There are, nonetheless, several points to be drawn from what has been done so far.

1. When we use the vocabulary of final cause, we are talking about an interpretation of the world in which the subjective intention is in some sense external to the realm of objectivity in which it is to be realized. It is precisely this internal dichotomy that has always made the teleological argument for the existence of a transcendent God so persuasive.

Nature is the realm of external relations—of space and time—in which independent things stand side by side. While history is the sphere of human action, which inevitably involves intentions and goals, it nonetheless takes place in time, and the individuals who act are not only spatially distinct, but centered consciousness isolates each one into his or her own subjectivity. It is precisely this feature of externality in both nature and history that makes the language of final cause so appropriate to them.

2. When we talk about final causes, we are talking of exploiting the processes inherent in the objective world for the purpose of some kind of conceptual end. On the one side are mechanical movements and chemical combinations, instinctive desires and blind passion, on the other is some kind of direction that has a sense of a unified whole. This whole can only be realized when determined into distinctive, interrelated parts, but at the same time, it ensures that these parts will never be dispersed into an unorganized diversity; in the end, any diversity will be reincorporated into the integrated unity originally intended. It is this complex that makes the phrase "cunning of reason" so appropriate for describing the teleological relation.

3. Kant's use of the term "teleology" to define the functioning of a living organism is misleading. In one sense, the self-determining and self-maintaining activity of life is an example of an end successfully maintaining itself in the objective world. It marks the resolution of all the conceptual problems inherent in our ordinary sense of final cause.

---

3. I have developed the logic of the idea of life in "Die Logik des Lebens als Grund der organischen Physik," as yet unpublished.

But if we are going to be precise in our use of language, organic wholes involve something quite distinct. For, as Kant himself saw, we have then to abandon the language of cause altogether. We have instead a self-maintaining process in which it is inappropriate to distinguish the subjective conception from its realization. The two are inextricably involved in a single dynamic.

For Hegel, history falls outside of any self-maintaining process. Art, religion, and philosophy all give evidence of spirit absolute—of spirit not relative to, or limited by, anything else. History, however, is the culminating stage of objective spirit, still bedeviled by externality, even if it incorporates the whole panorama of the world's past. For that past is a potpourri of diversity that acquires significance only from the achieved stage of the present. The present and the future, however, are indeterminate, subject to change and transformation, prey to the spontaneous passions of men and women. On its own, then, history cannot interpret itself. It does not manifest unambiguously any concept that it can actualize.

This would seem to condemn any attempt to determine the final causes that govern history. For we, as philosophers, do not live outside of time. We share in its ambiguities. Even the way we think is conditioned by the world in which we live.

Hegel does not fall prey to this modern despair. For while we are situated in history, there are nonetheless aspects of our lives that open up a vista into the principles that govern the universe. Great art offers an all-encompassing vision; religious devotion and practice integrates us into the universe; and philosophy makes explicit the network of relations that constitute the way the world is organized.

Philosophy alone makes the whole process self-conscious. So philosophers become the agents by which people situated in history can achieve self-knowledge. They tell us the nature of reason; and once we have acquired that insight, we can recognize the cunning reason uses in the course of world history.

That claim is intentionally self-reflexive. Philosophers emerge in history, conditioned not only by all of the past, but also by the insights they have gained in art and the transcendence they have encountered in religion. When they discover the nature of reason, they grasp the end that history is to achieve. This insight, which happens in time, identifies the final cause that governs the whole historical process.

It is no wonder that Hegel makes such a fuss about speculation and reflection. It is all a trick conjured up by mirrors, by specula. When the philosopher wants to know what history is all about, he only has to look at himself.

Let us first admit that Hegel is not the first one to translate his own image into an explanation of the world. What is Plato's *Republic* but the philosopher writ large? What is Hume's appeal to custom as the basis for our belief in cause but a sophisticated version of his Tory preferences? In a similar way, then, is Hegel situating his philosophy at the end of history not only because 1830 was the final point history had reached when he was lecturing, but also because his philosophy had captured the essence of everything that is, and will be?

Before we slide too easily into this Kojèvian conclusion,[4] we should look more closely. What, in particular, *is* Hegel's conception of the *telos* of history? How does he justify his claim that human passions are but instruments that must wear against each other to produce the end in view? For we may find that his answer is more subtle, and less easy to repudiate, than we at first imagine.

Let us go back to that passage about the cunning of reason: "It is what we may call the *cunning of reason* that it sets the passions to work in its service, so that the agents by which it gives itself existence must pay the penalty and suffer loss."[5]

Passions are the instruments or means that reason uses to accomplish its ends. The universal Idea, as something subjective, maintains itself inviolate and unscathed in the background in exclusive isolation. The passions with their immediate interest in particular ends are sent into battle—and here Hegel uses a term that recurs whenever he talks about the cunning of reason—"to wear each other out."[6]

*Abreiben* is the verb we would use for grating cheese; when it is used in the reflexive form *sich aneinander abreiben,* the image that comes to mind is a pebbly beach as the waves wash over it, rubbing the stones against each other until all are smooth. This verb, then, identifies the activity that reason initiates to accomplish its ends, whereas the passions are the entities—the stones, so to speak—that do it.

4. See Alexandre Kojève, *Introduction à la Lecture de Hegel* (Paris: Gallimard, 1947), 380; *Introduction to the Reading of Hegel,* ed. A. Bloom, trans. J. H. Nichols, Jr. (New York: Basic, 1969), 148ff.

5. G. W. F. Hegel, *Die Vernunft in der Geschichte,* ed. Hoffmeister (Hamburg: Meiner, 1955), 105. See *Lectures on the Philosophy of World History: Introduction,* trans. H. B. Nisbet (Cambridge: Cambridge University Press, 1975), 89.

6. The only exception to this is in paragraph 158 of the 1817 *Encyclopaedia.* It had been used in the more extended discussion of the larger *Logic,* a year earlier. The fact that it was explicitly reinserted as one of the few amendments to this paragraph in 1827 (§209) suggests that the conjunction of the two concepts had become firmer in Hegel's mind through his lectures. Not only did that happen in his lectures on world history, but the Zusatz to paragraph 245 of the Philosophy of Nature uses the verb *abreiben* when talking about our normal practical use of nature for our own finite ends. It is one of those key terms for understanding what Hegel has in mind when he talks about final cause.

Hegel here keeps reason well distanced from the passions, following the traditional conventions of philosophical wisdom. Reason is universal, the passions are particular; reason sits in its calm pavilion, while the passions struggle against each other in the pit. Where Hegel has diverged from the tradition is in suggesting that the passions are being used by reason. They are related as means to end. Reason as the subjective intention is immediately present in the passions. This is its initial move into objectivity. In other words, while reason is opposed to the passions as universal to particular, reason nonetheless determines its universality by abandoning itself to the particularity of the passions. Only in this way can its intention be realized. The passions are the means by which its initial subjective end is connected with its final purpose of making that end objective.

The achieving of the end, however, is not governed by reason. It follows the inherent development of the passions themselves. Each passion has its own particular focus; as passion, it has the energy and drive to push towards its own satisfaction. Once satisfied, it comes to an end, an end, however, that is not primarily its goal (since passions are seldom so self-conscious as to have a specific intention), but its termination. So each passion is inherently finite. Indeed there are many such finite, particular interests and concerns which conflict and struggle against each other. They wear each other down.

Hegel's peculiar claim is that this mutual struggle of particulars itself produces the universal which remains undisturbed through all the changes. In fact, the universal appears to be nothing else but this ongoing eruption and demise of particular passions. So if we are going to understand how the passions can be the instruments of reason, we must spell out both the original subjective intention and the nature of the achieved end.

Hegel says that the goal of history is freedom. By freedom, he does not mean absolute independence, isolation from all constraining influences, but self-determination. What does that term "self-determination" mean? In the first place, there is a self to be determined. It starts out as relatively indeterminate. In the second place, the self initiates a move to determine itself. That means it gives itself a character it did not originally have. It becomes different. In the third place, when it does become determinate, it constitutes itself. The determinations make up what it is to be. They are distinct, yet moments within its integrated unity.

Through such an integration of specific characteristics, the self is individuated and becomes an individual. On the one hand, it includes all the determinations and so becomes something general; on the other hand, it thereby makes itself so distinctive that it can only be named, not categorized. It becomes, to use Hegelian jargon, a concrete universal.

This is the nature of freedom: the goal of human history. But Hegel wants to say something in addition. This dynamic structure of freedom is nothing else but the nature of reason itself. Reason is a process of determining indeterminate universals and thereby becoming other than what it started out to be. It is a process of reflection that brings all the various determinations together into a single perspective. And it is a process of integration that understands the parts within a singular, all-inclusive unity.

The subjective end to be realized in history seeks to achieve such a freedom—to embody reason.

What does the achieved end look like? Hegel calls it the state. That sounds contradictory to our modern liberal age in which people's aim is to reduce the role of the state in society. The state is seen as the agent of repression, limiting the exercise of freedom, preventing people from fully determining themselves.

Individuals exercise their freedom, however, by responding to their passions. With basic instinctual needs, dissatisfied with the boring blandness of what they already are, their attention attracted and focused by their interests, they are driven to determine themselves in particular ways. The contingency and diversity of the passions inevitably leads to conflict. If one individual has come sufficiently to terms with herself to be a fully integrated individual, she nonetheless finds herself struggling against the interests and needs of another. His actions frustrate her ends. In the struggle, they wear each other down, developing over time customary responses that allow each to achieve satisfaction, and provide a more secure base for their free actions.[7] These conventions become some of the determinations that the self has initiated and that the self must reappropriate.

The state is the result of this interaction happening over and over again, a network of conventional institutions that has emerged over time as individuals have exercised their freedom. Each new structure has emerged because it enables some individuals, or groups of individuals, to determine themselves more adequately since they are less prey to external influences and the caprice of others. The complexity

---

7. In the *Phenomenology* and earlier, Hegel analyzes this process as the dynamic of recognition. See Robert R. Williams, *Recognition: Fichte and Hegel on the Other* (Albany: SUNY Press, 1991), and John W. Burbidge, "Language and Recognition," in *Method and Speculation in Hegel's* Phenomenology, ed. M. Westphal (Atlantic Highlands, N.J.: Humanities, 1982).

of modern society has come about because of the drive to full self-determination.

Social structures develop their own life. There is a division of labor that enables a society to determine itself—reflective agencies, decision-making agencies, executive agencies. In this way, the society too develops; it determines itself and thereby achieves its own freedom.

Just as individuals are not able to determine themselves absolutely but always find themselves determined by their environment, by their fellows, and by the state in which they live, societies do not live in a world of their own. States interact, their passions leading to struggles in which each is worn down until new conventions emerge—this time the conventions of international relations. In this way, freedom becomes more comprehensive, incorporating the total picture of human interaction.

There is, however, a fly in the ointment. For time passes, and the individuals who have been part of the development of social conventions die, to be replaced by others "who know not Joseph." Indeed, we need not be so melancholy. The individuals themselves change, and their interests and passions become different. The conventions alter in response to other interests and new passions. The structures that established individual freedom become fetters that restrict it—perhaps not for all, but for some. And passions erupt. New interests, not noticed before, emerge. Institutions are challenged, sometimes within the limits allowed by the constitution, sometimes so strongly that state and civil society are shattered.

This, too, is part of freedom's self-determination. Chaos comes again; passions are sent back into the struggle; they batter against each other, wearing each other out, and wearing each other down. Only through such a struggle do new conventions emerge, new institutional structures that are both more comprehensive and more liberating. There is no end to history. It continues in an infinite regress.

Yet there is an end or purpose to it all, nonetheless. That purpose is the process that history itself enacts: the process of reacting against what is already there as old hat, conventional, as something abstract and general; the process of introducing new particular determinations that are diverse and distinct; the process of allowing those passions to wear each other down. That process is itself freedom. And it progresses because each new outburst of passion responds to, and determines, the achievement already made.

Individuals and societies have finite ends. The freedom they achieve is inevitably limited. The only fully self-contained end is one in which the end and its objective means are one and the same—when freedom is the process. This is the final cause of history; but as Hegel points out, the language of cause is no longer appropriate. It is, instead, the life of history—the ideal integration of what history is to be and what it is.

There are two questions we still need to ask: The first concerns the role of nature, the second the role of God.

For Hegel, nature on its own is not a sphere of final cause; it is a set of mechanical and chemical processes. To be sure, animals, plants, and even geological processes are centered enough to maintain themselves as living. They use their environment as means to an end. But biology still describes a world of instinctive processes that simply follow whatever immediate direction is set. If anything, nature is instrument and activity, to be used by finite spirits. But taken on its own, it reveals neither subjective goal nor accomplished end.

We do not take it on its own, however. On the one hand, we know that nature is intelligible; we are able to understand its logic. This conviction is the basis for all science and for the theoretical conclusions of cosmology. The particulars of nature can be classified, and these classifications integrated into explanations that are genuinely predictive. All such explanations rely on concepts and implications that are inherently logical, that hold simply because of the meanings of the terms themselves. This is why nature can be included within a fully comprehensive philosophy.

But we do not simply comprehend nature and leave it there. We appropriate it and integrate it into our individual and cultural lives. We use it as technology; we exploit it to enhance the beauty of our cities; we adapt to it so that we can be genuinely free. The final end of nature is to be incorporated into, and used by, human society.[8]

What about God? The self-maintaining life that is the all-inclusive, self-determining end of history we have talked about as being the totality of human society. Yet teleology has traditionally been used to justify belief in God, in a transcendence that governs and directs all nature as well as history. Has Hegel abandoned God?

A transcendent God who is absolutely other than the world he has created is limited by that world, just as the world is itself limited by God's transcendence. Neither are fully free. Their particular passions must rub against each other and wear each other down through a process in which each side dies, or comes to an end, and in which each side rediscovers itself in a single, self-maintaining life. That process, suggests Hegel, has been fully presented in Christian doctrine, where

8. This is the point made by Hegel in paragraph 245 of the *Philosophy of Nature*.

God's passion of repudiated love particularizes itself into an individual man who dies, and where human passions end up in the despair of the dark night of the soul. Out of that mutual wearing each other down emerges the cultic life of the church which maintains itself through rituals that enshrine action, condemnation, confession, and reconciliation.[9]

Once, through the medium of religion and philosophy, we take full account of the doctrine of the Holy Spirit, we can recognize that the all-inclusive life of human history is the all-inclusive life of God. The absolute subjective end and the total realm of the objective world have collapsed into a unity. Concept and its realization are one. This is the ultimate achievement of Christian reconciliation that can be acknowledged and articulated by philosophy.

Immediately, the passions are stirred: how can we be so certain that this is the answer; is not discontinuity more ultimate than continuity? Christianity is being presumptuous once again. The passions rise up to mount their particular wars; we move to reject Hegel. But in a particularly frustrating way, he has been there already. His philosophy anticipates our passionate reaction. And while it does not tell us what the final product of that process will be, it does say that this very response is the expression of freedom, which is the real end of history. For only with such a passion will we be genuinely free and the cunning of reason attain its end. Hegel's achievement is at once both frustrating and liberating.

9. See my paper, "Is Hegel a Christian?," in *Hegel on Logic and Religion* (Albany: SUNY Press, 1992), 141–53, also in *New Perspectives on Hegel's Philosophy of Religion*, ed. D. Kolb (Albany: SUNY Press, 1992), 93–107.

# 9             The Anthropic Principle Today
## JOHN LESLIE

## I. Observational Selection

As first stated by Brandon Carter, the anthropic principle is "that what we can expect to observe must be restricted by the conditions necessary for our presence as observers."[1] An intelligent living being can observe only a time, a place, and a universe with properties allowing intelligent observership. This sets up the possibility of observational selection effects. It is by no means plain that every time, place, or universe—a time when all stars have burned out, perhaps, or the sun's center, or a universe lasting a mere fraction of a second—would be when or where observers could find themselves.

R. H. Dicke had used this idea before, to oppose P. A. M. Dirac. Dirac had suggested that a gigantic ratio between cosmologically important numbers remained the same at all times, which necessitated that gravity was growing weaker. But in a paper of 1961, Dicke held that the only necessity in this area was an observational one.[2] Observers could find themselves only at times when stars were beaming heat and light to planets whose complex elements (carbon in particular) had been produced inside earlier stars. Even without any variation in gravity, the gigantic ratio would hold at those times. Earlier, the universe would be too simple for observers to exist in it. Later on, it would be too cold and dark.

As Carter showed, similar reasoning could be used to oppose Eddington, who drew attention to a second gigantic ratio associated with gravity's extreme weakness.[3] Eddington regarded this ratio as confirm-

1. Brandon Carter, "Large Number Coincidences and the Anthropic Principle in Cosmology," in *Confrontation of Cosmological Theories with Observational Data*, ed. M. S. Longair (Dordrecht: Reidel, 1974), 291–98. Reprinted in John Leslie, ed., *Physical Cosmology and Philosophy* (New York: Macmillan, 1990), 125–33; quotation on 126.
2. R. H. Dicke, "Dirac's Cosmology and Mach's Principle," in Leslie, *Physical Cosmology*, 121–24.
3. Carter, "Large Number Coincidences," Leslie, *Physical Cosmology*, 130–33.

ing a very unconventional physics. Carter instead saw gravity's measured value as essential to long-lasting stable stars. In a universe where
gravity's pull was appreciably different, there could be no such stars
and so, presumably, nobody to observe that universe.

In effect, the anthropic principle can counterbalance the "Copernican" or "cosmological" principle which states that reality in its entirety is much like what you and I see. Users of the anthropic principle
follow in the steps of Hume and Kant who insisted that what we see
may be very atypical—something to be borne in mind when we examine the Teleological or Design Argument that God's creative action
is revealed by the properties of the universe as observed by us.

Recently all this has taken on considerable significance, for two main
reasons. First, physicists and cosmologists have been accumulating
much evidence that the observed universe is "fine tuned for producing
life" in the following technical sense: tiny changes in its general properties would have made it a universe in which no life-forms could appear. Notice that talk about fine tuning, when understood in this sense,
does not beg the question of whether God's hand is revealed here.
Which is important because, secondly, physicists and cosmologists have
also been developing theories which suggest that reality in its entirety
could include greatly many universes and that general properties could
vary from universe to universe. Instead, therefore, of introducing God
to explain why our universe is so well tuned to life's needs, we might
propose an "anthropic" observational selection effect. Among many
actually existing universes, we might be observing one of the rare ones
in which evolution can produce observers.

Naturally, this makes no sense if *a universe* has to be the whole of
reality, by sheer definition. But cosmologists now commonly talk of
multiple "worlds" or "universes," meaning huge domains of causally
interacting things, domains largely or entirely separated from one
another.

The evidence of fine tuning is strong. It is thus important, both to
philosophy and to science, to decide whether the only plausible way in
which fine tuning could be explained is a teleological/theistic way or
whether we could appeal instead to multiple universes and anthropic
observational selection.

## II. Fine Tuning

An early discovery of apparent fine tuning was inspired by F. Hoyle.
Carbon, crucial to all known life-forms, is manufactured abundantly in
stars, thanks to how the carbon nucleus just manages to "resonate" ap-

propriately and to how the oxygen nucleus just fails to resonate in a carbon-destroying fashion. Hoyle had confidently predicted the requisite delicate tuning of resonance levels, his confidence stemming from a belief that such matters varied from one huge domain to another. Obviously, he said, "we can exist only where those levels happen to be correctly placed."[4]

S. W. Hawking similarly drew much of his confidence from "anthropic" considerations when he developed the idea that galaxies could not have formed, had the early cosmic expansion rate been different by one part in a million.[5] (Later writers have argued that far smaller rate changes, corresponding to density changes by as little as one part in $10^{60}$, would have prevented their formation.) Tiny differences in early expansion rates would quickly have led to huge differences. A universe which had expanded marginally faster would soon have become very cold near-vacuum, while one expanding a trifle more slowly would equally soon have recollapsed. Hawking postulated the actual existence of greatly many universes expanding at different rates. It would then not be surprising that at least one expanded at the right rate for galaxy-formation: given sufficiently many monkeys typing at random, one or other of them would generate a sonnet. And without galactic clouds condensing into stars and planetary systems, we observers could not have evolved. It would thus be no surprise that a universe of galaxies was what we saw.

The list of factors seemingly in need of fine tuning is a long one. It includes the following further items, discussed in detail in the studies listed in the notes to this paper and especially in Davies, Barrow and Tipler, and Leslie.[6]

i. *Our universe's smoothness.* A Big Bang might be expected to give rise to immense turbulence, resulting in billion-degree temperatures and vastly many black holes, because large regions coming out of the Bang would seemingly not have had time to agree (so to speak) on how they would move. Penrose calculated that God, placing a pin to select our orderly, life-permitting universe from among the possibilities, could have needed precision to one part in 1 followed by $10^{123}$ zeros.[7]

4. Fred Hoyle, *Galaxies, Nuclei and Quasars* (London: Heinemann, 1965), 159.

5. S. W. Hawking, "The Anisotropy of the Universe at Large Times," in Longair, *Confrontation*, 283–86.

6. Paul Davies, *The Accidental Universe* (Cambridge: Cambridge University Press, 1982). John D. Barrow and Frank J. Tipler, *The Anthropic Cosmological Principle* (Oxford: Clarendon Press, 1986). John Leslie, *Universes* (New York: Routledge, 1989).

7. Roger Penrose, "Singularities and Time-Asymmetry," in *General Relativity: An Einstein Centenary Survey*, ed. S. W. Hawking and W. Israel (Cambridge: Cambridge University Press, 1979), 581–638.

ii. *Early inflation.* A currently popular claim, rejected by Penrose,[8] is that cosmic inflation at very early times led both to a galaxy-encouraging expansion rate and to cosmic smoothness. The story is that, with the Big Bang a small fraction of a second old, space began to expand exponentially fast, like an exploding rabbit population. After a very brief period, the cosmos had grown by perhaps a factor of $10^{1,000,000}$. Regions which had now become immensely far apart would earlier have been in causal contact so that they could have reached agreement on fairly orderly ways of behaving, and most of any remaining roughness would then have been smoothed out like the wrinkles on an inflating balloon. The inflation made space very "flat" (Euclidean) so that it thereafter automatically expanded at just the speed needed for galaxies to form. However, Davies, Ellis and others argue that such inflation would itself have needed very accurate tuning to occur at all and to leave roughness of just the right amount to lead to galaxies.[9] Two components of an inflation-driving "cosmological constant" might have had to balance each other with an accuracy of better than one part in $10^{50}$.

iii. Tiny alterations in the strength of *the nuclear weak force* would have destroyed all the hydrogen which now helps to make water and steadily burning stars.

iv. Tiny changes in *the nuclear strong force,* in *Planck's constant,* or in *the mass difference between the neutron and the proton* would seemingly have blocked the formation of protons, or made suns burn $10^{18}$ times faster or else unable to burn at all, or turned even small bodies into miniature neutron stars.

v. *The relative strengths of gravity and electromagnetism* may have needed tuning to one part in $10^{40}$ for there to be stable suns. Moreover, slight strengthenings of electromagnetism would seemingly have destroyed all atoms (by transforming quarks into leptons), or made hydrogen the only element (by making protons repel one another powerfully), or led to rapid decay of the proton, or made chemical changes immensely slow.

vi. *The masses of various superheavy particles* needed to be tuned so that there would be just the right excess of matter over antimatter when the universe cooled and so that protons would be stable enough for life's purposes. Here the risk was of getting a universe consisting almost entirely of black holes or almost entirely of light rays, or of

8. Roger Penrose, "Difficulties with Inflationary Cosmology," in *Fourteenth Texas Symposium on Relativistic Astrophysics,* ed. E. J. Fenyves (New York: New York Academy of Sciences, 1989), 249–64.

9. See, for example, Paul Davies, "What caused the Big Bang?" in Leslie, *Physical Cosmology,* 220–38.

having protons which decayed so rapidly that all matter was violently radioactive.

vii. *The electron-proton mass difference* must be great, for there to be solids and chemistry.

viii. A *top-quark mass* only a little above the actual one could cause space to collapse rapidly in a "vacuum instability disaster."

ix. *Space-time's topological and metrical properties* could differ from universe to universe, for reasons suggested by contemporary Unified Theories. Three spatial dimensions and "signature $+ + + -$" (in which the minus sign comes from Einstein's $-(ct)^2$) appear essential for stable atoms, stable stars and planetary systems, and even all particle-like states.

## III. Multiple Universes

Cosmologists have suggested numerous ways in which greatly many, greatly varied universes could be generated. They include the following (once again, details can be found in the studies listed in the notes, particularly those of Barrow and Tipler, and Leslie[10]).

i. *Oscillations.* J. Wheeler proposed that the cosmos oscillates, Big Bangs being succeeded by Big Collapses and then new Bangs, and that at each moment of greatest compression it "forgets" its properties, new properties then appearing in the next Bang in a probabilistic way.[11] Each oscillatory cycle could be counted as "a new universe."

Some writers have urged that only a single cycle would be possible, or only a few, but their reasoning is controversial. They assume, for example, that the cosmos would in fact "remember" its properties so that entropy would increase from cycle to cycle, and (see Sikkema and Israel[12] for one argument against this second assumption) that there would be no mass increase to dilute the entropy increase. Or they suppose that a Big Collapse would be irreversible because gravity would continue to be an attractive force, not a repulsive one, even at very high densities; yet this is now widely denied. Trying to explain why properties changed probabilistically from cycle to cycle, Wheeler did little more than wave a hand towards the quantum-fuzziness of everything at the tiny dimensions characterizing the start of each new Bang. However, recent studies in quantum cosmology by Hartle and Gell-Mann

10. Barrow and Tipler, *Anthropic Principle*, and Leslie, *Universes*.

11. J. A. Wheeler, "Beyond the End of Time," in Leslie, *Physical Cosmology*, 207–15, esp. 209–11.

12. A. E. Sikkema and W. Israel, "Black-Hole Mergers and Mass Inflation in a Bouncing Universe," *Nature* (3 January 1991): 45–47.

suggest that most universes growing from such tiny dimensions would indeed be greatly different from ours.[13] These universes would not even contain particles or readily detectable laws since they would be dominated by "chaotic, non-linear" effects and by "non-locality" (the breakdown of the distinction between being near and being far, so that any orderly systems would be disrupted by events which would otherwise be occurring at a safe distance). Further, the now popular "superstring" theories indicate that particle properties and even the dimensionality of space-time might vary from universe to universe according to how *compactification*—a rolling-up of some of a universe's dimensions as its temperature began to fall—chanced to proceed in each case. Finally and most significantly, modern theories of *symmetry-breaking* suggest that particle masses, which in turn help determine the strengths of nature's main forces, reflect the intensities of scalar fields which could vary probabilistically from one huge domain to another. Before the Big Bang cooled sufficiently for the scalar fields to appear, all particles were massless and all forces (with the possible exception of gravity) were "symmetrical," that is, virtually indistinguishable.

In short, modern theorists find it easy to invent mechanisms for making *apparent physics* and *overt properties* differ from one universe to another even when the underlying physics and the most fundamental properties remain always the same.

ii. *A gigantic or infinite space divided into domains.* Several writers, for instance Ellis, have pointed out that if the universe is "open" (instead of being "closed" like the surface of a sphere by gravitational bending), then it probably stretches infinitely and contains infinitely much material.[14] Huge regions could be contracting while others expanded at any of a great range of speeds; degrees of turbulence could vary widely from region to region; and modern theories—particularly of symmetry-breaking as discussed just a moment ago—could explain why particle masses and force strengths differed from region to region, making it more or less inevitable that some regions had properties appropriately tuned for giving rise to living organisms.

The notion that space is open and infinite is nowadays rather unpopular, yet this is due mainly to the popularity of the inflationary method (see above) for producing an almost "flat" cosmos from a tiny region which becomes gigantic while remaining closed. Now, inflation could provide plenty of room for properties to differ from place to

13. J. B. Hartle, "The Quantum Mechanics of Cosmology," in *Quantum Cosmology and Baby Universes,* ed. S. Coleman, J. B. Hartle, T. Piran, and S. Weinberg (Singapore: World Scientific, 1991), 65–151.

14. See, for example, Barrow and Tipler, *Anthropic Principle,* 434–36.

place. The volume at present visible to us, of radius about fifteen billion light years (the sort of distance light could have traveled towards us since the Bang), would be a minuscule fragment of the whole. If the cosmos quickly divided into domains with different properties, rather like the differently oriented crystals on a freezing pond, then the inflation theory suggests that even our own domain now stretches far beyond our present horizon. The fact that this domain interacts with others only at its vastly distant edges, and that its characteristics differ from theirs, could encourage us to speak of it as a separate world or small-u universe inside the greater Universe or cosmos.

Perhaps the most interesting variant of this is the "chaotic inflation" of A. D. Linde.[15] Linde's cosmos inflates for ever. Inside it, there constantly develop gigantic regions—universes or, as Russians like Linde often prefer to say, "metagalaxies"—which differ not merely in their particle masses and force strengths but also in their dimensionalities, in their metric signatures, in their "vacuum energy densities" (the intensities of the fields filling even "empty" space), in their "gauge symmetries" (which determine how many forces and types of particle are found in each), and in other ways as well.

iii. *Many-Worlds quantum mechanics.* First developed by Everett,[16] Many-Worlds quantum mechanics supplies a startling mechanism for generating regions separate enough to be called worlds or universes— and, as always, we could appeal to symmetry-breaking, and so on, to give different (overt) properties to those regions, thereby reinforcing our grounds for calling them worlds or universes. Everett started from the puzzle of why quantum theory's basic equations say nothing about wave-function collapse, the supposed process whereby fuzziness and probability are replaced by definiteness and actuality. His solution was that wave-functions never truly collapse. Instead the cosmos at each instant splits into branches, "worlds" (as they are usually named) which thereafter interact hardly at all: they "jostle" one another just sufficiently to set up, for instance, the strange effect seen in a double-slit experiment where *single electrons* appear to pass through *both* slits in a screen and then interact with themselves so as to help build patterns similar to those of wave interference. Observers, like everything else, are constantly splitting into multiple copies of themselves, each confined to one of the newest branches and unable to detect the thoughts and observations of his or her doubles in the other branches. All this

15. A. D. Linde, *Inflation and Quantum Cosmology* (San Diego: Academic Press, 1990).
16. Hugh Everett, "'Relative State' Formulation of Quantum Mechanics," *Reviews of Modern Physics* 29 (1957): 454–62. B. S. DeWitt and N. Graham, eds., *The Many-Worlds Interpretation of Quantum Mechanics* (Princeton: Princeton University Press, 1973).

might be no more fantastic than the phenomena which quantum theory seeks to explain.

iv. *Quantum-fluctuational universes.* Of the many other suggested mechanisms for generating multiple universes, perhaps the most important ones reflect the ideas of E. P. Tryon.[17] Tryon offers "the modest proposal that our universe is simply one of those things which happen from time to time."[18] Quantum theory portrays even "empty" space as a ferment of particles popping into existence and then vanishing before the energy accounts become more unbalanced than is allowed by Heisenberg's uncertainty principle. The smaller the energy tied up in any such particle, the longer it can survive. Tryon postulates a superspace in which entire universes jump into being and then last indefinitely long because their gravitational energy is (as is standardly the case with the physicist's "binding energies") *negative energy,* an energy balancing the positive energy of material particles and fields. While "vacuum fluctuations on the scale of our universe are probably quite rare," observers "always find themselves in universes capable of generating life, and such universes are impressively large," he comments.[19]

Later variants replace Tryon's superspace by a space-time foam or speak of universes quantum-tunnelling "from nothing" (where, however, the "nothing" has interestingly specific characteristics). People have tried to show that the properties of any such universe would be fairly firmly dictated, yet this now appears mistaken.

## IV. Anthropic Reasoning

There is wide misunderstanding of the anthropic principle and of how it can help explain things.

i. The word "anthropic" is frequently taken to mark some special concern with *anthropos,* with the human species. But the anthropic principle's original definer and baptizer, Carter, insists that he had in mind just a "cognizability principle" concerning the prerequisites of observers, *intelligent organisms* of whatever kind—it being assumed that such beings as immaterial angels are to be disregarded.

ii. It is often complained that the anthropic principle is a tautology, so can explain nothing. The answer to this is that while tautologies cannot by themselves explain anything, they can *enter into* explanations. The tautology that three fours make twelve can help explain why it is

17. E. P. Tryon, "Is the Universe a Vacuum Fluctuation?" in Leslie, *Physical Cosmology,* 216–19.
18. Ibid., 218.
19. Ibid., 219.

risky to visit the wood when three sets of four lions entered it and only eleven exited. The tautology that we could not exist in life-excluding conditions could help throw light on why we are not making our observations at the sun's center or at a time very early in the history of the universe.

iii. Carter distinguished a "weak" and a "strong" anthropic principle: the weak principle stated that our spatiotemporal location "is *necessarily* privileged to the extent of being compatible with our existence as observers," while the strong one said that our universe "must be such as to admit the creation of observers within it at some stage."[20] People have often imagined that he was proposing some deep philosophical division here. Their belief has been that the weak anthropic principle just reminds us that our surroundings must be life-permitting, whereas the strong principle declares dramatically that our universe, or absolutely any real universe, is forced to be life-containing. But although so many have had this belief that it may now no longer be wrong (since custom eventually gives respectability to many an error), Carter has repeatedly made clear that he intended nothing of the kind. Carter's weak principle reminds us of the obvious but oft neglected truth that our place and time must, granted that we are in fact there, be a place and time in which observers can exist: they are not, for example, fried immediately, as they would be shortly after the Big Bang. Carter's strong principle similarly reminds us that our universe must—as we do exist in it, don't we?—be a universe whose nature is not observer-excluding: it is not, say, a universe which recollapses a fraction of a second after beginning its expansion so that intelligent life has insufficient time to evolve. The "must" is in both cases like that of "The photo is marked WIFE, so *must* be of a woman." No suggestion that the photo *had to be* of a woman or that it is somehow especially easy to be a woman! The anthropic principle does not state that we live in a "cozy" universe, well-constructed for our comfort, a universe crammed with living intelligence from side to side and from start to finish, or even a universe in which life was almost certain to appear somewhere, some day.

In many cases there is actually quite a problem of deciding whether it is Carter's weak or his strong principle which applies. A spatiotemporal region that one cosmologist calls "just a time and a place," making it fall under the weak principle, is called by another "a world or universe" so that the strong principle covers it. Is each cycle of an oscillating cosmos a mere time or period, or shall we refer to it as a universe? Inside an inflationary cosmos, is a huge spatial volume a uni-

20. Carter, "Large Number Coincidences," in Leslie, *Physical Cosmology*, 127 and 129.

verse, or a mere place? It can be a trivial matter of verbal preference, and the distinction between "weak" and "strong" is then equally trivial and verbal.

iv. Correspondingly the anthropic principle, as Carter intended it to be understood, has nothing to do with teleology or theism. Not even Carter's strong principle says that God ensured that the universe's properties permitted or necessitated the evolution of intelligent life. Again, Carter's anthropic principle in no way declares, idealistically, that *to be* is the same as *to be observed,* either for philosophical or for quantum-physical reasons.

Nevertheless one must remember that *the evidence of fine tuning could well be interpreted teleologically or theistically* (or maybe even idealistically) instead of being explained in terms of many, very diverse universes and "anthropic" observational selection.

v. It is sometimes protested that users of the anthropic principle "reason back to front": they make our universe's character a consequence of our existence, whereas even fools should see that it is instead our existence which results from the universe's character. Oddly enough, some of the most vigorous protesters are philosophers. A philosopher ought to know that there are logical consequences as well as causal ones. When Hawking suggested that our observation of a universe whose early expansion rate allowed galaxies to form was "in a sense a consequence of our existence,"[21] he meant the (logical) sense in which being a woman is a consequence of being a wife, not the (causal) sense in which being a wife is a common consequence of being a woman.

vi. Still, users of the anthropic principle are not guilty of *replacing causal explanations by logical ones.* They do not deny that complex causal stories would be essential to full explanation of why a particular universe came to contain living beings. Compare, for a start, how saying that a square peg cannot be fitted into a round hole with the same cross-sectional area is not denying that a long, long story involving quark and electron movements would be needed for any really complete understanding of why any given peg resisted being thrust into any particular hole.

Suppose you want to know why you have managed to catch a fish neither too big for your net, nor so small as to fall through it. Suppose the net is so ridiculously designed that only fish of an extremely limited range of sizes could be caught. Why did the net catch a particular fish at a particular time? A full explanation would include the entire history

21. C. B. Collins and S. W. Hawking, "Why Is the Universe Isotropic?" *Astrophysical Journal* 180, no. 2 (1 March 1973): 317–34, quotation on last page.

of this fish from birth onwards. But a useful partial explanation would be that there were very many fish in the lake, fish of very varied sizes, so that it was quite likely that an appropriately sized fish would sooner or later swim by.

"Yet doesn't the partial explanation possess some redundant features? Once we know the complete life-story of the fish which was caught, don't we see that the other fish were irrelevant?" True enough, the life-stories of the other fish might be separate, either totally or in all relevant respects, from that of the caught fish. If *to explain* a fish-catching could only mean *to give its causal history,* then the other fish might indeed fall outside the explanation, the relevant causal tale. Still, we ought to distrust the idea that this tale concerned *the one and only fish in the lake.* The existence of many fish would help make it believable that there was one of the right size. It would throw light on the affair. It would reduce or remove reasons for puzzlement. Now, "an explanation" can mean that sort of thing too.

vii. The explanation would not involve claiming that the lake contained fish of all possible sizes—so it is strange to hear people suggesting that anthropic explanations presuppose that *all possible universes* actually exist. The most that such explanations could need would be *sufficiently many* universes to make it quite likely that observers would evolve inside one of them.

Again, no anthropic explanation of fine tuning need say that absolutely all of our universe's properties are crucial to the presence of life in it. This would be like a fisherman's claim that no fish could be caught by his net unless coming from exactly the right lake.

viii. Users of anthropic reasoning need not claim that the existence of many other universes had somehow *made it more likely that our universe would develop life-permitting properties* when it underwent early probabilistic compactifications or probabilistic symmetry-breakings. This would be like claiming that the existence of many other fish in the lake had made it more likely that the particular fish which was caught *would grow* to precisely the dimensions necessary for it to be caught; or that, in an experiment involving a sleeping man who was to be wakened only when triple-six was thrown with three fair dice, that the existence of many earlier throws of the dice would somehow have made triple-six more likely to occur when it did; or that when a forest is filled with many men, then all the men who were not in fact hit by the randomly flying arrow had somehow made it more likely that the particular man who was hit would be hit—rather than just making it more likely that some man or other would be.

The true situation is instead as follows. First, the presence of greatly many, greatly varied universes could render it unsurprising that one or several universes had life-permitting properties. And second, it would further be unsurprising that any living being would find himself, herself, or itself in one of the life-permitting universes and not in a life-excluding one.

Both of these points are crucial to making the fine tuning unsurprising. It is not enough to appeal just to the second point, saying that if our universe hadn't been appropriately tuned, then *we shouldn't be here to discuss it* and that therefore the fine tuning cannot be a sign of many universes. This would be like your saying that if all fifty riflemen in the firing squad hadn't missed, then you would be dead, unable to consider the matter, and that therefore their failure could show nothing. You would instead need to postulate something like a million firing-squad cases: sufficiently many to make it fairly likely that in at least one case all the bullets would miss. Or else you would need teleology: the riflemen wanted to miss, or God deflected the bullets. What has to be rejected is an inexplicable coincidence between a one and only universe and fine tuned observability.

Likewise, it is not enough to say that a life-permitting universe would quite probably occur somewhere, given sufficiently many, sufficiently varied universes. One needs the further point that *here,* the universe where we find ourselves, cannot (since we find ourselves here) be a life-excluding universe. It has to be life-permitting. Yet remember always that this *does not* mean that it *had to become* life-permitting: that it had, for example, been sure from the very first moment of its existence that the dice of quantum indeterminism *would* fall in such a way that early symmetry-breakings occurred life-permittingly. The universe which became "here" to us may not have been at all likely to become anyone's "here." When it initially came to exist, it might have been highly improbable that it would ever become life-permitting. (It could have been exactly as improbable, no matter how many earlier universes there had been—assuming, that is to say, that the universes were spread out in time, perhaps as cycles of an oscillating cosmos. Even the very first life-permitting universe could then, like the first triple-six thrown with three fair dice, be likely to have occurred *on some occasion or other* which was much later than the earliest possible occasion. Yet this does not say that *particular* later universes, the ninety-five trillionth universe, for example, would have been more likely to be life-permitting than the earliest one.)

ix. It is sometimes held that believers in multiple universes defy the principle that scientific theories (or perhaps all theories which are not utterly meaningless) must be supportable by evidence. How could we ever have actual evidence of the existence of other universes?

The quick answer is that people insisting always on *direct* evidence could nowadays do little science. How could we actually see quarks or superstrings or the situation in the first three minutes after the Big Bang, or the interior of a black hole? Scientists of today work with evidence that is very indirect. We have indirect evidence of something, when the existence of this something would throw light on the things whereof we have direct evidence: the lion is indirectly evidenced by the roaring sounds, and the quark by the elegance which its existence would bring to our understanding of bubble chamber photographs. Now, it is thoroughly question-begging to say that the existence of greatly many, greatly varied universes could not possibly throw light on the fine tuning which we see.

Bear in mind that the story of cosmic inflation is accepted by almost all cosmologists nowadays. It tells of gigantic regions ("worlds," "universes") which cannot possibly be directly observed: they are far beyond our present fifteen-billion-light-year horizon. Most of them may remain beyond the horizon at all future times.

x. It is sometimes protested that to believe in *greatly varied* universes is to defy the principle of induction, which states that we have grounds for belief in situations only when they are interestingly like others we have experienced. How could we ever have reason to accept universes with laws different from those familiar to us?

The answer to this is that, as indicated earlier, it need not be thought that the most fundamental laws differ from universe to universe. Instead *apparent physics,* the physics of derived laws and overt properties, can be what is imagined as varying. One and the same set of fundamental laws and properties could give rise to situations which seemed wildly different (supposing that anyone could experience them) when compactifications, symmetry-breakings, etc. had chanced to occur in different ways.

The same point refutes the following objection: that talk of our universe's improbable, fine tuned character must involve an absurd claim to know how frequently life-permitting universes appear in the field of all logically possible universes. The answer to this is that there is no need to consider so gigantic a field. We can limit our attention to the field of such possible universes as are, in their fundamental laws, recognizably like ours: universes which can have forces and particles and expansion rates, but where the forces have different strengths and the particles different masses, and where the expansion rates differ. While they are often wrong, cosmologists are not just guessing blindly when they suggest, for example, that if our universe had been expanding marginally less quickly, then it would have recollapsed long before life could appear.

Imagine a fly on a wall. Around it, an empty area stretches a yard in each direction. A bullet hits the fly. This can forcefully suggest that many bullets are hitting the wall or that the bullet was carefully aimed. One need not ask whether *distant* areas of the wall are crawling with flies so that almost any bullets hitting there would hit them. What is important is that *the area around this particular fly* is empty.

Rather similarly, a cosmologist arguing "anthropically" for many universes, or a theist concluding instead that God chose our universe's properties like a marksman deciding where to send a bullet, need not claim expertise about the properties of all possible universes, and the proportion of them which would be life-permitting.

xi. It is sometimes protested that there may well be just a single universe, in which case its nature cannot be "improbable" like the throwing of triple-six with fair dice. Probabilities can be estimated only when there are repetitions, or talk of probabilities is utterly meaningless unless there are repetitions.

The answer to this is that it would prove too much. It would show that our universe might well be in no way improbable even if electromagnetism were stronger than gravity by a factor of 112,012,100,202,100,021,011,211,021,112,100 —a figure spelling out MADE BY GOD when its zeros, ones and twos are interpreted as the dots, dashes, and spaces of Morse code.

The truth is that actual repetitions are inessential to the meaning of probability statements. The very most that could be required is that repetitions be conceivable. Even if there in fact exists just the one universe, it sounds bizarre to say there could not conceivably have existed any others or that the nature of this one universe could not possibly have depended on early probabilistic processes. At its earliest moments, our universe appears to have had a density at which quantum effects were greatly important. Quantum mechanics is usually viewed as very fundamentally probabilistic.

xii. It is sometimes said that appeal to multiple universes and anthropic observational selection is the lazy scientist's approach which could be used to "explain" almost anything.

This is unfair. It takes hard work to discover a plausible mechanism for generating many and varied universes and to show how various features of our universe are essential to the evolution of intelligent organisms. Further, great care is often needed to avoid the kind of trap into which Boltzmann fell.[22] Boltzmann pictured a cosmos extending

22. L. Boltzmann, "On Certain Questions of the Theory of Gases," *Nature* 51 (1895): 413–15.

so far spatially and/or temporally that it would be bound to contain domains which had fluctuated into the kind of thermal disequilibrium (low entropy) which is life's prerequisite. He pointed out that observers could find themselves only in such domains. Alas, his theory places us in a fluctuation much larger than is needed to explain our ability to observe things. A much tinier fluctuation, where our brains, bodies, and immediate surroundings were oases in a desert of disorder, would be far more probable, just as coin-tossing will far more probably yield fifty heads in a row, than fifty million.

xiii. Finally, it is often objected that users of anthropic reasoning wrongly assume that intelligent life is in special need of explanation, like a coin's falling heads a thousand times. Yet wouldn't just any universe be "fine tuned" to produce *something*? What is so special about life, rather than rocks or rubies? Indeed, aren't life's prerequisites just the prerequisites of long-lived stable stars, planets, water, carbon, and so forth; so why talk of tuning *for life* rather than for these?

The best reply involves asking why a run of a thousand heads should be thought special. Isn't this exactly as likely as any other observed single sequence of a thousand tosses? Yes, if the coin truly is a fair one instead of being double-headed, and if other sequences could equally easily be observed. But on witnessing even twenty successive heads, wouldn't you suspect double-headedness? Or, dragged into a room to observe twenty coins lying heads, suppose you knew all twenty were fair and had been tossed together. Wouldn't you suspect that the tosser had tossed for a long time before achieving this fine result and dragging you in? What is operating here is the Merchant's Thumb principle: the principle that a main ground for suspecting that something stands in special need of explanation is that a plausible explanation springs to mind. The thumb of a silk merchant cannot fail to be *somewhere,* yet if it covers a hole in the silk, then one suspects he positioned it carefully. A hand of cards which at first seems rubbish, a product of mere chance, can come to seem very special indeed—very much in need of an explanation in terms of cheating—when you recall that the rules of this particular game make this a powerful hand and that a million dollars are at stake.

In the case of the fine tuning we have, so to speak, a hundred factors conspiring to produce a fish of almost exactly 23.2576 inches. What is so special there, when every fish must have some length or other? (What's special in *life-encouraging* force strengths, particle masses, cosmic expansion rates, and so forth? All possible force strengths, masses, speeds, would yield *some* particular effects which slightly different factors would not yield.) Well, the fish comes to seem special, that is, specially in need of an explanation by something other than merest chance, when you discover that your fishing apparatus is exceptionally fussy, able to catch only fish of more or less exactly this length. For then two possible tidy explanations suggest themselves: first, that there are greatly many differently lengthed fish in the lake so that it was likely that the apparatus would catch one for you to observe, and second, that a well-wisher has reared a fish of exactly the right length for you to catch.

The second of these two explanations of course corresponds to the teleological or theistic explanation of the fine tuning. When the next section discusses "anthropic" predictions, bear in mind that sometimes no similar predictions would be made by those who prefer an explanation of the teleological or theistic kind—which is, remember, not anthropic at all, when "anthropic" is used in Carter's sense.

## V. Anthropic Predictions

The common claim that the anthropic principle leads to no predictions is based, usually, on recognizing that the principle is a tautology. Isn't it trivially obvious that life's prerequisites are satisfied, granted that we living beings exist? How could this lead to anything new?

Well, just as a tautologous anthropic principle can enter into explanations, as already discussed, so also can it enter into acts of prediction. It can *encourage* predictions without itself making them.

i. Recall that Hoyle felt encouraged to predict delicate tuning of carbon-producing resonance levels; also that Hawking felt encouraged to predict that basic physics did not dictate the universe's early expansion rate, so that in most universes galaxies would not form; and that anthropic considerations encouraged Dicke and Carter to predict that Dirac and Eddington were wrong in their explanations of various gigantic ratios.

ii. You cannot treat our universe's fine tuned characteristics as *observationally selected* unless believing that there actually exist universes with differing characteristics. People aware of the anthropic principle will be specially inclined to predict that at least one mechanism for generating many and varied universes will come to seem highly plausible. They may predict, for example, that the Higgs boson will shortly be found, reinforcing the theory that it is interactions with a Higgs scalar field which give particles their masses, and that it will next be confirmed that a Higgs field can take various stable or metastable values with almost equal potential energies so that such a field could well have settled down to different values in different domains of a cooling, "crystallizing" cosmos.

Several mechanisms might all contribute to producing variations between universes. Remember, there is no standard way of deciding what should be called a universe and what a huge spatiotemporal region. One mechanism could generate universes in great number; another might then generate vast domains inside them, domains which could themselves be called universes; and yet another might then give birth to still more domains/universes inside each of those. This would be very speculative. Being aware of the anthropic principle can make one more inclined to speculate—to predict tentatively not only that no Nobel prize will be earned for a Theory of Everything which dictates all physical force strengths and particle masses, but even that many mechanisms for making universes will survive detailed investigation.

It is curious to find Pagels arguing that the anthropic principle "never predicts anything" and then, in his next breath, that the principle has been refuted by new findings such as those that support the inflation theory (which allegedly shows why our universe came to expand at a life-permitting rate).[23] If anthropic reasoning cannot help predict anything, then it cannot be refuted by new findings, can it? Besides, inflation may (as already noted) itself require considerable tuning, on which the anthropic principle could throw light. And the inflation theory supplies us with a gigantic cosmos and also with reasons for thinking that it is divided into domains with differing characteristics. In fact, *without* inflation we should be hard pressed to explain why characteristics which had been settled probabilistically came to be settled in the same way right out to our horizon, some fifteen billion light years distant. An important "anthropic prediction" is thus that inflation will be confirmed.

iii. The anthropic principle reminds us that even if intelligent life were hard to achieve, we should find ourselves in a spatiotemporal region in which it had been achieved. This can encourage confidence that it really is hard to achieve and that no exotic life-forms exist in defiance of the alleged need for fine tuning. Life, then, will not be found in frozen hydrogen or at the Earth's or the sun's centre or in neutron stars or interstellar clouds or in the other strange places suggested by Feinberg and Shapiro.[24] It could even well be that carbon, which Hoyle and Dicke thought essential to it, truly is essential. And, once having accepted that observable situations could easily be unrepresentative of reality as a whole, we shall be more inclined to predict that many observed matters, which so far appear unimportant, will in due course

23. Heinz Pagels, "A Cozy Cosmology," in Leslie, *Physical Cosmology,* 174–80.
24. G. Feinberg and R. Shapiro, *Life beyond Earth* (New York: William Morrow, 1980).

be found to be crucial to observership, while other things still to be discovered will again turn out to be crucial.

At the same time, one must not forget that anthropic (observational-selection) explanations can run into the kind of trouble that destroyed Boltzmann's position. Steigman proposed that the observed excess of matter over antimatter reflected chance plus the fact that an excess was needed for observers to evolve.[25] He was wrong not only in fact (since the excess was soon successfully explained in another way) but also in inductive logic—for he should have reflected that the matter excess which we see is actually much greater than needed and, the greater the excess, the more unlikely it is that chance produced it. Weinberg took care not to imitate him when discussing the extremely small value of the cosmological constant.[26] Its smallness is essential to our existence because a universe in which it was large would be expanding or contracting violently. In a closed universe, Weinberg reasoned, this could be the basis of an anthropic explanation. In an open universe, in contrast, such an explanation would fail because slightly larger and apparently much more probable values of the constant would also be life-permitting. Anthropic considerations would thus have led us to expect those values instead.

iv. Clearly, anthropic explanations are very much open to refutation. The associated predictions (for example, that life will not be found in the sun or on waterless planets) may be disproved, or the explanations may be found to be technically faulty—based on wrong physics or on unimaginative biology or (cf. Boltzmann and Steigman) leading us to expect something much less impressive than what we actually see.

Anthropic explanations might even be faulty because various characteristics, which really are remarkably accurately tuned, are so because the universes which exhibit them *reproduce themselves better* like rabbits with wombs superbly formed for multiple gestations. Smolin suggests that the carbon-generating capacities of stars, which Hoyle interpreted anthropically, could equally well be explained by a tie between plentiful production of carbon and later production of numerous black holes.[27] Each black hole gives birth to another universe which tends to inherit the same superb ability to produce stellar carbon and black holes and more universes. (Any universe born from a black hole

25. G. Steigman, "Confrontation of Antimatter Cosmologies with Observational Data," in Longair, *Confrontation*, 347–56; see esp. 355.
26. S. Weinberg, "The Cosmological Constant Problem," *Reviews of Modern Physics* 61 (1989): 1–23, see esp. 8–9.
27. L. Smolin, "Did the Universe Evolve?" *Classical and Quantum Gravity* 9 (1992): 173–91.

expands into a space of its own, invisibly to us, so all this is not in obvious conflict with experience. Yet a seemingly simpler way of getting numerous black holes would be to have immense turbulence, so Smolin's story probably needs supplementation by the point that in immensely turbulent universes no observers can evolve.)

In Linde's eternally inflating, chaotic cosmos, where universes are constantly generating more universes, some of the universes have scalar fields so superbly tuned that they inflate enormously.[28] Perhaps only those universes are life-permitting; but even if others were too, living beings could most expect to see the enormously inflated ones since these are so large, so rich in places where living beings could evolve. And if a universe's inflationary prowess could be inherited by its offspring, wouldn't this too help to show that an enormously inflated universe was most likely to be observed? Each such universe would give birth to specially many further universes because there was specially much space inside it, space in which new universes could be born, and these further universes would in turn give birth to specially many.

v. It is tempting to use a "superweak" anthropic principle which reminds us (tautologically, as before) that if intelligent life's emergence, *no matter how hospitable the environment*, always involves very improbable happenings, then all intelligent living beings emerged where such happenings happened. Even if most planets, no matter how well provided with carbon and water, et cetera, remained lifeless because life's first beginnings require very, very improbable molecular combinations, our own planet would be one of the lucky ones, unsurprisingly.[29] Carter uses similar points to help explain why the time human intelligence took to evolve was roughly comparable to the total period available for its evolution, which he took to be the period between Earth's formation and the day of our sun's becoming a red giant. He suggests that it would be only extremely rarely that such high intelligence evolved fast enough—but, of course, our own species must (since we are discussing the matter) have been among those fortunate enough to beat the clock.[30]

Barrow and Tipler extend Carter's reasoning in complex ways, reaching the conclusion that mankind will probably become extinct

28. Linde, *Inflation*, 21.
29. M. H. Hart, "Atmospheric Evolution, the Drake Equation, and DNA: Sparse Life in an Infinite Universe," in Leslie, *Physical Cosmology*, 256–66.
30. Brandon Carter in *The Constants of Physics*, ed. W. H. McCrea and M. J. Rees, *Philosophical Transactions of the Royal Society, London* A30 (1983): 347–63. Carter, "The Anthropic Principle: Self-Selection as an Adjunct to Natural Selection," in *Cosmic Perspectives*, ed. S. K. Biswas, et. al. (Cambridge: Cambridge University Press, 1989), 185–206; see esp. 200–203.

within forty thousand or so years.[31] But, having criticized their argument elsewhere,[32] let me instead give another argument for a similarly pessimistic conclusion. It was discovered by Carter some ten years ago but first put into print by me and by Nielsen.[33] This "doomsday argument" says that *the risk that the human race will fairly soon become extinct has been systematically underestimated.*

Let us creep up on the doomsday argument by noting that observership's prerequisites are seldom entirely firm. For example, observers *just might* exist in the early universe, coming out of black holes. Black holes radiate particles in a random way so that, given sufficiently many such holes, some would (like monkeys typing sonnets) "emit . . . the works of Proust in ten leather-bound volumes" or even somebody just like Charles Darwin.[34] Still, no observer should *expect* to find that he or she had originated in this way. And likewise, nobody should expect that his or her race was the very first of many intelligent races to evolve— which suggests that either there are (or have been) many intelligent races besides ours, or else humans are more or less the only intelligent beings there ever will be.

Carter noticed that, very similarly, *one would have strong grounds for expecting not to be very exceptionally early in human population history.* One would not expect, for example, to be among the first 0.0001% of all humans who would ever be born. Now, if the human race were going to end soon then, obviously, we should not be exceptionally early; neither should we be very exceptionally late, since recent population growth means that roughly 10% of all humans who have so far been born are still alive today. If, on the other hand, the human race failed to end soon—if it survived for many more centuries even at its present size, let alone at the size it would soon reach if it started colonizing the galaxy—then we should indeed be very exceptionally early. Carter reasons that this ought to reduce any confidence that our race will have a long future. Compare how, if your name comes very early from a hat, then you have increased reasons for suspecting that the hat did not contain ten thousand names.

Admittedly this argument is weakened if the world is radically in-

---

31. Barrow and Tipler, *Anthropic Principle*, 564–67.
32. Leslie, "Anthropic Predictions," *Philosophia* 23 (1994): 117–44; see esp. 134.
33. Leslie, "Risking the World's End," *Bulletin of the Canadian Nuclear Society* (May 1989): 10–15, reprinted in *Interchange* 21 (1990): 49–58. Leslie, "Time and the Anthropic Principle," *Mind* 101 (1992): 521–40. H. B. Nielsen, "Random Dynamics," *Acta Physica Polonica* B20 (1989): 427–68; see esp. 447–59.
34. S. W. Hawking, "The Quantum Mechanics of Black Holes," *Scientific American* (January 1977): 34–40, quotation on 40. S. W. Hawking and W. Israel, eds., *General Relativity* (Cambridge: Cambridge University Press, 1979), 19.

deterministic and if the indeterminism is likely to affect how long the human race will last. Still, it could be powerful against the view that it is altogether probable that the race will last long, because the words "altogether probable" mark a belief that any indeterminism is unlikely to affect the matter.

Do not trust the first objection which springs to mind—for example, that later humans *are not alive yet* to observe their temporal positions; or, that we *know* we live in the 1990s and would be just as sure of this, no matter what our theories about our race's future; or, that genes like ours are common only near the 1990s, so we cannot fail to live then. If trustworthy, these objections would make nonsense not only of the doomsday argument but also of other forms of anthropic reasoning which are fairly obviously strong: for example, Dicke's reasoning starting from how one would most probably find oneself alive before most of the life-giving stars had burned out.

Carter has written to me that he considers the doomsday argument "obviously the most practically important application of the anthropic principle." As the argument is just for *a reduction in confidence* that our species will survive long, it encourages us to take great care with germ warfare, destruction of the ozone layer, et cetera. It does not tell us that the risk of imminent annihilation is exactly as high, no matter what precautions we take. Instead, it can persuade us to treat even seemingly slight dangers seriously, when humankind's survival is in question. Whereas, for example, nuclear bombs could seem able only to depress population figures temporarily, there would be no way in which the human race could survive a vacuum instability disaster brought on by experiments at very high energies, the sudden creation of a bubble which expands at nearly the speed of light and destroys everything.[35] The doomsday argument can suggest that we should be very careful to avoid *that*.[36]

## VI. The Teleological or Theistic Alternative

Let us now examine the teleological or theistic way of accounting for the fine tuning, and the predictions it might encourage. By a teleological approach to our universe, I mean one which explains it by reference to a purpose it fulfils. The most important teleological position is

35. J. Ellis, A. Linde, and M. Sher, "Vacuum Stability, Wormholes, Cosmic Rays, and the Cosmological Bounds on Top Quark and Higgs Masses," *Physics Letters* 252 B (1990): 203–11.

36. Such points are expanded in John Leslie, *The End of the World: The Science and Ethics of Human Extinction* (London: Routledge, 1996).

theism, the theory that God's power and goodness are responsible for our universe's existence and for its life-permitting properties. Theism *is compatible with* universes in great number and great variety, for why should God create just a single universe, or universes of just one kind? Nevertheless, theistic explanations *compete with* explanations that appeal to multiple universes and to anthropic observational selection. If we accept the one kind of explanation for the fine tuning, then there is less need to accept the other, and the two kinds tend to lead to different predictions.

How do things stand with respect to prediction of doomsday? It is unclear that theism affects this. Some would argue that God would have grounds to protect the human race, perhaps by making ours a universe in which no vacuum instability disaster could occur; yet mightn't we instead reason that God would create hugely or infinitely many universes so that there would be no lack of living-space even if one of them came to be uninhabitable? Using the words "anthropic principle" in a way that Carter rejects, Tipler has stated a "final anthropic principle" that conscious life will at no time die out.[37] Dyson and others had pioneered fascinating accounts of how it could survive indefinitely even in an ever-expanding cosmos, a cosmos constantly growing colder and more dilute, and Tipler's "Omega-point" theory has a Big Collapse reaching a final and timeless state as intelligent information-processing becomes infinite.[38] But while Tipler finds his picture ethically attractive and fully consonant with theism, not everyone would agree. At a papal workshop of 1987, John Polkinghorne condemned it as replacing ultimate fellowship with God by something comparable to a gigantic self-conscious encyclopaedia. (Tipler also offers non-theistic support for his final anthropic principle, associating it with a "participatory anthropic principle" defended by Wheeler.[39] The proposal is that quantum theory be interpreted idealistically: no reality is a reality unless it is observed. A criticism of this approach is that it appears "absurdly circular": it involves saying that observations collapse quantum wave-functions *"which must remain uncollapsed until*

37. Brandon Carter, "The Anthropic Selection Principle and the Ultra-Darwinian Synthesis," in *The Anthropic Principle*, ed. F. Bertola and U. Curi (Cambridge: Cambridge University Press, 1989), 33–59; see esp. 35–36. Barrow and Tipler, *Anthropic Principle*, 23 and 659.

38. See S. Frautschi, "Entropy in an Expanding Universe," *Science* 217 (1982): 593–99, and F. J. Tipler, "The Anthropic Principle: A Primer for Philosophers," in *Proceedings of the 1988 Biennial Meeting of the Philosophy of Science Association*, ed. A. Fine and J. Leplin (East Lansing, Mich.: PSA, 1989), 27–48.

39. See, for example, J. A. Wheeler, "Beyond the Black Hole," in *Some Strangeness in the Proportion*, ed. Harry Wolff (Reading, Mass.: Addison-Wesley, 1980), 341–75.

*observations occur* while at the same time the brains and bodies essential to those observations *themselves depend for the details of their evolution on how wave-functions collapse in particular ways.*"[40] However, Wheeler and Tipler view past, present, and future as tied together so intimately that such a criticism may amount merely to a complaint that their world-model is too complicated.)

With respect to other matters, the position is somewhat more clear. Thus, whether or not they believe in multiple universes, theists too should take an interest in the apparent fine tuning, predicting that further instances of it will be discovered. In fact they often oppose it, yet this seems just a case of their being reluctant to believe in things which might be evidence of God's hand, when doing so got opponents of Galileo and of Darwin into so much trouble. They have insufficiently appreciated that others besides theists can believe in such things. Fine tuning can be interpreted atheistically as well as theistically. Still, they should surely permit themselves some slight preference for interpreting it theistically. Theists should feel less pressure to accept that fine tuned force strengths, particle masses, and so on, are products of chance. Yes, they might perhaps picture God as creating immensely many universes, confident that probabilistic factors (symmetry-breakings or whatever) would sooner or later lead to a life-containing one. But they could at least equally well suppose that God created just one universe, or many universes of just one kind, and that he fine tuned things to suit life's needs—maybe by selection of the right values for force strengths, particle masses, et cetera, but perhaps instead by selecting fundamental laws which dictated the right values.

Atheists, in contrast, should be unwilling to accept that any laws dictated those values, for this would give them two unattractive positions to choose between: (a) One would be that there were greatly many universes obeying different laws and that the fine tuning of our universe was really fine tuning of its laws, laws observationally selected as the anthropic principle suggests—but here it seems right to protest that (unless produced by a deity who wanted variety) such variation in laws would be implausible, much harder to accept than any variation in force strengths and particle masses while the laws remained constant. (b) Yet the other position would be little better, for it would be that all the factors which seemed fine tuned to life's needs *were in point of fact dictated by the only fundamental laws which mathematical consistency allowed.* The idea of tuning a force strength or a particle mass should then be dismissed. It would be like that of "tuning" the ratio of an Euclidean

40. Leslie, *Universes,* 88–89.

circle's diameter to its circumference. Now, there are two defects in this position. First, it can appear easy enough to conceive universes with different laws, without running into mathematical inconsistency. And second, the position's dismissal of all the seeming evidence of fine tuning sounds far too similar to dismissing what looks like a long, readily intelligible message from extraterrestrials as "just a product of mathematical necessities." You might almost as well suppose that mathematical necessities had written GOD CREATED THE UNIVERSE inside every atom or that this message could be derived in a straightforward way from the first fifty prime numbers.

What could be said for reviving the Design Argument, on the basis of the observed fine tuning? (i) It should by now be evident that very general "refutations" of the Argument are often very unpersuasive. I particularly have in mind those alleged refutations which, if they were valid, would be valid also against all "fine tuning" arguments for multiple universes. It can be unpersuasive to claim, for instance, that probability theory tells us that there could be nothing improbable in fundamental physical laws, not even, for example, if those laws dictated that naturally occurring chain molecules should spell out the ten commandments. (ii) It could seem that making God responsible for the fine tuning was preferable to believing in greatly many universes and in probabilistic variations among them. After all, all multiple-universe theories are highly speculative and some may verge on the fantastic. In his defence of Design, Swinburne is particularly critical of Many-Worlds quantum mechanics, calling it "an enormous inverted pyramid of theory resting on a vertex of observation."[41] (iii) A force strength or a particle mass often appears to need tuning to its actual value, not just for one reason but for two or three or five. Yet evidently it could not have been tuned first in one way and next in another, to satisfy conflicting requirements. Must we then view it as inexplicable good fortune that the various requirements (for example, of long-lived stable stars, and of complex chemistry) were always in harmony? A better interpretation could seem to be that God selected, from among a great many possible sets of physical laws, one of the rare sets that led to no conflicts.

It is sometimes objected that God's existence could not be supported by any finite evidence, because God is infinite. The objection forgets that an infinite creator could be in a way much simpler than any finite one: compare how it could be simpler to have infinitely many vacuum-fluctuational universes rather than six hundred and forty-three. Again,

41. R. Swinburne, "Argument from the Fine-Tuning of the Universe," in Leslie, *Physical Cosmology*, 154–73; quotation from 171.

it is sometimes said that making God's mind the ultimate source of the order of the physical world only defers our problem: the question just becomes that of why God's mind is orderly. Yet it is unclear whether God even has a mind in any very ordinary sense; and if God has one, then we can, I think, see how its orderliness might perhaps be explained. My *Value and Existence* defends the doctrine—it has a lengthy history—that the ultimate reason for all actually existing things must lie in the eternal realm of platonic realities, and particularly in an unconditionally real ethical requirement, a requirement *which could itself necessitate* the existence of what is required.[42] Not logically, of course, for ethical requirements are not logical ones; yet not all firm necessitations need be logical necessitations. Contemplating their mere concept from an armchair, we cannot tell that ethical requirements are ever creatively powerful, but neither can we tell that they are always powerless. And the little matter of there existing any world at all, together with the strong semblance of fine tuning, can suggest that they are powerful at times, in cases where they have not entered into conflict with one another. Bear in mind that the standard defence against the Problem of Evil, of why a benevolent deity permits crimes and natural disasters, is that *ethical requirements very often do conflict*. The reason, therefore, why very many ethical requirements are powerless, might be that they have been overruled by other ethical requirements. As developed by Plotinus and Paul Tillich, this line of thought may lead to the conclusion that "God" simply names an ethical requirement which is responsible for the world's existence. But, alternatively, one could follow Ewing, picturing a divine mind as owing its existence and orderliness to its perfection, its supreme ethical requiredness.[43]

42. John Leslie, *Value and Existence* (Oxford: Blackwell, 1979).
43. A. C. Ewing, *Value and Reality* (London: Allen and Unwin, 1973), chap. 7.

# 10     Anthropic-Principle Cosmology: Physics or Metaphysics?

## GEORGE GALE

After a long, involved process, cosmology finally entered the secure ranks of a science. Recently, however, a small number of cosmologists began a research program which—according to the other cosmologists—ran the risk of putting metaphysics back into cosmology. This research program is based on a loose set of propositions called "the anthropic principle." In what follows, I trace out some of the history and structure of modern cosmology and lay out various aspects of anthropic-principle cosmologizing. In the end, I claim that anthropic-principle cosmologizing brings metaphysics back into cosmology just insofar as it brings teleological causality into the physical realm.

## 1. Cosmology: The Lay of the Land

Some activities are risky by their very nature. To do cosmology, for example, is to do what is by nature risky science. Cosmology is risky science because it teeters just on the balance between physics and metaphysics, between science and philosophy. One popular criterion used to distinguish between science and other fields, for example, philosophy, involves empirical observation: In order for a field to count as a science, it has to generate at least a modicum of empirical data. But for cosmology to satisfy this criterion proved a distressingly difficult task. Hermann Bondi, one of modern cosmology's great heroes, once noted that cosmology required using terrifyingly long chains of reasoning to apply observations, laws and principles extrapolated far beyond their originally intended scope. For this reason, it seemed to him that theory is always more reliable in cosmology than is observation.[1] Given such considerations as these, it is perhaps no surprise that modern cosmol-

---

1. H. Bondi, "Fact and Inference in Theory and in Observation," in Arthur Beer, ed., *Vistas in Astronomy*, vol. 1 (London: Pergamon Press, 1955), 155–62.

ogy was so late in arriving. By my own reckoning, modern scientific cosmology began on the 29th of September, 1931, on the occasion of the British Association for the Advancement of Science's special session devoted to "The Evolution of the Universe."[2] I pick this date simply because the session marked the achievement, on the part of all the principal cosmological practitioners, of a consensus view about the nature, structure, and origin of the universe. After this meeting, for roughly the next two decades, most mainstream cosmologists, if asked, would tell pretty much the same story about what the universe was like, where it had come from, and, most importantly, what evidence they had in favor of this view. The evidence, of course, wasn't much; but there was no denying that it *was* evidence, and, moreover, evidence of an acceptably scientific sort. In just a moment or two, we will take a look at some of that evidence and what it implied for cosmological theorizing.

Right now, however, I want to make—rather emphatically—two important points. First, as I noted in my second sentence, cosmology is risky science. Second, because of the nature of its origins, cosmology's risk is always that of slipping back down its just-climbed slippery slope into that non-science from whence it climbed—falling back into philosophy, or into theology, or into myth, or into poetry. Recently, however, for reasons which we will investigate later, a few cosmologists, particularly those investigating the so-called anthropic principle, have explicitly embraced this risk, and thereby embraced the possibility of an exhilarating revanchist slide back down the slope into philosophy, theology, or whatever. But most cosmologists have been quite leery of the risk, and, indeed, perhaps even a bit disdainful of their anthropic-principle colleagues who—in their eyes—have given in to the degrading temptations offered by this 'seamier' side of cosmology. This majority of cosmologists, ever mindful as they are of the late, difficult, and heavily panged birth of the *science* of cosmology, retains a very healthy guard against those artforms—philosophy, theology, myth, etc.—which, although midwives of their science's birth, should and must give up the newborn into science's nurturing arms. Our exploration today will prove, perhaps unfortunately, somewhat embarrassing for this majority. This is because I ultimately intend to focus upon the minority—anthropic-principle—style of cosmologizing, that risky business most of today's practitioners find disreputable. I think that the best way to introduce all this is to begin at the beginning . . . at the beginning of *cosmology*, of course—not at the beginning of the *cosmos!*

2. H. Dingle, *The Evolution of the Universe* (London: Nature, 1931), 699–722.

## 2. Some Intellectual Geography

A first major reason cosmology is risky business concerns its focus upon Big Questions. After all, it is not far from "What *is* All This Stuff?" to "Where did All This come from?," nor from "How does All This work?" to "Where is All This going?" And, as anyone can tell, it is not much of a slide from the latter query in each of these pairs to something more like "Who made All This?" or "Why is All This going where it is going?," neither of which is a recognizably respectable *scientific* question. Big Questions in cosmology, even undeniably scientific ones, have an unceasing dynamic striving to become Ultimate Questions, which are undeniably *unscientific* ones. It is here, in this fundamental dynamic, that the riskiness of cosmology is located.

Curiously enough, although cosmology developed in concert with another heavenly discipline—astronomy—the two fields were distinguishable even in their earliest versions. Astronomy began as an attempt to describe and predict the movements of the heavenly bodies; even in its origins, it was inextricably wedded to observational data of a clear and evident sort: the motions of the lights in the sky. Cosmology, however, was distinctly different from astronomy. In simplest terms, it was, from the first, an attempt to *add* to astronomy some sort of a cosmic theory, a theory of Everything, as it were. Cosmology thereby became humanity's fundamental theory about the nature, structure, origin and final destiny of the Universe.

In addition to its topical scope, cosmology differed from astronomy in another important respect. Cosmology relied from the start upon a different kind of reasoning procedure from astronomy. Whereas astronomy was relentlessly observational-data driven, cosmology relied upon argument from very general sorts of analogies based upon everyday experiences. Thus, Thales and water, Anaximenes and air, and so on down the line.

These first philosophical attempts were not anything close to what we would call 'scientific'; yet, for all that, they were still *empirical*, that is, cosmological speculations were firmly grounded in observations of the physical world and its processes. Unfortunately, during the ensuing 2,500 years, cosmology did not get much more scientific than what we see here. Indeed, during the late Medieval period and early Renaissance, it might be argued that cosmology got *less* scientific as its connections with Christian philosophy and theology strengthened. Even the rapid advances in astronomy which constitute the Scientific Revolution (c.1543–1686) did nothing to shake the status of cosmology as a philosophical enterprise. Moreover, the advances in astrophysics in the mid-nineteenth century, as the conceptual apparatus of chemistry and experimental physics were increasingly applied to heavenly bodies, similarly bypassed cosmology.

Quite possibly the most interesting question to ask about the intellectual history and geography we've been looking at here is a straightforward one: what prevented cosmology from entering the ranks of a science? Clearly, astronomy and astrophysics, which seem closely enough related both to each other and to the universe itself, had ascended into science. Why didn't the same happen to cosmology? The reason derives from what constitutes "science" on even its most simpleminded interpretation: a system of theories, some of whose concepts must have applications in material systems.[3]

By this definition, science consists of two related components, theories and their applications in material systems. I've chosen the latter term 'applications in material systems' fairly carefully, even though it sounds pretty vague. Yet, for all its vagueness, it is easy enough to illustrate. For example, when I say that geometrical optics has an application in the material system of my eyeglasses, I mean that by using the concepts and techniques of geometrical optics—tracing ray diagrams, computing indices of refraction, measuring focal lengths, etc.— I can help myself (and others) to see better. Similarly, to extend the notion a bit, when I say that Kepler's celestial dynamics has an application in the solar system, I mean that the solar system can be taken to be *a model* of Kepler's theory. And once a material system is a model for a theory, then all the powerful components of the theory can be used to explain, predict, manipulate, and discover features of the material system so modelled. Thus, another way to talk about a scientific domain is to talk about its theories and their models.

The problem with cosmology, at least until very recently, was that it had no *scientific* theories, and thereby, mutatis mutandi, no models. Consider the problem. In order to have a cosmological theory, one must have a theory of All There Is. That is, one must have in hand a theory of The Whole Universe as a Single Object, a single material system. Contrast this with, say, astrophysics. For an astrophysicist, any old heavenly body can function as the target material system—the sun, the moon, Jupiter's 5th satellite, even something as big as the nebula M31, Andromeda. But for a cosmologist, nothing else will do as a target material system than the whole shooting match, the whole nine yards, taken all together and all at once.

3. Frederick Suppe, *The Semantic Conception of Theories and Scientific Realism* (Urbana: University of Illinois Press, 1989).

One further difficulty perhaps remains hidden. Notice that there is a tight, even symbiotic relationship between theories and their material-system models. The theory in a strong sense not only specifies the nature and structure of what it is that constitutes the model-system itself, it also specifies which features of the model would constitute evidence of the correctness of the theory! Such chicken-versus-egg dilemmas are not at all unusual in science. They are usually worked around by using information and analogies gained from success in theories *other* than the one under development, in domains adjacent or above or below the developing one. But, in the case of the universe itself, what conceivable adjacent system *is* there to work with?

So, not only does a scientific cosmology require a theory of the whole universe taken as an object, discovering the features of a model material system which could be used to develop the theory *also* requires the theory. In short, you can't have scientific cosmology until you have a theory of the universe as a whole. Developing such a theory took no little bit of hard and creative genius.

## 3. A Bit of History

Einstein, of course, was the one who developed the theory, his General Theory of Relativity (GTR), which he offered in 1913 as a candidate to replace Newton's theory of gravity. In 1917, apparently simultaneously, Einstein and Willem deSitter realized that GTR could be applied to the cosmos as a whole. That is, they realized that the universe could be the model material system for GTR.

But it took another 12 years, until 1929, for Einstein, deSitter, and their colleagues to figure out enough of the details of the modeling relation to lead them toward possible observations connecting the theory's concepts with the behavior of the material system of the cosmos. Moreover, the startling observations made by Hubble forced them into the theory as well. We may quickly chart the developments like this:

Steps toward a Consensus 1917–29

|  | *Theoretical* | *Observational* |
|---|---|---|
| 1917 | Einstein, deSitter: world models | |
| 1922–24 | Friedmann: expanding model | Hubble: island universes |
| 1927 | LeMâitre: expanding model | Hubble + Humason: red shift |
| 1929 | Robertson: expanding model | proportional to distance |

Crucial theoretical developments were Friedmann's and LeMâitre's independent discoveries that the equations of GTR concealed a startling fact: any model system for the theory would be unstable—it would tend to either expand or contract. But for still unexplained reasons, Einstein and his co-workers, including Eddington in England, failed to understand the devastating significance of either Friedmann's or LeMâitre's work, even though each man's work had been examined personally by Einstein in both cases, and Eddington in LeMâtre's case! It took Hubble's observations to bring the theoretical contretemps to a fair head.

Hubble had the best glass in the world. Above Mt. Palomar, he also had the best seeing conditions in the astronomer's world. (Remember, this was long before Los Angeles was settled enough to emit either smog or nighttime photons!) Moreover, Hubble was that rarity, an observational astronomer who felt fairly well at home in the abstruse realm of Einstein's theory. (DeSitter was similar in this regard. But his Dutch glass and Dutch sky hardly matched Hubble's counterparts in southern California.) In 1924, Hubble's various observations of the nebulae convinced him that the universe was simply huge, and that the various nebulae were, in fact, galaxies—island universes—just like our home Milky Way.[4] Then, after several years of working with the incredibly sharp-eyed ex-muleskinner Humason, Hubble, in 1929, announced that all the other galaxies in the universe appeared to be red-shifted with respect to us. Even more interestingly, red-shifts appeared to increase with distance, thereby giving way to what came to be called 'Hubble's velocity-distance relation.' Almost at once, astronomers and cosmologists around the world inferred the astounding conclusion implied by Hubble's data: the universe was expanding. We should look briefly at the physical evidence underlying this dramatic sequence of events.

We are all familiar with the sound of a noisy vehicle—a screaming ambulance or a whistling train—first coming toward us, then just passing, then going away. Just as it passes, the sound undergoes a lowering of pitch, there to remain until silenced in the distance. Various investigations have uncovered the cause of this easily observed phenomenon: when moving toward us, the frequency of the sound is higher than when moving away from us. The human ear perceives this difference in frequency as a difference in pitch, with higher frequency perceived as higher pitch. Professor Doppler investigated the effect, thereby earning the right to be its namesake.

A similar phenomenon occurs in the case of light. When a light-

---

4. R. W. Smith, *The Expanding Universe* (Cambridge: Cambridge University Press, 1982).

emitting object is moving toward us, its frequency is higher than were it moving away. Human eyes perceive higher frequencies as blue, lower frequencies as red. Consequently, when Hubble and Humason's photo plates of the surrounding galaxies revealed certain key atomic spectra to be redder than those experienced in earthly labs, astronomers and cosmologists concluded that the surrounding galaxies were moving away from us.

The reaction to Hubble's astounding data was dramatic. Einstein, deSitter and Eddington suffered sudden cases of remembrance, exhuming Friedmann's and LeMâitre's works essentially overnight. Theory wedded data, and, at the aforementioned 1931 meeting of the British Association, consensus issued forth. At that point, a recognizable ancestor of what we now call Big Bang cosmology was born. It looked like this:

---

Consensus Cosmological Model, c. 1931

I. *The Universe Began in an Einstein State:* Dense and Static.

II. *It Then Collapsed into an Expanding Le Mâitre State.*

III. *It Will End in a deSitter State:* Diffuse and Ever-Expanding.

---

Unfortunately, despite the consensus, not all was to be well.

## 4. "Doing" Cosmology

We have already noted some of the difficulties involved in modeling GTR on the cosmos, worst among which resides finding observable behavior connectable to the theory. Interaction between Hubble's data and Friedmann/LeMâitre versions of GTR is just about the most beautiful example we could expect. But beyond this case, the theory just plain doesn't present many implications, nor does the cosmos-as-a-whole present much behavior, for ever the twain to meet. Moreover, within two short years, the theory itself was going to blow up in the face of the cosmologists. The problem is this: most equations have just one or two solutions. We all remember the general form of the solution to the quadratic equation: $x = (-b \pm \sqrt{[b^2 - 4ac]})/2a$. What should be noted is that two, and only two, solutions are indicated for the equation. Most equations, or sets of equations, work out this way. Consequently, when scientists work with the equations of a theory, they are, at the same time, working out which small set of solutions for the theory could serve as applications—models—in the physical world. But GTR turned out to be rather more nasty in this regard than previous theories had been.

When Einstein and deSitter had offered their cosmological models as applications of GTR, it was thought that their two solutions were the *only* solutions to the equations. Friedmann's and LeMâitre's solutions were essentially equivalent, and, according to Eddington and the others, provided the intermediate solution between the extremes of Einstein and deSitter.[5] Now there are three solutions. Still manageable. But several years more work revealed a vast succession of solutions to the equations. It became immediately obvious to all the practitioners that theory in this case was not to be of any major help in seeking models within the cosmos. And without theoretical constraints, observations, already difficult by the nature of the case, would become even more difficult to carry out: after all, it takes theory to tell us what counts as useful observations. Some shortcut or another would have to be taken. Enter Eddington and Dirac and their famous numerology.

Eddington and Dirac were the foremost theorists of their time. Dirac, indeed, is one of the foremost theorists of this century. Both men felt the unease any good theoretician feels when he finds himself forced toward experiment and observation in order to discover things about the world. Since Pythagoras and Plato, an unbroken stream of mathematical theorists—including such luminaries as Descartes, Kepler, and Leibniz—has held it possible to find knowledge through reason alone. These thinkers have, to a man, believed that introspection of reasoning itself, especially its mathematical content, should, could, and would reveal the frame of the world, the nature and structure of the cosmos. Eddington and Dirac were paid-up members of this illustrious club. Both, for various reasons we needn't go into here, fastened upon the fundamental constants of nature as sources of knowledge in and of themselves, independent of their empirical connections.[6]

The constants of nature are certain fundamental parameters that appear in the equations of physics. Examples of such constants are the masses of proton and electron, the speed of light, Planck's constant, the constants of the four forces (weak, strong, electromagnetic, and gravitational). In general, physicists find out about the constants by measuring them, a point which irritates theorists no end, because it implies that the constants are *arbitrary*—they aren't derived from anything more fundamental. Like Popeye, they just am what they am. Which drives theorists crazy, especially committed mathematical theorists such as Eddington and Dirac. Theorists would much rather *derive*

5. W. deSitter, "The Expanding Universe," *Scientia* 49 (1931): 1–10.
6. P. A. M. Dirac, "The Cosmological Constants," *Nature* (London) 20 (1937): 323. A. S. Eddington, *New Pathways in Science* (Ann Arbor: University of Michigan Press, 1959), chap. 11.

the values of the constants from something, anything, else, rather than measure them. And *real* theorists, ones such as Eddington and Dirac, have genuine philosopher's dreams about the whole project, as Whittaker's description notes well:

All the quantitative propositions of physics, that is, the exact values of the pure numbers that are constants of science, may be deduced by logical reasoning from qualitative assertions without making any use of quantitative data derived from observation.[7]

Eddington's project was to attempt to combine various constants in such ways that their dimensions disappeared, producing, thereby, dimensionless or pure numbers. What turns out to be puzzling about these efforts is that, apparently independently of which constants are compared, for example, the ratio of the strengths of the electrical and gravitational forces, it is found that the result of the comparison *always* ends up to be an extremely large number, about $10^{40}$, which is approximately equal to the ratio of the size of the universe to the size of an electron, which finding is patently absurd. Because of the rather astonishing equivalences between these very large numbers, they soon acquired the name "large number coincidences."[8] The final stage of Eddington's work was the attempt to demonstrate that the coincidental character of the large-number ratios dissolved once it was seen that they were rooted in the nature of the knowing being, rather than in aspects of Nature in and of herself.

Dirac did similar things. Dirac's jumping-off place was Eddington's work. After noting that Eddington most likely was generally correct in the cases of the smaller dimensionless numbers, Dirac argued that, in the case of the larger numbers, a new analysis should be made. Then Dirac made his fateful suggestion: careful manipulation of the fundamental constants revealed that many of them bore some connection to time. Moreover, if, as the consensus view held, the universe had existed only for some definite time since the initial Big Bang, then perhaps the values of the fundamental constants weren't arbitrary at all but were merely reflections of their existence during the present universal epoch. At earlier or later times, the values of the 'constants' would be different from their present values. In other words, the constants weren't really constant.

At this point, we have all we need to generate anthropic-principle

7. James R. Newman, *The World of Mathematics* (New York: Simon and Schuster, 1956), vol. 2, 1017.
8. See J. D. Barrow and F. J. Tipler, *The Anthropic Cosmological Principle* (Oxford: Oxford Univesity Press, 1988), 224–38.

cosmologizing. We have, first, a science which is difficult to do because it is difficult to connect theory and observations. Second, this science is rich, indeed, profligate in theories; something, anything, must be done to constrain theory proliferation. Third, major players in this science reveal themselves (as we should have expected) to be mathematicians in the rich tradition of Pythagoras, Plato, Descartes, Kepler, and Leibniz, committed thereby to the exploration and exploitation of rationalist mathematical speculation in the absence of data. Finally, we have Eddington and Dirac's efforts to manipulate the fundamental constants of nature, hoping thereby to find the correct theory of the cosmos. Together, these four elements strongly imply the emergence of anthropic-principle cosmology. What is surprising is that it took nearly 30 years for it to come into existence.

## 5. Dicke and the Modern "Coincidences"

Dirac had suggested that various 'numerological' relationships between the fundamental constants depended upon the fact that the universe had evolved for some particular period of time since the initial explosion. Princeton's R. H. Dicke proposed an underlying causal basis for the relationships. Note, he remarked, that Dirac's coincidences are strange only if time is allowed to vary independently. However, on the assumption of an evolutionary universe, it can be shown that $T$, the Hubble age of the Universe,

is somewhat limited by the biological requirements to be met during the epoch of man. The first of these requirements is that the universe, hence galaxy, shall have aged sufficiently for there to exist elements other than hydrogen. *It is well known that carbon is required to make physicists.*[9]

Dicke's suggestion is on the face of it outrageous. What he implies is that the cosmic coincidences are not coincidences at all. Rather, they in some sense reflect the fact that human beings are observing the universe, which necessitates certain features of the cosmos to be the case. As Dicke's example clearly implies, the physicist observing the interactions of the fundamental forces is a carbon-based living system. Obviously, the universe must be such that a being of this type could (and did) evolve. Since the initial state of the universe contained only hydrogen, a certain modicum of atomic evolution is called for in order to produce the higher chemical elements, for example, carbon. Atomic evolution takes place in the cores of stars. Then they blow up, spewing

9. R. H. Dicke, "Dirac's Cosmology and Mach's Principle," in John Leslie, ed., *Physical Cosmology and Philosophy* (New York: Macmillan, 1990), 122.

the trans-hydrogen elements into space. These remnants must then coalesce into a second stellar system, where, apparently, biological evolution begins. All these processes take time. Consequently, carbon-
based observers may look out upon only certain sorts of universes.
Other sorts would be forbidden. For example, no carbon-based observer could look out upon a very young universe, one whose stars had
only begun to transmute hydrogen into helium. Nor, of course, could
a carbon-based observer look out upon a universe consisting only of
geriatric stars, red giants and white dwarfs, whose radiation densities
would not support habitable planetary systems. Thus, reasoning *solely*
from the fact that he was there to observe the universe, Dicke concluded that the universe he observed *must* have certain special characteristics.

We need to pause for a moment to consider just how preposterous
Dicke's proposal in fact was. Consider first Copernicus. That noble
Canon had begun the movement to de-anthropomorphize cosmology.
Humankind, he suggested, is not at the center of the universe; rather,
we are in the third heaven, counting out from the sun. Kepler's work,
plus speculations of various others, went on to show that Copernicus's
suggestion needed strengthening. Not only are we not just three orbs
out from the center, there is no center: the universe is *infinite* in all
directions! From that time forth unto this day, the constant and resolute
intention of physicists, astronomers, astrophysicists, and cosmologists
has been to obey Canon Copernicus's dictum that humankind occupies
no special place in the universe, nor, indeed, was anything of importance in the universe to be correlated with humanity's existence. Dicke's
hypothesis that the observed values of the fundamental constants of
nature depended in a certain way upon the fact of humankind's existence flew directly, and scandalously, in the face of this 400-year-old
scientific tradition. Thirteen years later, Brandon Carter made things
even worse.

## 6. Carter Chooses a Name and Opens Pandora's Box

Brandon Carter had been taken with Dicke's reasoning and had
bruited about his own musings on the topic at various meetings of cosmologists and astrophysicists. Collins and Hawking had referred to his
work in passing,[10] and finally, John Archibald Wheeler, one of the
Grand Old Men of theoretical physics, asked Carter to say something

10. C. B. Collins and S. W. Hawking, "Why Is the Universe Isotropic?" *Astrophysical
Journal* 180 (1973): 317–34.

formally about his extensions of Dicke's work. The result was Carter's now famous (or, to some, notorious) paper, "Large Number Coincidences and the Anthropic Principle in Cosmology."[11] In this paper, Carter laid out a taxonomy of prediction-types based upon Dicke's analysis of the coincidences. He was up front about Dicke's inference ticket, even going so far as to name it: "these predictions do require the use of what may be termed the *anthropic principle* to the effect that what we can expect to observe must be restricted by the conditions necessary for our presence as observers."[12] Carter told me that he is sorry that he used the term "anthropic," since, as everyone immediately noted, two unhappy specters were incumbent upon this name: first, "anthropic" reminds people of "anthropocentric"; second, the central issue is that of the existence of an *observer*, and not of a *human* observer, which latter is suggested by "anthropic." Clearly, this latter point is well taken. Indeed, none of the principals (Dicke, Carter, Collins, and Hawking) restricted the argument to human observers alone. But if this allays doubts about the second problem, the first specter cannot be so easily dispelled: anthropic arguments *are* anthropocentric just insofar as they rely upon human observership as their starting point. "Back to Ptolemy!" is the import of anthropic-principle thinking, some critics feared. But other problems beyond its naming haunted Carter's exposition.

Carter's taxonomy of prediction-types introduced everyone, albeit only implicitly, to a problem with anthropic arguments which has plagued us to the present day. His taxonomy distinguishes between predictions "which only require the use of a 'weak' anthropic principle" (WAP) and "those which require the invocation of an extended (and hence, rather more questionable) 'strong' anthropic principle" (SAP). Later workers, especially Barrow and Tipler,[13] extended the taxonomic nomenclature into the soon-parodied WAP, SAP, FAP (final anthropic principle), and so on. The problem is obvious: the term "anthropic principle" stands for no one thing, but rather stands, it would seem, for a *style* or a *genre* of cosmological inferences and scenarios. Hence, the first task involved in understanding anthropic-principle cosmologizing is to come to some sort of an understanding of the various elements of the genre. Let's take a look at some examples.

11. Brandon Carter, "Large Number Coincidences and the Anthropic Principle in Cosmology," in Leslie, *Physical Cosmology*, 126.
12. Ibid.
13. Barrow and Tipler, *Anthropic Principle*.

## 7. Anthropic Arguments: A Taxonomy

Using the by-now-accepted terminology, anthropic arguments range from weak to strong to final. A likely start is to be made with an example of a 'weak' argument.

### 7.1. Weak Anthropic Principle: An Example

Collins and Hawking argue that "since it would seem that the existence of galaxies is a necessary condition for the development of intelligent life, the answer to the question 'why is the universe isotropic?' is 'because we are here'."[14] A perfectly straightforward rendering of this argument would be to conditionalize it to read:

> Human observers exist only if the universe is isotropic. (7.1)

This rendering illuminates Collins and Hawking's idea that the observed features of the universe provide necessary conditions for human observership. It seems to me that this statement, if understood as intended, is not only uncontroversial, it is innocuous. Indeed, it is hard to see how it could be useful to a cosmologist. One clue, however, could be Carter's idea that anthropic-principle inferences produce *predictions*. In this case, the consequent of 7.1 would need to be re-phrased to take account of the fact that it represented a whole class of heretofore unknown things:

> Human observers exist only if [all the conditions necessary for this to be true are in fact true]. (7.11)

I use this re-phrasing to indicate that at the present moment we don't know what all these conditions are; only in this way could anything of the general form of 7.1 ever hope to be called a 'prediction'. I should also note that several authors, especially during the initial stages of this sort of work, referred to 7.1 and its ilk as 'explanations.'[15] That is, they believed that, for example, the universe's isotropy, is 'explained' by the fact of human existence. This seems to me to be not only odd but unfortunate. Whatever methodological and/or heuristic value WAP-based arguments might possess, they most certainly don't possess any *explanatory* value. But stronger anthropic-principle arguments *do* exist, and they *do* possess explanatory power—at least they would, if they were acceptable, something which most cosmologists deny. Moreover, and here we come to the point of all this, their putative explanatory value

14. Collins and Hawking, "Isotropic," 332.
15. George Gale, "The Anthropic Principle," *Scientific American* 245 (1981): 154–71.

is linked to their undeniably *teleological* character. We'll examine these cases in the next section.

First, however, I would like to briefly note the relation between the style of anthropic cosmologizing discussed here—WAP cosmologizing—and our central issue, namely, the question whether cosmology is physics or metaphysics. It seems to me that use of anthropic-principle argument(s) to disclose observable features of the universe that are necessary to the existence of human observers is perfectly acceptable physics. There is no more metaphysics involved in reasoning from human existence to its necessary conditions than from pink litmus' turning blue to *its* necessary conditions. On this account, I find puzzling some of the hand-wringing which has gone on in certain quarters regarding anthropic-principle cosmologizing.[16] Yet, as we shall now see, not all uses of anthropic-principle arguments are so innocent of metaphysics.

## 7.2. *Strong Anthropic Principle: An Example*

Collins and Hawking's argument above can be given a different reading. Consider the following slight variation on 7.1: 'Because we are here, the universe is isotropic.' From this it is not such a long inferential leap to the rendering:

*The universe is isotropic in order to bring about human existence.* (7.2)

A reading such as this, it is argued, flows easily from what Barrow and Tipler give as the strong anthropic principle (SAP):

*SAP: The universe must have those properties which allow life to develop within it at some stage in its history.*[17] (7.21)

Even cursory examination of these two propositions reveals that everything depends upon the "must" in 7.21. If the "must" involves no more than the strength of an ordinary argument's "therefore," that is, the strength required to connect necessary conditions to their antecedent conditions, then we are left with only WAP-style argumentation. But 7.2 is clearly and straightforwardly *teleological* or *finalistic* in logical form; somehow, then, the "must" of 7.21 *must* be of a sort to support this much stronger form. I used to think that I understood how proponents of SAP cosmologizing got the job of supporting 7.2 accomplished . . . but I'm no longer quite so sure. But let me rehearse the moves in any case.

16. Heinz R. Pagels, "A Cozy Cosmology," in Leslie, *Physical Cosmology*, 174–80. Stephen Jay Gould, "Mind and Supermind," in Leslie, *Physical Cosmology*, 181–88.
17. Barrow and Tipler, *Anthropic Principle*, 21.

## 7.3. Fine Tuning and Many Worlds

Large-number coincidences led to initial efforts by Eddington and Dirac to produce new cosmologies. Dicke, inspired by Eddington's and Dirac's motives but not their cosmologies, suggested that the large-number coincidences were a relatively straightforward consequence of when, and by whom, the observations supporting the coincidences were being made. Carter and his colleagues called this argument genre "anthropic principle" and went on to distinguish various styles within the genre, each possessing its own peculiar strength (and, I suppose, attendant fascination). But it was immediately clear to many—most certainly to Carter—that any argument stronger than WAP couldn't be founded solely upon the coincidences, since their degree of puzzlingness was dissipated easily enough through WAP alone. Hence, since some cosmologists seemed to feel that there was more to anthropic-principle argumentation than merely the domain exploited by WAP, subsequent efforts explored the region beyond that of the merely puzzling large-number coincidences. What was found there was beyond puzzling; it was, in fact, just a bit unsettling. Whereas, in the case of the large-number coincidences, several distinct ratios between various constants have to roughly agree in value, further investigation revealed so many parameters that had to agree that it turned out to be just a bit scary. In other words, what had once seemed coincidental, now seemed conspiratorial. Let me use a homely example.

Consider Goldilocks. In order to make the Three Bears story work out, Goldilocks has to find overlapping filters or "windows" of acceptability: the porridge, say, has three *independent* dimensions whose windows of acceptability must overlap—temperature: can't be too hot or cold; sweetness—can't have too much sugar or too little; size—bowl can't be too large or too small. Only if acceptable values for each of these three dimensions are *conjointly* present, will the porridge be acceptable. Note that the *im*probability of this conjunction occurring goes up directly as the number of dimensions—the number of windows which must overlap—increases. Moreover, if Goldilocks is very sensitive to each of these parameters (temperature, sweetness, and size), if she is picky, picky, picky, the size of each individual window goes down, again increasing the *im*probability of her liking what she finds. For Goldilocks to accept it, the porridge must indeed be fine-tuned to her tastes.

If we take the suitability of the universe for life as the analogue of the acceptability of the porridge, then life itself is the analogue of Goldilocks. And, as it turned out, not only is life picky, picky, picky (very sensitive to small changes in values of the variables), the number of variables involved in suitability for life is horrifically large. For both these reasons, some *real* fine tuning is required for suitability for life. Goldilocks had only three dimensions of acceptability; life has an enormously large number, no one knows how many. But, to put it bluntly, the result of all this is that the existence of life no longer looks coincidental, it looks suspect. So enters the problem of fine tuning: too many too-tiny windows had to line up perfectly for life apparently to have passed through them *at all*, let alone easily.

Fine-tuning 'co-incidences' appear at all scales. On the largest scale, that of the cosmos itself, two global features are exceedingly improbable: isotropy and flatness. Isotropy is a feature of the peculiar electromagnetic radiation observed at all angles in the sky. Namely, this radiation appears of uniform character to within one part in $10^4$. According to Collins and Hawking, the initial conditions required to bring about such uniformity are extremely unlikely. Flatness is an equally disturbing feature of the universe. The term 'flatness' refers to a qualitatively singular member of the set of possible fates of the Universe's expansion. The two predominant (and opposed) consequences of the expansion of the universe are its being *open*, or its being *closed*. In the latter condition, the expansion will at some point cease, and gravity will subsequently bring about the Universe's collapse, thereby bringing about Big Crunch, and, perhaps, another Big Bang. An open Universe, on the other hand, is one which will expand forever, eluding eternally the forces of gravity straining to end the expansion. Yet, open and closed are not the only two possible characters of the universe; a third, and quite singular, possibility exists as well: the *flat* Universe. The flat Universe is the precise intermediate state between the other two. In that state, the Universe is slowing down *at precisely the rate of expansion*. In other words, there is an exact balance between the two rates. Cosmologists today estimate that it is likely that the Universe is flat. It is also estimated that the initial conditions of the Universe would have had to have been tuned to one part in $10^{55}$ to bring this about.[18]

But fine-tuning apparently occurs in the middle dimensions as well as at cosmic scale. Barrow and Tipler, for example, devote a dense chapter to the various stringencies life places upon biochemistry.[19] Carbon, oxygen, and nitrogen, for example, each has its own peculiar properties relevant to the existence of life as we know it. The chapter

18. B. J. Carr, "On the Origin, Evolution and Purpose of the Physical Universe," in Leslie, *Physical Cosmology*, 134–53.
19. Barrow and Tipler, *Anthropic Principle*, chap. 8.

climaxes with a ten-item list of "crucial steps in the evolution of Man." Crucial step 1, for example, is the "development of the DNA-based genetic code," while crucial step 10 concludes the list with the evolution of *Homo sapiens* in the chordate line.

Fine-tuning at the smallest scale, the quantum dimension, is no less evident. Among many other instances, Carr and Rees note that if the weak fine-structure constant $\alpha_w$ were only slightly different, than either the universe would consist entirely of helium, or contain no helium at all.[20] Insofar as helium is the first-stage product of thermonuclear burning in stars, extravagances or dearths of the gas would bode ill for chemicals synthesized from it—carbon, for example. Leslie compiles many of these smallest-scale fine-tuning necessities into a very impressive litany.[21] A few examples:

Strong force 2% stronger: no atoms.

Strong force 5% weaker: no neutron-based nuclear burning.

Electromagnetic fine-structure constant stronger by 1 part in $10^{40}$: only red stars.

Electromagnetic fine-structure constant weaker by 1 part in $10^{40}$: only blue stars.

Gravitational fine-structure constant 10% stronger: small, hot stars.

Gravitational fine-structure constant 10% weaker: perhaps no stars.

Other authors mention other examples, but the main point is quite clear in all this: There is a large number of basic parameters that are implicated in the existence of observers in the Universe. Moreover, and perhaps even more disconcertingly, the values that *each* of these parameters *must* take if life is to come into existence, can vary, if at all, within a distressingly narrow interval. In other words, there are a number of windows through which life must pass *in series*, and each of the windows is exceedingly small. Life appears implausibly improbable.

Apparently only two hypotheses might serve to explain away our unease at the degree of difficulty life's existence faced and conquered: (1) Someone *aimed* life perfectly well, thereby successfully navigating it through the difficult passage, through the narrow, deep straits, constituted by the immense stack of windows; or, alternatively, (2) life had so very many shots at the lined-up windows that eventually it successfully passed through the straits. Hypothesis 1 is obviously a contemporary version of the Design argument, as so ably argued by Barrow

20. B. J. Carr and M. J. Rees, "The Anthropic Principle and the Structure of the Physical World," *Nature* (London) 278 (1979): 605–12.

21. John Leslie, *Universes* (London: Routledge, 1989), chap. 2.

and Tipler, and defended so well by John Leslie. Hypothesis 2 is the Many Worlds hypothesis, about which more in a moment.

To look back at the question how to justify the SAP and its teleological interpretation in 7.2, most certainly a theistic interpretation of the design argument will do the job. The "must" of 7.21 carries the same strength that any "must" would in a statement such as, for example, "The door must be placed here, for that's where the Architect planned it to be." On this account, to say that the universe *must* be such as to admit life, is to say no more than that the universe is *designed* to admit life. Again I return to our initial question: is this sort of cosmologizing physics or metaphysics? The answer seems straightforward enough: using SAP argumentation to entrain a Designer is metaphysics. Period. Is there an alternative? Yes. Is the alternative equally metaphysical? Yes. No. I don't know. Maybe. Which brings us to the hypothesis of Many Worlds.

Instead of invoking a Designer, Who organizes the whole thing from the ground up in order that it might contain life, thereby passing through the narrow straits of the lined up windows, an alternative invocation is The Infinity Mechanism. We are all familiar with The Infinity Mechanism, since, after all, it is the device driving the plausibility of all those monkeys and all those typewriters writing all those sonnets of Shakespeare. It is the device relied upon by Aristotle when he claimed that some motion must be eternal, since, if it weren't but time were, at some time no motion would exist. And, most appositely, it is the device entrained by the quantum physics dictum "Everything permitted, is required." That is to say, each and every event with a non-zero probability will occur, given an infinite series of time and/or events.[22] Obviously, if the occurrence of life has a non-zero probability—a fact we are quite sure of, no matter *how* narrow the straits formed by the lined-up windows—then it is required. Life, on this account, *must* occur. This is simple enough. What is really interesting, however, is the mode of physicalizing The Infinity Mechanism. In modern cosmology, The Infinity Mechanism, when coupled to a realistic interpretation of probabilistic quantum measurement, becomes the Many Worlds.

Although the 'parallel worlds' theme—many worlds in adjacent 'dimensions'—has long been a favorite in science fiction stories, it has not found much favor (or use) in science, ancient or modern. Indeed, Leibniz's notion of possible worlds was the first such model ever deployed. Among contemporary theories, only quantum mechanics has em-

---

22. E. P. Tryon, "Is the Universe a Vacuum Fluctuation?" in Leslie, *Physical Cosmology*, 216–19.

ployed a version of such a structure. It developed as a possible solution to a stubborn problem in quantum measurement. Quantum theory is inherently statistical, that is, its formalism inescapably entrains probability statements in its description of the world. For example, when used to predict where electrons emerging from a slit will strike a screen, the quantum formalism couches its predictions in strictly probabilistic terms in a "wave function": there is, for example, a 21% probability that the electron will impact at point A, and a 28% probability it will impact at A' . . . and so on. Yet, when the electron in fact impacts, it impacts at one point and one point only, no matter how long the string of probabilities called out in the wave function. In this situation, what is one to make of the string of probabilities? What is their status, given that one and only one of the predicted probabilities can be accurate? Since measurements are inherently unique, and quantum predictions are inherently statistical, how are we to conceive of the relationship between the world as measured and the world as quantum predicted?

A majority of physicists hold to the Copenhagen Interpretation, which proposes that the probabilities are accurate until the measurement is made, at which point, and with infinite speed, the probabilities collapse into the unique value measured, which, obviously, at that point, itself becomes accurate. Some physicists are uncomfortable with the Copenhagen Interpretation: "the wave function collapse postulated by the Copenhagen Interpretation is dynamically ridiculous, and this interpretation is difficult if not impossible to apply in quantum cosmology."[23] Doubts such as these prompted Hugh Everett, alone at first, and later with B. S. DeWitt, to develop an alternative interpretation of what happens during measurement on quantum mechanical systems.[24]

According to this interpretation, which, for obvious reasons is called the Many-Worlds Interpretation, the wave function is interpreted realistically, that is, it is interpreted to be *literally true*: each of the probabilities calculated applies to some particular world in which, were the measurement to be carried out, the value would correspond to the probable value in the wave function. From this it follows that measurement does not 'collapse' the probability function into a unique value; rather, it simply moves the observer along his or her own world's own worldline among the infinitely many possible ones. All of the probable states exist together, each in its own world, all "parallel" in some sense to one another in the quantum phase-space dimension.

23. Barrow and Tipler, *Anthropic Principle*, 496.
24. B. S. DeWitt and N. Graham, eds., *The Many-Worlds Interpretation of Quantum Mechanics* (Princeton: Princeton University Press, 1973).

Starting from this notion of the Everett ensemble of many-worlds, cosmologists began to invent ways in which the universe might multiply itself. Driven from the first by worries about the existence of life, means have been found for the universe to propagate itself in space, in time, and in nearly every other conceivable dimension.

What is at issue here, as I once called it, is Cosmological Fecundity.[25] If life is incredibly improbable, how can we reduce our wonder at its existence? One way to bring about the reduction is with an increase in the number of tries the universe gets to make. In other words, if the universe is not one but very many, then most certainly life will come to be in at least one of the worlds, no matter how improbable this occurrence might be. If an infinite number of monkeys can write all of Shakespeare, then most certainly an infinite number of universes can at least once contain life.

This is neither the time nor the place to go any further into the various intricacies of how to create many universes. Suffice it to say that multiple-universe theory is a major research area in physical cosmology. It's extremely difficult to work one's way through all these hypotheses, especially since some are so bizarre. Open universes, closed universes, flat universes, universes side-by-side in time. How is one to choose? My own suspicion is that our universe is a closed one, that each Big Bang is both preceded *and* succeeded by a Big Crunch, and that the reason we're here to observe the highly improbable fact of our own existence is due to nothing more than being in the right spacetime in the right universe.

Is there anything finalistic or teleological about *our* existence? On this account, the Many Worlds account, no, certainly there's nothing teleological about our having come to be. But suppose we imbed the issue into sort of a *super*-Universal domain, and go on to say the following:

*Super-SAP: The ensemble of all universes must have those properties which allow life to develop within it at some stage in its history.* (7.3)

What can we say about the "must" here? Would it support a teleological statement such as 7.2, with its claim that isotropy exists in order to bring about life? I honestly don't know. Moreover, I don't want much to think about it at this late stage of our analysis, because it generates both a headache and an infinite regress.

Again, our initial theme returns in yet another guise: is many-worlds

25. George Gale, "Cosmological Fecundity: Theories of Multiple Universes," in Leslie, *Physical Cosmology*, 189–206.

cosmologizing "metaphysical"? Probably. Especially if the reactions of many scientists are any clue to metaphysical status! Most certainly the various physical mechanisms chosen as instantiations of The Infinity Mechanism have been violently criticized by astrophysicists and cosmologists alike. Quantum-theoretical many-worlds mechanisms in particular have been vilified as "comic book," "science fiction," "metaphysical monstrosities" and so on. Yet, in my own examination of the situation, at least *some* of the many-worlds mechanisms come quite close to quietly tunneling through the barrier separating metaphysics from physics, thence to reside safely on the physics side. Many-worlds-in-time mechanisms, for example (oscillating universes, as they're sometimes called), propose reasonably plausible, not unfamiliar, physical processes as prime movers in the bang-crunch-bang-crunch cycle. Of course it is true that we have no theory that can safely guide us through the entropy-scrambling maelstrom of Big Crunch, yet, it is easy enough to envisage what might happen. And, most importantly, no mysterious forces, mystic entities, or supernatural powers are required to make the thing work. Probably. But, if we define science so as to require possibilities for observation, what we're talking about here ain't science. It's metaphysics. As a closing shot, I'd like to bring up what I personally take to be the most outrageous bit of anthropic-principle argumentation, John Archibald Wheeler's participatory anthropic principle (PAP).

### 7.4. Observership

John Archibald Wheeler takes quantum mechanics seriously. Moreover, Wheeler is not unfamiliar with the wiles of philosophers, especially metaphysicians, idealistic metaphysicians.[26] These two propensities of Wheeler have led him into what some take to be the most bizarre of all anthropic-principle interpretations. But far from being bizarre, Wheeler's interpretation evidently is quantum-mechanically orthodox to its core. In other words, Wheeler's position isn't bizarre, *quantum mechanics* is bizarre! Here's how the scheme works.

In quantum mechanics, epistemology often slides over into metaphysics. In fact, the elision is typical. Heisenberg's uncertainty principle, for example, is often taken to mean that a particle's conjoint momentum/position is in reality fuzzy; that is, the fuzziness isn't limited to our knowledge. Many-worlds versions of quantum mechanics, another example, are nothing more than strictly metaphysically realistic interpretations of the probability calculus which is the heart of quan-

26. John A. Wheeler, "Genesis and Observership" in *Foundational Problems in the Special Sciences* ed. R. E. Butts and J. Hintikka (Dordrecht: Reidel, 1977), 32.

tum theory. But the third example of this tendency for epistemology to slide into metaphysics is the most central one. I refer here to the 'quantum observability principle.'[27] According to the dictates of this principle, quantum variables have no values until measured. Slightly stronger versions of the principle go so far as to state that not only the values of the variables, but particle properties associated (causally) with the variable, don't exist. In other words, if we, say, measure a particle's spin at the experiment's entrance, and then measure it again at the exit, we are not only not allowed to claim that we know what the spin value *was* during the unmeasured interval, we are not allowed to claim that the particle even *had* a spin during the interval. Put pithily, the quantum reality principle states that what is not observed, doesn't exist.

Wheeler takes the quantum reality principle as Gospel. Moreover, he has read his Berkeley and the German Idealists carefully.[28] It is no wonder that he quite enthusiastically endorses the consequence of the conjunction of the two themes, which come together in what is called the participatory anthropic principle (PAP):

*PAP: Observers are necessary to bring the Universe into being.*

If what was desired was a mechanism to justify the SAP, well, this mechanism does the job with a vengeance! Most certainly, the teleological statement of SAP at 7.2 ("the universe is isotropic in order to bring about human existence") follows with facility from PAP. But, in what can only be called quantum 'justice', the statement, "Humans exist in order to bring about an isotropic universe" is equally true. Causality is circular (or, at least circular-in-time, which makes it sort of spiral, I suppose), a kind of feedback loop, or, as Wheeler has said, "a self-excited circuit." This latter notion refers to those well-known oscillator circuits whose very layout bring about generation of a radio frequency wave. In that sense, the underlying mechanism is no more nor less mysterious than the Infinity Mechanism underlying the many-worlds interpretations; nor, I suppose, than the Deity underlying the Designer interpretation. Clearly, however, there is genuine, out-there-in-the-world teleology only in the first or third interpretation, albeit genuine teleology generated via different means. The Designer's purposes undergird the finalistic tendencies of the designed universe in the first interpretation; the Observer's purposes play the same role in the third, participatory universe. But the second interpretation, the many-worlds

27. Barrow and Tipler, *Anthropic Principle*, 470.
28. John A. Wheeler, "Beyond the Black Hole," in *Some Strangeness in the Proportion: A Centennial Symposium to Celebrate the Achievements of Albert Einstein*, ed. Harry Wolff (Reading, Mass.: Addison-Wesley, 1980), 374.

universe has no genuine, metaphysical, out-there-in-the-world teleology. It is only upon looking *from* our present position in that second type of universe, back *towards* our highly unlikely beginnings, that the appearance of teleological forces swims into view. These forces, however, are merely the result of our perspective, our 'Whiggish' perspective, on the question how such an unlikely event as our own existence came to be.

Of course our initial issue raises its ugly but fascinating head once again: Is Wheeler's PAP physical or metaphysical? It seems to me fairly clear that it's metaphysical, and this not the least because it is so clearly teleological. Imputation of teleological processes—*correct* imputation, that is—to physical systems inevitably relegates that physical system to metaphysics. In the end, then, anthropic cosmologizing—insofar as it involves teleological processes such as those seen in the strong and participatory versions of the anthropic principle—is metaphysical in an old-fashioned, nonscientific sense. Many-worlds causal accounts of anthropic cosmologizing, however, are not inevitably metaphysical in the old-fashioned, nonscientific sense. In other words, it seems possible (but only 'just') to do anthropic cosmologizing in a many-worlds context, and still stay upon the secure path of a science. Of course there are a number of philosophers and cosmologists who disagree with this view. But the dispute in and of itself doesn't require us to disallow all anthropic cosmologizing. There's still room for observers in the universe!

# 11     Modern Natural Science and the Intelligibility of Human Experience

## RICHARD F. HASSING

*Yet prudence is always endangered by false doctrines about the whole of which man is a part, by false theoretical opinions; prudence is therefore always in need of defense against such opinions, and that defense is necessarily theoretical. The theory defending prudence is, however, misunderstood if it is taken to be the basis of prudence.*

—Leo Strauss[1]

The title of this paper embraces topics of immense breadth, defining a subject matter lying well beyond the bounds of what can be competently undertaken in a brief essay. I would like, nevertheless, to discuss these things because of widespread beliefs that natural science either contradicts the intelligibility of human experience or is the very best ground on which to make human experience intelligible. My intention is to criticize these beliefs. These two beliefs correspond to two conceptions of the unity of science: the conventional reductionist paradigm and the new holist paradigm.[2] The conventional reductionist paradigm originates in the physics and philosophy of the seventeenth century. Supplemented by philosophic interpretation of twentieth-century physics, the reductionist paradigm receives its canonical articulation within philosophy of science in the positivist unity-of-science program culminating in the 1950s.[3] The new holist paradigm, on the

---

1. "An Epilogue," in *Essays on the Scientific Study of Politics*, ed. Herbert J. Storing (New York: Holt, Rinehart and Winston, 1962), 308; reprinted in Strauss, *Liberalism Ancient and Modern* (New York: Basic Books, 1968), 206.

2. The correspondence between believers and paradigms is different in the two cases. (By paradigm I mean predominant or authoritative model; the Kuhnian sense of radical incommensurability is not intended.) The belief that natural science makes human experience unintelligible is held by many students of the history of philosophy as a despairing reaction to longstanding claims made by the proponents of reductionism; believers are not the proponents. The opposite belief—that (recent) natural science is the best basis for understanding the human—*is* held by certain proponents of evolutionary holism, as discussed in section 4 of this paper.

3. *International Encyclopedia of Unified Science*, eds. O. Neurath et al. (combined

other hand, arises within the recent ferment in natural science in connection with what is called "the evolutionary sequence," an unpretentious name for a very large item, namely, the entire evolving universe, from the alleged Big Bang, through emergent structures, to the present order of chemical elements and compounds, living species, and astronomical systems.[4] The core of the reductionist conception is the old materialist doctrine that complex wholes are in principle reducible to simple parts. The core of the new conception, in fundamental contrast, is that complex wholes emerge in the course of cosmic evolution in such a way that they are, in principle, irreducible to simpler parts.[5]

The dichotomy of reductionism versus evolutionary holism thus expresses a fundamental philosophical opposition concerning the relation between natural wholes and their parts. The theme of wholes and parts is one of the two guiding themes by which we shall take our bearings in this paper. The second guiding theme is that of essential heterogeneity in nature, or specific difference, or normative natural kind.

---

edition), vol. 1 in 2 parts (Chicago: University of Chicago Press, 1955). See also *Logical Positivism*, ed. A. J. Ayer (New York: The Free Press, 1959) with extensive bibliography.

4. The term 'evolutionary sequence' has been used by Sidney W. Fox; see "The Evolutionary Sequence: Origin and Emergences," *American Biology Teacher* 48 (March 1986): 140–49.

5. This simple formulation facilitates the clear dichotomy appropriate for a beginning, but it masks a diversity of scientific theory and philosophic interpretation in the burgeoning study of evolutionary emergence. In particular, the terms 'holist' and 'in principle irreducible' would merit extended discussion. The following brief remarks must suffice for the present. We can distinguish several senses in which a whole is said to be irreducible to its parts or more than the sum of its parts. (1) Ontological: the being of the whole determines the being of the parts, that is, the parts are what they are only in terms of the whole. To separate part from whole is not only to change the whole but to make of the part something other than it was (see note 17, below). Living things (eyes in an animal) and quantum systems (electrons in an atom) are candidates for ontological holism. (2) Historical: the whole is produced through a unique temporal process, perhaps arising from a chance event, resulting in a structure that cannot be deduced from prior knowledge of the parts and cannot be understood independently of its historical genesis. (3) Information-theoretical: the quantitative or Shannon information (in bits) of the whole is greater than the sum of the informations of the parts. This is the widest and weakest sense of "irreducibility," for it is neutral to ontological or causal distinctions, and applies to everything from organisms to machines to electronic circuits to the arrangement of bricks in a wall. (4) Based on mathematical complexity: it is common in the modeling of physicochemical systems to develop equations of motion that are easy to write down but impossible to solve due either to many-particle interactions or to nonlinearity, or both. One says that mathematical complexity prevents derivation of system behavior from elementary components and interactions. It would seem, however, that in such cases the *causes of motion* are completely represented in the equations, and so there would be no basis for a claim of ontological holism. Thus, how these four senses of irreducibility may or may not be related is an issue for further study.

This is no longer a familiar notion, in significant part because of modern science, and some discussion will be required to make its meaning clear. Suffice to say for the moment that essential heterogeneity is intimately a matter of teleology and the intelligibility of human experience. My argument focuses on the intersection between the whole-part theme and the teleology theme.

The principal conclusions of this paper are: (1) The basic philosophical problem attendant to modern natural science and posed by both unity paradigms, the reductionist and the evolutionist, is that science inclines us to understand the human in terms of the non-human.[6] (2) But the severity of this problem differs greatly according to which unity paradigm and associated image of nature one believes. (3) On grounds of the reductionist paradigm, the problem is extreme. Were this paradigm adequate to nature, then, indeed, natural science would contradict the intelligibility of human experience.[7] The reason is simply that, on the reductionist account, neither mind nor soul can be a cause of motion in any body whatsoever. But the case for the universality of reductionism was, from its seventeenth-century beginnings, and has remained, weak and unpersuasive. (4) On grounds of the new evolutionary holism, the basic philosophical problem remains, because the contemporary scientific evolutionary picture of nature, of and by itself, appears to offer no clear ground for the essential status of rationality in the human animal. But this perplexity, although deep indeed, is not so drastic; it can be philosophically accommodated, if we are willing to live with something like the type of dualism that we find in Plato's *Phaedo*. These are my principal conclusions; they amount to a defense of the autonomy of the humanities against the unity of the sciences. Now to the argument proper in which the terms 'reductionism,' 'evolutionary holism,' 'essential heterogeneity,' and 'the intelligibility of human experience,' must be defined and interrelated. We can best begin in the *Phaedo,* for there we see most concretely that the necessary condition of human self-knowledge is that there be psychic causes of physical motion; specifically, that opinion can be a cause of motion in human bodies.

---

6. See the discussion of Leo Strauss and modern science in the introduction to this volume.

7. Two philosophical alternatives would then remain: existentialism (that is, the denial of all rational bases for human action) and German Idealism (that is, physical nature is mere appearance and in truth an emanation of Mind), so that it would be a mistake to continue to teach ancient, medieval, and early modern philosophy.

## 1. The Intelligibility of Human Experience

*Nature does nothing in vain . . . man alone among the animals has speech.*
                                                                —Aristotle[8]

In the *Phaedo*, 95–99, we find Socrates in jail, awaiting his execution. A distressed friend wants to hear a proof of the immortality of the human soul, but an adequate proof would require a general inquiry into the cause of generation and corruption, for which there is not enough time. And so Socrates offers instead an account of his own experience in the search for causes of generation, and passing away, and existence—his own experience in "the investigation of nature."[9] There follows the famous autobiographical passage on Socrates' disappointment with the contemporary physics and the failure of Anaxagoras to supply the defect, culminating in Socrates' "second sailing," his turn to political philosophy and the study of things as reflected in speech. His disappointment with physics consists at least partly in this: the physicists tried to explain the activities of all natural things in terms of their material parts. And this is like saying that the cause of Socrates' sitting in jail is the composition of his body from "bones and sinews, and the bones are hard and have joints . . . and the sinews can be contracted and relaxed . . . and so . . . make me able," says Socrates, "to bend my limbs now, and that is the cause of my sitting here with my legs bent."[10] Such an explanation—by the reduction of wholes to parts—is not adequate to our constant experience of ourselves as human beings. What is this experience? Socrates says, "by the dog, these bones and sinews of mine would have been in Megara or Boeotia long ago *carried by an opinion of what is best* if I did not think it more just and nobler" to stay.[11] (It is clear from the context that, with the help of his friends, Socrates could have escaped from jail.) Socrates' body is put in motion or remains at rest by his opinions of what is right. As human, we constantly move our bodies or remain at rest according to our opinions of what is best for us to do. In fact, we see from Socrates' situation in the *Phaedo* that the most important causes of the most important motions of human bodies often are opinions, about the highest or most compelling things. Opining involves perception, desire and aversion, thought, and most of all, speech among other human beings. There follow judgment and choice, then bodily motion. Aristotle says, "man is by nature a po-

8. Aristotle, *Politics*, 1253a9–10.
9. Plato, *Phaedo*, 96a.
10. Ibid., 98d.
11. Ibid., 99a; emphasis added.

litical animal . . . man alone among the animals has speech."[12] Think carefully about these words. To be an animal means to metabolize and reproduce, like plants, but also, and specifically, to have the powers of perception and self-motion. Animals perceive—form internal images of—objects of desire and aversion. They have the correlative ability to move themselves in pursuit or avoidance of objects of appetition. To say that man is the animal possessing speech means that the perception and bodily motion of *this* animal cannot be understood without understanding his speech, because, in *this* animal, opinion is a cause of perception and self-motion. Opinion is a cause of human perception. For example, consider a burning building in Sarajevo. We ask nearby human beings, all of whom receive the same physical stimuli at the optically active surfaces within their eyes, what do they see? Their answers fall into two groups: one says, "that is a burning hospital in which innocents are dying;" the other says, "that is an enemy command center masquerading as a hospital." They perceive differently because of their different views of their own histories, views passionately held but partial—they perceive differently through their different opinions. And opinion is a cause of motion in human bodies, for the two groups move in very different ways: the first group runs toward the burning building, in spite of great danger, trying to rescue people or put out the fire, while the second climbs up surrounding hills and drops shells down mortar tubes. In a much better, and less destructive way, we who are here now in this room moved our own bodies to this lecture because of our opinion that it would be good to meet and try to understand some things.

If our bodies, at the moment of decision, failed to move as we intended, then not only our major decisions but all of our daily activities would be nonsense. We could not function as human beings. Subhuman animate or vegetative functions might continue, but our specifically human capacities, our characteristically human way of being, and being in motion, thus our *telos* would be impossible. Therefore, the teleology of the human kind requires as a necessary condition that opinions can be causes of our bodily motions. This is what I want to isolate as essential in our experience of ourselves as humans. This is what I mean by the intelligibility of human experience, whereby our experience is subject to inquiry, for the sake of both theoretical and practical life. In fact, Socratic analysis of opinion is fundamental human physics.[13] And the problems Socrates works on after his second

---

12. *Politics*, 1253a3, a10.
13. The separation of psychology and physics is, to a large extent, a post-Cartesian development alien to premodern science.

sailing are among the deep and abiding problems connected with our specifically human way of being, like the tension between our natural partiality, or love of one's own, and openness to truth. What does modern natural science have to do with this?

General knowledge of physical nature unavoidably borders on, or makes contact with, the domain of human experience in a manner that, however tangential, nevertheless affects the way we understand ourselves. This is clear from the fact that the intelligibility of human experience depends upon a necessary condition involving physics: it must be possible for an opinion to be a cause of bodily motion in human beings. (Note that there is a second condition of possibility: it must be possible for the good to cause an opinion, otherwise, our opinions could never give access to any moral or ethical truth. Although I realize that this second condition may be of greater interest for many readers, it is a more difficult issue and requires a different kind of inquiry than analysis of natural science, to which I now return.) Is physical nature so constituted that an opinion could be a cause of motion in human bodies; is such a thing possible on grounds of the modern science of nature? The prescientific answer is that physical nature *must* be so constituted because it is immediately obvious to each of us that we do move according to our beliefs, judgments, and choices. But we still ask, as Socrates did in his early researches into nature, how does this work; *how* do psychic causes—our opinions of what is best—produce physical motion? As far as I know, the Socratic "second sailing," away from reductionist physics and into the dialogue, leaves this question unanswered. Does Plato then reject general physics or just reductionist physics, the Presocratic reduction of wholes to parts, of Socrates to bones and sinews? We know that Plato's great student, Aristotle, offers a nonreductionist general physics—a physics of irreducible natural substances—the core of which is formal and final causality. It is to Aristotle that we shall turn, in the second part of this paper, for the notion of natural kind, or essential heterogeneity in nature. My aim in what follows (on physical reductionism) is not to explain how psychic causes originate physical motion in living bodies, something no one has succeeded in doing, but rather to execute a negative strategy and refute an allegedly scientific argument that psychic causes of physical motion are impossible.

## 2. Physical Reductionism

*Le bon Dieu est dans les détails*
—Traditional French aphorism

Is nature so constituted that an opinion could be a cause of motion in human bodies? My answer is, yes, because the most complete argument against this possibility—that of universal determinist reductionism based on Newtonian physics—is weak and unpersuasive. And arguments for reductionism based on quantum physics can only be weaker.[14] To prepare the technical analysis, let us set out in advance the difference between universal physical reductionism and what we find in the *Phaedo*. In the *Phaedo*, no claim is made that the two distinct accounts of the motion and rest of Socrates' body—the one in terms of physical parts, the other in terms of an opinion of the just—are contradictory or incompatible. Rather, Socrates' opinion and judgment of what is right is clearly affirmed as a better causal explanation, whereas the configuration of his bodily parts is only a necessary condition.[15] How exactly opinion and judgment work through bodily parts is unexplained. The two accounts are not unified; they are left standing "side by side" in a relation that we could call problematic compatibility. I believe that our knowledge of the problem today is the same. It would be a very different matter if a claim were raised that the account in terms of bodily parts provided a fully sufficient and causally exclusive explanation of the motion and rest of Socrates' body. For such a claim would exclude any causal contribution by what we as whole human beings experience as an opinion of the good and a judgment of what is right. Precisely such a claim—for sufficient and causally exclusive explanation—is made by universal physical reductionism (also called ontological or constitutive reductionism). Why is this claim weak and unpersuasive; where does the argument go wrong? To see where, we

14. The holistic features of quantum physics are well known. For example, "phenomena in atomic physics possess a new property of *wholeness*, in that they cannot be dissected into part-phenomena without changing the entire phenomenon substantially every time [a measurement] is attempted" (W. Pauli, "Naturwissenschaftliche und Erkenntnistheoretische Aspekte der Ideen vom Unbewussten," *Dialectica* 8 (1954), 285). Wave-particle duality and the Pauli exclusion principle make it impossible to conceive an atom as composed of nucleus and electrons in the same way that the solar system is composed of sun and planets. In an atom, the parts are not neutral to the whole; in the solar system, they are. For an account of the recent Aspect experiments validating the reality of EPR correlations, see N. D. Mermin, "Is the moon there when nobody looks? Reality and the quantum theory," *Physics Today* (April 1985): 38–47, and "Spooky Actions at a Distance: Mysteries of the Quantum Theory," in *The Great Ideas Today* 1988 (Chicago: Encyclopedia Britannica, 1988), 3–53.
15. *Phaedo*, 99a–b.

must review the anatomy of the paradigmatic reductionist argument. This argument consists of certain pieces of Newtonian physics, or classical mechanics, and a specific philosophical interpretation thereof. We find the needed pieces of physics in Newton's gravitational theory applied to the solar system. Now the solar system is a whole composed of parts, namely, sun, nine planets, and occasional comets. (I realize this is an odd way of speaking, but it facilitates the remarkable analogy on which classical reductionism is based, namely, every whole in nature is like a solar system writ small.) The great accomplishment of Newtonian physics is this: from the observed position and velocity of any planet or comet at one point in time, to calculate the position and velocity of the body at any desired future time or past time.[16] The empirically determined values of position and velocity with which the calculation begins are called initial conditions. The completed Newtonian calculation of future position and velocity, subject to initial conditions, is then, amazingly, found to match the empirical observation thereof, within limits of precision of measurement. Let us review the important features of this accomplishment and then look at the principles on which it is grounded.

After Newton, we can *predict* (or retrodict) the local motions of planets and comets as well as natural and artificial satellites and projectiles. For the positions and velocities of these bodies at one moment *determine*, through the principles of Newtonian physics, their positions and velocities at the next moment. More generally: the state of the system at each moment in time fully determines (without choice, without chance) its state at the next. This is the definition of determinism. Furthermore, there is no more to the local motions of the whole system, say the whole solar system, than the quantitative properties and local motions of its parts—motions along trajectories in space predetermined according to the principles of Newtonian physics. Whatever we want to know about the behavior of the whole is fully answered in terms of the motions and properties of the parts. The whole is *reducible* to the parts in that the activity of the whole is entailed by the motions and properties of the parts without need of any principle specific to the whole as such—like soul—whereby the activity of the whole would determine the parts, in addition to being determined by the parts.[17] Here,

16. Orbital calculations become unreliable for sufficiently long times, due to the complexity of many-body effects, but the essential point (to be made shortly) stands: the solar system is a deterministic system.

17. Hegel gives an incisive formulation of ontological holism: "The notion of the whole is to contain parts: but if the whole is taken and made what its notion implies, i.e., if it is divided, it at once ceases to be a whole. Things there are, no doubt, which cor-

in the domain of celestial mechanics, the parts are (ontologically and epistemologically) prior to the whole. The whole is no more than the sum of the parts. The philosophically important features of the Newtonian account of gravitational systems are: predictability, determinism, reductionism.

What, then, are the principles of Newtonian physics upon which this account is based, and what are the alternative principles that are, therefore, not needed, that are thereby rendered superfluous?

The essential elements of the Newtonian theory are as follows: the three laws of motion, the law of gravitation, the parallelogram rule for composition of forces. We must consider each of these in turn. *First, the three universal laws of motion,* whereby forces in general—pushes and pulls—are quantified and related to local motion by means of equations:[18]

L I    Every body continues in its state of rest or of uniform motion in a right line, unless it is compelled to change that state by forces impressed upon it.
(Momentum $\mathbf{p}$ = constant if and only if $\mathbf{F}_{net}$ = 0)

L II   The change of motion is proportional to the motive force impressed; and is made in the direction of the right line in which that force is impressed.
($\mathbf{F}_{net}$ = $d\mathbf{p}/dt$)

L III  To every action there is always opposed an equal reaction: or, the mutual actions of two bodies upon each other are always equal, and directed to contrary parts.
($\mathbf{F}_{a\,on\,b}$ = $-\mathbf{F}_{b\,on\,a}$)

Prediction of trajectories, however, is not possible on grounds of the three laws of motion alone, which three laws, accordingly, provide no

respond to this relation: but for that very reason they are low . . . existences. . . . The relation of whole and parts . . . comes very easy to reflective understanding; and for that reason it often satisfies when the question really turns on profounder ties. The limbs and organs, for instance, of an organic body are not merely parts of it: it is only in their unity that they are what they are, and they are unquestionably affected by that unity, as they also in turn affect it. These limbs and organs become parts, only when they pass under the hands of the anatomist, whose occupation, be it remembered, is not with the living body but with the corpse. Not that such analysis is illegitimate: we only mean that the external and mechanical relation of whole and parts is not sufficient for us, if we want to study organic life in its truth." *Encyclopedia Logic,* sec. 135, note, in *Hegel's Logic,* trans. William Wallace (Oxford: Oxford University Press, 1975), 191. See also sec. 38, note, and sec. 126, note.

18. Newton, *Principia Mathematica,* trans. Andrew Motte and Florian Cajori (New York: Greenwood Press, 1962), 13; the equations are standard and can be found in mechanics textbooks.

sufficient basis for determinism. Nor do the three laws of motion alone
entail any particular relation between bodily wholes and parts. Accordingly, they provide no basis for reductionism. Therefore, Newton's
three laws of motion, of and by themselves, have no philosophical implications concerning matter and causality. Such implications can arise
only on grounds of a larger foundation, one that includes but goes beyond the three universal laws of motion.[19] Hence, *second, the law of gravitational attraction* between any two bodies, whereby a particular type of
force—gravitation—is expressed in terms of the masses, M, and m, of,
and distance, R, between, the two bodies:[20]

$$F = -GMm/R^2$$

Joining the law of gravitation with the laws of motion (specifically the
second law) yields a differential equation of motion and makes possible
the predictive calculation of the trajectories of two bodies gravitationally interacting. From this calculation begins the philosophical argument for determinism based on classical physics. But we need more.
For Newton's law of gravitation refers only to *two* bodies—each interacting only with the other—whereas the whole solar system contains
ten or more bodies or parts (including comets and asteroids), all of
which interact, and natural wholes in general may contain billions of
parts interacting by various kinds of forces. We need an additional rule
to answer the following key question: if a given body, the planet Mars,
for example, is subject to the gravitational force of not just the sun, but
also another planet, Jupiter, say, so that Mars is subject to the simultaneous gravitational forces of both Jupiter and the sun together, then
how do we proceed to calculate the one net force on Mars resulting
from the two conjoint gravitational attractions of the sun and Jupiter?
In general, how do we relate the force exerted by one whole (sun +
Jupiter) to the forces exerted by its two or more parts (sun, Jupiter)?
Within the principles of classical physics, the answer is given by Corollaries I and II of the *Principia*, usually referred to as, *third, the parallelogram rule for the composition of forces* (due to the geometric figure used
in the procedure):[21]

C I    A body, acted on by two forces simultaneously, will describe the
       diagonal of a parallelogram in the same time as it would de-
       scribe the sides by those forces separately.

19. This is explained in detail in Richard F. Hassing, "Animals versus the Laws of
Inertia," *Review of Metaphysics* 46 (1992): 29–61.
20. Newton, *Principia*, Book III, Prop. VII and Cor. II, 414–15.
21. Ibid., 14–15.

C II  And hence is explained the composition of any one direct
force AD, out of any two oblique forces AC and CD; and, on
the contrary, the resolution of any one direct force AD into
two oblique forces AC and CD: which composition and resolution are abundantly confirmed from mechanics.

In the conclusion of his derivation of this rule, Newton states that "on
what has been said depends the whole doctrine of mechanics."[22] Thus,
the parallelogram rule is an important item. We shall see that it is at
the heart of the argument for universal reductionism based on classical
physics, a universality proclaimed, not by Newton, we should note, but
by Laplace.[23] The parallelogram rule says that, to obtain the one effect
of two (or more) forces acting simultaneously on a body, we add up the
effects of each force, as if that force acted independently of the other
force (or forces). In Newton's formulation of Corollary I (in which the
forces are impulsive), the key word is the last word: "separately." It is
the key to understanding the whole-part relation in terms of motion
and force; thus, the key to understanding the whole-part relation as
embraced within the framework of Newton's mathematical principles.
For Newton here assumes that the agencies—whatever they may be—
that produce the two simultaneous forces, whose combined effect we
seek, act independently of each other. Although temporally together,
each agent behaves as if the other did not exist. By assumption, they
cannot influence each other when acting simultaneously. If we regard
the two things exerting the simultaneous forces in Corollary I as parts
of a whole, then Newton's tacit assumption would mean that, for this
whole, the parts do not modify their behavior in function of the whole
they compose. It would mean that the parts act as they do independently of the whole and, in this sense, are *dynamically independent* in
whatever forces they exert on "A body" (C I) external to the whole. The
strength and persuasiveness of the classical reductionist argument depends precisely on the validity and, above all, the generality of this implicit assumption; that is, are *all* wholes in nature composed of dynamically independent parts, parts which are then describable in terms of
elementary force laws like that of gravitation? In an older terminology,
the universal validity of Newton's assumption would entail the exclusion from nature of all potency to form, since elementary parts would
always be fully actual in the whole, as they are in artifacts. I maintain
that the classical reductionist argument is weak and unpersuasive pre-

22. Ibid., 17.
23. Laplace, *A Philosophical Essay on Probabilities*, trans. F. W. Truscott and F. L. Emory
(New York: Dover, 1951), 4.

cisely because this assumption of the dynamical independence of jointly acting forces—implicit in the application of the parallelogram rule to physical compounds—is not universal in its application to bodies and forces in nature; rather experiment and observation make clear that the assumption of dynamical independence does apply to some wholes, but there is no reason to believe that it applies to *all* the wholes in nature.

This has been a comment on Corollary I of Newton's *Principia.* We have not yet seen the main structure of the argument for classical reductionism and how the parallelogram rule necessarily enters into it. Before descending further into an unavoidably technical explanation, let us stand back, survey the terrain we have crossed, and remember the proximate question that led us directly into physics, namely, what are the principles of Newtonian physics on which the account of the solar system is based, and what are the principles thereby rendered superfluous? To this question we can now give an answer.

Employment of Newton's laws and the force composition rule (of Corollaries I and II) leads to a description of planets and comets, satellites and projectiles by means of mathematical equations whose solutions are the orbits or trajectories of the bodies under study. These equations entail no reference to celestial soul, separated intelligences, or divine superintendence. Planets and comets, satellites and projectiles just move along curved paths in space predetermined according to initial conditions and the laws of motion and gravitational force. No other causes of motion are needed. Notions of soul, will, intellect are superfluous in the explanation of the continuing operation of the solar system within classical physics.[24]

24. The continuing operation of the solar system means the continuance of the motions of the planets in their nearly concentric and coplanar orbits. As explained in section 3 of this paper, the type of universality characteristic of Newton's gravitational law is such that the *particular* shapes of the orbits (besides being conic sections) are unexplained. There is no necessity intrinsic to the gravitational principle from which arises any specific pattern of motion. The particular, determinate shapes of orbits or, in general, trajectories resulting from Newton's equations of gravitational motion derive rather from initial conditions (positions and velocities imposed at the beginning of motion). The determinate structure of the solar system thus derives from primordial initial conditions in the remote past. What accounts for them? Newton fills this explanatory gap with a famous theological statement in his General Scholium, added to the second edition of the *Principia* (1713): "and the planets and comets will constantly pursue their revolutions in orbits given in kind and position, according to the laws above explained; but though these bodies may, indeed, continue in their orbits by the mere laws of gravity, yet they could by no means have at first derived the regular position of the orbits themselves from those laws. . . . This most beautiful system of the sun, planets, and comets, could only proceed from the counsel and dominion of an intelligent and powerful Being." (543–44) Newton thus provides an early example of what came to be known as a "God-of-the-gaps" ar-

The philosophical argument for universal reductionism now consists in generalizing the Newtonian theory from the particular domain of planets, comets, satellites and projectiles—the motions of bodies resulting from gravitational forces—to all the motions of all the bodies in nature. This extraordinary generalization is accomplished by the remarkable assumption that every body—including yours and mine—is a vast assemblage of tiny particles that interact by mathematically describable forces and move along trajectories just as astronomical bodies by gravitational force. The analogy here proposed is thus that every body is like a solar system writ small, not in the sense that every body *looks* like the solar system but in the sense that the most basic principles are the same. Here is Newton's own formulation:

. . . I derive from the celestial phenomena the forces of gravity with which bodies tend to the sun and the several planets. Then from these forces . . . I deduce the motions of the planets, the comets, the moon, and the sea. I wish we could derive the rest of the phenomena of nature by the same kind of reasoning from mechanical principles, for I am induced by many reasons to suspect that they may all depend upon certain forces by which the particles of bodies, by some causes hitherto unknown, are either mutually impelled towards one another, and cohere in regular figures, or are repelled and recede from one another. These forces being unknown, philosophers have hitherto attempted the search of nature in vain; but I hope the principles here laid down will afford some light either to this or some truer method of philosophy.[25]

The fact that planets and comets, the sun, the moon and the sea, are very big bodies, whereas the particles hypothesized in this incredible analogy are very small, and furthermore, the bodies of plants and animals are medium sized and very different from comets and planets, is, apparently, not important. For, as Newton says, "nature is exceedingly simple and conformable to herself. Whatever reasoning holds for greater motions should hold for lesser ones as well."[26] This assertion implies the rejection of what I earlier referred to as essential heterogeneity in nature, or specific differences, or natural kinds. The assertion thus betokens a fundamental transformation in our understanding of nature. It betokens what I'll call species neutrality, as discussed in section 3, below.

---

gument, a new type of natural theology in which God is required to supply what the necessitarian and universal laws of physics cannot: a principle to account for the otherwise contingent conditions that determine the laws to their specific effects. In this type of natural theology, God is not understood as a cause in act required to complete a hierarchial chain of causes taken to be *per se* determined to the specific effects we now see.

25. Newton, *Principia*, First Preface, xviii.
26. "Unpublished Conclusion of the *Principia*," in *Unpublished Scientific Papers of Isaac Newton*, eds. A. R. and M. B. Hall (Cambridge: Cambridge University Press, 1962), 333.

Here in the *Principia,* Newton proposes physical reductionism as a research program; he says, let's try it as a working hypothesis—let's try the particles and forces approach to see how far we can go with it. He does not really claim that all the wholes in nature universally are reducible to their parts in the way that the solar system is reducible to its parts. After all, how could he explain, on grounds of such a claim, his own whole body, moved as it was by the love of physics in his own soul? Laplace and others, however, are not thinkers of Newton's caliber; they lack his moderating awareness of larger problems. Laplace does proclaim, in the following notorious passage, the exclusive universality of physical reductionism:

We ought then to regard the present state of the universe [not just the solar system] as the effect of its anterior state and as the cause of the one which is to follow. Given an intelligence that could comprehend at one instant all the forces by which nature is animated and the respective situation of the beings who compose it—an intelligence sufficiently vast to submit these data [initial conditions] to analysis—it would embrace in the same formula the movements of the greatest bodies in the universe and those of the lightest atom; for it, nothing would be uncertain and the future, as the past, would be present to its eyes. . . . The regularity which astronomy shows us in the movements of the comets doubtless exists also in all phenomena. The curve described by a simple molecule of air or vapor is regulated in a manner just as certain as the planetary orbits; the only difference between them is that which comes from our ignorance.[27]

All the motions of all the wholes in nature, then, are entailed exclusively by laws of motion and force expressed as differential equations, in terms of physical properties, like mass and charge, position and velocity, of parts and particles. The causes of motion in nature are, thus, in principle fully comprehended. Psychic causes of physical motion are excluded. Mind or soul cannot be a cause of motion in any body whatsoever. Therefore, it is not possible for an opinion to be a cause of motion in human bodies. Rather, an opinion must itself be a strange effect of elementary particles and forces.

Newton's reductionist research program was splendidly corroborated in particular domains of physics—in celestial mechanics, fluid dynamics, the kinetic theory of gases, and all sorts of engineering mechanics problems. My disagreement is not with Newton but with those who, like Laplace, claim the complete adequacy and exclusive universality of the reductionist model of nature, who think that the entire universe is nothing more than a vast assemblage of deterministic microparticles. As stated above, the philosophical heart of this claim concerns

27. Laplace, *A Philosophical Essay on Probabilities,* 4, 6.

the applicability of the parallelogram rule for composition of forces. Let me finish my description of this and thereby complete my criticism of the reductionist argument.

The argument for universal reductionism goes through only if we can write down the general equations of motion whose solutions determine the trajectories of particles. To obtain these equations, we must use not only Newton's laws of motion (specifically the second law) and an assumed force law (mathematically analogous to gravitation) but also and necessarily the parallelogram rule for compositon of forces.[28] This is because any individual particle, say q, is attracted or repelled by many other particles simultaneously, just as the body referred to in Corollary I is acted on by multiple forces simultaneously. This employment of the parallelogram rule entails the assumption that the net or whole force on the given particle, q, exerted by all other particles in the universe is always given by adding up the effects on q (accelerations) due to each particle as if its elementary force on q were independent of, and unmodified by, the presence of any other particles. Thus, setting up the deterministic equations celebrated by Laplace for the trajectory of any particle, q, entails *a priori* the assumption that each particle, say p, in the universe behaves in relation to q as if no other particles existed, except p and q. This is the meaning of the key word "separately" in Corollary I when the force composition rule is incorporated, as it must be, in the implicit logic of Laplace's claim for universal reductionism. The argument goes through only if we assume at the outset that, in the analysis of every system of particles or bodily compound in nature, we can arrive at a level of elementarity in which the constituent particles are dynamically independent. The argument, therefore, *presupposes* that *all* wholes in nature are reducible to parts that are what they are and act as they do (that is, interact according to mathematical force laws) independently of the whole they compose. Thus, no whole acts *as such* but only as a sum of dynamically independent parts. But this is precisely what the reductionist argument was supposed to prove. The classical argument for the universality of reductionism in fact presupposes its conclusion by presupposing the universal applicability of the parallelogram rule to imagined elementary parts of natural wholes. The argument rules out *by assumption* the possibility that certain systems of particles, certain subsets of all the particles in the universe, might be privileged in possessing a special unity whereby the parts are what they are, and function as they do, only in

28. A detailed account of this point is given in Richard F. Hassing, "Wholes, Parts, and Laws of Motion," *Nature and System* 6 (1984): 195–215.

terms of the whole they compose. Such parts could not be adequately or fully described by deterministic equations of motion, and thus neither could the wholes they compose. Living things, the things we call "alive," continue to be the most immediate candidates for compounds enjoying this special type of unity; the phenomena of biology compel us to speak in terms of *organic* unity. Atoms, molecules, chemical substances are another example, involving quantum physics, on which we shall comment in section 3.

If my criticism is correct, then the applicability of the parallelogram rule for composition of forces is properly an empirical matter: we find some wholes that are reducible to parts that are dynamically independent and behave according to simple force laws, but we find other wholes with properties and characteristics not derivable from their parts, like animals, among which ourselves. These wholes would be compatible with—they would not violate—the mathematical laws of physics, but their motions would never be derivable from, or fully entailed by those laws. On this account, there *can* be psychic causes of physical motion. Even though no one can explain exactly how an opinion can produce motion in our own bodies, there is no plausible argument that it cannot. Since this causality is, and always has been, massively self-evident, we recover the dualism of Plato's *Phaedo*, the dualism of problematic compatibility.

This completes my analysis and criticism of the reductionist argument. Clearly, a fully adequate treatment would require a detailed historical study of the parallelogram rule for composition of forces. What does Newton himself think about Corollaries I and II of the *Principia*? This we can answer now. But other thinkers come immediately to mind, especially Kant, who exerted a great influence on the philosophical interpretation of classical physics in Germany.[29] Let us at least look at Newton.

Corollary I of Newton's *Principia* provides the rule for combining the effects (velocities) resulting from two (impulsive) forces assumed

---

29. Kant, *Metaphysical Foundations of Natural Science*, trans. James Ellington, in *Kant's Philosophy of Material Nature* (Indianapolis: Hackett Publishing Co., 1985). Composition of motions, not forces, is discussed on 30–37. It is significant that, in reflecting critically on his principle of the complete comprehensibility of nature, Helmholtz cites the early influence of Kant. See Helmholtz, "Ueber die Erhaltung der Kraft," in *Wissenschaftliche Abhandlungen* (Leipzig, 1882), vol. 1, 15–16 and 68–69. Note also that, for John Stewart Mill, the distinction between systems reducible in the sense of the parallelogram rule, that is, mechanical systems, on the one hand, and chemical and biological systems, on the other, is "so radical, and of so much importance, as to require a chapter to itself," namely, chapter 6 of *A System of Logic* (London: Longmans, Green and Co., 1941), book 3, titled "Composition of Causes," 242–47 (quotation on 242).

not to influence each other when acting simultaneously. The compound effect on the body subject to these two forces (the velocity, which is constant, and thus the distance travelled in a given time) is then simply the vector sum of the separate effects of the independent forces. Corollary I defines what we could call the mechanical relation of whole and part. Corollary II then states the mathematical rule for vector addition employed in relating force vectors to calculationally convenient components:

> And hence is explained the composition of any one direct force AD, out of any two oblique forces AC and CD; and, on the contrary, the resolution of any one direct force AD into two oblique forces AC and CD; which composition and resolution are abundantly confirmed from mechanics.[30]

The essential point is that Corollaries I and II are not given further demonstration in the *Principia*, but rather they are illustrated by means of application to typical mechanics problems. The dynamical independence of forces is assumed throughout. It is important to emphasize that this assumption is not entailed by the laws of motion, or by the general concept of force (as whatever effects, or tends to effect, acceleration). As Ernst Mach shows, against Daniel Bernoulli, the parallelogram rule is not "a *geometrical* truth, independent of physical experience."[31] Validation of the assumption of dynamically independent forces consists in the success of the resulting description in each particular case, the particular case of gravitational systems being, of course, a world-historic success.[32] As Newton says, "the use of this Corollary [II] spreads far and wide, and by that diffusive extent the truth thereof is further comfirmed." In other words, for Newton, the parallelogram rule for composition of forces is certified empirically. This is why I believe that Newton, who proposes physical reductionism as a research program, would, nevertheless, not subscribe to Laplace's proclamation of *universal* reductionism. In general, I strongly suspect that there has never been in the history of philosophy a sound science-based argument for the universal reduction of wholes to parts.

The belief in reductionism supplied the unifying principle for the unity-of-science program embraced by logical positivism during its ascendancy from the 1930s to the 1950s. Needless to say, the assimilation of Einstein's relativity and quantum physics to the reductionist model involves technically sophisticated analysis of language and empiricist methodology. The distinction between methodological reductionism

---

30. Newton, *Principia*, Corollary II, 15. It is crucial not to confuse physics with mathematics in looking at these two corollaries.
31. Mach, *Science of Mechanics* (Lasalle, Ill.: Open Court, 1960), 51.
32. Newton, *Principia*, Bk. III, Prop. VII and Cor. II, 414–15.

and physical (or ontological) reductionism is a real distinction of some importance. For our purposes here, however, we could sum up the reductionist unity-of-science paradigm by reference to a well known 1958 article by Paul Oppenheim and Hilary Putnam, called "Unity of Science as a Working Hypothesis."[33] The crux of this article is that wholes ought to be explained in terms of parts, and what now is ought to be explained in terms of what came before. Oppenheim and Putnam justify their methodological reductionism ontologically; that is, reduction (synchronic and diachronic) as a method in science is best because ultimately wholes really are reducible to parts. The evidence for this consists in the partial successes of reductionist explanation in particular domains of science, plus the overall picture of universal evolution, serious gaps notwithstanding.

Karl Popper's view is different in a most interesting way. In a 1974 article titled "Scientific Reduction and the Essential Incompleteness of All Science," Popper writes as follows:

There do not seem to be any good arguments in favour of *philosophical* [i.e., physical or ontological] reductionism. . . . But I . . . suggest that we should, nevertheless, on methodological grounds, continue to attempt reductions. The reason is that we can learn an immense amount even from unsuccessful or incomplete attempts at reduction, and that problems left open in this way belong to the most valuable intellectual possessions of science.[34]

Popper is right—impressively so—insofar as he is talking about physics, chemistry, and biology. But what happens if we force the human sciences into the reductionist mold? What happens if we try to understand the human compound in terms of physical parts and prehuman species? Here is a sample.

In the spring of 1992, there appeared an article in *The Washington Post* titled "Science and Sensitivity" describing, among other things, some research on violent human behavior. The research, done in Finland and at the University of Wisconsin, was based on the fact that "the human genetic code is more than 98-percent identical to the chimpanzee code." The objective of the work was thus to understand "the roots of human violence" by the study of monkeys:

experimenting on caged rhesus monkeys, [the research] . . . showed that babies deprived of a mother grew up to be severely warped in personality, unable to

33. Paul Oppenheim and Hilary Putnam, "Unity of Science as a Working Hypothesis," in *Minnesota Studies in the Philosophy of Science,* eds. H. Feigl, M. Scriven, and G. Maxwell (Minneapolis: University of Minnesota Press, 1958), 3–36.

34. Karl Popper, "Scientific Reduction and the Essential Incompleteness of All Science," in *Studies in the Philosophy of Biology,* eds. F. Ayala and T. Dobzhansky (Berkeley and Los Angeles: University of California Press, 1974), 260.

fit into monkey society—and that they were prone to random acts of violence. . . . Work in [this] lab also provided evidence . . . that deprived and be-
haviorally impaired monkeys could be rescued by exposing them to younger,
normal monkeys for as little as an hour a day. . . . So close is the human-
monkey kinship in behavioral terms, in fact, that the series of human developmental stages worked out by Jean Piaget, the late French child psychologist,
is much the same as for rhesus monkeys—up to the age at which language
becomes a major factor in children's behavior. . . . Evidence for a dramatic bio-
chemical difference among the [monkey] personality types has emerged in recent years. . . . the scientists have discovered a striking chemical marker of
violent behavior—low levels of a molecule that is a breakdown product of a
substance called serotonin, a powerful messenger molecule that brain cells in
all species use to carry certain signals. It has turned out that the more aggressive monkeys have low levels of serotonin and the least aggressive have high
levels. Outcast males have the lowest levels. The same chemical differences have
also been found in humans and, again, the correlation is with violent behavior
of a certain type. . . . What makes an individual's serotonin high or low? The
research shows that genes play a role, as does environment. . . . 'What interests
many of us is that the serotonin levels of monkeys—and their personality differences—can be traced back to the animals' early beginnings,' [one of the re-
searchers] said. 'It makes a big difference what kind of mothers they had and
what their genetic heritage was. It's an interaction of the two—genes and environment—that shapes the animal's personality.' By deliberately manipulating
the circumstances under which young rhesus monkeys grow up, [the research]
has shown that environmental factors can reshape personality types begun under the influence of genes. Young monkeys born with low serotonin put into
peer groups with . . . [a] mother monkey that [only] supplied milk grew up
more likely to display impulsive, violent behavior. But those placed with especially nurturing mothers grew up to be more normal. Nurture had overcome
nature.[35]

The two lessons of this newspaper article are: first, that serotonin
might be effective in ameliorating violent psychoses, and this indeed
could be useful; but, second, the essential cause of criminal violence in
America is the collapse of the family; this is true but hardly new—it is
obvious to any careful observer of American society.[36]

Here then man is understood in terms of molecules and monkeys;
wholes in terms of parts, what now is in terms of what came before. This
means that what is specific to the human is necessarily discounted (for
example, the role of language in children's behavior, above, duely cited

35. Boyce Rensberger, "Science and Sensitivity," *The Washington Post*, 1 March 1992,
C4.
36. See, for example, Barbara D. Whitehead, "Dan Quayle was Right," *The Atlantic
Monthly*, April 1993, and George F. Will, "The Tragedy of Illegitimacy," *The Washington
Post*, 31 October 1993. "Federal officials estimate that 70 percent of children in juvenile
court are from single-parent households. In the last 30 years, the proportion of single
mothers has grown from one in 20 to one in four." *The Washington Post*, 2 January
1994, A19.

and strikingly ignored); no account of the human on its own terms can count as science. This amounts to a kind of intellectual gravitational pull that affects our self-understanding. It is the basic philosophical problem attendant to modern natural science. Let us now address the subject that I mentioned earlier: species neutrality and the rejection of essential heterogeneity in nature, that is, rejection of natural kinds or specific differences.

## 3. Species Neutrality

*That which is common to all, and is equally in a part and in the whole, does not constitute the essence of any particular thing*

—Spinoza[37]

We saw that Newton proposed a "method of philosophy" based on the idea that "the same kind of reasoning" discovered to work for "the planets, the comets, the moon, and the sea" should also work for "the rest of the phenomena of nature." But how could anyone come to think that the principles of the motions of planets should apply to animals, say? For these are radically different kinds of things. The sizes and shapes of planets are completely different from the sizes and shapes of cats and dogs and people. Above all, these two kinds of bodies—planets and animals—move in utterly different ways. Planets just follow their cyclic orbits. They don't eat, excrete, perceive, reproduce, age, die. Planets don't start and stop themselves, and scamper around in unpredictable ways, as we animals do. How could anyone come to think that things that move in such vastly different ways could be understood by "the same kind of reasoning"? Is it not obvious that things that move in very different ways have correspondingly different material compositions? For example, whatever can initiate and terminate its own local motion, and change its own direction—whatever is a self-accelerator—must have a diversity of hard and soft parts, and the hard parts must have flexible joints, as Socrates described while sitting in jail. Since astronomical bodies do not move in this way, they should not be composed of parts in this way. And they aren't.

We can see this way of thinking about body, motion, and causality in Aristotle's *Physics*. In *Physics* VIII.1, Aristotle raises the crucial question whether motion is eternal. He makes clear that physical motion—as opposed to the motion of a mathematical object, like a point—must be understood in relation to its subject. He says "for each motion [that

---

37. Benedict Spinoza, *Ethics* II.37, in *Spinoza, On the Improvement of the Understanding, The Ethics, Correspondence*, trans. R. H. M. Elwes (New York: Dover, 1955), 109.

is each kind of motion], it is the subject capable of that motion which has that motion."[38] For example, listen to how Aristotle explicates the essential difference between elemental bodies and living things in *Physics* VIII.4:

> To say that [elemental bodies, like water or fire] are moved by themselves is impossible, for this is an attribute of living things and is proper to them. . . . if it were up to fire itself to go up, clearly it would also be up to fire itself to go down [so there is a fundamental difference between the motion, and associated cause of motion in a bird, say, as compared to fire]. It is also unreasonable that [what can move by itself, like a bird] should be causing only one motion in itself [indeed a bird changes direction by itself, whereas fire just goes up]. . . . [And] how can something that is continuous and [of uniform composition] cause itself to be moved? For insofar as a thing is one and [uniformly] continuous [like fire or water, without joints] it is incapable of being acted upon [by itself]; but insofar as a separation has been made, one [part] can by nature act and the other, be acted upon [like muscle and bone]. So none of [the elemental bodies] causes itself to be moved (for each is of uniform composition). . . .[39]

In this passage, kind of motion, kind of mobile, kind of causality are all thought together. In general, it is vividly evident from our ordinary experience of things all around us that the way a thing moves— the way it can undergo change—depends on its size and shape and internal structure. That is to say, the activity characteristic of the kind of thing it is, essentially and not by accident, is intimately related to its visible looks or, more generally, to its properties as given in unassisted sense perception. Think of any animal. In the Aristotelian science of nature, form—the fundamental intelligible—is not at all "blind" or "indifferent" or "neutral" to the matter it energizes. In Aquinas's succint formulation, "natural form . . . requires determinate quantity."[40] We could say that the intelligible universal principles—the forms—lie close to, or within, the sensible particulars. Indeed, Aristotle says that "form . . . does not exist separately from the thing except in speech."[41]

Maimonides takes this linkage between the way a thing moves and the kind of matter it has, and the causes of its motion, to be of the greatest importance. In discussing certain problems in the medieval physics of the heavens (related to the well known scandal of Ptolemaic astronomy), he says that, if "the form of the motion of the [celestial]

<hr>

38. Aristotle, *Physics* VIII.1, 251a14.
39. Ibid., VIII.4, 255a6–17.
40. Aquinas, *In phys.* VIII, n. 1067; *Commentary on Aristotle's Physics*, trans. Richard J. Blackwell, Richard J. Spath and Edmund Thirlkel (New Haven: Yale University Press, 1967), 529.
41. Aristotle, *Physics* II.1, 193b5–6.

spheres would not be indicative of their matter, [then] this would be the ruin of all principles."[42]

To summarize: things that move in essentially different ways as manifested to our senses possess essentially different kinds of matter and sources of motion. They have different natures. Thus, celestial bodies are essentially different from terrestrial bodies, and among the latter, living things are essentially different from non-living things. And among animals, the kind that speaks and opines in order to be what it is—the rational political animal—is essentially distinct. There are natural kinds of things, and they are essentially, not accidentally, heterogeneous. The stable differences in the way things appear to ordinary sense perception are effects that proceed *per se*, not *per accidens*, from intelligible causes and principles accessible to natural prescientific reason. This means that what the different kinds have in common is not as fundamental as what differentiates and specifies them.

What then happened in the rise of modern science and philosophy to overpower this powerfully common-sensical way of thinking nature and speaking the phenomena? What happened that enabled Newton to say that, "Whatever reasoning holds for greater motions should hold for lesser ones as well;" that enabled Laplace to say that, "The regularity which astronomy shows us in the movements of the comets doubtless exists also in all phenomena. . . . the only difference . . . is that which comes from our ignorance," not from different natures?

A good answer to this question would involve us deeply in the seventeenth century. We would need to study Galileo, Bacon, Hobbes, Descartes, Spinoza—not a short term project. But we have Newton at our disposal, and we can use him again to see another feature of his gravitational theory, one that nicely exemplifies the species neutrality of classical physics. By "species neutrality," I mean a relation between sensible effects and intelligible causes unlike the traditional one, the one we have just reviewed in Aristotle and the commentators.

The fundamental intelligible and universal governing principle in Newton's account of the solar system is his law of gravitational attraction: between any two bodies, there is a force of attraction proportional to the product of their masses and inversely proportional to the square of the distance between. This is usually written algebraically as $F = -GMm/R^2$, where M and m are the masses of the two bodies, and R is

---

42. Maimonides, *Guide of the Perplexed* II.22, 49b; trans. Shlomo Pines (Chicago: University of Chicago, 1963), 319. It is not the ruin of *all* principles but only of the *comprehensivess* of the Aristotelian teleology. Partial teleologies (in biology and human affairs, say) can remain, but the purposive unity of the whole can no longer be viewed by natural reason.

the distance between them. The terms "mass" and "distance" have an obvious characteristic on which we previously touched but did not fully elaborate. They are properties *common* to all the kinds or *species* of bodies. *Every* body—regardless of size, shape, kind, internal structure, and function—has mass. Similarly, every body has spatial position relative to other bodies, and so any two bodies have between them a distance. This means that from the masses and positions of bodies alone we cannot determine what kind of bodies are present. The same is true of all the basic terms derived from mass, position, and time, which are used in classical physics, for example, linear and angular velocity, acceleration, momentum, and kinetic and potential energy. The idea that terms and properties common in this sense, and not Aristotle's species or natural forms, can ground the true account of nature is a major theme in Bacon, Descartes, and Spinoza. It is part and parcel of the idea of *method* in early modern philosophy. Spinoza states it bluntly: "That which is common to all . . . and which is equally in a part and in the whole, does not constitute the essence [read Aristotelian form] of any particular thing. . . . Those things which are common to all, and which are equally in a part and in the whole, cannot be conceived except adequately."[43] Spinoza is referring to extension and local motion, two crucial terms of Cartesian physics, but mass and interparticle distance fit his characterization just as well. Newton's three laws of motion, and law of gravitational force, and the resulting equations of motion are algebraically composed entirely of such species-neutral terms. Because of this, these laws and equations are independent of, or indifferent to, the size, shape, kind, internal structure, and function of the bodies gravitationally interacting. This is why, in celestial mechanics (where bodies don't bump into each other, which would demand non-gravitational, repulsive forces of some sort), extended, shaped, divisible bodies can be taken as unextended, indivisible points, namely, mass-points. Here is a recent textbook formulation by a well-known specialist: "Newtonian mechanics studies the motion of a system of point masses in three-dimensional euclidean space."[44] Therefore, the fundamental intelligible and universal governing principle—the law of gravitational force —is blind, indifferent, neutral to the different kinds of bodies and patterns of motion it governs.[45] Unlike a natural form, the law of gravitation does not require determinate quantity in order to be. And so,

43. Spinoza, *Ethics* II.37–38; Elwes, 109–110.
44. V. I. Arnold, *Mathematical Methods of Classical Mechanics* (New York: Springer-Verlag, 1989), 1.
45. The only "structure," "end," or "*telos*" to which a gravitational system (Newtonian or Einsteinian) is *per se* directed is a black hole, which is unintelligible.

for example, the equation, $F = -GMm/R^2$, is the same for planetary elliptical orbits, for an open hyperbolic orbit, for terrestrial parabolic trajectories. Newton's law of gravitation is invariant under these large distinctions in orbital structure, in visible patterns of motion. This is true in general of Newtonian mechanics. What accounts for these large differences are the initial conditions, that is, the position, direction and speed with which the body was projected at some time in the past. The different initial conditions leading to different particular orbits or visible patterns of motion are external to, are not entailed by, the general laws and equations of motion. If—and this is a significant "if "—we regard the initial conditions as simply contingent or per accidens, then we can immediately see the radical break with the previous understanding of local motion in nature. Planets in the heavens and rocks on the earth do not possess essentially different kinds of matter and sources of motion. Phenomena previously thought to manifest two essentially distinct natures—celestial and terrestrial, for example, the moon and a rock—in virtue of the great differences in their observable motions, are found instead to be derivable from the same principles. The difference in their observed motions is taken to be merely per accidens, namely, the result of the different impulses that happened to occur at the beginning of motion. If we are motivated to generalize this result—motivated by a philosophical interest in attacking formal and final causality in nature—then we would hold that the true principles of nature do not conform to what we apprehend by our senses. Thus, great differences in visible patterns of motion, and the sensible features of bodies, are no guide to the real nature of the things being moved.

The idea of a new, species-neutral intelligibility or aspect of nature is, of course, a major theme in the philosophy of Newton's predecessors, Bacon and Descartes. Both present a philosophical, thus extra-scientific attack on formal and final causality in nature.[46] Let me briefly comment on Bacon. In the *New Organon*, he says that

in nature nothing really exists besides individual bodies [thus no species] performing pure individual acts [thus no potency] according to law . . . in philosophy this very law . . . is the foundation as well of knowledge as of operation. And it is this law . . . that I mean when I speak of *forms* . . . whosoever is acquainted with forms [that is, laws] embraces the unity in materials the most unlike, and is able therefore to detect and bring to light things never yet

46. See, for example, Bacon, *New Organon*, ed. Fulton Anderson (Indianapolis: Bobbs-Merrill, 1978), I.15; Descartes, *Le Monde*, trans. Michael S. Mahoney (New York: Abaris, 1979), chaps. 6 and 7.

done. . . . From the discovery of forms therefore results truth in speculation and freedom in operation.[47]

Bacon refers to "materials the most unlike," such as lunar material and earthly artifacts, or a metal bar magnet and living flesh. They are linked through an underlying unity of laws that will "bring to light things never yet done," such as going to the moon or magnetic resonance imaging in medical diagnostics. In general, the branches of physics dealing with gravitation, with heat, and especially with electromagnetism seem to exhibit Baconian features. They attest to the reality of a previously unanticipated aspect of nature. Thus, the idea of species neutrality, and the corresponding rejection of formal and final causality in nature—the strategy of method—is a large and crucial part of the whole of early modern philosophy. This idea means that what the different kinds of bodies have in common is more fundamental than what specifically differentiates them. I suggest that this idea, of which Newton and Laplace were surely aware, is what enabled them to propose in so unreserved a manner that remarkable analogy of theirs, on which reductionism is based. Look at Hypothesis III of the first Latin edition of Newton's *Principia:* "Every body can [in principle] be transformed into another, of whatever kind, and all the intermediary degrees of qualities can be successively induced in it"[48]—by controlling the initial and boundary conditions on the particles of which every body is composed. As discussed in the introductory essay, this is a noteworthy instance of "transformism" in early modern philosophy.

The species neutrality of classical physics is so radical that it provokes one of the two great scientific revolutions of the twentieth century, namely, quantum physics. The reason is that the strictly deterministic character of the Newtonian account (as well as classical electromagnetism) makes unintelligible all phenomena in which a system reconstitutes itself, or recovers a privileged state of the whole following an external disturbance.[49] The most conspicuous of such phenomena is

---

47. Bacon, *New Organon* II.2 and II.3.

48. *Isaac Newton's Philosophiae Naturalis Principia Mathematica*, eds. Alexandre Koyre and I. Bernard Cohen (Cambridge: Harvard University Press, 1972), 550.

49. Self-reconstitution can of course be modeled by negative feedback, a nonlinear effect, for example, think of a room with a furnace and a thermostat. I do not believe, however, that nonlinear science weakens the fundamental distinction (about to be described) between the type of stability exhibited by classical deterministic systems, on the one hand, and the type of stability characteristic of organisms and atoms, on the other. My reasons are twofold: (1) The thermostat has no tendency to repair itself if it gets broken, unlike an organism. See Douglas Ehring, "Negative Feedback and Goals," *Nature and System* 6 (1984): 217–20. (2) Perhaps it is conceivable that quantum mechanics will be superseded by a nonlinear space-time description (facilitating unification with

somatic health; that is, healing, or the resistence of living organisms to disease and injury. Without the living body's own internal tendency to recover a good way of physical functioning specific to its kind, there would be no such thing as medicine.

Less conspicuous, but more important for the history of physics, is the stability of atoms and molecules, that is, the stable behavior of the chemical species. The contradiction between classical physical theory and the phenomena of atomic and molecular stability led to the quantum revolution in physics. Listen to the following statement by Neils Bohr, as paraphrased by Heisenberg:

> My starting point was . . . the stability of matter, a pure miracle when considered from the standpoint of classical physics. . . . By 'stability' I mean that the same substances always have the same properties, that the same crystals recur, the same chemical compounds, etc. In other words, even after a host of changes due to external influences, an iron atom will always remain an iron atom, with exactly the same properties as before. This cannot be explained by the principles of classical mechanics. . . . Nature clearly has a tendency to produce certain forms . . . and to recreate these forms even when they are disturbed or destroyed. . . . All this, far from being self-evident, is quite inexplicable in terms of the basic principles of Newtonian physics, according to which . . . the present state of a phenomenon or process is fully determined by the one that immediately preceded it. [Thus there is no sense in which a future state as norm or goal could be a cause of present motion.] This fact used to disturb me a great deal when I first began to look into atomic physics.[50]

On grounds of classical physics, both atoms and organisms are "quite inexplicable" precisely because of their respective self-reconstitutive stabilities (health in living species, the ground state of atomic and molecular species). Newton, victorious over the solar system, is finally undone by atoms and organisms. But we must note that there are fundamental differences between atoms and organisms. The specific structure of atoms—miraculous on grounds of species-neutral classical physics—is successfully described by quantum physics. Although I associated Bacon with the idea of species neutrality, and thus with Newton, atomic physics is nevertheless Baconian in at least three important respects: First, atoms and molecules are elements common to the many distinct species of visible bodies, and in this sense, they are themselves species-neutral principles. Second, unlike plants and animals, atoms are not given in ordinary sense perception, but are only inferred

---

general relativity on grounds of the latter), but it seems extraordinarily unlikely. Nevertheless, see Mendel Sachs, *Quantum Mechanics from General Relativity* (Boston: Kluwer Academic, 1986).

50. Heisenberg, *Physics and Beyond*, trans. Arnold J. Pomerans (New York: Harper Torchbooks, 1972), 39.

through ingeniously devised experiments. Third, and most important, atoms and molecules lend themselves to powerful technological exploitation (in chemistry, solid state physics, not to mention nuclear physics) in a way that living things do not. The question whether molecular biology, the locus of the outstanding problem of biogenesis (briefly discussed in section 4), is Baconian or Aristotelian,[51] or something else, and the meaning of non-locality, the most bizarre of all quantum effects (now empirically verified), will probably remain open well into the next century. My basic point is that the issues between Aristotle and the commentators, Newton and his early modern predecessors, and quantum physics—issues concerning astronomical systems, organisms, and atoms—are complicated. We could sum this up in a very rough way by saying that nature is less Aristotelian than Aristotle thought, but more Aristotelian than modern science thinks.

This completes my discussion of physical reductionism and species neutrality. We have obtained the following results: (1) On grounds of natural science, it is possible for an opinion to cause human bodily motion because there does not yet exist a good science-based argument against psychic causes of physical motion. The best such argument is weak due to its unwitting assumption of universal reductionism in the very premises with which it begins. (2) Applied to human phenomena, the reductionist attitude to scientific knowing gives rise to a pervasive tendency to try to understand the rational in terms of the non-rational. This is not useless, but it tends to obfuscate a knowledgeable understanding of our own specifically human perennial problems—the problems of ethics and politics. It remains to consider what I earlier referred to as evolutionary holism, a new paradigm for unity of science.

## 4. Evolutionary Holism

*For philosophers, the most important discovery of modern science has been the history of Nature.*
—Carl Friedrich von Weizsäcker[52]

The thoughts in this section are tentative and provisional. The dichotomy of species neutral laws of nature and humanly experienced

---

51. Molecular biology is Aristotelian in the sense that the genetic plan of an organism is a kind of (quasi-)unmoved mover, as described by Max Delbrück, "Aristotle-totle-totle," in *Of Microbes and Life*, eds. Alexandre Koyre and I. Bernard Cohen (New York: Columbia University Press, 1971), 50–55. Molecular biology is Baconian by virtue of the apparently open-ended potential of genetic engineering, that is, the possibilities for overcoming barriers previously regarded as by nature insurmountable.

52. Forward to Bernd-Olaf Küppers, *Der Ursprung biologischer Information* (Munich: R. Piper & Co., 1986); *Information and the Origin of Life*, trans. Paul Woolley (Cambridge: MIT Press, 1990), xi.

specific difference—the homogeneity of laws and the heterogeneity of kinds[53]—is the guiding idea. The basic logic is as follows. Universal physical reductionism is species neutral and (obviously) reductionist. It claims (erroneously) that psychic causes of physical motion are impossible and would thus imply that human experience is unintelligible in the sense described in section 1. The thesis of the present section is that evolutionary holism is species neutral but nonreductionist. Thus, like physical reductionism, it gives rise to a prejudice towards understanding the human kind in terms of what is common to both man and non-man, towards understanding the rational in terms of the non-rational. But, unlike physical reductionism, it does not compel us to reject the specifically human, for it makes no claim that psychic causes of physical motion are impossible, no claim that opinion cannot be a cause of motion in human bodies. The evolutionist paradigm for unity of the sciences thus permits a relation of problematic compatibility between natural science and human experience. The *compatibility* is as follows. As we have seen, all things having mass, regardless of kind, obey the universal law of gravitation; as we shall see, all systems having energy and definable entropy obey the universal laws of thermodynamics. (The significance of thermodynamics will be explained momentarily.) Thus, for example, the operations of a living cell in its environment obey, and in this sense are compatible with, the first and second laws of thermodynamics, yet from those laws alone one cannot derive what is specific to living cells, namely, that nucleotide sequences are the carriers of encoded information.[54] In a similar way, the local motions specific to animals are compatible with, but not derivable from or entailed by, the law of universal gravitation common to all masses. The completion of this analogy is that the opinion-based motions specific to human animals (discussed in section 1) are compatible with, but not derivable from or entailed by, the species-neutral principles of modern natural science. This idea is not new, although its justification by detailed analysis of the natural sciences is regrettably rare.[55] And it may

53. This rather cryptic but succint and felicitous formulation is due to the late Thomas Prufer.

54. The problem of the relation between thermodynamic entropy and biological (intrinsic structural) information is thus central to the research programs aimed at unification of biology and physics. See, for example, D. R. Brooks and E. O. Wiley, *Evolution as Entropy* (Chicago: University of Chicago Press, 1988), 31–52, and Bruce H. Weber, David J. Depew, and James D. Smith, eds., *Entropy, Information, and Evolution* (Cambridge: MIT Press, 1990).

55. The importance of the problem of the specific versus the species-neutral is, in general, recognized by biologically interested scientists; see John H. Campbell, "Evolution as Nonequilibrium Thermodynamics: Halfway There?," in Weber, Depew, and

be true, as David L. Hull has remarked, that "compatibility is a weak relation,"[56] but a weak pluralism of the sciences is preferable to a strong but one-sided unity that distorts our self-understanding. What is *problematic* in any species-neutral account of nature is simply this: how is the specific to be understood? Is it a product of chance, possessing only a history, or does it possess its own necessary principles, whereby it has a transhistorical nature? Is a living whole adequately to be understood only in terms of its origins rather than its present characteristics, in terms of the process rather than the product? Must it be so understood precisely because its present appearance and operation are only *per accidens* effects of causes *per se* aimed at something indifferent to the present order of things? Is it thus mistaken to understand man as the animal possessing speech (with all that this definition entails), because this characteristic is posterior to something more fundamental, such as differential reproduction rates or maximum energy flow? In the modern evolutionary universe, the problem is acute, because all the species now living did not exist a finite time ago (before the formation of the solar system), *and are, on strictly scientific grounds, candidates for further open-ended changes.*[57] This gives rise to the prejudice that the knowable in nature can only be the common, law-governed evolutive process from which all specific products randomly emerge. The process is necessary and intelligible, the products are accidental; to take them as essential is to be self-deceived.[58] In this sense, the contemporary scientific evolutionary picture of nature, of and by itself, appears to offer no clear ground for the essential status of rationality in the human animal. Let me complete the account by explaining more fully what I mean by evolutionary holism, illustrating the basic logic of my critique by means of excerpts from the burgeoning literature on this subject. The two essential points are that the new unity of science paradigm is (1) species neutral, but (2) nonreductionist.

Smith, *Entropy*, 278, and John Collier, "The Dynamics of Biological Order," 230–32. For the nonspecialist, the issue is stated with force and clarity by Leon Kass, *Toward a More Natural Science* (New York: The Free Press, 1985), 1–14, and esp. 37.

56. David L. Hull, introduction to Weber, Depew and Smith, *Entropy*, 2.

57. "Before us still lies evolution from man to mankind, from single humans with various degrees of social organization to a true human society. . . . The process of creation is by no means at an end, although no one can predict what is to come. . . . Man is still a relative newcomer to the planet Earth, and the creation of humanity has only just begun." Manfred Eigen, *Steps Towards Life* (New York: Oxford University Press, 1992), 48–49.

58. "The human understanding is of its own nature prone to abstractions and gives a substance and reality to things which are fleeting. . . . Matter rather than forms should be the object of our attention, [and] its . . . law of action or motion; for forms are figments of the human mind. . . . " Bacon, *New Organon* I.51, Anderson, 53.

"Evolutionary holism" is a name I have made up to designate a new and, at best, loosely coherent alternative to the traditional reductionist paradigm for unity of science.[59] The term "holism" is provisional, since it is not clear that, within this inchoate understanding, there would be a consensus that natural wholes are ontologically prior to their parts. There is a consensus that many-particle systems open to their environment possess emergent properties that cannot be derived from simpler antecedent components. The new understanding is, therefore, non-reductionist, even if not holist in the strong sense.[60]

Despite its present incompleteness, evolutionary holism is significant because it is a view of nature that includes the human; it claims natural science as its warrant, and employs methods recently developed and widely acclaimed, namely, "the new sciences of complexity."[61] Evolutionary holism is based on (1) a grand empirical fact and (2) a confluence of recent (since the 1940s) theoretical developments. Let us look at these items.

First, a grand empirical fact: the structures we find in the universe are not eternal, but came into being out of simpler materials, which materials in turn came from yet simpler elements. Thus, atoms of hydrogen and helium, galaxies and stars, the heavier chemical elements ejected from supernovae, the solar system, the earth's oceans and atmosphere, biopolymers, cells, organisms, and the ordered diversity of the biosphere are known with high confidence to have appeared sequentially out of originally uncombined elementary particles and radiation. (Quantum physics is crucial for the processes of combination, and for the specific properties of atomic and molecular structures.) The latter (particles and radiation) are believed to have been ultimately produced in the primordial Big Bang, an event currently dated approximately fifteen billion years ago, detailed knowledge of which is unavoidably speculative.[62] The net directedness of this process is its

59. On the looseness of the unity, see Brooks and Wiley, *Evolution as Entropy*, 1.

60. See note 5, above. For an important account of the supersession of reductionism *within* physics in favor of "investigation of emergent phenomena" resulting in the stratification of physics itself "into independent levels with stable basic principles," see Silvan Schweber, "Physics, Community and the Crisis in Physical Theory," *Physics Today* (November 1993): 34–40.

61. "I am convinced that the societies that master the new sciences of complexity and can convert that knowledge into new products and forms of social organization will become the cultural, economic, and military superpowers of the next century." Heinz Pagels, *The Dreams of Reason* (New York: Simon & Schuster, 1988), 53.

62. Hence the Big Bang itself—the earliest moments of the expanding universe—should be regarded as a hypothesis less corroborated than the formation of the solar system 4.5 billion years ago. The recent (announced April 23, 1992) discovery by the COBE satellite of minute inhomogeneities in the cosmic background radiation strength-

most striking feature. "For fifteen billion years, matter has been evolving toward ever higher states of organization, complexity, and performance."[63] We know the *fact* of this extraordinary cosmogony without, however, possessing complete knowledge of *how*, at each and every step, the more complex whole emerged from simpler parts. Gaps in the theoretical understanding of emergence—especially the emergence of life and, above all, of mind—coexist with the empirical facts and partial theories of the evolutionary sequence. The natural sciences can then be placed on the timeline of cosmic history according to the emergent structures and processes with which each science is primarily concerned. Because certain theories of physics are species neutral, they extend over the entire cosmogony (with the exception of the earliest moments), applying to structures on (almost) all scales of size from large to small—galaxies and stars, atoms and molecules, organisms and ecosystems.[64] These theories are gravitation, electromagnetism, and thermodynamics. We could call them "structure-neutral" as an alternative to species-neutral. As briefly discussed in section 3, quantum physics is not species- or structure-neutral in the sense that nuclei and electrons can combine and can interact with electromagnetic radiation only in certain ways, namely, as the stable (no-longer evolving) species of atoms and molecules with characteristic structures and discrete energy spectra—the materials of, and radiation from, all the kinds of things we now see in the universe. Major advances, beginning in the 1940s, in the extension of thermodynamics (specifically the law of increasing entropy) to phenomena of spontaneous organization (wherein

---

ens this hypothesis. According to one enthusiast, the COBE discovery "has set the seal on twentieth-century science's greatest achievement—the Big Bang theory which explains the origin of the Universe and everything in it, including ourselves." John Gribbin, *In the Beginning* (Boston: Little, Brown and Company, 1993), ix. But the fundamental problem of twentieth-century physics remains unsolved, namely, the failure to synthesize quantum physics and general relativity. We cannot exclude the possibility of a great revolution in physics in the next century, deriving from the solution to this outstanding problem, whereby the Big Bang model could be either corroborated *or refuted*. The thermodynamics, biochemistry, and molecular biology of organisms, ecosystems, and emergence on earth, however, are "intermediate-level" sciences that would probably survive a new "deep-level" physics of quantum gravity. See note 60, above. Regarding John Gribbin's remark, above, it is a principal purpose of this paper to question whether any scientific theory of the *origin* of man could be an adequate theory of the *nature* of man.

63. Hubert Reeves, *The Hour of Our Delight* (New York: W. H. Freeman, 1991), 6. I use the term "net directedness" because life on earth seems not to have evolved monotonically: "numerous authorities have argued that after the Cambrian, life on earth has been a matter of ups and downs," David L. Hull in Weber, Depew, and Smith, *Entropy*, 3.

64. The limitations involve quantum-gravitational effects and the Planck units of time and distance; see, for example, John D. Barrow and Frank J. Tipler, *The Anthropic Cosmological Principle* (New York: Oxford University Press, 1988), 292.

242     RICHARD F. HASSING

local entropy decreases) mark the first origins of evolutionary holism.[65] The application of the second law of thermodynamics to the expanding universe and, especially, to evolutive processes in the biosphere constitute the research areas most important for the new unity-of-science paradigm. How are the emergence and the evolution of life on earth to be understood in terms of entropy? The attempt to unify physics with biology will be our main focus in the following.[66] Other specialties are, however, important. The thermodynamics of evolution is one of three major theoretical developments forming the substance of evolutionary holism. The other two are the mathematics of non-linear equations, known popularly as "chaos," and molecular biology, the study of the molecular bases of replication, mutation, and metabolism in organisms. Each of these is today a vast domain of rich and highly specialized scientific research. Brief descriptions are bound to be woefully inadequate to their intellectual charm and importance. For present purposes, however, the following remarks must suffice. I begin with the thermodynamics of evolution or nonequilibrium thermodynamics, also known as self-organizing systems theory.

*Nonequilibrium Thermodynamics (Self-Organizing Systems)*

Research on the thermodynamics of chemical reactions, especially by the Brussels School of Ilya Prigogine, features examples of chemical systems in which there emerge remarkable, visible (macroscopic),

65. E. Schroedinger, *What is Life?* (London: Cambridge University Press, 1945); I. Prigogine and J. M. Wiame, "Biologie et thermodynamique des phenomenes irreversibles," *Experientia* 2 (1946), 451–53; I. Prigogine, *Étude Thermodynamique des Phenomenes Irreversibles* (Liege: Desoer, 1947); Alan Turing, "The Chemical Basis of Morphogenesis," *Philos. Trans. Royal Soc. Lond.* B237 (1952): 37–72. Also of importance for the origins of the Brussels School is T. DeDonder, *L'Affinité* (Paris: Gauthier-Vallars, 1927).

66. The application of physics to the evolutionary sequence from (just after) the Big Bang up to the emergence of life on earth (currently dated about 3.8 billion years ago) is conceptually well grounded. Indeed, the "anthropic principle" can be regarded as a body of research in physics persuasively showing that the known principles of the physical universe—laws, initial conditions, constants—are *per se* aimed at a universe containing all the chemical elements of the periodic table, rather than a universe containing only hydrogen, helium or iron. The extension of physics into biogenesis and biological evolution (see note 54) is not as well grounded due to a diversity of opposed opinions on the correct relation between entropy, information, organization, and complexity and a corresponding diversity of biogenesis scenarios. (The terms "order" and "disorder," traditional among physicists, are not adequate for the study of biological phenomena.) See, for example, Hubert Yockey, *Information Theory and Molecular Biology* (Cambridge: Cambridge University Press, 1992); also David Hull's remarks in Weber, Depew, and Smith, *Entropy*, 5–7; also Harold Morowitz, *Beginnings of Cellular Life* (New Haven: Yale University Press, 1992), 126. The notion of a law of increasing informational entropy (as opposed to increasing thermodynamic entropy of matter and energy) proposed by Brooks and Wiley, *Evolution as Entropy*, 31–52, is a new departure with respect to conventional physics.

spatio-temporal patterns of order that are compatible with, but not predictable from, the temporally preceding state of the system.[67] "[F]ar from equilibrium, new types of organization of matter appear. . . . entirely new properties arise. The structure and properties of the solution below the instability point cannot be extrapolated even in a first approximation."[68] Such spontaneous formation of order from a previously homogeneous state is called self-organization. By "spontaneous" is meant proceeding from sources internal to the system in the given environment. The role of the environment is important.

According to traditional equilibrium thermodynamics, the spontaneous formation of the more complex and differentiated (a chick) from the simpler and more homogeneous (an egg) would violate the second law, the law of monotonically increasing entropy.[69] The organization and evolution of living things thus gave rise in the latter part of the nineteenth century to a well known perplexity as to whether life contradicts the second law of thermodynamics, and how best to reconcile Darwin with entropy. The discussion continues today.[70] Prigogine's generalization of thermodynamics to nonequilibrium (and nonlinear) systems is a major contribution. Systems open to flows of energy and matter from their environment can undergo a decrease in local entropy consistent with a compensating increase in the total entropy of the system plus environment.[71] They are nonequilibrium systems because the flows that feed increasing internal organization arise from differences in temperature and chemical potential in and around the system, differences maintained and prevented from spontaneously equilibrating by certain constraints imposed on the system. To produce and maintain their organization, such thermodynamically constrained systems must exhaust or dissipate energy in the form of waste heat, and are thus also called dissipative systems. "The study of such a new organization, the

67. The reactions discovered by Belousov and Zhabotinski, *Biofizika* 9 (1964): 306–11, are a paradigm for self-organizing systems theory. Pictures of Belousov-Zhabotinski reaction patterns appear prominently in most of the books by Prigogine and his collaborators.

68. P. Glansdorff and I. Prigogine, *Thermodynamic Theory of Structure, Stability and Fluctuations* (London: Wiley-Interscience, 1971), 42–43.

69. The cream in our coffee spontaneously mixes until it is uniformly distributed. Were the light brown fluid spontaneously to separate into two distinct layers (of cream and coffee), we would be astonished. We know such processes never occur by themselves but only by some agent's working on the system and expending energy to reverse its tendency toward homogeneity; for example, a refrigerator engine expends energy in forcing heat to flow from a lower temperature to a higher one.

70. Hubert Yockey's charming book, *Information Theory and Molecular Biology*, has significant things to say on this topic, 7, 70, 241, 281, 310–13.

71. Nicolis and Prigogine, *Self-Organization in Nonequilibrium Systems* (New York: Wiley-Interscience, 1977), 24–25.

so-called *dissipative structure,* arising from the exchange of matter and energy with the outside world, appears as one of the most fascinating subjects of macroscopic physics. . . ."[72] Since biological phenomena provide the most vivid examples of organization emerging from homogeneity, for example, embryonic development, the new thermodynamics suggested the possibility of a unification of physics and biology:

> We can already feel the possibility of a new, nonequilibrium order principle. . . . This is of obvious interest for living systems; the biosphere as a whole is a nonequilibrium system, as it is subject to the flow of solar energy. . . . Although much work remains to be done, it already clearly appears that self-organization is an emerging paradigm of science . . . in which nonlinear processes and nonequilibrium conditions play a significant role.[73]

Therefore, instead of being the result of either extraordinary causality (God) or extraordinarily improbable natural events (blind chance), the emergence and evolution of life would be embedded in the laws of nature as the likely outcome of ordinary physico-chemical processes.[74]

Far from being outside nature, biological processes follow from the laws of physics, appropriate to specific nonlinear interactions and to conditions far from equilibrium. Thanks to these specific features, the flow of energy and matter may be used to build and maintain functional and structural order.[75]

72. Glansdorff and Prigogine, *Thermodynamic Theory,* 73, also 41–43. See also the presentation of chemical cycling in energy flow systems in Harold Morowitz, *Energy Flow in Biology* (New York: Academic Press, 1968), 1–33. The term "self " in self-organization thus refers to the removal of the need within traditional equilibrium and linear nonequilibrium thermodynamics for appeal to the extraordinary (either God or chance) in accounting for evolutive development. The term "self " is thus dependent on the historical context of nineteenth-century physics, and does not refer to our prescientific experience of personal awareness and interiority; that is, it has no psychological meaning.

73. Nicolis and Prigogine, *Self-Organization,* 25 and 474. "Concepts such as coherence, complexity, and order . . . have long been an integral part of biology, but until recently they were outside the mainstream of physics. The possibility of using these fundamental concepts to describe the behavior of quite ordinary physical systems as well as living things is a major development that science could not have forecast even just a few years ago." G. Nicolis and I. Prigogine, *Exploring Complexity* (New York: W.H. Freeman, 1989), 13. For recent statements by evolutionary biologists on the status of unification, see Weber, Depew, and Smith, *Entropy,* especially David L. Hull's remarks on 2–3.

74. Concerning ultimate causality, however, there would remain the metaphysical question of the source of the biogenetic laws of physicochemical nature. See Paul Davies, *The Mind of God* (New York: Simon and Schuster, 1992).

75. Nicolis and Prigogine, *Self-Organization,* 13–14. In the context of the present discussion, "these specific features" are *common* to both prebiotic chemical systems and biological organisms. More recently, Stuart Kauffman has suggested that "we can think of the origin of life as an expected *emergent collective property* of a modestly complex mixture of catalytic polymers. . . . I believe that the origin of life was not an enormously improbable event, but law-like and governed by new principles of self-organization in complex webs of catalysts." Kauffman, *The Origins of Order* (New York: Oxford University Press, 1993), xvi. Similarly, "Our view is . . . that nonequilibrium models can provide a set of

It is now widely accepted that the organic must be understood within the theory of dissipative systems.[76] But are nonlinear kinetic equations and nonequilibrium thermodynamic constraints *sufficient* to account for the apparent differences between living and nonliving things? Will these differences then be shown by the theory of self-organizing systems to be merely superficial and no more essential than the difference between celestial and terrestrial motions? As Stuart Kauffman correctly observes, "deeply embedded in the tradition of science from Newton, lay the ideal of accounting for the diversity of superficially heterogeneous phenomena on the basis of relatively few underlying universal principles."[77] On the molecular level, the most striking organic phenomenon is the genetic code.[78] Does the genetic code amount to superficial or essential heterogeneity? Before turning to molecular biology, we must consider a development in mathematics.

*Nonlinear Mathematics (Chaos)*

The manual analysis of non-linear equations (algebraic and differential) is, in general, prohibitively time-consuming due to the "feedback" terms that make them non-linear. Effective study of these equations, therefore, became possible only with the advent of modern high-speed computers. There resulted the extension of mathematical treatment to phenomena previously regarded as hopelessly random, or chaotic, and thus inaccessible to mathematical modeling. Remarkable

principles showing why the evolution of biological systems is something to be expected, rather than something that needs to be explained against a theoretical background that does not strongly anticipate it. . . ." David J. Depew and Bruce H. Weber, "Consequences of Nonequilibrium Thermodynamics for Darwinism," in Weber, Depew, and Smith, *Entropy*, 318.

76. "Everyone agrees, we presume, that organisms are far-from-equilibrium dissipative structures. By this we mean that organisms are 'working systems' that require a continuous input of free energy inorder to maintain themselves in a steady state." Brooks and Wiley, *Evolution as Entropy*, 33. "All natural organizations (as opposed to machines) are nonequilibrium systems that operate, and autocatalytically produce themselves, by degrading energy resources. . . . understanding the organism as an informed dissipative structure is enormously important to the Kantian project of connecting life with the rest of nature, and in making in-principle restrictions on the hand of variation in evolutionary processes." Jeffrey Wicken, "Thermodynamics, Evolution, and Emergence," in Weber, Depew, and Smith, *Entropy*, 165, 166. "A fundamental problem for statistical mechanics is to explain why dissipative systems (those in which entropy is continually being produced and removed to the surroundings) tend to undergo 'self-organization,' a spontaneous increase of structural complexity, of which the most extreme example is the origin and evolution of life." Charles H. Bennett, "Dissipation, Information, Computational Complexity and the Definition of Organization," in *Emerging Syntheses in Science*, ed. David Pines (Redwood City, Calif.: Addison-Wesley, 1988), 215.

77. Kauffman, *The Origins of Order*, 4.

78. See, for example, Ernst Mayr, *Toward a New Philosophy of Biology* (Cambridge: Harvard University Press, 1988), 2.

regularities (visible not to sense but to the eye of the mathematical mind) were discovered to underlie processes that seemed both irregular and unrelated, such as turbulent flow in fluids and the variation of insect populations.[79] Among the most interesting results of nonlinear mathematics is the confirmation of the ubiquitous character of "sensitive dependence on initial conditions," an effect originally predicted by Henri Poincaré, wherein trajectories initially adjacent (in phase space) rapidly diverge and possess a seemingly random, irregular character.[80] This result means that natural processes that are thoroughly deterministic but which possess nonlinear features can become completely unpredictable after a finite time. For example, long-term weather prediction has always been impossible, and now, by means of the mathematics of chaos, we understand why this must be the case. The concept of *trajectory*, the fundamental concept of classical dynamics, is thus revealed to be only *partially* applicable to nature, and not fully adequate to nature.[81] "Contrary to what Isaac Newton may have believed, the deterministic equations of classical mechanics do not imply a regular, ordered universe."[82]

A second result of nonlinear mathematics is directly relevant for evolutionary holism. Physicochemical systems governed by nonlinear equations can (under nonequilibrium conditions) exhibit alternative time evolutions, or bifurcations. The system, as it were, comes to a fork in the road, and "chooses" one branch or the other unpredictably.[83] In such cases:

Nothing in the description of the experimental setup permits the observer to assign beforehand the state that will be chosen; only chance will decide, through the dynamics of [unpredictable microscopic] fluctuations. . . . the system becomes a historical object in the sense that its subsequent evolution depends on this critical choice.[84]

79. Mitchell Feigenbaum, "Universal Behavior in Nonlinear Systems," *Los Alamos Science* 1 (Summer 1980): 4–27, reprinted in *Physica* D7 (1983): 16–39; James Gleick, *Chaos* (New York: Viking, 1987).

80. Henri Poincaré, *Science and Method* (New York: Dover, 1950), 67–69; Edward N. Lorenz, "Deterministic Nonperiodic Flow," *J. Atmos. Sci.* 20 (1963): 130–41; Gleick, *Chaos*, 9–32.

81. Joseph Ford, "How Random is a Coin Toss?," *Physics Today* 36 (1983), 40; I. Prigogine and I. Stengers, *Order Out of Chaos* (New York: Bantam Books, 1984), 264. Quantum mechanics yields the same conclusion, in the form of the Heisenberg uncertainty principle, but for different reasons.

82. Roderick Jensen, "Classical Chaos," *American Scientist* 75 (1987): 168.

83. Nicolis and Prigogine, *Self-Organization*, 70–71.

84. Nicolis and Prigogine, *Exploring Complexity*, 72. Similarly: "Evolution of the non-equilibrium structure depends on some singular factor that happens to occur at the right time, at the right place: it depends on chance." Prigogine, "Nonequilibrium Thermo-

It is important to ask what actual physical systems exhibit this behavior? What kinds of natural compounds are self-organizing systems with bifurcation histories determined by chance fluctuations? In general, a great diversity of physical systems exhibit characteristics (such as deterministic chaos, spontaneous pattern formation, and coherent structures) now described by nonlinear mathematics.[85] For present purposes, three examples, nicely presented by Nicolis and Prigogine,[86] raise with unusual clarity the issue of species neutrality in the evolutionist paradigm for unity of science. They are Benard convection cells in heated liquids, the Belousov-Zhabotinski (BZ) reaction in inorganic chemistry, and the phenomenon of aggregation in populations of the amoeba *Dictyostelium discoideum,* or slime mold.

Benard cells are patterns of contiguous rolling motions in a horizontal fluid layer that is heated from below and is thus subject to a temperature difference vertically from its lower (hotter) surface to its upper (cooler) surface. The cells appear abruptly as the temperature difference is increased beyond a characteristic critical value. Once formed, alternate cells rotate in alternately clockwise and counterclockwise directions. The formation of the cells can be repeated at will by restoring the temperature difference to zero and then reheating the liquid from below to the critical temperature difference at which the spatial structure of Benard convection cells reappears.

[T]his phenomenon is therefore subject to a strict determinism. In contrast, the *direction* of rotation of the cells is unpredictable and uncontollable. Only chance, in the form of the particular perturbation that may have prevailed at the moment of the experiment, will decide whether a given cell is right- or left-handed. We thus arrive at a remarkable cooperation between chance and determinism, one that is reminiscent of the duality of mutation (chance) and natural selection (determinism) familiar in biology since Darwin's era. . . . nonequilibrium has enabled the system . . . to transform part of the energy communicated from the environment into an ordered behavior of a new type, the *dissipative structure*: a regime characterized by symmetry breaking, multiple choices [bifurcations], and correlations of a macroscopic range. We can therefore say that we have witnessed the birth of complexity. True, the type of complexity achieved is rather modest; nevertheless, it presents characteristics that usually have been ascribed exclusively to biological systems. More important, far from challenging the laws of physics, complexity appears as an inevitable consequence of these laws when suitable conditions are fulfilled.[87]

---

dynamics and Chemical Evolution: An Overview," in *Aspects of Chemical Evolution*, ed. G. Nicolis, Seventeenth Solvay Conference on Chemistry (New York: Wiley, 1984), 48.

85. See the concise overview by David K. Campbell, "Nonlinear Science," *Los Alamos Science* 15 (1987): 218–62.

86. Nicolis and Prigogine, *Exploring Complexity*, 8–26, 31–36.

87. Ibid., 14, 15.

The remaining two examples, the BZ reaction and the aggregation of slime mold, exhibit spontaneous formation of mobile spatial patterns, or waves. In the mixture of inorganic chemicals (far from chemical equilibrium) in the BZ reaction, concentric or spiral waves appear.[88] In the life cycle of a population (about 100,000 cells) of the amoeba, starvation causes the initially independent, and independently functioning, cells to coalesce into a single multicellular body. This aggregate acts as one organism (!), whose cells now perform distinct functions in order to optimize control over scarce food supplies. The condition of starvation is the analogue of a nonequilibrium constraint. During the phase of cooperative behavior, the motion of the whole collection "gives rise to density patterns among the cells that look very much like the wave patterns in the BZ reagent."[89] Here we find similar visible patterns in two completely different materials (inorganic chemicals and amoebae) under analogous conditions of nonequilibrium constraint. Common to both are nonlinear processes (feedback or autocatalysis). Such examples of physical, chemical, and biological self-organization phenomena and the accompanying mathematical description lead Nicolis and Prigogine to the following remarkable assessment:

If instead of the Benard flow we were interested in the Belousov-Zhabotinski reaction, the aggregation of *Dictyostelium discoideum*, or in practically any other transition phenomena, and if we constructed bifurcation diagrams for these systems, we would find the same qualitative structure. The only differences would concern terminology, which is necessarily specific to each particular problem. Thus we find a deep unity among widely diverse systems, and this allows us to assert that the passage toward complexity is intimately related to the *bifurcation* of new branches of solutions following the *instability* of a reference state, caused by the nonlinearities and the constraints acting on an open system. . . . [Thus] we have succeeded in formulating, in abstract terms, the remarkable interplay between chance and constraint, between fluctuations and irreversibility. . . . Note the similarity between these ideas and the notion of mutation and selection familiar from biological evolution. As a matter of fact, we can say that fluctuations are the physical counterpart of mutants, whereas the search for stability is the equivalent of biological selection. Even the very structure of a bifurcation diagram is reminiscent of the phylogenetic trees employed in biology.[90]

88. Ibid., 22.

89. Ibid., 35, also I. Prigogine, *From Being to Becoming* (New York: W. H. Freeman, 1980), 74–75.

90. Nicolis and Prigogine, *Exploring Complexity*, 73. For Mae-Wan Ho, the "similitude between biological and physico-chemical forms [that is, the visible patterns] demonstrates a deep order in nature that transcends both detailed mechanisms and the particular material substrates involved." "Reanimating Nature: The Integration of Science with Human Experience," *Leonardo* 24 (1991): 610. Other specialists are more reserved in their estimation of the biological significance of generalized thermodynamics: "[T]he

Evidently, the terminologies specific to self-organization phenomena in "widely diverse systems," for example, living and nonliving, do not refer to anything essential, so that what these different kinds of systems have in common (certain nonlinear equations of motion) is more fundamental than what specifically differentiates them. Does the fundamental order underlying what we call "life" then transcend what currently seem to be the specifically organic characteristics—metabolism, replication, variation, and selection, in a material basis of informational nucleic acids and proteins? This is the tantalizing suggestion of Nicolis and Prigogine in the passage above.[91] Stuart Kauffman offers a similar opinion: "the template-replicating properties of DNA and RNA are not essential to life itself (although these properties are now essential to *our* life). The fundamental order lies deeper, the routes to life are broader."[92]

But the strongest claims for the new evolutionist paradigm concern its application to human phenomena. "It is, of course, very tempting to apply these considerations . . . to problems of sociocultural evolution."[93] Not all workers in this extremely diverse domain of research

---

irreversible behavior of certain biological systems has a quite different basis from that exhibited by purely physical dissipative structures. . . . biological systems exhibit order and organization based on properties that are inherent and heritable. Physical dissipative structures lack these characteristics." E. O. Wiley, "Entropy and Evolution," in Weber, Depew, and Smith, *Entropy,* 176. "Thermodynamics thus allows discussion of evolutionary whys apart from mechanistic particulars, and provides general rules or guidelines for *kinds* of mechanisms. It cannot comment, however, on their specifics." Jeffrey Wicken, "Thermodynamics, Evolution, and Emergence," in Weber, Depew, and Smith, *Entropy,* 153. "The richness of biology lies in the molecular hardware, the power of genetic coding, the great historical testing of niches, the remarkable pattern generation of morphogenesis, and other such empirically rooted approaches. There will be theories to make sense of these, but to think in terms of predictive grand, unified theories based on thermodynamics is simply dreaming." Harold Morowitz, *Beginnings of Cellular Life,* 77.

91. Their view is more cautious on page 32 of *Exploring Complexity.* And, in an earlier work, Nicolis is careful to distinguish dissipative structures in nonequilibrium *chemical* systems from biological organization: "To avoid misunderstanding, it should be stressed that the form of dissipative structures discussed in this review is probably not yet the exact prototype of biological structures in the usual sense of the term (macromolecules, membranes, cells as a whole, and so on). Indeed, the drastic lowering of entropy and the increase of entropy production which characterize these structures does not occur as a general rule in the dissipative structures analyzed [here]. What the theory of dissipative structures can explain, however, are some aspects of functional order, once the existence of macromolecules and their interactions is taken for granted. . . . future work may prove that the concept of dissipative structures is even more fundamental, and is one of the necessary prerequisites for life." G. Nicolis, "Stability and Dissipative Structures in Open Systems Far From Equilibrium," in *Advances in Chemical Physics* XIX, eds. I. Prigogine and S. A. Rice (New York: Wiley Interscience, 1971), 209–323; quotation from 315.

92. Kauffman, *The Origins of Order,* xvi. Note Kauffman's parenthesis: an originally accidental effect can become, in some sense, essential.

93. Nicolis and Prigogine, *Self-Organization in Nonequilibrium Systems,* 473.

succumb to this temptation. It is worth a brief look at some remarks of the Brussels School, however, for they illustrate the persistence, within the new paradigm, of the basic philosophical problem of modern natural science: the effect it produces on our own self-understanding.

Concerning dissipative systems near a bifurcation point, Prigogine writes that, "a small fluctuation may start an entirely new evolution that will drastically change the whole behavior of the macroscopic system. The analogy with social phenomena, even with history, is inescapable."[94] Accordingly, Nicolis and Prigogine consider self-organization in human systems:

Our everyday experience teaches us that adaptability and plasticity of behavior, two basic features of nonlinear dynamical systems capable of performing transitions in far-from-equilibrium conditions, rank among the most conspicuous characteristics of human societies. It is therefore natural to expect that dynamical models allowing for evolution and change should be the most adequate ones for social systems.[95]

The specifically human is acknowledged as follows:

The evolution of such a system is an interplay between the behavior of its actors and the impinging constraints from the environment. It is here that the human system finds its unique specificity. Contrary to the molecules, the actors in a physico-chemical system, or even the ants or the members of other animal societies, human beings develop individual *projects and desires*.[96]

The plasticity of human desires and projects poses the fundamental question,

whether . . . the overall evolution is capable of leading to some kind of global optimum or, on the contrary, whether each human system constitutes a unique realization of a complex stochastic process whose rules can in no way be designed in advance. In other words, is past experience sufficient for predicting the future or is a high degree of unpredictability of the future the essence of human adventure, be it at the individual level of learning or at the collective level of history making?[97]

There results mathematical modeling based on the logistic equation, a paradigm for nonlinear dynamics and historically used in the study of variations in insect populations. In accounting for the difference between humans and ants, as Nicolis and Prigogine point out in their

94. Prigogine and Stengers, *Order Out of Chaos*, 14.
95. Nicolis and Prigogine, *Exploring Complexity*, 238.
96. Ibid.
97. Ibid.

earlier work, "the main difficulty is to determine the relevant variables. . . . one needs to introduce such elusive variables as 'quality of life' [i.e., justice and happiness] which are much more difficult to handle in a quantitative manner."[98] Accordingly, a real variable, $A_i$, is introduced, which represents the *attractiveness* of option i in a set of options, 1 . . . K. We can easily find examples of contemporary options: dealing drugs, helping the poor, abandoning one's child, being a responsible parent, joining an extremist political faction, or working for democratic pluralism are six typical and timely options for our projects and desires. In the model, the attractiveness of option i is taken to depend, as it should, on the number of people (easily quantified) "envisaging this option," but not on the intrinsic worth of the option ("difficult to handle in a quantitative manner").[99] A complicated set of equations for the number of people in option i as a function of time is then derived.[100]

As the equations are highly nonlinear, it is expected that there will be several solution branches exhibiting a complicated set of bifurcation phenomena. Different initial conditions will place the system in different basins of attraction, thus switching on different evolutions, different histories.[101]

Computer-assisted analysis yields results of interest. "We now have sufficient elements at our disposal to answer the [basic] question," namely, "is past experience sufficient for predicting the future, or is a high degree of unpredictability . . . the essence of human adventure"?[102] The key result is that, in the mathematical model, the spontaneous formation of patterns of populations and options cannot be controled from initial conditions.

This illustrates the dangers of short-term, narrow planning based on the direct extrapolation of past experience. Such static methods threaten society with fossilization. . . . The principal message of the dynamical modeling advocated [here] is that the adaptive possibility of societies is the main source allowing them to survive in the long term, to innovate of themselves, and to produce originality.[103]

But can human problems be knowledgeably understood and ameliorated? Can human disasters be averted by wise policy?[104] Or is human society so evolving and open to wholly new futures that there are no

98. Nicolis and Prigogine, *Self-Organization in Nonequilibrium Systems,* 473; also *Exploring Complexity,* 218.
99. Nicolis and Prigogine, *Exploring Complexity,* 239.
100. Ibid., 240, Eq. 6.15.          101. Ibid., 241.
102. Ibid., 241 and 238.          103. Ibid., 242.
104. See, for example, Winston Churchill, *The Gathering Storm* (Boston: Houghton Mifflin, 1948), iv and ix.

abiding problems, no objective meaning to the virtues of courage, wisdom, justice, and moderation—and their corresponding vices? The latter seems to be the preferred answer given by the above variant of the evolutionist paradigm. And so the permanent tension between eros and justice that we learn from Plato's *Republic,* the problem of our partiality that extends through the entire history of political philosophy, the meaning of moderation as a moral condition of good judgment in Aristotle's *Ethics,* the crucial importance of institutional arrangements in *The Federalist*—arrangements that not only limit power but promote the conditions of rational deliberation because factional conflict is the greatest threat to democracy—human learning of this type finds no more place in the new unity-of-science paradigm than it did in the old. Is criminal violence in America better understood in terms of logistic equations and attractiveness functions, or in terms of the collapse of the family and the rise of a generation of anomic adolescents? Is the Yugoslav war better understood in terms of entropy production and distance from equilibrium (even granting the exceedingly unlikely assumption that these concepts could be meaningfully defined) or from human accounts like the following?

> When Milosevic came into power, he did a very simple thing: he replaced all the key persons in the media. . . . And then the big game of openly blaming others, whoever they might be, could start. Of course the name for it was nationalism. . . . this was a process which many faithful totalitarian minds had prepared for over six or seven years. They worked to legitimize national hatred. And they succeeded.[105]

Is it not the case that, of the specifically human problems, whatever might be understood in terms of the evolutionary paradigm can be better understood without it?

Let us return from the most radical extensions of the evolutionist paradigm, to the scientists most familiar with the phenomena of the organic: the biochemists and molecular biologists. This is the third major theoretical development on which the evolutionist unity-of-science paradigm is based. Here we find a most appropriate debate, one that is both intrascientific yet germane to our central theme of natural science, essential heterogeneity, and human self-knowledge.

## Molecular Biology (DNA)

The briefest remarks must suffice. I comment on the recent accounts of the origin of biological information (that is, the genetic plans encoded in the DNA of organisms) by Bernd-Olaf Küppers of the "Göt-

---

105. Slavenka Drakulic in *Partisan Review* LIX (1992), No. 4, 739.

tingen school" of molecular Darwinism, and Hubert Yockey.[106] Molecular Darwinism offers a physico-chemical explanation of the emergence
and function of biological macromolecules. It presupposes nonequilibrium thermodynamics and nonlinear mathematics as its theoretical
basis. As its name implies, molecular Darwinism extends the Darwinian
principles of random mutation and environmental selection back into
the prebiotic phase of molecular interactions.[107] The emergence of self-
replicating populations of nucleic acids subject to adaptive selection is
thereby embedded in the laws of nature as the likely outcome of ordinary physico-chemical processes.[108] On grounds of this new account
of evolutionary emergence, what then is the status of the universal genetic code (whereby nucleotide triplets code for amino acids),[109] and
what is the status of the particular genomes of organic species? Are
they products of chance, possessing only a history, or do they possess
their own specific principles? In other words, of the determinate order
of living things that we now see, what can and what cannot be explained
*scientifically* in the sense of the new unity-of-science paradigm? A complete answer to this question would require an extensive study. Let us
give a provisional answer by means of the following excerpts:

Since the elementary events (mutations) that lead to evolutionary change are
completely indeterminate,[110] every evolutionary process is historically unique.
It is thus clear that the molecular-Darwinistic approach a priori can explain
the origin of biological information in itself, but not the detailed structure of
this information. . . . The modern theory of the origin of life is a physicochemical theory. As such, it attempts to base the historical process of biological self-
organization upon its fundamental, unchanging principles and mechanisms.

106. Yockey, *Information Theory and Molecular Biology,* and Küppers, *Information and
the Origin of Life.* Küppers is a coworker of Manfred Eigen, Director of the Max Planck
Institute for Biophysical Chemistry at Göttingen, and founder of the group that has
developed the highly influential "nucleic-acids-first" self-organization biogenesis sce-
nario. See especially Eigen, "Self-Organization of Matter and the Evolution of Biological
Macromolecules," *Naturwissenschaften* 58 (1971): 465–523, and M. Eigen and P. Schuster,
*The Hypercycle* (Heidelberg: Springer Verlag, 1979).
    107. "These models of self-organization (so-called hypercycles) are all based upon
the assumptions that selection and evolution in the Darwinian sense is already effective
at the molecular level *and* that the nucleic acids were able to reproduce themselves in the
prebiotic phase of evolution without the help of the proteins." Küppers, *Information and
the Origin of Life,* 136.
    108. Küppers, *Information and the Origin of Life,* chap. 12.
    109. Ibid., 18.
    110. Ibid., 150. Mutations are completely indeterminate, according to Küppers, be-
cause they are "based ultimately on quantum-mechanical uncertainty" (167). Since 1988,
however, biologists have been aware of (astonishing) evidence that certain mutations may
not be simply random; see J. Cairns, J. Overbough, and S. Miller, "The Origin of Mutants," *Nature* 335 (September 1988): 142–45, and Boyce Rensberger, "Choosing the
Right Mutation?," *The Washington Post,* 20 April 1992.

The theory does *not* claim to be able to reconstruct the process in its historical details [thus it does not explain] the origin of a plan [e.g., a specific genome] in its detailed structure. . . . [The theory predicts] *that* biological structures exist, but not *what* biological structures exist. . . . The concrete content of biological information can not be deduced from the laws of physics and chemistry.[111]

Here, "the historical process of biological self-organization [will be based] upon its fundamental, unchanging principles and mechanisms." And so it seems indeed that the scientifically knowable can only be the common, law-governed evolutive process from which all specific products randomly emerge. Therefore, *insofar as they are objects of scientific explanation*, the genetic code and specific genomes must be taken as products of chance; *insofar as possessing natures*, they are merely objects of "phenomenological description."[112]

It is important to note that Küppers's concept of scientific explanation plays a significant role in his argument. Specifically, his adherence to methodological reductionism while rejecting both ontological reductionism and holistic principles betokens a distinctive (and somewhat perplexing) position.[113] The point I wish to emphasize is that, as presented by Küppers, molecular Darwinism (1) rejects reductionism in the philosophically decisive sense of physical or ontological reductionism, (2) regards holistic principles as *nonscientific*, but (3) affirms that the "value of a holistic viewpoint *on the descriptive level* of biology is . . . incontestable."[114]

Here it would seem that a relation of problematic compatibility can obtain between study of the specific and species-neutral natural science. The genetic code, specific genomes, and, ultimately, the specifically human—although relegated to being objects of phenomenological description rather than science—are not rejected as simply unreal or mere appearance, as they would be within the reductionist unity-of-science paradigm. In turn, the problem of the relation between natural science and human self-knowledge now includes the issue of phenomenology: what exactly is the distinction between phenomenological description and scientific explanation?

A stronger defense of the scientific autonomy of biology is given in Hubert Yockey's argument for the genetic code as an axiom or first principle of molecular biology. Yockey and the Göttingen school thus constitute two sides of a valuable debate. In its barest essentials, Yockey's

111. Küppers, *Information and the Origin of Life*, 150, 164, 169, and 177.
112. Ibid., 130.
113. Ibid., chap. 11, and 131.
114. Ibid., 127, emphasis added.

position is a transformation of Bohr's 1933 hypothesis of a complementarity principle for organisms (analogous to wave-particle duality in quantum phenomena). According to Bohr,

we should doubtless kill an animal if we tried to carry the investigation of its organs so far that we could describe the role played by single atoms in vital functions [thus reduction of living wholes *qua* living to elementary parts is not possible]. . . . the idea suggests itself that the minimal freedom we must allow the organism in this respect is just large enough to permit it, so to say, to hide its ultimate secrets from us. On this view, the existence of life must be considered as an elementary fact that cannot be explained, but must be taken as a starting point in biology, in a similar way as the quantum of action, which appears as an irrational element from the point of view of classical mechanical physics, taken together with the existence of elementary particles, forms the foundations of atomic physics.[115]

It is Yockey's intention "to show that the sequence hypothesis . . . [which] states that the sequences of nucleotides and amino acids carry the information that controls the folding and activity of proteins . . . may be taken as a starting point or axiom of molecular biology and play the role called for by Bohr."[116] Accordingly, an essential part of Yockey's argument is the criticism of current self-organization biogenesis scenarios, including that of the Göttingen school.[117] His criticism is that, based on the mathematical theory of information, these scenarios are not scientifically plausible. Yockey's position is a transformation of Bohr in that it is the universal genetic code, rather than the life of the individual organism, that is the irreducible principle. This principle then grounds phenomena the knowledge of which "complements" physics and chemistry, although there is no irreconcilability of the quantum type (between wave description and particle description according to mutually exclusive observational arrangements), and apparently no "ultimate secrets" in the molecular physics of organic reproduction of like from like. Thus, unlike Bohr's 1933 hypothesis, Yockey's position seems not to entail a holistic understanding of the individual living thing and might be consistent with a greater degree of reductionist explanation than Bohr envisaged prior to the discovery of DNA in 1953.[118]

115. Niels Bohr, "Light and Life," *Nature* 131 (1933): 421–23 and 457–59. Quoted by Yockey, *Information Theory and Molecular Biology*, 2.
116. Yockey, *Information Theory and Molecular Biology*, 1 and 3.
117. Ibid., 271–83.
118. See Gunther Stent, "Light and life: Niels Bohr's legacy to contemporary biology," in *Niels Bohr: Physics and the World*, eds. H. Feshbach, T. Matsui and A. Oleson (New York: Harwood Academic Publishers, 1988), 231–44; also Küppers, *Information and the Origin of Life*, 74–75.

Broadly stated then, evolutionary holism is a conflation of mathematics, physics, chemistry, biology, and information theory yielding what we could call, in analogy to Newton, the mathematical principles of evolution, whereby the emergence of life is embedded in the underlying physics of the evolutionary flow. This general characterization covers a diversity of positions and fundamental issues. Two such issues are: first, clarification of the concepts of entropy, information, order, randomness, organization, and complexity, especially in regard to causality; second, what is scientific explanation in relation to phenomenological description?

In its strongest version,[119] evolutionary holism purports to be a major advance in the understanding not only of living species in general, but of the human species in particular, and even of revolutionary human events; it purports to be the best ground on which to make intelligible both evolution and revolution. Of the specifically human problems, however, I believe that whatever might be understood in terms of the strong evolutionary paradigm can be better understood without it.

On grounds of the more moderate versions of evolutionary holism (essentially based on molecular biology) the scientific quest for common or species-neutral principles of origin appears to be compatible with phenomenology of specific natures—thus compatible with prescientific knowledge of the human. Indeed, as the phenomenological psychologist Erwin Straus put it, "With all due respect for the accomplishments of those early [prehuman] ancestors, we should not forget to investigate our own situation. Man is not only the end of a long development; he also represents a new beginning."[120]

119. That of Prigogine, also Erich Jantsch, *The Self-Organizing Universe* (Oxford: Pergamon Press, 1980).

120. Erwin Straus, *Phenomenological Psychology* (New York: Basic Books, 1966), 140.

# Contributors

*John W. Burbidge* received his Ph.D. from the University of Toronto in 1971, and he has taught at Trent University since 1970 where he is currently Chairman of the Department of Philosophy. His research focuses on Hegel's logic and philosophy of nature, on the relation between syntax and reasoning, and on religion in Canada. He is the author of *Being and Will: An Essay in Philosophical Theology* (1977), *On Hegel's Logic: Fragments of a Commentary* (1981), *Within Reason: A Guide to Non-Deductive Reasoning* (1990), *Hegel on Logic and Religion: The Reasonableness of Christianity* (1992), and *Real Process: How Logic and Chemistry Combine in Hegel's Philosophy of Nature* (1996).

After receiving his Ph.D. in Letters from the Sorbonne in 1955, *Ernest Fortin* has taught at Assumption College and was Visiting Professor at Laval University from 1965–72, where he studied with Charles DeKoninck in the philosophy of nature. Since 1971, he has been Professor of Theology at Boston College, specializing in religion and political theory. He has published *Christianity and Philosophic Culture in the Fifth Century* (1959), *Medieval Political Philosophy: A Sourcebook* (1973), and *Philosophy and Dissidence in the Middle Ages: Dante and His Antecedents* (1980). He is co-editor of *Saint Augustine's Political Writings* (1994). A three-volume edition of his collected essays, *The Birth of Philosophic Christianity, Classical Christianity and the Political Order,* and *Human Rights, Social Justice, and the Common Good,* appeared in 1997.

Currently a member of the Department of Philosophy at the University of Missouri at Kansas City, *George Gale* received his Ph.D. from the University of California at Davis in 1971. He is a specialist in Leibniz and in the history of modern cosmology. He has published *Theory of Science* (1979), and numerous articles, among which "The Anthropic Principle" in *Scientific American*, "Rationalist Programmes in Early Modern Cosmology" in *Astronomical Quarterly*, "Leibniz" and "Leibniz-Clarke Correspondence" in the *Encyclopedia of Time*, edited by Samuel

Macey, and "The Physical Theory of Leibniz" in *Leibniz: Critical Assessments,* edited by R. S. Woolhouse (1994).

A life member of Clare Hall, Cambridge, *Allan Gotthelf* received his Ph.D. from Columbia University in 1975, and he is currently Chairman of the Department of Philosophy and Religion at The College of New Jersey. He has edited *Aristotle on Nature and Living Things* (1985) and *Philosophical Issues in Aristotle's Biology* (1987). His numerous publications include "Aristotle's Conception of Final Causality" in *Review of Metaphysics,* "First Principles in Aristotle's *Parts of Animals*" in *Philosophical Issues in Aristotle's Biology,* and "The Place of the Good in Aristotle's Natural Teleology" in *Proceedings of the Boston Colloquium in Ancient Philosophy* (1989). He is currently preparing David Balme's posthumous edition with commentary of *Historia Animalium* for publication by Cambridge University Press.

*Richard F. Hassing* received his Ph.D. in theoretical physics from Cornell University in 1971 and has continued his studies in philosophy and political theory as a faculty member of the School of Philosophy at The Catholic University of America. He specializes in history of physics and philosophy of nature with emphasis on the relations between natural science and human self-understanding. His essays include "Wholes, Parts, and Laws of Motion" in *Nature and System,* "Animals versus the Laws of Inertia" in *Review of Metaphysics,* and *The Federalist Post-1989* (1995).

*John Leslie* holds the degree of M.Litt. (Oxon.). He joined the faculty of the University of Guelph in 1967 and is currently Professor of Philosophy, specializing in philosophy of religion and the philosophical interpretation of physical cosmology. He is the author of *Value and Existence* (1979), *Universes* (1989), *The End of the World: the Science and Ethics of Human Extinction* (1996), and has edited *Physical Cosmology and Philosophy* (1990). Among his numerous publications are "The Theory That the World Exists Because It Should" in *American Philosophical Quarterly,* "Mackie on Neoplatonism's 'Replacement for God'" in *Religious Studies,* and "Time and the Anthropic Principle" in *Mind.*

*Francis Slade* has taught philosophy and political theory at St. Francis College since 1957. He has translated "A Discussion between Ernst Cassirer and Martin Heidegger" (the Davos Exchange) and has published *The Existentialist Tradition,* edited by L. Langiulli (1971). His research focuses on the comparison between modern state and ancient polis. His articles include "On Sovereignty" in *The Truthful and the Good, Essays in Honor of Robert Sokolowski,* edited by John Drummond and James G. Hart (1996), and "Was ist Aufklärung? Notes on Maritain, Rorty, and Bloom" presented at the 1995 Maritain Conference, University of Charleston.

Currently Associate Professor in the School of Philosophy, The Catholic University of America, *Richard L. Velkley* received his Ph.D. from Pennsylvania State University in 1978. His research centers on the relations between morality, reason, and nature in modern philosophy with emphasis on the German tradition. He is the author of *Freedom and the End of Reason* (1989), and, most recently, has edited and introduced *The Unity of Reason: Essays on Kant's Philosophy* (1994), a collection of essays by Dieter Henrich. His articles include "Realizing Nature in the Self: Schelling on Art and Intellectual Intuition" in *Figuring the Self,* edited by D. Klemm and G. Zoeller (forthcoming), "Kant on the Primacy and Limits of Logic" in *Graduate Faculty Philosophy Journal,* and "Edmund Husserl" in *History of Political Philosophy,* edited by L. Strauss and J. Cropsey (1987).

*William A. Wallace,* professor emeritus of philosophy and history at The Catholic University of America, holds doctorates in philosophy and theology from the University of Fribourg. He turned to intellectual life and the Dominican Order after serving in the U.S. Navy from 1941 to 1946, during which period he pioneered in techniques later known as operations research. His philosophical work has focused on the Aristotelian understanding of nature and on the methodological roots of modern science with special emphasis on Galileo. In addition to numerous articles, he is the author of the two-volume *Causality and Scientific Explanation* (1972 and 1974), *Galileo's Early Notebooks* (1979), *From a Realist Point of View: Essays on the Philosophy of Science* (1979, 2d ed., 1983), *Prelude to Galileo* (1981), and *Galileo and His Sources* (1984). His more recent work, *Galileo's Logical Questions,* with its companion volume, *Galileo's Logic of Discovery and Proof* (1992), establishes the connection between the Renaissance development of Aristotle's *Posterior Analytics* and Galileo's research program in the mathematical science of nature. His latest book is *The Modeling of Nature* (1996) which develops in detail the thesis proposed in his contribution to this volume.

*David A. White* received his Ph.D. from the University of Toronto in 1973 and has taught at DePaul University since 1982. His research centers on philosophy and literature with special emphasis on Heidegger and Plato. His numerous books and articles include *Heidegger and the Language of Poetry* (1978), *The Grand Continuum: Reflections on Joyce and Metaphysics* (1983), *Logic and Ontology in Heidegger* (1985), *Myth and Metaphysics in Plato's* Phaedo (1989), and *Rhetoric and Reality in Plato's* Phaedrus (1993).

# Bibliography

Angier, Natalie. "Matter over Mind: The Curse of Living within One's Genes." *The New York Times,* 18 December 1994.

Aquinas, Saint Thomas. *Commentary on Aristotle's Physics.* Translated by Richard J. Blackwell, Richard J. Spath, and Edmund Thirlkel. New Haven: Yale University Press, 1963.

———. *The Division and Methods of the Sciences, Questions V and VI of the Commentary on the De Trinitate of Boethius.* Translated by Armand Maurer. Toronto: The Pontifical Institute of Mediaeval Studies, 1963.

———. *In octo libros physicorum Aristotelis expositio.* Turin and Rome: Marietti, 1965. Translated by Richard J. Blackwell, Richard J. Spath, and Edmund Thirlkel, *Commentary on Aristotle's Physics* (New Haven: Yale University Press, 1963).

———. *On the Power of God.* Translated by the Dominican Fathers. Westminster, Md.: The Newman Press, 1952.

———. *Summa Theologiae.* 4 vols. Turin: Marietti, 1948.

———. *Treatise on Law (Summa Theologica, Questions 90–97).* Chicago: Henry Regnery Gateway, 1965.

Aristotle. *The Politics.* Translated by Carnes Lord. Chicago: University of Chicago Press, 1984.

———. *Aristotle's* De Motu Animalium*: Text with Translation, Commentary and Interpretive Essays.* Translated and edited by Martha C. Nussbaum. Princeton: Princeton University Press, 1978.

———. *Aristotle's* De Partibus Animalium I *and* De Generatione Animalium I *(with passages from II.1–3).* Translated by David M. Balme. Oxford: Clarendon Press, 1992.

———. *Aristotle's* Metaphysics. Translated by H. G. Apostle. Grinnell, Iowa: The Peripatetic Press, 1979.

———. *Aristotle's* On the Soul. Translated by H. G. Apostle. Grinnell, Iowa: The Peripatetic Press, 1981.

———. *Aristotle's* Physics. Translated by H. G. Apostle. Grinnell, Iowa: The Peripatetic Press, 1980.

———. *Nicomachean Ethics.* Translated by H. Rackham. Vol. 19 of *Aristotle.* Loeb Classical Library. Cambridge: Harvard University Press, 1982.

Arnold, V. I. *Mathematical Methods of Classical Mechanics.* New York: Springer-Verlag, 1989.

Atkins, P. W. *The Creation.* Oxford: W. H. Freeman, 1981.

Augustine, Saint. *The City of God.* Translated by Marcus Dods. New York: Random House Modern Library, 1950.

Averroes. *Ibn Rushd's Metaphysics.* Translated by Charles Genequand. Leiden: E. J. Brill, 1984.

Avicenna. *Sufficientia*. In *Opera omnia*. Venice, 1508.

Ayer, A. J. *Logical Positivism*. New York: The Free Press, 1959.

Bacon, Francis. *The New Organon*. Edited by Fulton H. Anderson. Indianapolis: Bobbs-Merrill, 1960.

Bagley, Paul. "On the Practice of Esotericism." *Journal of the History of Ideas* 53/2 (April–June 1992): 231–47.

Balashov, Y. V. "Resource Letter AP1: The Anthropic Principle." *American Journal of Physics* 59 (1991): 1069–76.

Balme David. "Teleology and Necessity." In *Philosophical Issues in Aristotle's Biology*, edited by Allan Gotthelf and James G. Lennox. Cambridge: Cambridge University Press, 1987.

Barrow, John D., and Frank J. Tipler. *The Anthropic Cosmological Principle*. Oxford: Clarendon Press, 1986.

Bazan, J. Carlos, Eduardo Andujar, and Leonardo Sbrocchi, eds. *Moral and Political Philosophies in the Middle Ages*. Ottawa: Legas, 995.

Bennett, Charles H. "Dissipation, Information, Computational Complexity and the Definition of Organization." In *Emerging Syntheses in Science*, edited by David Pines. Redwood City, Calif.: Addison-Wesley, 1988.

Berns, Walter. "Comment on 'Christians, Politics, and the Modern State,' by E. R. Norman." *This World* 6 (1983): 96–101.

Bertola, F., and U. Curi, eds. *The Anthropic Principle*. Cambridge: Cambridge University Press, 1989.

Binswanger, Harry. *The Biological Basis of Teleological Concepts*. Los Angeles: Ayn Rand Institute Press, 1990.

———. "Life-Based Teleology and the Foundations of Ethics." *The Monist* 75 (1992): 84–103.

Bohr, Niels. "Light and Life." *Nature* 131 (1933): 421–23 and 457–59.

Bondi, H. "Fact and Inference in Theory and Observation." In *Vistas in Astronomy*, vol. 1, edited by Arthur Beer. London: Pergamon Press, 1955.

Boltzmann, L. "On Certain Questions of the Theory of Gases." *Nature* 51 (1895): 413–15.

Bradie, Michael, and Fred D. Miller, Jr. "Teleology and Natural Necessity in Aristotle." *History of Philosophy Quarterly* 1 (1984): 133–45.

Brooks, D. R., and E. O. Wiley. *Evolution as Entropy*. Chicago: University of Chicago Press, 1988.

Burbidge, John W. "Is Hegel a Christian?" in *Hegel on Logic and Religion*. Albany: SUNY Press, 1992.

———. "Language and Recognition." In *Method and Speculation in Hegel's Phenomenology*, edited by M. Westphal. Atlantic Highlands, N.J.: Humanities Press, 1982.

Butts, Robert E. *Kant and the Double Government Methodology*. Dordrecht: Reidel, 1984.

———. "Teleology and Scientific Method in Kant's *Critique of Judgment*." *Nous* 24 (1990): 1–16.

Cairns, J., Overbough, J., and Miller, S. "The Origin of Mutants." *Nature* 335 (1988): 142–45.

Campbell, David K. "Nonlinear Science." *Los Alamos Science* 15 (1987): 218–62. Reprinted as a *Los Alamos Science* Special Issue.

Campbell, John H. "Evolution as Nonequilibrium Thermodynamics: Halfway There?" In *Entropy, Information, and Evolution*, edited by Bruce H.

Weber, David J. Depew, and James D. Smith. Cambridge: MIT Press, 1990.

Cantor, Norman F. *Inventing the Middle Ages: The Lives, Works, and Ideas of the Great Medievalists of the Twentieth Century.* New York: W. Morrow, 1991.

Carr, B. J. "On the Origin, Evolution and Purpose of the Physical Universe." In *Physical Cosmology and Philosophy,* edited by John Leslie. New York: Macmillan, 1990.

Carr, B. J., and M. J. Rees. "The Anthropic Principle and the Structure of the Physical World." *Nature* 278 (April 1979): 605–12.

Carter, Brandon. "The Anthropic Principle: Self-Selection as an Adjunct to Natural Selection." In *Cosmic Perspectives,* edited by S. K. Biswas, et al. Cambridge: Cambridge University Press, 1989.

———. "The Anthropic Selection Principle and the Ultra-Darwinian Synthesis." In Bertola and Curi, eds., *Anthropic Principle.* Cambridge: Cambridge University Press, 1989.

———. "Large Number Coincidences and the Anthropic Principle in Cosmology." In *Physical Cosmology and Philosophy,* edited by John Leslie. New York: Macmillan, 1990.

Cassirer, H. W. *A Commentary on Kant's Critique of Judgment.* New York: Barnes and Noble, 1938.

Charles, David. "Aristotle on Hypothetical Necessity and Irreducibility." *Pacific Philosophical Quarterly* 69 (1988): 1–53.

———. "Teleological Causation in the *Physics.*" In *Aristotle's Physics: A Collection of Essays,* edited by Lindsay Judson. Oxford: Clarendon Press, 1991.

Charlton, William. "Report on Recent Work." In *Aristotle's* Physics, Books I and II. Reprint, new impression. Oxford: Clarendon Press, 1992.

———. "Aristotle and the Harmonia Theory." In *Aristotle on Nature and Living Things,* edited by Allan Gotthelf. Pittsburgh: Mathesis Publications, 1985.

Churchill, Winston. *The Gathering Storm.* Boston: Houghton Mifflin, 1948.

Churchland, Paul. *Engine of Reason, Seat of the Soul.* Cambridge: MIT Press, 1995.

Cohen, Sheldon. "Aristotle on Hot, Cold, and Teleological Explanation." *Ancient Philosophy* 9 (1989): 255–70.

Collier, John. "The Dynamics of Biological Order." In *Entropy, Information, and Evolution,* edited by Bruce H. Weber, David J. Depew, and James D. Smith. Cambridge: MIT Press, 1990.

Collins, C. B. and S. W. Hawking. "Why is the Universe Isotropic?" *Astrophysical Journal* 180 (1973): 317–34.

Cooper, John M. "Aristotle on Natural Teleology." In *Language and Logos,* edited by M. Schofield and M. C. Nussbaum. Cambridge: Cambridge University Press, 1982.

———. "Hypothetical Necessity." In *Aristotle on Nature and Living Things,* edited by Allan Gotthelf. Pittsburgh: Mathesis Publications, 1985.

———. "Hypothetical Necessity and Natural Teleology." In *Philosophical Issues in Aristotle's Biology,* edited by Allan Gotthelf and James G. Lennox. Cambridge: Cambridge University Press, 1987.

Da Vinci, Leonardo. *The Notebooks of Leonardo da Vinci.* Edited by Jean Paul Richter. 2 vols. New York: Dover, 1970.

Davies, P. C. W. *The Accidental Universe.* Cambridge: Cambridge University Press, 1982.

————. *The Mind of God.* New York: Simon and Schuster, 1992.
Dawkins, Richard. *The Selfish Gene.* Oxford: Oxford University Press, 1976.
De Sanctis, Francesco. *Saggi critici.* Milan: n.p., 1933.
DeDonder, T. *L'Affinite.* Paris: Gauthier-Vallars, 1927.
Delbrück, Max. "Aristotle-totle-totle." In *Of Microbes and Life,* edited by J. Monod and E. Borek. New York: Columbia University Press, 1971.
Demaret, J., and C. Barbier. "Le principe anthropique en cosmologie." *Revue des Questions Scientifiques* 152 (1981): 181–222 and 461–509.
Depew, David J., and Bruce H. Weber. "Consequences of Nonequilibrium Thermodynamics for Darwinism." In *Entropy, Information, and Evolution,* edited by Bruce H. Weber, David J. Depew, and James D. Smith. Cambridge: MIT Press, 1990.
————. *Darwinism Evolving.* Cambridge: MIT Press, 1995.
Descartes, Rene. *Discourse on Method.* In *The Philosophical Writings of Descartes,* vol.1, translated by John Cottingham, Robert Stoothoff, and Dugald Murdoch. Cambridge: Cambridge University Press, 1985.
————. *Le Monde.* Translated by Michael S. Mahoney. New York: Abaris, 1979.
————. *Oeuvres.* Edited by Charles Adam and Paul Tannery. 13 vol. Paris: n.p., 1964.
————. *Treatise on Man.* In *Philosophical Writings,* vol. 1, translated by John Cottingham, Robert Stoothoff, and Dugald Murdoch. Cambridge: Cambridge University Press, 1985.
DeSitter, W. "The Expanding Universe." *Scientia* 49 (1931): 1–10.
Dewey, John. *Experience and Nature.* La Salle, Ill.: Open Court, 1929.
DeWitt, B. S., and N. Graham, eds. *The Many-Worlds Interpretation of Quantum Mechanics.* Princeton: Princeton University Press, 1973.
Dicke, R. H. "Dirac's Cosmology and Mach's Principle." In *Physical Cosmology and Philosophy,* edited by John Leslie. New York: Macmillan, 1990.
Dingle, H. *The Evolution of the Universe.* London: Nature, 1931.
Dirac, P. A. M. "The Cosmological Constants." *Nature* 20 (February 1937): 323.
Drakulic, Slavenka. "Intellectuals and Social Change in Central and Eastern Europe." *Partisan Review* 59, no. 4 (1992): 736–40.
Dyson, F. "Energy in the Universe." *Scientific American* (September 1971): 51–59.
Earman, J. "The SAP Also Rises: A Critical Examination of the Anthropic Principle." *American Philosophical Quarterly* 27 (1979): 307–17.
Eddington, Arthur S. *New Pathways in Science.* Ann Arbor: University of Michigan Press, 1959.
Ehring, Douglas. "Negative Feedback and Goals." *Nature and System* 6 (1984): 217–20.
Eigen, Manfred. "Self-Organization of Matter and the Evolution of Biological Macromolecules." *Naturwissenschaften* 58 (1971): 465–523.
————. *Steps towards Life.* New York: Oxford University Press, 1992.
Eigen, Manfred, and P. Schuster. *The Hypercycle.* Heidelberg: Springer-Verlag, 1979.
Einstein, Albert, and Leopold Infeld. *The Evolution of Physics.* New York: Simon and Schuster, 1966.
Ellis, G. F. R. "The Homogeneity of the Universe." *General Relativity and Gravitation* 11 (1979): 281–89.
————. *The Universe: Cradle of Our Existence.* London: Bowerdean Press, 1992.

Ellis, J., A. Linde, and M. Sher. "Vacuum Stability, Wormholes, Cosmic Rays and the Cosmological Bounds on Top Quark and Higgs Masses." *Physics Letters* 252B (1990): 203–11.

Ewing, A. C. *Value and Reality*. London: Allen and Unwin, 1973.

Feigenbaum, Mitchell. "Universal Behavior in Nonlinear Systems." *Los Alamos Science* 1 (1980): 4–27. Reprinted in *Physica* D7 (1983): 16–39.

Feinberg, G., and R. Shapiro. *Life Beyond Earth*. New York: William Morrow, 1980.

Finnis, John. *Natural Law and Natural Rights*. Oxford: Clarendon Press, 1980.

Ford, Joseph. "How Random Is a Coin Toss?" *Physics Today* 36 (April 1983): 40–47.

Forrest, P. "Anthropic Answers and the Existence of God." *Proceedings of the Russellian Society* 7 (1982): 1–13.

Fortin, Ernest. "Sacred and Inviolable: *Rerum Novarum* and Natural Rights." *Theological Studies* 53 (1992): 203–33.

Fox, Sidney W. "The Evolutionary Sequence: Origin and Emergences." *American Biology Teacher* 48 (March 1986): 140–49.

Frautschi, S. "Entropy in an Expanding Universe." *Science* 217 (1982): 593–99.

Friedman, Michael. *Kant and the Exact Sciences*. Cambridge: Harvard University Press, 1992.

Furley, David. "The Rainfall Example in *Physics* II.8." In *Aristotle on Nature and Living Things*, edited by Allan Gotthelf. Pittsburgh: Mathesis Publications, 1985.

Gale, George. "The Anthropic Principle." *Scientific American* (December 1981): 154–71.

———. "Cosmological Fecundity: Theories of Multiple Universes." In *Physical Cosmology and Philosophy*, edited by John Leslie. New York: Macmillan, 1990.

Glansdorff, P., and I. Prigogine. *Thermodynamic Theory of Structure, Stability and Fluctuations*. London: Wiley-Interscience, 1971.

Gleick, James. *Chaos*. New York: Viking, 1987.

Glenn, G. D. "Inalienable Rights and Locke's Argument for Limited Government: Political Implications of a Right to Suicide." *The Journal of Politics* 46 (1984): 80–105.

Godfrey of Fontaines. *Quodlibet 8*. In *Philosophes Belges* 4 (1924): 105.

Goethe, J. W. "Anschauende Urteilskraft." In *Schriften zur Botanik und Wissenschaftslehre*. Munich: Deutscher Taschenbuch Verlag, 1963.

Gotthelf, Allan, ed. *Aristotle on Nature and Living Things*. Pittsburgh: Mathesis Publications, 1985.

———. *Aristotle's Conception of Final Causality*. Ann Arbor: University Microfilms, 1975.

———. "Aristotle's Conception of Final Causality." *Review of Metaphysics* 30 (1977): 226–54. Reprint with additional notes and "Postscript 1986," *Philosophical Issues in Aristotle's Biology*, edited by Allan Gotthelf and James G. Lennox. Cambridge: Cambridge University Press, 1987.

———. "First Principles in Aristotle's *Parts of Animals*." In *Philosophical Issues in Aristotle's Biology*, edited by Allan Gotthelf and James G. Lennox. Cambridge: Cambridge University Press, 1987

———. "The Place of the Good in Aristotle's Natural Teleology." Vol. 4 (1988) of *Proceedings of the Boston Colloquium in Ancient Philosophy*, edited by J. J.

Cleary and D. C. Shartin. Lanham, Md.: University Press of America, 1989.

———. "Report on Recent Work." In *Aristotle's* De Partibus Animalium *and* De Generatione Animalium I *(with passages from II.3)*. Translated by David Balme. Oxford: Clarendon Press, 1992.

———. "Teleology and Spontaneous Generation: A Discussion." In *Nature, Knowledge and Virtue,* edited by R. Kraut and T. Penner. *Apeiron* Special Issue 22.4 (1989).

———, ed. *Aristotle on Nature and Living Things.* Pittsburgh: Mathesis Publications, 1985.

Gotthelf, Allan, and James G. Lennox, eds. *Philosophical Issues in Aristotle's Biology.* Cambridge: Cambridge University Press, 1987.

Gould, Stephen Jay. "Mind and Supermind." In *Physical Cosmology and Philosophy,* edited by John Leslie. New York: Macmillan, 1990.

Gratian. *Decretum Magistri Gratiani.* Edited by E. Friedberg. Corpus Juris Canonici, vol. I. Leibzig: Tauschnitz, 1879.

Gribbin, John. *In the Beginning.* Boston: Little Brown, 1993.

Grotius, Hugo. *De iure belli et pacis.* Lausanne: Bousquet, 1751–52.

Guth, A. H., and P. J. Steinhardt. "The Inflationary Universe." *Scientific American* (May 1984): 116–28.

Guyer, Paul. "Reason and Reflective Judgment: Kant on the Significance of Systematicity." *Nous* 24 (1990): 17–43.

Guyer, Paul, and Ralph Walker. "Kant's Conception of Empirical Law." *Proceedings of the Aristotelian Society,* Supplemental vol. 64 (1990): 221–58.

Hacking, Ian. "The Inverse Gambler's Fallacy. The Argument from Design. The Anthropic Principle Applied to Wheeler Universes." *Mind* 96 (1987): 331–40. Responses to Hacking by three writers in *Mind* 97 (1988): 259–72.

Hall, A. R., and M. B. Hall. *Unpublished Scientific Papers of Isaac Newton.* Cambridge: Cambridge University Press, 1962.

Hamilton, Alexander, James Madison, and John Jay. *The Federalist Papers,* edited by Clinton Rossiter. New York: Mentor, 1961.

Harman, Gilbert. *The Nature of Morality.* New York: Oxford University Press, 1977.

Hart, H. L. A. *The Concept of Law.* Oxford: Oxford University Press, 1961.

Hassing, Richard F. "Animals versus the Laws of Inertia." *Review of Metaphysics* 46 (1992): 29–61.

———. "Wholes, Parts, and Laws of Motion." *Nature and System* 6 (1984): 195–215.

Hawking, S. W. "The Anistropy of the Universe at Large Times." In Longair, M. S., ed., *Confronation of Cosmological Theories with Observational Data.* Dordrecht: Reidel, 1974.

———. "The Quantum Mechanics of Black Holes." *Scientific American* (January 1977): 34–40.

Hawking, S. W., and Israel, W., eds. *General Relativity.* Cambridge: Cambridge University Press, 1979.

Hegel, G. W. F. *The Encyclopedia Logic,* edited by Geraets, et. al. Indianapolis: Hackett, 1991.

———. *Gesammelte Werke.* Hamburg: Meiner, 1968–.

———. *Hegel's Logic.* Translated by William Wallace. Oxford: Clarendon Press, 1975.

———. *Hegel's Phenomenology of Spirit.* Translated by A. V. Miller. Oxford: Clarendon Press, 1977.

———. *Hegel's Philosophy of Nature.* Translated by A. V. Miller. Oxford: Clarendon Press, 1970.

———. *Hegel's Science of Logic.* Translated by A. V. Miller. London: Allen and Unwin, 1969.

———. *Lectures on the Philosophy of World History: Introduction.* Translated by H. B. Nisbet. Cambridge: Cambridge University Press, 1975.

———. *Die Vernunft in der Geschichte.* Edited by Hoffmeister. Hamburg: Meiner, 1955.

Heidegger, Martin. *Kants These über das Sein.* In *Wegmarken.* Frankfurt: Klostermann, 1967.

Heisenberg, Werner. *Physics and Beyond.* Translated by Arnold J. Pomerans. New York: Harper Torchbooks, 1972.

Helmholtz, Hermann. "Über die Erhaltung der Kraft." In *Wissenschaftliche Abhandlungen.* Vol. 1. Leipzig: n.p., 1882.

Henry of Ghent. *Quodlibet 9.* In *Opera Omnia,* edited by Raymond Macken. Vol. 13. Leuven, Belg.: University Press, 1983.

Ho, Mae-Wan. "Reanimating Nature: The Integration of Science with Human Experience." *Leonardo* 24 (1991): 607–15.

Hobbes, Thomas. *De Cive.* Edited by Howard Warrender. Oxford: Clarendon Press, 1983.

———. *Elements of Law.* Edited by F. Tönnies. London: Cass, 1969.

———. *Leviathan.* Edited by C. B. Macpherson. New York: Penguin, 1985.

Hoyle, Fred. *Galaxies, Nuclei and Quasars.* London: Heinemann, 1965.

Hull, David L. Introduction to *Entropy, Information, and Evolution,* edited by Bruce H. Weber, David J. Depew, and James D. Smith. Cambridge: MIT Press, 1990.

Irwin, Terence H. *Aristotle's First Principles.* Oxford: Clarendon Press, 1988.

Jantsch, Erich. *The Self-Organizing Universe.* Oxford: Pergamon Press, 1980.

Jensen, Roderick. "Classical Chaos." *American Scientist* 75 (1987): 168–81.

Jerome, Saint. *In Amos.* In *Commentarii in prophetas minores.* Part I.6 of *S. Hieronymi Presbyteri Opera.* Corpus Christianorum. Turnhout: Brepols, 1969.

Judson, Lindsay, ed. *Aristotle's Physics: A Collection of Essays.* Oxford: Clarendon Press, 1991.

Kahn, Charles H. "The Place of the Prime Mover in Aristotle's Teleology." In *Aristotle on Nature and Living Things,* edited by Allan Gotthelf. Pittsburgh: Mathesis Publications, 1985.

Kant, Immanuel. *Critique of Pure Reason.* Translated by Norman Kemp Smith. New York: St. Martin's Press, 1965.

———. *Erste Einleitung in die Kritik der Urteilskraft.* In *Kants gesammelte Schriften.* Preussische Akademie der Wissenschaften. Vol. 20. Berlin: Walter de Gruyter and Predecessors, 1902.

———. *Foundations of the Metaphysics of Morals.* Translated by Lewis White Beck. Indianapolis: Bobbs-Merrill, 1959.

———. *Critique of Judgment.* Translated by Werner S. Pluhar. Indianapolis: Hackett, 1987.

———. *Kritik der Urteilskraft.* In *Kants gesammelte Schriften.* Preussische Akademie der Wissenschaften. Vol. 20. Berlin: Walter de Gruyter and Predecessors, 1902.

———. *Lectures on Ethics*. Translated by Louis Infeld. New York: Harper and Row, 1963.

———. *Metaphysical Foundations of Natural Science*. Translated by James Ellington. In *Kant's Philosophy of Material Nature*. Indianapolis: Hackett, 1985.

———. "Perpetual Peace." Translated by Lewis White Beck. In *Kant on History*, edited by Lewis White Beck. Indianapolis: Bobbs-Merrill, 1963.

Kass, Leon. *Toward a More Natural Science*. New York: The Free Press, 1985.

Kauffman, Stuart. *The Origins of Order*. New York: Oxford University Press, 1993.

Kennington, Richard. "Bacon's Critique of Ancient Philosophy in *New Organon* I." In *Nature and Scientific Method*, edited by Daniel O. Dahlstrom. Washington, D.C.: The Catholic University of America Press, 1991.

———. "Rene Descartes." In *History of Political Philosophy*, edited by Leo Strauss and Joseph Cropsey. 3rd ed. Chicago: University of Chicago Press, 1987.

———. "Strauss's *Natural Right and History*." In *Leo Strauss's Thought*, edited by Alan Udoff. Boulder: Lynne Rienner Publishers, 1991.

Kitcher, Philip. "Kant's Philosophy of Science." In *Self and Nature in Kant's Philosophy*, edited by Allen W. Wood. Ithaca: Cornell University Press, 1984.

———. "Projecting the Order of Nature." In *Kant's Philosophy of Physical Science*, edited by Robert E. Butts. Dordrecht: Reidel, 1986.

Klein, Jacob. "Aristotle, an Introduction." In *Jacob Klein Lectures and Essays*, edited by Robert B. Williamson and Elliott Zuckerman. Annapolis, Md.: St. John's College, 1985.

Körner, S. *Kant*. Harmondsworth: Penguin, 1955.

Kojève, Alexandre. *Introduction to the Reading of Hegel*, edited by A. Bloom and translated by James H. Nichols, Jr. New York: Basic Books, 1969.

Kolb, D., ed. *New Perspectives on Hegel's Philosophy of Religion*. Albany: SUNY Press, 1992.

Kraut, R., and T. Penner, eds. *Nature, Knowledge and Virtue: Essays in Memory of Joan Kung*. *Apeiron* Special Issue 22.4 (1989).

Küppers, Bernd-Olaf. *Information and the Origin of Life*. Translated by Paul Woolley. Cambridge: MIT Press, 1990.

Kuiper, B. H., and G. D. Brin. "Resource Letter ETC1: Extraterrestrial Civilization." *American Journal of Physics* 57 (1989): 12–18.

Lagarde, G. de. "Individualisme et corporatisme au moyen âge." In *L'Organisation corporative du moyen âge à la fin de l'Ancien Régime*. Louvain: Bureaux du Recueil, Bibliotèque de l'Université, 1937.

Laplace, Pierre Simon. *A Philosophical Essay on Probabilities*. Translated by F. W. Truscott and F. L. Emory. New York: Dover, 1951.

Lawrence, J. "Logos and Eros: The Underlying Tension in Kant's Third *Critique*." *Idealistic Studies* 12 (1992): 130–43.

Lee, Kwang-Sae. "Kant on Empirical Concepts, Empirical Laws and Scientific Theories." *Kant-Studien* 72 (1981): 398–414.

Leslie, John. "Anthropic Predictions." *Philosophia* 23 (1994): 117–44.

———. "Efforts to Explain All Existence." *Mind* 87 (1978): 181–94.

———. *The End of the World: The Science and Ethics of Human Extinction*. London: Routledge, 1996.

———. "Mackie on Neoplatonism's 'Replacement for God'." *Religious Studies* 22 (1986): 325–42.

————. "Risking the World's End." *Bulletin of the Canadian Nuclear Society* (May 1989): 10–15. Reprinted in *Interchange* 21 (1990): 49–58.

————. "The Theory That the World Exists Because It Should." *American Philosophical Quarterly* 7 (1970): 286–98.

————. "Time and the Anthropic Principle." *Mind* 101 (1992): 521–40.

————. *Universes.* London: Routledge, 1989.

————. *Value and Existence.* Oxford: Blackwell, 1979.

————, ed. *Physical Cosmology and Philosophy.* New York: Macmillan, 1990.

Linde, A. D. *Inflation and Quantum Cosmology.* San Diego: Academic Press, 1990.

Locke, John. *An Essay Concerning Human Understanding.* Edited by A. C. Fraser. 2 vols. New York: Dover, 1959.

————. *Questions Concerning the Law of Nature.* Translated by Robert Horwitz, Jenny Strauss Clay, and Diskin Clay. Ithaca: Cornell University Press, 1990.

————. *The Reasonableness of Christianity.* Washington, D.C.: Regnery Gateway, 1965.

————. *The Second Treatise of Government.* Edited by Thomas Peardon. Indianapolis: Bobbs-Merrill, 1952.

————. *Two Treatises sf Government.* Edited by Peter Laslett. New York: Mentor, 1965.

Longair, M. S., ed. *Confrontation of Cosmological Theories with Observational Data.* Dordrecht: Reidel, 1974.

Lorenz, Edward N. "Deterministic Nonperiodic Flow." *Journal of Atmospheric Science* 20 (1963): 130–41.

Mach, Ernst. *The Science of Mechanics.* Lasalle, Ill.: Open Court, 1960.

Machiavelli, Niccolo. *The Discourses.* In *The Prince and the Discourses.* edited by Max Lerner. New York: Random House, 1950.

————. *The Prince.* Translated by Harvey C. Mansfield, Jr. Chicago: University of Chicago Press, 1985.

Macpherson, C. B. *The Political Theory of Possessive Individualism.* Oxford: Oxford University Press, 1962.

Maimonides. *The Guide of the Perplexed.* Translated by Shlomo Pines. Chicago: University of Chicago Press, 1963.

Mansfield, Harvey C., Jr. *Taming the Prince.* New York: The Free Press, 1989.

Maritain, Jacques. *The Person and the Common Good.* Translated by John J. Fitzgerald. Notre Dame, Ind.: University of Notre Dame Press, 1966.

————. *Les Droits de l'homme et la loi naturelle.* New York: Éditions de la Maison francaise, 1943.

Marsilius of Padua. *Defensor Pacis.* Translated by Alan Gewirth. Toronto: University of Toronto Press in association with the Medieval Academy of America, 1990.

Masters, Roger D. *Beyond Relativism.* Hanover, N.H.: University Press of New England, 1993.

————. "Evolutionary Biology and Natural Right." In *The Crisis of Liberal Democracy,* edited by Kenneth L. Deutsch and Walter Soffer. New York: SUNY Press, 1987.

Matthen, Mohan. "The Four Causes in Aristotle's Embryology." In *Nature, Knowledge and Virtue,* edited by R. Kraut and T. Penner. *Apeiron* Special Issue 22.4 (1989).

Mayr, Ernst. *Toward a New Philosophy of Biology.* Cambridge: Harvard University Press, 1988.

McCrea, W. H., and M. J. Rees, eds. "The Constants of Physics." *Philosophical Transactions of the Royal Society, London* A310 (1983): 209–363.

McFarland, John D. *Kant's Concept of Teleology.* Edinburgh: Edinburgh University Press, 1970.

Mermin, N. D. "Spooky Actions at a Distance: Mysteries of the Quantum Theory." In *Great Ideas Today* 1988. Chicago: Encyclopedia Britannica, 1988.

Meyer, Susan Sauve. "Aristotle, Teleology, and Reduction." *Philosophical Review* 101 (1992): 791–825.

Mill, John Stewart. *A System of Logic.* London: Longmans, Green and Co., 1941.

Miller, Fred D., Jr. *Nature, Justice and Rights in Aristotle.* Oxford: Clarendon Press, 1995.

Milton, John R. "The Origin and Development of the Concept of the 'Laws of Nature'." *Archives Europennes de Sociologie* 22 (1981): 173–95.

Monachus, Johannes. *Glossa Aurea.* Paris: n.p., 1535.

Morowitz, Harold. *Beginnings of Cellular Life.* New Haven: Yale University Press, 1992.

———. *Energy Flow in Biology.* New York: Academic Press, 1968.

Munitz, Milton K. *Cosmic Understanding.* Princeton: Princeton University Press, 1986.

Neurath, O., et al., eds. *International Encyclopedia of Unified Science.* Chicago: University of Chicago Press, 1955.

Newton, Isaac. *Philosophiae Naturalis Principia Mathematica.* Edited by Alexandre Koyre and I. Bernard Cohen. 2 vols. Cambridge: Harvard University Press, 1972.

———. *The Mathematical Principles of Natural Philosophy.* Translated by Andrew Motte and Florian Cajori. New York: Greenwood Press, 1962.

———. *Opticks.* New York: Dover, 1979.

Newman, James R. *The World of Mathematics.* New York: Simon and Schuster, 1956.

Nicholas of Cusa. *De Concordantia Catolica.* Vol. 14 of *Opera Omnia*, edited by Gerhard Kallen and Anna Berger. Hamburg: Felix Meiner, 1968.

Nicolis, G. "Stability and Dissipative Structures in Open Systems Far from Equilibrium." In *Advances in Chemical Physics,* vol. 19, edited by I. Prigogine and S. A. Rice. New York: Wiley-Interscience, 1971.

Nicolis, G., and I. Prigogine. *Exploring Complexity.* New York: W. H. Freeman, 1989.

———. *Self-Organization in Nonequilibrium Systems.* New York: Wiley Interscience, 1977.

Nielsen, H. B. "Random Dynamics." *Acta Physica Polonica* B20 (1989): 427–68.

Nussbaum, Martha C. "Aristotle." In *Ancient Writers,* edited by T. J. Luce. New York, 1982.

———. "Aristotelian Dualism: Reply to Howard Robinson." *Oxford Studies in Ancient Philosophy* 2 (1984): 197–207.

———. *Aristotle's* De Motu Animalium*: Text with Translation, Commentary and Interpretive Essays.* Princeton: Princeton University Press, 1978.

———. "The 'Common Explanation' of Animal Motion." In *Zweifelhaftes in Corpus Aristotelicum: Studien zu Einigen Dubia,* edited by P. Moraux and J. Wiesner. *Akten des 9. Symposium Aristotelicum.* Berlin, 1983.

———. "Review of *Substance, Body, and Soul: Aristotelian Investigations,* by E. Hartman." *Journal of Philosophy* 77(1980): 355–65.

Oakeshott, Michael. *On Human Conduct*. Oxford: Clarendon Press, 1990.

Ockham, William of. *Dialogus*. Edited by M. Goldast. Frankfurt: n.p., 1614.

———. *Quaestiones in librum secundum Sententiarum*, II. In *Opera Theologica*, vol. 5, edited by G. Gal and R. Wood. New York: St. Bonaventure, 1981.

Offler, H. S. "Three Modes of Natural Law in Ockham: A Revision of the Text." *Fransiscan Studies* 15 (1977): 207–18.

Oppenheim, Paul, and Putnam, Hilary. "Unity of Science as a Working Hypothesis." In *Minnesota Studies in the Philosophy of Science*, edited by H. Feigl, M. Scriven, and G. Maxwell. Minneapolis: University of Minnesota Press, 1958.

Orwin, Clifford. "Machiavelli's Unchristian Charity." *American Political Science Review* 72 (1978): 1217–28.

Pagels, Heinz. "A Cozy Cosmology." In *Physical Cosmology and Philosophy*, edited by John Leslie. New York: Macmillan, 1990.

———. *The Dreams of Reason*. New York: Simon and Schuster, 1988.

Parfit, D. "Why Does the Universe Exist?" *Times Literary Supplement*, 3 July 1992.

Pauli, Wolfgang. "Naturwissenschaftliche und Erkenntnistheoretische Aspekte der Ideen vom Unbewussten." *Dialectica* 8 (1954): 285.

Penrose, Roger. "Difficulties with Inflationary Cosmology." In *Fourteenth Texas Symposium on Relativistic Astrophysics*, edited by E. J. Fenyves. New York: New York Academy of Sciences, 1989.

———. "Singularities and Time-Asymmetry." In *General Relativity*, edited by S. W. Hawking and W. Israel. Cambridge: Cambridge University Press, 1979.

Plato. *Apology*. Translated by H. N. Fowler. In *Plato*. Vol. 1. Loeb Classical Library. Cambridge: Harvard University Press, 1982.

———. *Phaedo*. Translated by H. N. Fowler. In *Plato*. Vol. 1. Loeb Classical Library. Cambridge: Harvard University Press, 1982.

———. *Republic*. Translated by Paul Shorey. Cambridge: Harvard University Press,, 1935.

———. *The Republic of Plato*. Translated by Allan Bloom. New York: Basic Books, 1968.

Poincare, Henri. *Science and Method*. New York: Dover, 1950.

Polkinghorne, J. C. *One World: The Interaction of Science and Theology*. London: SPCK, 1986.

Popper, Karl. "Scientific Reduction and the Essential Incompleteness of All Science." In *Studies in the Philosophy of Biology*, edited by F. Ayala and T. Dobzhansky. Berkeley and Los Angeles: University of California Press, 1974.

Prigogine, I. *Étude thermodynamique des phenomenes irreversibles*. Liege, Belgium: Desoer, 1947.

———. *From Being to Becoming*. New York: W. H. Freeman, 1980.

———. "Nonequilibrium Thermodynamics and Chemical Evolution: An Overview." In *Aspects of Chemical Evolution* (17th Solvay Conference on Chemistry), edited by G. Nicolis. New York: Wiley, 1984.

Prigogine, I., and I. Stengers. *Order Out of Chaos*. New York: Bantam Books, 1984.

Prigogine, I., and J. M. Wiame. "Biologie et thermodynamique des phenomenes irreversibles." *Experientia* 2 (1946): 451–53.

Primasius of Hadrumetum. *Commentarius in Apocalypsin*. Edited by A. W. Adams. Turnhout, Belgium: Brepols, 1985.

Prufer, Thomas. *Recapitulations*. Washington, D.C.: The Catholic University of America Press, 1993.

Pufendorf, Samuel. *The Law of Nature and Nations*. Translated by Basil Kennett. London: n.p., 1749.

Rand, Ayn. *The Virtue of Selfishness: A New Concept f Egoism*. New American Library, 1964.

Rees, M. J. "Black Holes, Galactic Evolution and Cosmic Coincidences." *Interdisciplinary Science Reviews* 14 (1989): 148–61.

Reeves, Hubert. *The Hour of Our Delight*. New York: W. H. Freeman, 1991.

Rensberger, Boyce. "Choosing the Right Mutation?" *The Washington Post*, 20 April 1992.

———. "Science and Sensitivity." *The Washington Post*, 1 March 1992.

Roque, Alicia Juarrero. "Self-Organization: Kant's Concept of Teleology and Modern Chemistry." *Review of Metaphysics* 39 (1985): 107–35.

Rozental, I. L. *Big Bang, Big Bounce*. Berlin: Springer-Verlag, 1988.

———. "Physical Laws and the Numerical Values of Fundamental Constants." *Soviet Physics Uspekhi* 23 (1980): 296–305.

Ruby, Jane E. "The Origins of Scientific 'Law'." *Journal of the History of Ideas* 57 (1986): 341–59.

Russell, R. J., W. R. Stoeger, and G. V. Coyne, eds. *Physics, Philosophy and Theology*. Vatican City States: Vatican Observatory, 1988.

Sachs, Mendel. *Quantum Mechanics from General Relativity*. Boston: Kluwer, 1986.

Sakharov, A. D. "Cosmological Transitions with the Alteration of Metric Signature." *Soviet Physics JETP* 60 (1984): 214.

Saxonhouse, Arlene. *Women in the History of Political Thought*. New York: Praeger, 1985.

Schelling, F. W. J. *Vom Ich als Prinzip der Philosophie*. In vol. 1, bk. 1 of *Schellings Sämmtliche Werke*, edited by K. F. A. Schelling. Stuttgart: Cotta, 1856–61.

Schrader, George. "Kant's Theory of Concepts." In *Kant A Collection of Critical Essays*, edited by Robert Paul Wolff. Garden City, N.J.: Anchor Books, 1967.

———. "The Status of Teleological Judgment in the Critical Philosophy." *Kant-Studien* 45 (1953–54): 204–35.

Schrock, Thomas. "The Rights to Punish and Resist Punishment in Hobbes *Leviathan*." *The Western Political Quarterly* 44 (1991): 853–90.

Schroedinger, Erwin. *What is Life?* London: Cambridge University Press, 1946.

Schweber, Silvan. "Physics, Community and the Crisis in Physical Theory." *Physics Today* (November 1993): 34–40.

Sedley, David. "Is Aristotle's Teleology Anthropocentric?" *Phronesis* 36 (1991): 179–96.

Seidler, Michael. Introduction to *Samuel Pufendorf's On the natural state of men*. Translated by Michael Seidler. Lewistown, N.Y.: Edwin Mellen Press, 1990.

Shakespeare, William. *The Complete Works of William Shakespeare*. New York: Avenel Books, 1975.

Sikkema, A. E., and W. Israel. "Black-Hole Mergers and Mass Inflation in a Bouncing Universe." *Nature* 3 (January 1991): 45–47.

Smart, J. J. C. *Our Place in the Universe*. Oxford: Blackwell, 1989.

Smith, Q. "World Ensemble Explanations." *Pacific Philosophical Quarterly* 67 (1987): 73–86.

Smith, R. W. *The Expanding Universe*. Cambridge: Cambridge University Press, 1982.

Smolin, L. "Did the Universe Evolve?" *Classical and Quantum Gravity* 9 (1991): 173–91.

Sorabji, Richard. *Necessity, Cause, and Blame: Perspectives on Aristotle's Theory.* Ithaca: Cornell University Press, 1980.

Spinoza, Benedict. *The Ethics.* In *Spinoza, On the Improvement of the Understanding, the Ethics, Correspondence,* translated by R. H. M. Elwes. New York: Dover, 1955.

———. *A Theologico-Political Treatise and a Political Treatise.* Translated by R. H. M. Elwes. New York: Dover, 1951.

Stent, Gunther. "Light and Life: Niels Bohr's Legacy to Comtemporary Biology." In *Niels Bohr: Physics and the World,* edited by H. Feshbach, T. Matsui, and A. Oleson. New York: Harwood, 1988.

Straus, Erwin. *Phenomenological Psychology.* New York: Basic Books, 1966.

Strauss, Leo. *Natural Right and History.* Chicago: University of Chicago Press, 1953.

———. "An Epilogue." In *Essays on the Scientific Study of Politics,* ed. Herbert J. Storing (New York: Holt, Rinehart and Winston, 1962) Reprinted in *Liberalism Ancient and Modern.* New York: Basic Books, 1968.

———. *The City and Man.* Chicago: University of Chicago Press, 1964.

———. "Marsilius of Padua." In *History of Political Philosophy,* edited by Leo Strauss and Joseph Cropsey. Chicago: University of Chicago Press, 1987.

———. "Political Philosophy and the Crisis of Our Time." In *The Post-Behavioral Era,* edited by George J. Graham and George W. Carey. New York: David McKay, 1972.

———. *Studies in Platonic Political Philosophy.* Edited by Thomas L. Pangle. Chicago: University of Chicago Press, 1983.

———. "The Three Waves of Modernity." In *Political Philosophy: Six Essays by Leo Strauss,* edited by Hilail Gildin. Indianapolis: Bobbs-Merrill, 1975.

———. *Thoughts on Machiavelli.* Seattle: University of Washington Press, 1969.

Squires, E. J. "Do We Live in the Simplest Possible Interesting World?" *European Journal of Physics* 2 (1981): 55–57.

Steigman, G. "Confrontation of Antimatter Cosmologies with Observational Data." In

Longair, M. S., ed. *Confrontation of Cosmological Theories with Observational Data.* Dordrecht: Reidel, 1974.

Suarez, Francisco. *De Legibus.* Edited by Luciano Parena. Madrid: Consejo Superior de Investigaciones Cientificas, Instituto de Francisco de Vitoria, 1971.

———. *De Triplici Virtute Theologica: De Caritate.* In vol. 13 of *Opera Omnia,* edited by Charles Berton. Paris: Vives, 1859.

Suppe, Frederick. *The Semantic Conception of Theories and Scientific Realism.* Urbana: University of Illinois Press, 1989.

Sylvan, R. "Toward an Improved Cosmo-Logical Synthesis." *Grazer Philosophische Studien* 25/26 (1986): 135–79.

Tierney, Brian. "Aristotle and the American Indians—Again." *Cristianesimo nella storia* 12 (1991): 295–322.

———. "Conciliarism, Corporatism, and Individualism: The Doctrine of Individual Rights in Gerson." *Cristianesimo nella storia* 9 (1988): 81–111.

———."1492: Medieval Natural Rights Theories and the Discovery of America." In *Moral and Political Philosophies in the Middle Ages,* edited by J. Carlos Bazan, Eduardo Andujar, and Leonardo Sprocchi. Ottawa: Legas, 1995.

————. "Marsilius on Rights." *Journal of the History of Ideas* 52 (1991): 5–17.

————. "Natural Rights in the Thirteenth Century: A Quaestio of Henry of Ghent." *Speculum* 67 (1992): 58–68.

————. "Origins of Natural Rights Language: Texts and Contexts, 1150–1250." *History of Political Thought* 10 (1989): 615–46.

————. "Tuck on Rights, Some Medieval Problems." *History of Political Thought* 4 (1983): 429–40.

————. "Villey, Ockham and the Origin of Individual Rights." In *The Weightier Matters of the Law*, edited by John Witte, Jr. and Frank Alexander. Studies in Religion, no. 51. American Academy of Religion. Atlanta: Scholars Press, 1988.

Tipler, Frank J. "The Anthropic Principle: A Primer for Philosophers." In *Proceedings of the 1988 Biennial Meeting of the Philosophy of Science Association*, edited by A. Fine and J. Leplin. East Lansing, Mich.: PSA, 1–989.

————. "Extraterrestrial Intelligent Beings Do Not Exist." In *Frontiers of Modern Physics*, edited by T. Rothman, et al. New York: Dover, 1985.

Tryon, E. P. "Is the Universe a Vacuum Fluctuation?" In *Physical Cosmology and Philosophy*, edited by John Leslie. New York: Macmillan, 1990.

Tuck, Richard. *Natural Rights Theories: Their Origin and Development*. Cambridge: Cambridge University Press, 1979.

Tucker, Robert C. *The Soviet Political Mind: Studies in Stalinism and Post-Stalin Change*. New York: Praeger, 1963.

Tully, James. *A Discourse on Property: John Locke and His Adversaries*. Cambridge: Cambridge University Press, 1980.

Turing, Alan. "The Chemical Basis of Morphogenesis." *Philosophical Transactions of the Royal Society of London* B237 (1952): 37–72.

Vilenkin, A. "Creation of Universes from Nothing." *Physics Letters* 117B (1982): 25–28.

Villey, Michel. *La Formation de la pensée juridique moderne*. Paris: Dalloz, 1975.

————. "Genèse du droit subjectif chez Guillaume d'Occam." *Archives de philosophie du droit* 9 (1964): 97–127.

Wallace, William A. "Aquinas's Legacy on Individuation, Cogitation, and Hominization." In *Thomas Aquinas and His Legacy*, edited by David Gallagher. Studies in Philosophy and the History of Philosophy, vol. 28. Washington, D.C.: The Catholic University of America Press, 1994.

————. "Cosmological Arguments and Scientific Concepts." In *From a Realist Point of View*. Washington, D.C.: The Catholic University of America Press, 1983.

————. "The Intelligibility of Nature: A Neo-Aristotelian View." *Review of Metaphysics* 38 (1984): 33–56.

————. "Nature as Animating: The Soul in the Human Sciences." *The Thomist* 49 (1985): 612–48.

————. "Nature, Human Nature, and Norms for Medical Ethics." In *Catholic Perspectives on Medical Morals: Foundational Issues*, edited by E. D. Pellegrino, J. P. Langan, and J. C. Harvey. Philosophy and Medicine, vol. 34. Boston: Kluwer Academic Publishers, 1989.

Wardy, Robert. "Aristotelian Rainfall or the Lore of Averages." *Phronesis* 38 (1993): 18–30.

Waterlow [Broadie], Sarah. *Nature, Change and Agency in Aristotle's Physics*. Oxford: Clarendon Press, 1982.

Weber, Bruce H., David J. Depew, and James D. Smith, eds. *Entropy, Information, and Evolution*. Cambridge: MIT Press, 1990.

Weinberg, S. "The Cosmological Constant Problem." *Reviews of Modern Physics* 61 (1989): 1–23.

Weisheipl, J. A. "The Axiom 'Opus naturea est opus intelligentiae' and Its Origins." In *Albertus Magnus—Doctor Universalis 1280–1980*, edited by G. Meyer and A. Zimmerman. Mainz, Germany: Matthias-Grünewald-Verlag, 1980.

Wheeler, J. A. "Beyond the Black Hole." In *Some Strangeness in the Proportion: A Centennial Symposium to Celebrate the Achievements of Albert Einstein*, edited by Harry Wolff. Reading, Mass.: Addison-Wesley, 1980.

————. "Genesis and Observership." In *Foundational Problems in the Special Sciences*, edited by R. E. Butts and J. Hintikka. Dordrecht: Reidel, 1977.

Whitehead, Barbara D. "Dan Quayle was Right." *The Atlantic Monthly*, April 1993.

Whitrow, G. J. "Why Physical Space Has Three Dimensions." *British Journal for the Philosophy of Science* 6 (1955): 13–31.

Wicken, Jeffrey. "Thermodynamics, Evolution, and Emergence." In *Entropy, Information, and Evolution*, edited by Bruce H. Weber, David J. Depew, and James D. Smith. Cambridge: MIT Press, 1990.

Wieland, W. *Die aristotlesche Physik*. Göttingen, Germany: Vandenhoeck Ruprecht, 1970.

Wiley, E. O. "Entropy and Evolution." In *Entropy, Information, and Evolution*, edited by Bruce H. Weber, David J. Depew, and James D. Smith. Cambridge: MIT Press, 1990.

Will, George F. "The Tragedy of Illegitimacy." *The Washington Post*, 31 October 1993.

Williams, Robert R. *Recognition: Fichte and Hegel on the Other*. Albany: SUNY Press, 1991.

Wolff, Christian. *Institutiones Iuris Naturae et Gentium*. Vol. 26 of Gesammelte Werke. Halle, 1750.

Wootten, D. "Lucien Febvre and the Problem of Unbelief in the Early Modern Period." *Journal of Modern History* 60 (1988): 695–730.

Wright, Larry. *Teleological Explanations*. Berkeley and Los Angeles: University of California Press, 1976.

Yockey, Hubert. *Information Theory and Molecular Biology*. Cambridge: Cambridge University Press, 1992.

Zel'dovich, Y. B. "Birth of the Closed Universe and the Anthropogenic Principle." *Soviet Astronomy Letters* 7 (1981): 322–24.

Zhabotinskii, A. M. "Periodic Movement in Oxidation of Malonic Acid in Solution" (in Russian). *Biofizika* 9 (1964): 306–11.

Zycinski, J. M. "The Anthropic Principle and Teleological Interpretations of Nature." *Review of Metaphysics* 41 (1987): 317–33.

# Index

Rees, M. J., 204
Reeves, Hubert, 241n. 63
regulative idea, 111, 117, 119, 128
Rensberger, B., 229n. 35
*Republic. See* Plato
rights: active, 88; ecclesiastical, 90; individual, 86, 87, 89; natural (*see* natural right); objective, 87, 89, 92, 99; passive, 88; subjective, 86, 87, 89, 91–92, 99
Roque, Alicia J., 130n. 6
Rousseau, 107–9, 113–15, 123
Ruby, Jane E., 31n. 83, 32n. 85

Sanctis, Francesco de, 10n. 19
Saxonhouse, Arlene, 88
Schelling, 107, 108, 120
Schiller, 108
Schopenhauer, 107
Schrader, George, 127n. 4
Schrock, Thomas C., 97n. 43
Schroedinger, E., 242n. 65
science. *See* natural science
Sedley, David, 74, 75
Selden, J., 88
self, 45
self-determination, 46–47, 110–11, 114–15, 152, 155, 158, 160, 161
self-legislation, 107, 111, 113–14, 124
self-maintaining life, 155, 156, 161
self-organizing systems, 50, 240–52, 254
self-preservation, 34, 37–38, 95, 98–102, 105
serotonin, 229
Shakespeare, 2n. 3, 205
Shapiro, R., 179
Sher, M., 183
Shulman, Adam, 21n. 45
Smith, James D., 2n. 2, 238n. 54, 244n. 73
Smith, R. W., 193n. 4
Socrates' second sailing, 4, 216–17
Sorabji, Richard, 76
soul, 5, 41, 43–45, 63, 101, 218, 222, 224
species, 46–48, 58–61, 67–68, 112, 116–17, 120–24, 128–49, 170, 181, 183, 233, 236, 239, 241, 253, 256. *See also* natural kind; specific difference
species-neutrality, 42–43, 50–51, 223, 230–38, 241, 247–56
specific difference, 12–13, 51, 212, 223, 229–30, 237–39, 248–54. *See also* natural kind; species
Spinoza, 230, 233
stability of matter, 236
state, 159–60

state of nature. *See* nature, state of
Stalin, Joseph, 32n. 86
star, 19, 163–67, 177, 180, 183, 186
Steigman, G., 180
Stengers, I., 250n. 94
Straus, Erwin, 256
Strauss, Leo, 7, 10–22, 25, 36, 38, 86, 88, 211
Suarez, 88–89
substance, 56, 58, 64–66, 68, 71–72, 216, 236
Suppe, F., 191n. 3
Swinburne, R., 186

teleology, 2, 5, 6–8, 10, 11, 15, 19, 22, 26, 39–40, 44–46, 50, 52, 59–60, 67, 71, 75–82, 102, 106–8, 112–16, 119, 120, 122–24, 125–26, 137, 151–52, 155, 164, 172, 174, 178, 183–88, 205–10, 213, 215. *See also* causality, final
Thales, 190
*The Federalist*, 252
thing in itself, 110, 113
Tierney, Brian, 88–94, 97, 100, 104–5
Tillich, Paul, 187
Tipler, F. J., 165, 181, 184, 196n. 8, 199, 201, 203, 206n. 23, 241n. 64
Tocqueville, 86, 102
trajectory, 218–25, 234, 246
transformism, 31–32, 34, 38–44, 235. *See also* mastery of nature
Tryon, E. P., 170, 205n. 22
Tuck, Richard, 87, 89
Tucker, Robert C., 32n. 86
Tully, James, 86
Turing, Alan, 242n. 65

unconditioned, 108–9, 122, 124
unity, 125–32, 135–38, 142–49, 158–59, 162, 225–26, 235, 248
unity of the human being, 107–8, 112, 120
unity of science, 50, 211–13, 227–28, 237–42, 247, 252–54
universality, 110, 113, 114, 213, 221–25, 227
universe, 19, 163–86, 212, 224, 239–42. *See also* multiple universes

Villey, Michel, 87, 88, 89
virtue, 12, 25, 31, 32, 36, 37, 45, 252
von Weizsäcker, C. F., 237

Walker, Ralph, 126n. 3
Wallace, William A., 6, 16n. 34
Waterlow, Sarah, 75, 80